Praise for *Elemental Witchc...*

"Heron Michelle shares her personal practice in an inclusive volume that is part reference text, part study guide, and part road map ... As a beautiful bridge between witchcraft's history and present-day application, *Elemental Witchcraft* could very well become the twenty-first century's version of Buckland's 'Big Blue.' A must-have!

—Raina Starr, host and producer of
Desperate House Witches Podcast

"*Elemental Witchcraft* goes way beyond the basics of 'how to' books on Witchcraft. It is an erudite book that provides for experienced practitioners new ideas and insights to deepen their practice and teaching, which for newcomers offers a vision of how contemporary witchcraft can provide a path to deep spiritual transformation.

—Dr. Vivianne Crowley, author of
Wicca: The Old Religion for the New Millennium

"Heron Michelle writes with sass and style and shares a powerful vision of Witchcraft that's firmly rooted in the past, yet very much a part of the progressive present. There's something for every Witch in this book, no matter their level of experience."

—Jason Mankey, author of *The Horned God of the Witches*

"*Elemental Witchcraft* is a magnificent work, an analysis of the Old Religion following the path of the Elements ... There's a wealth of information here, presented with the author's wit, charm, and attention to detail ... This is a book you'll be going back to again and again."

—Miles Batty, author of *Teaching WitchCraft*

"In Heron Michelle's brilliant book, she lays a fantastic overview of the foundational elements of this path, combining the ancient wisdom of the past with modern revelation and innovation."

—Mat Auryn, author of *Psychic Witch*

"Heron Michelle's work is an insightful integration of Hermetics and Witchcraft into a distinctive path of witchery. With the elements as both foundation and framework, the Pentacle Path reveals a tradition writ whole."

—Canu Nodiad, Faery Seer, Georgian
Wicca Elder and community witch

ELEMENTAL WITCHCRAFT

About the Author

Heron Michelle (Greenville, NC) is a Witch, priestess, artist, and mom. She is the founding high priestess of the Sojo Circle Coven, having created a training program in Modern Witchcraft, taught publicly since 2010. Heron is the owner of the Sojourner Whole Earth Provisions metaphysical shop, a Reiki master, tarot diviner, and clairvoyant. She writes the blog *Witch on Fire* at Patheos Pagan, and she regularly lectures at local universities, festivals, and conferences.

HERON MICHELLE

Anna!
Blessings upon
the Pentacle
Path.
~Heron ⛤
Michelle

ELEMENTAL WITCHCRAFT

A GUIDE TO
LIVING A MAGICKAL LIFE
THROUGH THE
ELEMENTS

LLEWELLYN PUBLICATIONS
WOODBURY, MINNESOTA

FIRST EDITION
First Printing, 2021

Book design by Samantha Peterson
Cover design by Shannon McKuhen
Interior illustrations on pages 88, 241, 274, 316, 350, 392 and 393 by Heron Michelle
Interior illustrations on pages 19, 50, 60, 63, 89, 94, 96, 113, 115, 116, 118, 130, 131, 172, 175, 184, 192, 234 and 413 by Llewellyn Art Department
Interior illustrations on page 120, 139, 147, 167, 177, 187 and 194 by Mickie Mueller

Llewellyn is a registered trademark of Llewellyn Worldwide Ltd.

Library of Congress Cataloging-in-Publication Data
Names: Michelle, Heron, author.
Title: Elemental witchcraft : a guide to living a magickal life through the elements / Heron Michelle.
Description: First edition. | Woodbury, Minnesota : Llewellyn Publications, [2021] | Series: The pentacle path; 1 | Includes bibliographical references. | Summary: "Elemental Witchcraft provides rituals, meditations, spells, and journal reflections to develop partnerships with elemental allies and deities, work with the four classical elements, and construct your own astral temple. Michelle explores the principles of Hermeticism, the five bodies, and the paths of power, truth, love, sovereignty, and completion on the Wheel of the Year"— Provided by publisher.
Identifiers: LCCN 2021040233 (print) | LCCN 2021040234 (ebook) | ISBN 9780738766034 (paperback) | ISBN 9780738766263 (ebook)
Subjects: LCSH: Witchcraft. | Four elements (Philosophy)—Miscellanea. | Religious calendars—Wicca. | Magic.
Classification: LCC BF1566 .M335 2021 (print) | LCC BF1566 (ebook) | DDC 133.4/3—dc23
LC record available at https://lccn.loc.gov/2021040233
LC ebook record available at https://lccn.loc.gov/2021040234

Llewellyn Publications
A Division of Llewellyn Worldwide Ltd.
2143 Wooddale Drive
Woodbury, MN 55125-2989
www.llewellyn.com

Printed in the United States of America

Dedicated with gratitude to my beloved L. B., my guiding star;
for my children Lauren and Nathan, my heart and purpose;
for Sondra, Solomon, Linda, and Heather Anne,
my inspiration to live authentically;
for Guardian Tree, the tulip poplar priest under
whose branches these thoughts took form;
and for Aphrodite and Hermes, this offering of love is in your honor.

Disclaimer

This book contains suggestions that can enhance holistic balance in all aspects of wellness: physical, mental, emotional, and spiritual. However, these suggestions do not attempt to diagnose or prescribe treatment for any condition. This spiritual system is most effective when considered alongside the advice of licensed physicians and mental health professionals. Always take safe candle-burning and fire-tending precautions. Do not ingest herbal preparations without prior clearance from your physician. Never ingest essential oils; take caution to properly dilute essential oils before any contact with skin. Beware the potentially harmful effects that some plant materials and essential oils may have upon household pets and small children. Witchcraft returns responsibility for cultivating healthy balance to the individual; therefore, it is practiced at your own risk. The author and publisher accept no liability for any unintended effects your Witchcraft may incur.

Contents

Section 1
Religious Foundations of Modern Witchcraft

Section 2
Elemental Magick and the Fivefold Self

Section 3
Walking the Pentacle Path of Elemental Witchcraft

Exercises, Spells,
Rituals, and
Meditations

Chapter 16

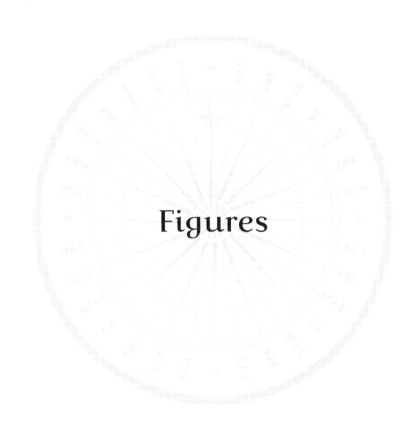

Figures

Foreword

My first introduction to Heron Michelle was several years ago when she took part in a study group for one of my books, *Wicca: Another Year and A Day*. I remember thinking she might be shy, hanging out in the sidelines as she did. When she contributed, she did so humbly. Because of that, very few of us in that group witnessed her integrative brilliance. It was a year later that I discovered Heron was a contributor to *Patheos* where she served up sizzling-smart insights.

When considered against the historical backdrop of what was once expectable and acceptable in the sometimes overly traditional Wiccan path, some old-timers in the Craft might have considered her modern offerings to be a radical and provocative overshare. Not in the least. In my estimation, Heron and her efforts are bent on waking us up.

When I began writing, I did so out of fulfillment of my obligation to the gods and to those who taught me. After reviewing her inaugural book *Elemental Witchcraft*, I can see this same drive urging Heron forward. We are lucky today that Heron has generously shared the treasures she's unearthed during her very personal heroine's journey. From it, she's brought back a roadmap we can all follow that is meant to take us ever closer to magical empowerment.

I wrote my first books during the last part of the twentieth century. There were cell phones, but they were big and clunky and reserved for people we didn't like to talk about. The internet came across as little more than a novelty. It was a time when the dissemination of witchcraft information, of magical lore and custom, was an in-person affair and done under very specific circumstances.

Once upon a time in Wicca, there were *Very Strict Rules* we had to follow. The parties sharing information had to be Craft initiates and had to be "properly prepared" through magical methods. They also must be enclosed by a magic circle. Fast forward nearly thirty years when almost all Pagan authors and I offer instruction and guidance online to initiates and non alike. A vastly different experience by any account.

But these differences have been necessary for the magical traditions of Wicca and Witchcraft to thrive amid a new generation of seekers, many of whom have known nothing of that nearly barbaric pre-internet world. The traditional ways of relaying magical methods changed in order to be relevant. Nowadays, "properly prepared" nearly means having a laptop and a good Wi-Fi signal.

Before readers plunge into the comprehensive offering Heron provides us, I think it is worthwhile for readers to pause a moment to understand the context of Wicca's transition from guarded and secret practice to one that proliferates across cyberspace like magic mushrooms, and which contributed, in part, to the book you hold in your hands.

In the 1980s when I was formally initiated, American Wiccans had barely begun to embrace a "build-it-yourself" ethic. There were still very traditional foundations one had to observe in order for the others on the path to consider you "legitimate." But on the sly, many practitioners were exploring and expanding what they knew. It was a daring thing to do given the scrutiny of fellow initiates who were a little like spies that might turn you in for straying from strict adherence to old formulas.

The founders of British Traditional Wicca—Gerald Gardner, Doreen Valiente, and by all accounts, English occultist Aleister Crowley—never planned on any of the social or technological advances of the latter decades when stirring the cauldron to create the

Wiccan tradition in the 1940s and '50s. But when Raymond Buckland and others transported Wicca to the United States, they did so during the dawning of the Age of Aquarius.

The cultural revolution of the 1960s was, at its heart, a repudiation (or at least a reimagination) of the traditions and values that underpinned the social fabric of America. Young people everywhere were smashing open the known forms of custom, culture, and belief, not because these no longer held value, but because they sought to unearth whatever impeded human potential and freedom. All social, cultural, and religious ideas were fodder for deconstruction and reintegration. And right on cue, almost as symbolic as anything from a Freudian dream, the moon itself—once a deity and a sphere of veneration—become a place for humans to step foot and explore.

In his book *The Religious Crisis of the 1960s*, Hugh McLeod notes that the period from 1958 to 1975 marked an explosive change in religious thinking fostered by a surge in political, secular, and theological reexamination. Social and spiritual revolution produced a rupture in traditions as profound as that brought about by the Reformation. These same forces affected how folks approached traditions such as Wicca and witchcraft.

It's worth mentioning again that there have always been "hard-core" traditionalists within the ranks of Wicca who seem to engage with a Pagan spiritual process with an ethic reminiscent of Western Christian Fundamentalism. All forms of fundamentalism become obsessive and often overheated about historical preservation. That approach might be necessary for developing a history or science book—undertaking some work based on verifiable facts, logical conclusions, and measurable outcomes. However, when we undertake a spiritual journey, such as the one that Heron prescribes, we need to acquiesce to a process and to a language of symbol, poetry, and energy. We need to understand what the symbols mean rather than take symbols at face value.

The previous decades of revolution and revelation had worked their magic for the most part by the time of my initiation into Gardnerian Wicca. A good portion of American Craft initiates (at least in hippie California) sought practices that informed their personal journey, led to growth, healing, expansion, and awareness, or simply helped them live life with sanity. People didn't want to cast a circle, grind up herbs, light a candle, ring a bell, and call that "spirituality."

In the Los Angeles Gardnerian coven called *Oruborus et Ova*, our initiating priestess made cultivating complementary studies that enriched Wiccan understanding a prerequisite for elevation to the second and third degrees. That's not anything Gerald Gardner required of his initiates, as far as I know. But it was an intelligent requisite.

With that green light, our coven members began reading mythologist Joseph Campbell and psychologist Carl Jung, Marija Gimbutas, cultural anthropologist Michael Harner, Wade Davis, Bruno Bettelheim, and Carlos Castaneda. We went to African drum and dance circles. We attended Santeria ceremonies. Two of us graduated with masters degrees. Mine was in clinical psychology. The ground upon which I developed my personal gnosis stemmed from our teacher's requisite and included diverse sources such as modern Druidism, ceremonial magic, shamanic-ecstatic practices, and Eastern mysticism.

At the same time, writers such as Starhawk pointed out how feminism, ecology, and politics fit into the magical mix and informed the practices of witchcraft. Dancer and musician Gabrielle Roth showed us how to reach the ecstatic realm in an urban life. Celebrated ceremonialists, such as author Lon Milo DuQuette, adamantly confirmed that magic was art, not science. The Craft was no longer comprised solely of folks looking for restricted occult "secret formulas." It had become a genuine holistic path that expanded into and informed every facet of life.

Here we are in the second decade of the new century, and we arrive at Heron Michelle's *Elemental Witchcraft*—a book that lets me know that all of my risk-taking efforts will continue. I see Heron has taken that baton and will further urge Wicca's newest participants to engage the path as a transformative spiritual journey. She's opening up a great big, tricked-out limousine, swinging the door wide, and inviting us all to go for a great ride. Not everyone wants this kind of ride, nor do they wish to sit in the trunk Jacuzzi. And that's okay. There's enough space still for everyone on the path to "build-it-yourself." Find your own adventure.

Heron has understood (and lets us know) that while initiatory Wicca has its place, it isn't the only place. Folks just starting on this path—and even those who've been doing this for a long time—don't need to worry that they're doing something "wrong" because they don't have an initiation or a coven to authenticate their experience and their journey.

Heron's followed the lead of so many pioneers, and she's pulled from countless sources as vast and disparate as the *Tao-te Ching* and the ancient alchemical treatises. Heron announces her eclectic choices, pieces them together for the reader in a way that illustrates their underlying principles, and stands up for these choices with nary a whisper of self-consciousness. Thank the gods. In fact, she makes them zing with life force. As Joseph Campbell said, a hero must come along now and then to renew the word. To teach with the authority of fire that burns in the belly (or whatever chakra you'd like) and show us all the way. Enter Heron.

She's announcing from the mountain her clear-eyed vision of witchcraft's future—that it does not get stuck in the concrete of traditional forms and practices. It reaches far into the vast unknown and helps you conjure up your authentic self. It evokes the deepest resources of the mind, the body, and the spirit and helps you to know that every action you take has meaning. She gives permission to find Spirit in the ordinary. And when we go looking for it right here under our own feet, we discover, like Dorothy who eventually finds she's been on the farm all along, there's no place like home.

—Timothy Roderick, June 2021, Los Angeles

Introduction

I consider this Pentacle Path I tread to be a form of panentheist, Neopagan, Hermetic, Modern Witchcraft. It is a syncretism born of all the various influences in my life, including in-depth comparative study of anthropology and religion, and the magick I find in the deepest roots of this planet earth. I was mostly raised in Taylors, South Carolina, where my mother took us three times a week to the evangelical, conservative, bigoted, hellfire and brimstone, "fear and admonition of the Lord" variety of Christian churches. However, from ages nine through twelve, my father's work moved us to Jeddah, Saudi Arabia, which is an Islamic theocracy, a mere thirty-minute drive from the holy city of Mecca. Despite what strangeness that might suggest, I enjoyed a loving home full of international adventure and eye-opening experiences. With time, I shed the religious strictures of my youth to become a self-made Witch and priestess.

As a child, I always felt … different … like an alien observer wearing a human meat-suit. I retained memories from my most recent past life and death. I remembered PTSD-like flashbacks being a male soldier in the US Army, fighting and dying in France during the First World War. When you're a little kid, it's hard to know that your way of perceiving the world is different than how other people perceive it. In hindsight, I had a natural ability for clairvoyant psychism. I dreamed true in déjà vu so prolifically that in each moment I hardly knew if I was seeing the past, present, or future. I could see energy flowing like colored light within and around everything. In bed at night, I'd play with moving the flows of colors with my mind, swirling them into patterns. Similarly, I could see auras of light around people and other living things. I called them halos, and from that halo I knew their mood and emotions. It would take until my mid-forties to understand that this hyperawareness, hyper-feeling, hyper-focus, hyper-communication were the "H" in my neurodivergency, which is often how ADHD (attention-deficit/hyperactivity disorder) expresses in cis females.

I spent my early childhood wandering the woods, climbing trees, wading in creeks, kindling illicit campfires, and dreaming up to the moon. My neighborhood trees were my friends, and the interconnection I felt with the woods was like my family. As weird as I knew myself to be, comparatively speaking, I never really felt alone in my woods. Not like the desperate "otherness" I felt while inside my mother's church. That dissonance led to deep preteen depression and the existential crises of rejecting my family's religion entirely.

The most important night of my life came when I was around thirteen years old. A particularly bright full moon night, I was awakened to a divinity vastly different than what I'd been questioning in Sunday school. I call it my "burning bush moment" when I could actually hear the chorus of divinity singing within the moonlight, encouraging me onward to fulfill my destiny along a different kind of spiritual path.

By 1992, as I turned eighteen, I'd found my spiritual home in the early books on the goddess religion of Wicca. For ten years I mostly hid my interest and was too intimidated to venture any further than the covers of books like this one. By twenty-eight years old, during my first Saturn return I gave birth to my first child, and the Great Goddess herself appeared in clairvoyant vision as my midwife. Childbirth was a cataclysmic initiation! Like a memory from the between, I tapped momentarily into the ecstasy of unified creation. My inner *witchflame* fully ignited into an inferno of sacred purpose that could no longer be shuttered. Since then, I've been a *Witch on fire.* From that soul-searing moment of clarity, I was devoted to exploring the mysteries, teaching Witchcraft, community organizing, and eventually opening a Neopagan bookstore and spiritual supply shop called The Sojourner Whole Earth Provisions.

At The Sojourner, we created sacred space as a publicly accessible Pagan haven in the broad daylight of Greenville, North Carolina. Through a decade of magick performed in our classroom since then, The Sojo Circle Coven came into form, and I was honored to be elected the founding high priestess. Along the way, I've been attuned to master level in the Lotus Blossom lineage of Usui Reiki, a method of natural healing. I've also attained proficiency in the Thoth tarot card divination system, and offer consultations and past life retrieval for others. In 2015, I took vows as a priestess and answered the call to service of humanity by Aphrodite, goddess of love, grace, and beauty, and Hermes, god of wisdom, magick, and communication. I pledged to share their message of Divine Love through my writing. Which brings us to this auspicious moment, on these pages, and the fulfillment of their commission.

I tell my story to convey that the Witch I am today is the result of determined aspiration and following the breadcrumbs of divine guidance along a self-initiatory path. Any expertise I may have is the result of grassroots partnerships and self-actualization. I cannot boast any bestowed Witchcraft initiations from well-regarded lineages, despite my respect for those kinds of credentials. But I have enjoyed the mentorship of several outstanding Witches to whom I owe much gratitude for deep conversations, invitations to their public rituals, and their written works. While I've had no access to "oath-bound" Wiccan materials, neither do I have secrets to keep. I just kept showing up at the crossroads of magick to do lots of hard work, ask questions, and figure it out on my own. Like an occult explorer, I've mapped my way here, and here is pretty good. That is the nutshell instruction to Witchcraft that I can share.

With a thousand acts of stubborn will, Witches pursue a relationship with the God/dess, who beckons from the wild fringes of nature, and *nature* is our best instructor. Lessons sung as breezes through branches, from moonbeams, smoldering fire, and scourging rain. The Witches in our self-starter coven all just kept turning the sacred wheel of sabbats and seeking divine inspiration. Then we *did the inspired things* and compared notes on what we'd discovered. Not that it was easy, or more correct to take the self-initiatory path, but it worked out well for me. The Great God/dess never failed to deliver.

Modern Witchcraft

By my definition, Modern Witchcraft is a path of wisdom. This path emphasizes a radical new form of personal sovereignty, truth-seeking, empowerment, and responsibility that stands proudly on the cultural and religious foundations of our ancestors. Yet, we craft a meaningful connection to nature that will serve our future.

Modern Witchcraft is also a spirituality, which blends scientific knowledge and ancient mysticism with the goal of evolving beyond the pitfalls of other *religions*. We work to conquer the fears that drive *superstition* and create a new mode of being that brings healing, peace, and balance to the seeker, striving to create a healthy way of life in this crazy modern world that we can enjoy. It provides the lens through which we can maintain a balanced perspective, offering a structure through which we can process life's challenges and grow through them with grace.

Treading the witching path is a lot like a dance to the rhythm of nature. We move through the dance in partnership with the God/dess. Sometimes it is a waltz; sometimes it is a mosh pit, but Witchcraft teaches us to lace up our combat boots and jump right in.

The form of Modern Witchcraft this book shares is a reclaimed form of Neopagan religion. Specifically, the *panentheism* influenced by the Greco-Egyptian philosophy known as *Hermetics*. It is also an occult magickal system emerging within the Western Esoteric Traditions: Neoplatonic philosophy, Hermetic alchemy, Rosicrucian Order, Theosophy, Freemasonry, theurgy, qabala, astrology, tarot cards, yoga, chakra systems, Wicca, New Thought, New Age, metaphysics, and psychology. All these mystery schools and systems codify the path of seeking our way back to union within Spirit. They all applied poetic structures and developed techniques of meditation, ceremony, and tricks of the mind so folks of exceptional conscience and perception could better cope with life. Compost them all down to basics, and they're mystical applied forms of psychotherapy. Modern Witchcraft may be a new sapling within this noble forest, but her roots draw nutrients from that fertile soil, then leans hopefully into a new light. Despite the ancient sources, the cosmology and paradigm of Hermetics easily aligns with advances in scientific discoveries and provides a naturally progressive, ecologically sustainable, culturally transformative, and radically inclusive framework through which we evolve into a globally aware twenty-first century.

The Pentacle Path

I've come to call this particular style of witchery, which coalesced over a decade of coven practice and teaching, the Pentacle Path of Modern Witchcraft. A benefit to sharing Witchcraft with many diverse people is that you start to notice how predictably the universal tides ebb and flow through life. Obvious patterns form, syncopating in a Witch's understanding over time. What seems so random and chaotic at the beginning eventually settles into simple elegance.

Mind you, this Pentacle Path isn't always a tango through the moonflowers; sometimes we're dragged screaming by the scruff through some wickedly thorny brambles. The path a Witch treads jigs and jags through both sunlight and shadow, ecstasy and agony, beauty and horror, gain and loss. To purposefully tread the Witch's path with sensitivity is not easy. Our beingness is challenging but our work is necessary, and I am grateful that you're here.

Witchcraft is a set of skills anyone can employ, but I think of *witchery* as a spiritual orientation. The *is-ness* of a true Witch is just encoded into our bones. Once our witchflame fully ignites, the desire for a meaningful existence screams up from our depths and cannot be quelled. Spirit stirs relentlessly within us, felt as deepest yearnings for interconnection. Memories of divine ecstasy and enchantment burble up through all the cracks between …

Once a Witch willingly sets foot to the Pentacle Path, we realize we've always been here. Now we carry the torch of our Divine Will to light the way. No life is without struggle, but at least we acknowledge that much going in! Witchcraft offers us methods to cope with life's challenges effectively while purposefully celebrating joy and triumph at every possible occasion.

The first lesson of Witchcraft I want to convey is this: the entirety of the natural cosmos, and all life within it, is sacred, including you. To *live* is to worship that sacredness. There is no distinction between the sacred and the mundane. Every act, whether it be a high altar ceremony, preparing a meal, clearing out the pesky junk drawer, or throwing a Yule party, are all acts of magick. We are charged to "drink the good wine to the Old Gods, And dance and make love in their praise."[1] Our holy duty is to enjoy this life we're given.

I call it the *Pentacle Path*, because just like drawing the five-pointed star in a continuous, clockwise-flowing series of equal lines, the path a Witch treads makes regularly scheduled pit stops through the elemental and divine mysteries. These mysteries are mapped to the

---

1. Doreen Valiente, "The Charge of the Goddess" in *The Charge of the Goddess: Expanded Edition with New and Previously Unpublished Poems* (The Doreen Valiente Foundation, 2014), 19–21.

Neopagan ritual cycle of eight solar holidays we call the Wheel of the Year. This way, as we turn the wheel, we remain mindful of the elemental lessons in larger context. Elemental, lunar, and solar tides are celebrated as an interwoven pattern against the backdrop of the starry cosmos. Life becomes a magickal sigil of balance, power, and protection that we embody through our rituals.

This Witchcraft provides a handy and adaptable structure through which we enjoy our incarnation here on Earth. By connecting to nature, a Witch regularly aligns their individual spirit, mind, will, heart, and body to the transcendent Spirit of God/dess. In fivefold interconnection, we awaken to their Divine Mind, their Divine Will, and to their Divine Love. Remember that our bodies are divine! That doesn't sound daunting at all! Where do we begin?

The Chinese proverb from the *Tao-te Ching* wisely advises "The journey of a thousand miles begins beneath one's feet."[2] In other words, bundle up your gumption and strike out from wherever you're at right now. The first and most enduring lesson of Witchcraft begins by becoming fully present exactly where we live: on planet Earth in these gorgeous magickal bodies during these bizarre times. To fully explore how spiritually interconnected we all are, we'll begin with the alchemical lessons taught to us by the elements of air, fire, water, earth, and spirit.

Human beings are the embodied pentacle. As we engage in the praxis of Elemental Witchcraft, we successfully balance and align these energies in ourselves, which reveals the very crossroads of magick at our core. Your power, the temple of divinity, control over your life, and the God/dess you seek were never "out there." These have always been at the center of your being. The Wiccan liturgical poem known as "The Charge of the Goddess" assures us, "that if that which thou seekest, thou findest not within thee, thou wilt never find it without thee. For behold, I have been with thee from the beginning; and I am that which is attained at the end of desire"[3]

What to Expect in This Book

The heritage of occult wisdom is an integration of thought and practice from both East and West that really knows no borders. Wicca is sometimes mistaken to be exclusively

---

2. Ralph Keyes, *The Quote Verifier: Who Said What, Where, and When* (New York: St. Martin's Griffin, 2006), 107. Often attributed to Lao Tzu.

3. Valiente, *The Charge of the Goddess*, 12–13.

derived from European and British pagan cultures. However, it has just as many African, Middle Eastern, East and Southeast Asian influences. The Modern Witchcraft offered in these pages is eclectic, syncretic, intersectional feminist, progressive, egalitarian, and radically inclusive. It reconciles the divine paradox: in Spirit we are *one*; yet in the God/dess's family, all diverse distinctions we bring to the party are a sacred gift we're here to fully celebrate. These spiritual tools are offered as a means to transform our culture, correct our human course, and resolve the issues we face in the twenty-first century.

Elemental Witchcraft lays a foundation for a magickal practice with the goal of figuring out who we are as individuals and where we fit in the cosmic scheme of things. We figure out what is "true," recalibrate our moral compass, establish personal sovereignty, internalize our source of empowerment, and develop our divine relationships. After we heal ourselves, then we can endeavor to heal the earth and her people. We can transform the toxicity of the patriarchal dominator culture into the cooperator culture of the God/dess. Through the integration of our physical, mental, emotional, will, and spiritual bodies, we unlock our human potential.

This system of Modern Witchcraft is distinct for several reasons:

- Built upon a *panentheistic* paradigm: Divinity being both inherent within nature and having transcendent consciousness, being radically inclusive of all other-*isms*.
- The Great Goddess and Great God are engaged as "the Two Who Move as One" because they are divinity in reflection, a mirrored spectrum of all possibility. For ease in writing, I refer to them as "*God/dess*," all-gender inclusive.[4]
- Based in the ancient *Hermetic philosophies* attributed to Hermes Trismegistus of Greco-Egyptian origin. Hermeticism established the esoteric sciences of astrology, alchemy, and the Hermetic principles. These inform Witchcraft's calendar of auspicious timing, formulary, and magickal practices.
- Takes inspiration from Wiccan mythos of Moon Goddess and Horned God, inspired by Wicca's rituals and sacred poetry, such as "The Rede of the Wiccae" presented by Lady Gwen Thompson and "The Charge of the Goddess" and "The Witches Creed" by Doreen Valiente. Yet, Modern Witchcraft provides an individualized, self-initiatory system of attainment that approaches Spirit directly.

---

4. I first heard the phrase "the Two Who Move as One" in a workshop ritual with author Christopher Penczak and later throughout his Temple of Witchcraft series of books.

- Engages in the alchemical Great Work of Magick, intent on evolving human consciousness but doing so each Witch at a time.
- Follows the *Pentacle Paths* of sovereignty, truth, power, love, and completion as a means of achieving wellness and wholeness, recognizing that humans are multidimensional divine beings within a multidimensional cosmos.[5]
- Utilizes the praxis of *ritual magick, journey work, and spellcraft* to fully engage with the powers of nature.
- Explores the elemental mysteries symbolically as *the Witch's Jewel of Power,* based on the platonic solid known as an octahedron or bipyramid.
- Introduces the *nine Divine Love Conditions* of the God/dess to further understand and apply the Wiccan ethos of Perfect Love and Perfect Trust.
- Offers the *Four Rules for Personal Sovereignty* as an ethical framework for reconciling the paradox of sovereignty within an interconnected web of existence.
- Instills tools of *equality and cooperation* within the honeymoon paradigm of goddess loving god, reconciling paradoxes along continuums: profane into sacred, banefulness into benevolence, violence into peace, etc.

When to Start

Whenever you pick up this book is an excellent time to dive right in. The readings and meditations of sections one and two may be explored any time of year. There are exercises that will prepare you in advance for the applied Elemental Witchcraft lessons of section three. Those elemental chapters are synchronized to the Wheel of the Year and will tap into the astrology and seasonal flows specific to those seasons as experienced in the Northern Hemisphere. For Witches of the Southern Hemisphere, the mysteries are mirrored onto the opposite side of the zodiac and may be translated. It is most magickally auspicious to begin the elemental lessons of earth immediately following the sabbat of Samhain. (Northern, 15 degrees Scorpio. Southern, 15 degrees Taurus.) Prior to beginning the magickal workings, review the preparation chapters and collect the necessary materials.

---

5. I named the four elemental paths for the "internal ingredients" symbolized by the Witch's altar tools, as named by Christopher Penczak in his book *Outer Temple of Witchcraft* on page163. The path of completion's name was inspired by Vivianne Crowley's teachings within *Wicca: The Old Religion in the New Millennium,* chapter 12.

Section One: Foundations of Modern Witchcraft

First, we will define Modern Witchcraft and explore some history and theological foundations within Neopaganism, Wicca, and Hermetic philosophy. We'll explore the panentheistic paradigm and ethical considerations through the lens of Wiccan sacred poetry. Then, we'll map it all to the Great Work of Magick as it is enacted throughout the Witch's Wheel of the Year celebrations: elemental, lunar, solar, and stellar.

Section Two: Elemental Magick Basics

Next, we'll dive into the lore and history of elemental magick and the mysteries revealed through the *Witch's Jewel of Power*. Altogether, this road map reveals the repeating patterns that mirror above and below, within and without. They give us both a foundation and a structure around which to build our personal elemental practice in section three.

Section Three: Turning the Wheel Through Elemental Witchcraft

Section three is where we dig into the praxis of Witchcraft and begin applying all that we've learned. Each chapter provides a guided tour through the elemental mysteries, synchronized to the seasonal tides of the year. Again, they begin after the sabbat of Samhain and assume that the reader is celebrating those concurrently.

These lessons are designed to be appropriate for the beginner but can also deepen the experience for those who've walked the path a long time. Through each year's magick, we renew our balance as we evolve our practice. Our goal in part three is to develop relationships with the Great God/dess of nature and our elemental allies.

By the conclusion, the reader will create a personal altar with the selection and consecration of the Witch's traditional ritual tools. Exercises will establish a meditation practice, teach ritual techniques like casting a circle and opening the elemental gateways to the Plane of Forces, and evoking the God/dess and ancestors. Each elemental chapter includes a magickal herbalism formulary with instructions for creating your own charged candles, incenses, oils, and assorted lotions and potions necessary for the rites and spells. By the end of this work, your magickal cupboards will hold everything you need for a robust spellcrafting practice in the future.

The rituals of this year build upon each other, guiding the construction of your energetic temple layer by layer. First, we make the introductions, then we put those powers to use through magickal spells to create change in your life. Overall, this Great Work culminates in the Pentacle Path's rite of completion: fivefold balance within divinity at the crossroads of yourself.

Build Your Own Temple

The beauty of this Witchcraft is that you get to build your own temple. Regardless of how you construct it, when you choose to celebrate the auspicious moments, or which techniques you use, I implore you to seek a logical, internal consistency that transcends empty religiosity. Life has great meaning, but it is up to you to discover it, assign it value, and then celebrate that meaning. Do as you will but do it as beneficially and meaningfully as you can muster!

The framework to the Great Work of Magick proposed through this system could be applied to any form of magickal or Neopagan religious devotion. To that end, the Wiccan-esque ritual structures presented here remain simple, calling on natural, archetypal metaphors for divinity without being pantheon or culture specific. We'll keep it general to the seven celestial spheres of planetary magick, and from there I encourage you to adapt the rituals to your preferred deities and cultural mythos in creative ways.

Discernment Is Key

As you study, I challenge you to accept no blind faith or superstitious "just do as I say" malarkey into your Witchcraft, starting with this book. Though I suggest you try techniques presented here at least once, feel free to customize them to your personal practice once you figure out what works for you and what doesn't. True understanding of the Craft takes a lifetime. Remember that sometimes the old-fashioned, analogue way that the Witches of old did things can be exactly the cure you need in this fast-lane, tech-crazed modern life. Other times, new technology can aid your Craft in ways our ancestors would envy.

In modern society we get used to instant gratification. With a smartphone, we have vast data at our fingertips. The ancients would have called it a "sorcerer's tablet" or something grand, and we'd be the most powerful being they'd ever met. Which, as a matter of course, would likely get us burned at the stake! However, knowledge is different than *wisdom*. You could have all the data in the world and unless you thoroughly unpack that information and apply it in a personal way, it won't help you much.

A critical task for any student of the occult is separating historical accuracy from the hubris and honest mistakes found in nineteenth- and twentieth-century texts. We are challenged to adapt as more accurate information comes to light, lest we fall into the traps of stubborn fundamentalism. Sadly, just because a bit of lore or someone's pet theory was printed in occult books that everyone referenced for decades, that doesn't necessarily make it factual. For example, early anthropological works like *The Witch-Cult in Western Europe* by Margaret Murray and *The Golden Bough* by Sir James Frazer. Despite launching renewed interest in paganism, their theories later proved to be faulty. Yet, divinity moved through those books to take root in the modern imagination in very real and beneficial ways. Mythical truth is a nuanced beast.

I beseech you to critically examine everything you've ever heard about Witchcraft. Do your own research, search your intuition, try things out with a healthy dose of scientific skepticism, and then draw your own conclusions. That includes this book. The speed of communication and availability of information allows any factoid to be instantly verified with the Google equivalent of the Library of Alexandria in our pockets. Ignorance is an option no one has to take. By the same token, just because some Witchcraft meme is trending on social media does not necessarily make it accurate either; discernment is key.

Okay. Enough with the introductions. Welcome to the boldly wandering, beautiful and challenging, rapturous and humbling Pentacle Path of Modern Witchcraft.

Section 1

RELIGIOUS FOUNDATIONS OF MODERN WITCHCRAFT

Besides being a spiritual practice, there isn't much that the varied traditions of the Craft can agree on, so any discussion of "foundations" requires a few caveats. There are Witches whose devotional practices resurrect the polytheistic "paganism" we call the "Old Religion." There are also Witches who vehemently argue that their Witchcraft is neither pagan nor a religion at all. Personal sovereignty demands that we are each entitled to define our own identities and beliefs and then to live accordingly. For clarity, when referring to "Witches" or "Witchcraft," know that I can only speak from my own experience. In section one, we'll define the Pentacle Path of Modern Witchcraft as one of the Neopagan religious traditions, which is newly emerging, and its foundational influences in ancient philosophy and magickal practices.

At what point does spirituality also qualify as a *religion*? I agree that Witchcraft practices are equally effective for atheists, as they are for devotional polytheists, because the practices align with the *is-ness* of cosmic mechanics. Those mechanisms don't much care what you call them. However, "religions" do have common qualities, and those qualities have the potential to deeply enrich a witching life.

Religions attempt to answer the same existential questions. Based on those answers, religions define systems of ethics and lifestyle choices. They offer celebrations of meaningful auspicious moments with ritual practices that exemplify that meaning. Religions answer questions like: How did the cosmos and humans come into being? By what creative power? Was it a god? A goddess? What is our relationship with that divinity? And, now that we're here, what purpose do we serve? What happens when we die? Humans can only theorize, but those worldview theories establish a religion's *paradigm* or framework for understanding our cosmos. A religious paradigm then leads to methodologies through which we experience that cosmos. What sort of society would best reflect this paradigm? What values and ideals would someone within that paradigm hold dear? What behaviors uphold those ideals? What is the point of it all?

Throughout the chapters of section one, we'll attempt to answer the existential questions defining the unique qualities of this Modern Witchcraft from a Hermetic, God/dess-balanced, Neopagan perspective. We'll explore the historical and philosophical foundations that inform our thealogy (with an "a"), our ethics, and build our practices. We'll examine those concepts as they are expressed through the inspired liturgy and mythos presented in modern Wicca. This offers a rediscovery of the cooperator culture of the God/dess that could solve the modern problems we face and better support our health and happiness into the twenty-first century and beyond.

Chapter 1
Witchery for the Twenty-First Century

One might think a journey along the Pentacle Path begins, as journeys tend to do, at the beginning. But where is that? Nature teaches us that all life is a cycle without beginning or end, such that each "present" moment hangs in the balance between cause and effect, past and potential. Before we can attend to the business of balancing our lives through Elemental Witchcraft, we're going to need some context. From whence did this witching path come? Who cleared the road for us up to here and left all these mysterious signposts and mile markers along the way? To get the lay of the land, we'll begin with a *very* brief and incomplete history of the Wiccan and Witchcraft contributors over the last eighty years. Then we'll define a Neopagan, panentheistic, Wiccan-inspired, Modern Witchcraft and how that fits in context to the over-culture. Finally, we'll introduce the magickal tools of the God/dess that can transform our culture, evolving to meet the demands of our future.

Paving the Witching Road

The magickal religion of Wicca and practices known as Witchcraft emerged into diverse forms over the last one hundred years. This movement is so young that some of its founders are still living as of this writing. Our foundational texts and sacred poetry are still protected by copyright. There is no common Witchcraft canon, no religious laws, unifying tenets, nor any central authority to define or enforce such. We like it this way. Well-informed Witches tend to be "people of the library," because the seeds of knowledge must be collected from many sources, which often contradict each other. So, you just about have to forge your own path through firsthand experience. However, let's start with a brief mention of a few of those foundational texts and the Wiccan founders who authored them.

Founders of Wicca and the Neopagan movement took inspiration from the anthropological and folkloric works of the late 1800s and early 1900s. These include important works by archaeologists such as Margaret Murray's *The Witch-Cult in Western Europe* (1921) and *The God of the Witches* (1933); and works by folklorists such as Charles Godfrey Leland's *Aradia, or, The Gospel of the Witches* (1899), Sir James George Frazer's *The Golden Bough* (1890), and *The White Goddess: A Historical Grammar of Poetic Myth* (1948) by poet and classicist Robert Graves. Graves was especially influential to modern God/dess religion, as he is believed to have channeled an unorthodox, feminist mythology in reverence of the Great Goddess of love, destruction, and inspiration, who was worshipped in the matriarchal cultures of the ancient past prior to being supplanted by patriarchal gods of war, logic, and reason.[6]

Upon those foundations, add the twentieth-century writings of ceremonial magician and infamous occultist Aleister Crowley (1875–1947), the Rosicrucian influences from The Hermetic Order of the Golden Dawn, of which Crowley was a member (1898), and MacGregor Mathers's translation of *The Key of Solomon* (1888). Now, add in the Theosophical and Jungian psychology influences of another former Golden Dawn member, Dion Fortune (1890–1946), in her books *The Mystical Qabalah* (1935), *The Sea Priestess*

---

6. "The White Goddess," Encyclopedia Britannica, accessed February 5, 2021, https://www.britannica.com /topic/The-White-Goddess; Robert Graves, *The White Goddess: A Historical grammar of Poetic Myth*, ed. Grevel Lindop (New York: Farrar, Straus and Giroux, 2013), n.p.

(1935), and *Moon Magic* (1956, published posthumously). Then, blend in the ritual techniques of the Co-Masons and the *Ordo Templi Orientis* (Crowley's occult organization.) Now, filter all that through the experience of a career spent as a civil servant and archeologist in Malaysia.[7] Add the nudist lifestyle of naturism and a secret 1930s initiation into a Witch's coven in the New Forest region of England.[8] From this life full of mystical experiences, a new dream of the God/dess came to form through the magick of an Englishman named Gerald Brousseau Gardner (1884–1964), who is the acknowledged "father" of Modern Witchcraft.[9]

After the anti-Witchcraft laws were finally repealed in England in 1951, Gardner presented his hybrid Witchcraft religion to the public through his published books *High Magic's Aid* (1949) and *Witchcraft Today* (1951), which included an introduction by Margaret Murray. This tradition of his own creation would come to be called "Gardnerian Wicca."

In 1953, Doreen Valiente (1922–1999) was initiated into Gardner's coven, and would help to rewrite the rituals and liturgy of his Book of Shadows. Those would go on to be hand-copied into the Books of Shadows of initiates in their lineage. Notable among her contributions is her prose poem adaption of "The Charge of the Goddess," which blended passages from Leland's *Aradia*, and her own poetry inspired by classical Greek mythology. Valiente and Gardner also collaborated on his book *The Meaning of Witchcraft* (1959), further introducing Wicca to the world. Valiente is widely considered the mother of Modern Witchcraft. Her keen discernment and research skills, in-depth occult scholarship, and beautiful poetry enormously influenced the Witchcraft resurgence along many diverse paths through the God/dess's garden.

During the same period, another Englishman named Alexander Sanders (1926–1988), having received an initiation and copy of the Gardnerian Book of Shadows, established an Egyptian-influenced tradition with his then-wife Maxine Sanders (b. 1946), a previously initiated priestess of the Egyptian gods.[10] Their lineage came to be known as

---

7. "Gardner, Gerald Brousseau," World Religions Reference Library, Encyclopedia.com, April 15, 2021. https://www.encyclopedia.com/religion/encyclopedias-almanacs-transcripts-and-maps/gardner -gerald-brousseau.

8. Philip Heselton, "Lighting the Shadows and Searching for Dorothy" in *Doreen Valiente Witch* (Doreen Valiente Foundation and The Centre for Pagan Studies, Woodbury, MN: Llewellyn Publications, 2016), n.p.

9. Heselton, *Doreen Valiente Witch*, 81.

10. Maxine Sanders, *Fire Child: The Life and Magick of Maxine Sanders, 'Witch Queen'* (Oxford: Mandrake, 2007), 28–35.

"Alexandrian Wicca." Throughout the 1960 and '70s, they often worked with journalists and theater companies and as consultants for television and movie productions, bringing their practice of Witchcraft into broad popular awareness.[11]

Throughout the remaining twentieth century these original British covens initiated many priests and priestesses, hiving off covens worldwide whose initiates would themselves go on to refine the craft and publish influential books over the following decades. Thus, the initiatory traditions of Wicca proliferated.

Concurrent to the revelation of Gardner's Wicca, an entirely independent form of traditional Witchcraft of Britain also came to light, primarily through Robert Cochrane (1931–1966) and his coven the Clan of Tubal Cain. Cochrane's correspondences with a Witch named Joseph Wilson would be widely distributed among covens in America, founding the 1734 tradition among others. Interestingly, after breaking with Gardner in 1957, Doreen Valiente was later initiated by Cochrane in 1964 and spent a year in his coven before eventually breaking with him as well. She later co-authored a book of their rituals with Evan John Jones called *Witchcraft: A Tradition Renewed* in 1990.[12] Valiente authored several influential books of her own, notably *Witchcraft for Tomorrow* (1978) and *The Rebirth of Witchcraft* (1989).

Witchcraft has come a long way in a relatively short period of time and is rapidly evolving. From Wicca's first revelation, her poignant beauty inspired generations of Witches all over the world who would further apply the Craft to aid progress in feminism, environmentalism, and civil and social rights. Like dandelion fluff on the wind, Witchcraft germinated, flowered, and diversified into hundreds of fantastic varieties. However, as the next generations tended the God/dess's wild garden of Wicca, each coven, priest, and priestess did their bit of pruning and grafting, cultivating her strengths into hybrid bloom, each progressing our cultural transformation. The Pentacle Path continues this age-old tradition, anchored by deep roots in the *is-ness* of ancient paganism and occultism, yet leaning into a new light.

Seeking the Is-ness

The Modern Witchcraft presented in this work came to be a religion of both science and poetry. It is a poetic paradigm, one of metaphor and correlation and questioning—

---

11. Sanders, chapter 14, in *Fire Child*.

12. Heselton, *Doreen Valiente Witch,* 266.

not meant to be taken literally. Within the range of what we call "nature," where do the knowings of sciences like physics, chemistry, and biology intersect with the knowings of the metaphysical sciences of occultism? How do those compare to the knowings of the organized world religions and mystical spiritualities? How have these knowings been reflected in human culture as unearthed by archaeologists and interpreted by cultural anthropologists? How have all these human knowings been expressed through the art, literature, folk customs, and magick of our world?

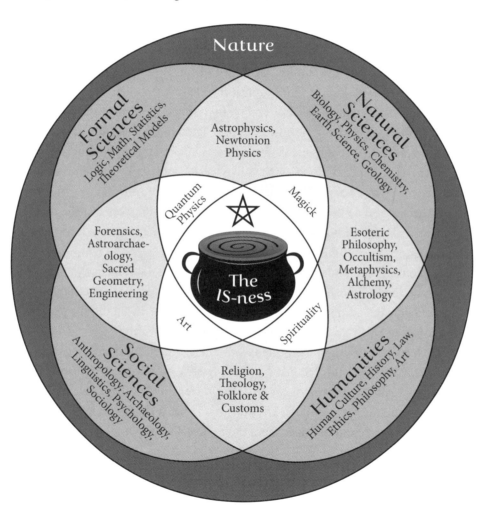

Figure 1: The is-ness

Like a huge Venn diagram of overlapping systems, there is a place of commonality where they align. In the liturgical poem "The Charge of the Goddess," we are advised: "For mine is the secret door which opens upon the Land of Youth; and mine is the Cup of the Wine of Life, and the Cauldron of Cerridwen, which is the Holy Grail of Immortality."[13] This gray spot in the middle of the Venn diagram is like a keyhole to the secret door that Modern Witchcraft opens. That door leads down a liminal path, a transition across a threshold between known and unknown, that can take you anywhere you want to go.

I call this keyhole the *is-ness*. Forgive my silly word for a complex notion, but the language fails me. Witchcraft is built upon the foundation stones of what *is*; this reality in which we find ourselves, not the illusion of separateness we find in the consensus reality.[14] The *is-ness* is the truest true thing regardless of context or perspective, regardless of who is in charge or who gets paid for it. It just *is what it is*.

On the deepest, basement-level of reality, there must be some naked cosmic truth that remains after you strip off the costumes of religion, culture, and language. I choose to believe that the *is-ness* that remains would be fundamentally benevolent and affirming of every form of existence in the cosmos. The *is-ness* would apply no matter what planet we're on or what star we are orbiting in any galaxy. For the time being, I'm content to figure out the best way to be human here on Earth. I'd dare to guess that the fundamental purpose of all the various Witchcraft practices is just that: effective and meaningful human existence.

To figure out what that meaning for humanity might be, I've dug back to ask how the earliest humans lived as they gathered in cooperation to build settlements, craft tools and vessels, wield fire, and cultivate the land so they could thrive. What did the people of the Neolithic Mother-Earth-goddess-worshiping settlements around "Old Europe" know? Prior to 4500 BCE their culture appears to have been agricultural, egalitarian, matrifocal, matrilinear, and peaceful.[15] Similarly, what mysteries would the temple priestesses of Çatalhüyük in Anatolia, Turkey, or the priestess-queens of Minoan Crete have to teach us about the veneration of a goddess? On the flip side, what did the warrior priests of the proto-Indo-European cultures know about their gods of war, mountain, sky, and animal?

---

13. Valiente, "The Charge of the Goddess" in *The Charge of the Goddess:*, 12–13.

14. Consensus reality is defined as the things that are generally accepted to be real as shared by a group of people.

15. Marija Gimbutas, *The Goddesses and Gods of Old Europe, 6500–3500 BC: Myths and Cult Images*, new and updated ed. (Los Angeles: University of California Press, 1982), 9.

From 4500–2500 BCE they invaded on horseback from the Asiatic steppes with their herds, integrating their patriarchal, nomadic, pastoral, and war-oriented pagan culture.[16] How did these pagan cultures celebrate divinity while still so closely linked to nature's cycles?

In her book *The Chalice and the Blade,* social systems scientist and cultural historian Riane Eisler offers a beautiful telling of this history, and in it one recurring answer to these questions. As revealed through the mythical images of ancient Crete, she writes that in "the Goddess as Mother of the universe, and humans, animals, plants, water, and sky as her manifestations here on Earth—we find the recognition of our oneness with nature."[17] What about the megalith monument builders of Stonehenge in Britain and Göbekli Tepe in Turkey? The pyramid builders of Egypt and Mesoamerica? The ancient societies of Greece, Rome, China, Persia, and India? Studied through a comparative cultural lens, there were many similarities intuited or revealed among our ancestors from all over the earth. In recent decades, we've come to describe the religious beliefs of these indigenous cultures as "ancient paganism."

Defining Paganism

The word *pagan* comes from the Latin *paganus.* In the beginning this word meant something akin to "country dweller" or "of the land" and described those folks far from town who managed to keep to their indigenous nature religion the longest.[18] Over time, the term pagan came to be applied to anyone who refused to convert to the new conquering religion of Rome. Thus, an innocent, wholesome word was twisted into a slur and condemnation.

The prominent ancient religions excavated as "paganism" today include the classical Greeks and Romans of the Mediterranean, the Norse and Celtic cultures of Northwestern Europe, the Sumerian, Babylonian, and Phoenician cultures of the Middle East, and the Egyptians of North Africa (among many others all over the world). These paganisms are themselves a blending of cultures before they emerged into recorded history after the Iron Age. Ancient pagan cultures didn't grow up in a vacuum. Through refugee migration after

---

16. Gimbutas, *The Goddesses and Gods of Old Europe*, 9.

17. Riane Eisler, *The Chalice and the Blade: Our History, Our Future* (San Francisco: Harper Collins Publishers, 1995), 36.

18. Christopher Penczak, *The Inner Temple of Witchcraft: Magick, Meditation, and Psychic Development* (St. Paul, MN: Llewellyn Publications, 2004), 42.

natural disasters, sharing along trade routes and shipping channels, invading and conquering, adaptation and struggle, there was a lot of cross-pollination in the fields of early civilization. To use another agricultural metaphor, the branches of diverse mythologies and deities grafted themselves into the "world trees" of every patch of the ancient world. One result appears to be that ancient paganism bore a resilient hybrid fruit that modern people still find to be spiritually nutritious.

Today, we reclaim the term *pagan*, redefining it as the indigenous beingness that grew from nature over the millions of years that life has been evolving on planet Earth in all the hybrid varieties. Every being on Earth grew up out of this mud, and so we are perfectly suited to this earthy religion. We carried the primordial waters within us in our wombs and adapted in perfect accord with our environments. From what we intuited from that accord, humankind wrote diverse symbolic stories and developed diverse religious practices. Each uniquely celebrates the interconnection with the land from which they grew. Archeological remains from the earliest settlements like Çatalhüyük on the Anatolia plain in modern Turkey and Minoan Crete show that there was a vibrant goddess religion practiced with little separation between the spiritual and mundane aspects of their lives. They also show abundant evidence that these early goddess-centered cultures were artistic, relatively joyful, peaceful, and "remarkably equalitarian" for thousands of years.[19]

Pagans are *of the land*, yet despite how varied their landscapes, when you boil each of the natural religions down to their essence, there are commonalities:

- Sacredness of all nature, including all genders of human; worship of many goddesses and gods who are associated with natural phenomena; more sexually permissive.
- Celebration of repeating cycles of nature linked with continuation of life, death, and rebirth.
- Techniques for reunion with Spirit that we experience as ecstasy.
- Interconnection of consciousness within all things, with mutual responsibility throughout.
- Veneration of hosts of spiritual entities within multiple dimensions; some benevolent, some baneful, but usually complex with various levels of agency.
- Hidden magick just beneath the obvious, which may be tapped to affect change.

19. Eisler, *The Chalice and the Blade*, 25, 37.

Every patch of planet Earth has an indigenous belief system with some measure of these essential commonalities. I call that common essence *paganism*.

Neopaganism, or *new* paganism, describes the re-emergence of those ancient indigenous religions and their cultural wisdom into the modern era. With the aid of archaeology and anthropology, we intentionally excavate these cultures and usher the beneficial parts back into the modern world. We do not delude ourselves with any fantasy that these were perfect utopias. Far from it. Some aspects of classical paganism, like the subjugation of women, invasion and warfare, or human sacrifice, need to be resigned to the past. The gods evolve, and so must our practices. Neopaganism is the next evolution of nature-based religion, which reclaims our power in hopes of correcting the course of human evolution back toward benevolence and ecological sustainability.

Neopaganism asserts that the land *is* divine; all cultures are expressions of divinity in that time and place; all of divinity's faces and names are exactly as they are meant to be known. Creation is still in progress, and divinity is evolving right along with us. I am interested in resurrecting this natural paganism because it is apparent to me that as long as we maintain that natural accord, we can know ease and fulfillment. It is when our culture began to forsake our relationship with nature and subverted the natural spiritual flow that we began to suffer. Considering the dire state of global climate change and the heaping ecological disaster now looming, the instinctual yearning that Neopagans feel to restore harmony with a natural divinity may be the old gods once more stepping in to help us to survive.

Shedding the Invasive Orthodoxies

By the definition of Neopaganism outlined above, the only non-pagan religions are those that are divorced from nature, exclusively monotheistic, and who invaded and colonized from outside their indigenous home long after the "Common Era" of history began. For the sake of discussion and without feeding any further power into their names, I'll call these religions of the Western over-culture the "invasive orthodoxies." *Invasive* because they have a religious mandate to bully their way into other cultures, dominate and subjugate, and eradicate the worship of the local gods and goddesses through coercion. *Orthodoxies* because they impose their exclusive "right beliefs" as the only possible gateway to one, exclusively male, god, then condemn and threaten violence upon all who refuse the one gateway they control.

It is the invasive orthodoxies who continue to enforce the patriarchal dominator culture under which the world suffers today. The paradigms of these religions control through a fear of being "cast-out" from the love of divinity; their message is to comply with the absolute authority of their specific god or be tortured eternally. The invasive orthodoxies have been running their extortion racket for less than two millennia, leaving much of humanity hijacked, kneecapped, and exploited.

These coercive tenets are a form of spiritual violence and not in harmonious accord with nature. Evil, which Neopaganism would say flows through fear-based choices, emerges from the subversions of the natural order. By Neopagan standards, the tenets of the invasive orthodoxies are an aberration, and all humans have the free will to ignore them. Even if generations of our ancestors were immersed in one of these patriarchal religions, we may still choose to reclaim the inherent, indigenous paganism that is our human birthright. We may choose to lay down their patriarchal weapons and abandon their battlefield in peace.

Elemental Tools to Transform Our Culture

The Elemental Witchcraft presented in this book is an application of anthropologist Riane Eisler's cultural transformation theory. This gender-holistic approach envisions a potential future for our human culture, which is informed by the goddess-venerating societies who thrived for thousands of years during the Neolithic period, prior to the first patriarchal invasions by the pastoral Indo-European tribes from the Russian steppes. Cultural transformational theory describes two basic models underlying human societies throughout history: dominator and partnership.[20]

Dominator Model

- Societies organized through "ranking" by sex into hierarchies based on superiority, authoritarian, backed by threat of violence and force.

- Established through warfare, control of resources, creating false scarcity.

- Typically, also a patriarchy (what Eisler terms an "androcracy" or male ruled). Could potentially describe a "matriarchy" by traditional definition if female rule is based on superiority/inferiority ranking.

---

20. Eisler, introduction to *The Chalice and the Blade*, xvii.

- Acquires wealth by developing technologies of destruction.
- Venerates the power of life-taking and fear of death.
- Symbolized by the blade.

Partnership or Cooperator Model:
- Societies organized through "linking" in egalitarian cooperation among all sexes.
- Established through peacefulness and shared abundance.
- Would also be what Eisler termed a "gylany" (ruled equally by all sexes).
- Acquires wealth by developing technologies of production.
- Venerates the power of life-giving and nurturance with acceptance of a natural cycle of life, death, and rebirth.
- Symbolized by the chalice.[21]

To streamline these complex terms for our Witchcraft, like Eisler, we'll define patriarchy as a dominator culture: focused on a solely male deity, ranking males as superior, and subjugating all others through threat of force. As a more applicable alternate system than *matriarchy*, Eisler coined the term "gylany," which is a cooperative partnership culture focused on an array of gender-inclusive deities linking us all in divine interrelationship with each other in an equal and egalitarian way.

Despite the Latin root words *patr-* meaning father and *matr-* meaning mother, these distinctions still aren't about the sex or gender of the people in charge. Men are just as much victims of any toxic dominator system. Rather, these words define a culture by their fundamental approach to power. The patriarchy of the invasive orthodoxies we are most familiar with in the West have a battlefield paradigm rooted in their "good vs. evil" mythos. The patriarchal approach to power is a cosmic fight for dominance maintained through threat of violence and abandonment. No matter who wins the war, we're all left traumatized on their fields of destruction. If you live almost anywhere on Earth in the early twenty-first century, this warzone is what you're experiencing right now.

By contrast, the potential for a gylanic, cooperator culture of Modern Witchcraft would be based in a honeymoon paradigm of goddess loving god, whose approach to

---

21. Eisler, *The Chalice and the Blade*, 105–106.

power is unity. Here everyone lives in the bower of creation. A culture inspired by a Great God/dess implies an egalitarian organization shared through mutual cooperation of all people. Rather than domination, a gylanic form of "matriarchy" would build strength from loving inclusivity because Mama loves all her babies just the same; it is a family approach.

Why are these models of society important to a personal practice of Witchcraft? Well, the first step of magick is identifying the problem that needs changing. Slapping salve on a symptom isn't nearly as effective as eliminating the root cause of a disease. Divinity reveals to me that the emergence of Wicca as a new religion, with her imperfectly resurrected Neopagan rites and mythos, could be the Great Work of Magick that collectively saves our planet from human-imposed destruction. I propose that this "fear and dominance" based culture is the root cause of the "disease" eating away at our collective spirit. Magick that restores the goddess to the divine balance can restore our personal balance and teach us true love and cooperation again. As our magick individually transforms each Witch, so our culture is transformed collectively.

To that end, it has become a common battle cry among Witches to "smash the patriarchy," and I absolutely understand that impulse. However, our word choices might be part of the problem. Allow me to plant this seed of thought: We cannot smash the patriarchy using patriarchal weapons.[22] The tools of the patriarchy are fear, oppression, and domination. Smash things and we've only staged a coup with a change of bully regime and improved nothing. It's just a perpetuation of violence and a transference of privilege. Modern Witchcraft offers a new paradigm, a new approach to power, and a new set of matriarchal *tools* rather than weapons. These tools of the God/dess have the potential to transmute the toxicity, heal our wounds, clear the wreckage from the fields, and once more cultivate beauty and abundance among us.

The most powerful tools a Witch can command are encoded within the traditionally "feminine" or receptive side of the elemental mysteries of earth, air, water, and fire. Elemental Witchcraft shifts us away from *ye olde clenched fist of stingy doom* into the *opened heart of loving potential.* This magick results in both personal and societal evolution. A happy by-product of this progress is a more just society and a healthier planet for our children to inherit. Ultimately, this evolution is the goal of the Great Work of Magick this book presents in section three.

---

22. A proposition first stated to me in conversation with Lipbone Redding.

Defining Panentheism

Let's define some common religious terms so we can triangulate our position within the many-isms of Neopagan religions.

Monotheism: The belief in one god responsible for the creation, maintenance, and judgment of all things. Invasive orthodoxies tend to be monotheistic.

Duotheism: Characterized as having two main aspects along a polarity, often an equally powerful god and goddess.

Polytheism: A belief in many distinct gods and goddesses who can exist within a collective pantheon but have individual agency.

Animism: A belief that natural forces, natural objects, and phenomena have individual spirits.

Pantheism: A belief that divinity is immanent within nature. Everything exists as a manifestation of an unknowable and impersonal spirit.

Panentheism: A belief that divinity is both immanent within nature (all matter) but also has a transcendent consciousness with whom we may interact personally; divinity interpenetrates every part of the cosmos and extends timelessly beyond it. Therefore, everything in the cosmos has a spirit and is interconnected at a fundamental level. People, plants, minerals, animals, stars, planets, individual deities, all beings of spirit are all aspects of divinity, which is fundamentally benevolent.

Now, keep driving down that panentheist road of thought, and you arrive at the truth that no part of the cosmos could possibly be separated from divinity. Therefore, all humans are incarnations of divinity. Congratulations! We couldn't possibly be "cast out" no matter how poor our choices. Damnation would not be possible. Life is not a cosmic death match to win the dream vacation. Best of all, because we are interconnected to ultimate cosmic power, we can work cooperatively as co-creators. It is this linkage and partnership throughout the divine universe by which a matriarchal cooperator culture is empowered.

Each -*ism* above describes a puzzle piece in the greatest occult mystery of all: What is the meaning of life? Panentheism attempts to describe the entire puzzle picture, the *ineffable*, or that which is so beyond human comprehension that it can't really be put into words. So, panentheism reconciles all of our various philosophies, experiences, and personal revelations. They can all fit together as we all navigate our spiritual path and be simultaneously *true-ish*.

The etymology of panentheism means *all-in-god* from the ancient Greek.[23] This term was coined in 1828, by German philosopher Karl Christian Friedrich Krause (1781–1832).[24] It is formed primarily from Greek Neoplatonic philosophy, which is a cornerstone of Hermeticism and Elemental Witchcraft. It also aligns with much of ancient Hindu and Buddhist thought.

Panentheism heavily influenced New England transcendentalists like Ralph Waldo Emerson and the New Thought movement. This concept of panentheism most certainly did not originate with Modern Witchcraft, nor is it unique to us. The notion that the God/dess is manifest within nature is repeated throughout our founding Witchcraft texts of the twentieth century. This passage by Starhawk in *Spiral Dance* illustrates this beautifully: "The Goddess is not separate from the world—She *is* the world, and all things in it: moon, sun, earth, star, stone, seed, flowing river, wind, wave, leaf and branch, bud and blossom, fang and claw, woman and man. In Witchcraft, flesh and spirit are one."[25]

In the liturgical poem arranged by Doreen Valiente, "The Charge of The Goddess," Witches are informed directly that the God/dess is nature, and that this divine nature is calling us home. "I, who am the beauty of the green earth, and the white moon among the stars, and the mystery of the waters, and the heart's desire, call unto thy soul. Arise and come unto me."[26] To acknowledge that the tangible stuff of nature is divine requires no faith on our part. Nature just is. Trees grow, winds blow, seasons change, regardless of any human viewing them or believing in them.

Spelling God/dess Thealogy into Modern Form

Before we get much further into the panentheistic thealogy of Modern Witchcraft, let's make a pit stop into my choices of spelling and punctuation. Within panentheistic Witchcraft, words like *nature, universe, cosmos, Great Spirit, Divine Mind, Source, the*

23. John Culp, "Panentheism," *The Stanford Encyclopedia of Philosophy*, ed. Edward N. Zalta, fall 2020 ed., updated June 17, 2020, https://plato.stanford.edu/entries/panentheism/.

24. Encyclopedia Britannica, "Karl Christian Friedrich Krause," May 2, 2021, https://www.britannica.com /biography/Karl-Christian-Friedrich-Krause.

25. Starhawk, *The Spiral Dance: A Rebirth of the Ancient Religion of the Great Goddess.* 10th anniv. ed. (San Francisco: HarperSanFrancisco, 1989), 22.

26. Valiente, *The Charge of the Goddess*, 13.

All, become interchangeable words for the wholeness of divinity, with their own transcendent consciousness and aggregate agency. Wiccans often focus on the interplay of the Great Goddess and Great God—as shorthand proper names in their invocations and prayers—thus these words are reverentially capitalized. Christopher Penczak proposed the title "the Two Who Move as One" in his *Temple of Witchcraft* series of books. I have lovingly adopted this title, as they are mirror reflections of the full range of divinity. For my own shorthand, and as an act of intentional magick, I write their title as *God/dess.* In this way, we cannot forget that divinity is inclusive of all gender, all possibility, and all phases of the cycle of life. God/dess, a title referring to infinite names and identities, is therefore referred to with the plural pronouns *they/them.*

Similarly, a discussion of the religion of the God/dess would be their *thealogy.* This is my "spell" to dismantle the patriarchy. *Theology* (with an "o") is derived from the ancient Greek word *theos* meaning god. It is the study of religion primarily from the masculine viewpoint. The etymology links to the fourteenth century French use *theologie* referring to the philosophy of Christian doctrine. *Thealogy* (with an "a") is derived from the ancient Greek word *theas* meaning goddess. As such, it is the study of religion from a feminist perspective. I choose the inclusive spelling that best reflects the cooperative culture of the God/dess that panentheist Witchcraft creates. As words have power, I choose to "spell" this change into reality.

Defining Modern Witchcraft

Modern Witchcraft is a relative newcomer to the Neopagan scene and is still coalescing into form. The tradition presented in this book syncretizes an applied practice from the threads of Wicca and traditional Witchcraft, which emerged from Britain. It is interwoven with ancient pagan mythology, folk magick practices, and the occult sciences and ritual techniques derived from Hermetic alchemy. We keep the romantic witching aesthetic of old-world mystery—of burning incense, bubbling cauldrons, brooms, candlelight, and enchanting spells. We ditch the dualism, patriarchal colonization, sexism, homophobia, and unquestioning hierarchical obedience. Reclaimed Neopaganism feeds a deep, ancestral yearning for mystery and meaning. However, we are no longer the peoples of an ancient society. Neither are the old gods static. Everything in nature is evolving; therefore, our practices are intended to suit the needs of an evolving people, in partnership with an evolving divinity, to solve modern problems.

There are several defining characteristics of Modern Witchcraft: our influences are both syncretic and eclectic, resulting in an orthopraxy that is intended to reclaim our personal sovereignty, resulting in an internalized control of our lives.

Syncretic and Eclectic

If you really dig down to the roots, you find that every major world religion, and every flavor of ancient paganism and Witchcraft, are both syncretic and eclectic. This is what I learned from Modern Witchcraft founders by their example, if not by creed. *Syncretism* results from the attempt to blend and reconcile varying, and sometimes opposing, principles and practices within philosophy and religion. *Eclectic* means keeping what one considers to be the best elements, not following any one particular system, instead forging a new system from many parts.

Orthopraxy vs. Orthodoxy

Witchcraft is better defined by what Witches do rather than what they believe or who they are. Note the emphasis on the *Craft*. An *orthodoxy* defines what an adherent must believe in order to play for their team, as is standard in the invasive orthodoxies. An *orthopraxy* suggests doing particular actions. Witchcraft offers time-tested techniques through which you will be challenged to think for yourself. Then, through experience and divine revelation, a Witch can discover what they believe on their own.

Witchery is more about personal improvement right here and now rather than worrying over the aesthetics, worshipping the old gods, or even what happens when we die. While not unimportant, those are secondary considerations. A Witch's life is the poetry of meaningful presence, and all metaphors are divine. Within Modern Witchcraft, we may each write a new poem with our lives. That enacted poetry is the Great Work of Magick, which can also transform our culture.

Witchery should have an internal consistency that makes sense, no faith required. It holds as a moral imperative that Witches take nothing at face value. The very definition of *occult* is that there is hidden wisdom to be found beneath the obvious. Learn to trust your own perceptions and experiences, take confidence in your growing power and accomplishments along the journey. Then forge a personal Craft of your own.

Personal Sovereignty

Most importantly, Witchcraft reclaims sovereignty over our own lives and spirits, repossessing what the invasive orthodoxies long ago colonized. We take authority over our own minds, hearts, bodies, and lives. With our ritual practices, we calibrate our moral compass to highest divine guidance. This way we grow into spiritual maturity and heal the wounds inflicted on us by the dominator culture.

Once we shift into the matriarchal mindset of cooperation, nurturing, and compassion among equals, sovereign Witches are ready to step up as co-creators of a re-enchanted world. We are prepared to tear down the aberrant structures that would further oppress us. In this "new age," a partnership with God/dess emerges again, and the impediments of social class, religion, gender, race, ethnicity, ability, and custom are dissolved.

With our sentience, human Witches are like the priesthood of the animal realm, just as trees are the priests of the plant realm, and mountains are the priests of the mineral realm. Together this diverse priesthood enters into service to protect nature as defenders and caretakers, as weavers of the interconnected web of life.

Internalizing the Locus of Control

In our Neopagan cooperator culture, we are reclaiming the *agency* that is our God/dess given right. In the social sciences, agency refers to "the thoughts and actions taken by people that express their individual power … agency is the power people have to think for themselves and act in ways that shape their experiences and life trajectories."[27] Within psychology, the *locus of control* refers to the *location* of where we believe the source of control over our lives originates: within me or outside of me? This concept was first introduced in the 1950s by psychologist Julian Rotter.[28] It is a simple idea, but it holds great significance in the way that it influences a person's beliefs.

Patriarchy purposefully installed an *external locus of control* with the belief that outside forces are calling all the shots and you have no say in the matter. Like a leaf being tossed about on the wind, you might think you are helplessly pushed around by forces beyond your control. If you like where that wind blows, you may consider yourself "blessed." If

---

27. Nicki Lisa Cole, "How Sociologists Define Human Agency," ThoughtCo., updated January 22, 2019, https://www.thoughtco.com/agency-definition-3026036.

28. Nichola Tyler, Roxanne Heffernan, and Clare-Ann Fortune, "Reorienting Locus of Control in Individuals Who Have Offended Through Strengths-Based Interventions: Personal Agency and the Good Lives Model," *Frontiers in Psychology* (September 15, 2020), https://doi.org/10.3389/fpsyg.2020.553240.

you don't like what is happening, then you can conveniently blame that force for whatever awful thing is victimizing you and think you're "cursed."

This externalized control could be a belief that the outside force is "god," some predestined fate, a generational curse, the government, or mind-controlling aliens. Because we create reality by our own thoughts, you might be unwittingly fulfilling your own prophesy and handing over your power to that imagined controller. Even the good things you accomplish would still be attributed to that outside force, and you never take responsibility for your own life. This is the powerlessness required to keep dominators of the invasive orthodoxies in control.

On the other hand, if you believe that *you* hold control over your life, that is called an *internal locus of control.* If you know you are master of your own destiny and have the necessary power to create the life you choose, then that is the reality you will manifest. You make your own choices, and you live with your consequences. You are also allowed to claim your own victories! If your Elemental Witchcraft accomplishes one thing, use it to internalize control of your spiritual journey. Shift your mindset from powerless victim to powerful victor in full possession of your beautiful life. We'll attend to this directly during the elemental lessons.

The Path of Return

Practicing a Witchcraft "tradition" and working through a book like this one is a lot like following an established map. They are very handy artifacts from those who've trod the path before us, but we know that change to the landscape is inevitable through time, and the experience is unique to the traveler. We can start with the maps that other travelers left for us, but slavishly retracing their steps is at best just empty religiosity and at worst becomes meaningless fundamentalism. We can stack all the various mystical, magickal, religious, scientific, philosophical, and occult maps on top of each other, shine the divine light of possibility through them, and look for what is both internally consistent and useful. Through this open-minded exploration, through trial and error, modern Witches can triangulate their way to the *is-ness* of their personal universe. This is how we will discover God/dess within ourselves, like the X marking the spot where treasure can be found. We still have to follow the clues, make the trip, and dig it up for ourselves. For me, this is the "secret door that opens upon the Land of Youth" and is "the Holy Grail of Immortality" spoken of in Wicca's "The Charge of the Goddess" liturgy.[29]

This long road of exploration is what completes the Pentacle Path of Return—a return back into proper relationship with the God/dess of nature and into your empowerment as a fully actualized Witch. For a practical Witchcraft in this current life, our path begins at the crossroads of spirit, earth, air, fire, and water found at the core of our being. This ancient system internalizes the three loci of power (plural for locus or location):

1. *Control* over our physical lives.
2. *Authority* to trust our instincts and make sound choices for ourselves.
3. *Security* felt along with self-confidence, and empowerment that is gained when divine power is rediscovered within ourselves.

As "The Charge" so eloquently advises, "know thy seeking and yearning shall avail thee not, unless thou know this mystery: that if that which thou seekest thou findest not within thee, thou wilt never find it without thee."[30]

Witchery for the Twenty-First Century

I conclude that this form of Modern Witchcraft is the emerging spirituality that can empower necessary solutions to the twenty-first century problems inherited from the dominator culture. Problems such as sexual repression, gender inequality, homophobia and transphobia; toxic masculinity, exploitation and violence toward women and children; systemic racism, the resurgence of authoritarianism and fascism with continual warmongering, the threat of global annihilation at the push of a button; the growing mental and physical healthcare crises, and the inevitable doom of environmental pollution and climate change.

As we will explore in the coming chapters, a Neopagan culture founded in the loving partnership of the God/dess would be fundamentally progressive and cooperative. It mirrors the vision of the intersectional feminist movement. The ethics of panentheistic thealogy require that we preserve our environment as good stewards of the earth and offers equal compassion for all genders, sexes, races, sexual orientations, and our neighbors for full participation in the democratic dream of "life, liberty and the pursuit of happiness."

---

29. Valiente, *The Charge of the Goddess*, 12.
30. Valiente, *The Charge of the Goddess*, 13.

Best stated in the concluding sentence of *The Chalice and the Blade*, Riane Eisler envisions this potential future world of the God/dess, where "our drive for justice, equality, and freedom, our thirst for knowledge and spiritual illumination, and our yearning for love and beauty will at last be freed. And after the bloody detour of androcratic [patriarchal] history, both women and men will at last find out what being human can mean."[31]

Getting Started: Book of Mirrors Journal

For these studies, you'll need to find a journal to serve as your *Book of Mirrors* throughout the year. A Book of Mirrors is a romantic word for a Witch's personal journal. This is not the same thing as a Witch's *Book of Shadows*, or *grimoire*. Those books are more like your procedure manual and recipe book for your magickal practice.

For a Book of Mirrors, I use inexpensive composition notebooks, and I may go through two or three in a year. I don't mind scribbling, sketching, and note-taking away in them, because they are inexpensive, and I can always get more. I do decorate the covers with images inspiring to the work at hand, which matches my yearly dedication candle. I especially like reusing the art prints of witchy calendars from the previous years. You can choose whatever journal makes you feel comfortable to express your personal journey along the Pentacle Path.

I cannot recommend strongly enough the value you'll find from a regular practice of writing down your thoughts, challenges, and experiences as they unfold. Like the moon reflecting the sun, the journaling process helps bounce our conscious thoughts off of our subconscious depths, illuminating our path here on Earth more clearly. It is harder to notice patterns to the forest while you are still wandering through the trees. These entries will allow you to look back on your progress and begin to see patterns and themes emerging. They are a "reflection" of where you are along your path—a snapshot in time—but they become the mirror in which we can see ourselves more clearly. The goal of Witchcraft is to provide some aim to this journey, and these entries will become the breadcrumbs you drop yourself along the way. This way, when the cycle spirals around again—but at a higher octave—you may navigate more easily.

---

31. Eisler, *The Chalice and the Blade*, 203.

Critical Thinking Skills

Since any book on Witchcraft worth its pulp won't tell you what to believe, it's up to you to apply these methods, along with critical thinking skills, and figure out what you believe on your own. Sadly, our modern society actively discourages critical thinking. I encourage you to question everything about your world, existence, and spirituality; dissect it, rearrange it, test-drive it until the wheels fall off. Dismiss what offends your soul, as they say, and then repeat the things that ring true for you. Choose to dive deeply into the why of the things you do, both spiritual things and mundane things. This starts with critically reexamining what you consume and how you engage with society. In order to delete the insidious patriarchal programming we've all received since birth, we have to make a fresh study of all our assumptions, actions, and motivations in life. Then only keep what is aligned with our moral compass and is internally consistent. Then we do what is effective and beneficial to our lives as sovereign beings.

In order to discover what is most effective, we have to study, experiment, and then record our findings. These journal entries are how we'll keep the process of spiritual evolution constantly honing us into powerful Witches.

Since Witchcraft is an orthopraxy, meaning right action, it is critical that Witches actually do the things. Simply reading this book won't get you nearly as far as putting it into practice. Neither will mindlessly following instructions without dissecting how they affect your life. Investigate how these witchy practices affect you. That is magick. Whatever you write down is going to be subjective—there are no wrong answers in a journal entry, so don't censor yourself. You can let your Divine Mind flow in a stream of consciousness! Nevertheless, you still have to subject your experiences to scrutiny. Otherwise, what is the point of doing it?

Magickal Handwriting

A field of science known as haptics proves that the physical act of handwriting creates physical changes in the brain.[32] Using your body to spell out nonmaterial ideas with symbols that tap an egregore of power fed by billions over millennia, forming words that transmute thoughts into form will embed that power here in the Middleworld. Sound familiar? It doesn't affect the brain in the same way in a digital format or using a voice

---

32. Anne Mangen and Jean-Luc Velay "Digitizing Literacy: Reflections on the Haptics of Writing," *Advances in Haptics*, ed. Mehrdad Hosseini Zadeh, *IntechOpen* (April 1, 2020): https://doi .org/10.5772/8710.

recorder. This could be why everyone feels more lost during this technological age. Plus, Witchcraft is quaintly anachronistic for good reasons. So, get yourself a good pen and a notebook, and get started!

⚜ Journal Reflection: Daily Entry ⚜

Daily reflections are a personal journal entry to record your daily happenings within a witching context. Begin a practice of taking a few minutes of quiet reflection or meditation each morning before you begin your day, and then write in your journal for a few minutes. Start with the date, the sun's position within the zodiac, the moon's phase and position within the zodiac, and which elemental mystery tide you're working through at the time. For this, having a *Llewellyn Witches' Datebook* or a good astrology app will be necessary. For smartphones, I like the "TimePassages" app for daily astrological positions and descriptions.

Make note of dreams, synchronicities and recurring numbers that keep popping up for you. Have an unusual encounter with a wild animal? See the same image everywhere from cloud formations to swirls in your latte foam? A friend unexpectedly gifts you with a rare variety of stone? Write it down. Then do a quick reference search online to make notes about the metaphysical and occult attributes behind those things. Pay attention to see if those energetic attributes apply to the goings-on in your life in the moment. How do you feel physically today? Sleep well? If you menstruate, include anything noteworthy about your cycle. Has anything interesting happened today?

Reflect on what you've learned so far this chapter. Record your emotional reactions and thoughts on the subject. As you write, keep in mind that you are a multidimensional being with mental, emotional, will, physical, and spiritual selves. Check in with each aspect of yourself and jot down anything at all about your state of being.

Chapter 2
Hermetic Foundations

The occult disciplines that are easily associated with Witchcraft today were founded in large part upon Hermetic philosophy. It is from the Hermetic paradigm that many traditions of occultism derive answers to the existential religious questions about cosmic creation, the nature of divinity, and our ongoing divine relationships and human purpose.

Hermetics is an amalgam of Greek, Egyptian, Persian, and Hebrew mysticism, which alchemists and Hermeticists of many traditions then put into spiritual practice. What emerged from their experimentations grew into the *Western Esoteric Sciences* like astrology and theurgy. It is through alchemy that the Wiccan lore of the four elemental powers of air, fire, water, and earth were found. By understanding where our foundational ideas come from, we can deepen and authenticate our "Modern" Witchcraft even further. To that end, let's start with an exploration of the history, tenets, and cosmology of Hermetic philosophy, which established the systems of astrology, planetary magick, and formulary for spellwork. Then let's follow that Hermetic thread into the modern era with an exploration of the seven Hermetic principles as presented in *The Kybalion*.

Hermetic Philosophy

Hermetic philosophy emerged in Alexandria, Egypt, during the first three centuries of the Common Era. It eventually became a syncretic blending of ancient paganisms from Egypt, Greece, Persia, and the Middle East. Hermetic philosophy takes its name from the mythical figure of Hermes Mercurius Trismegistus, which translates as "thrice-greatest Hermes."[33] *Thrice Greatest* was a common Egyptian epithet for the ibis-headed god named Thoth, or Tehuti.[34] Philosophers in Alexandria, being both Egyptian by heritage and educated in Greek philosophy, saw their ancient god Thoth shining through the Greek god Hermes and Roman god Mercury. These deities of wisdom, writing, communication, and magick were seen as three faces of an evolving god tasked by the Supreme Intelligence of the cosmos to teach the mysteries of magick to humanity … but only those humans who were prepared for the truth.

Some scholars suggest that Hermes Trismegistus was the first man who attained gnosis, or spiritual knowing by divine revelation, who then taught others to attain gnosis. Upon his death, the sage became a god, as anyone could.[35] His students would then become his priesthood, and that wisdom would be passed sage to sage in their temples, preserving and teaching his mysteries.

Hermes Trismegistus is credited as the source of *The Corpus Hermeticum*, a collection of eighteen texts, or tractates, which reveal the cosmology and teachings of Hermes. However, these texts emerged much later from many individual teachers in Roman-ruled Alexandria, Egypt, who credited Hermes with authorship, as was the common practice at the time. Florian Ebeling, in his book *The Secret History of Hermes Trismegistus*, describes the figure and philosophies attributed to Hermes Trismegistus as being "the product of the syncretic, Hellenistic philosophy of nature, which itself was a conglomera-

---

33. Pronounced her-MEEZ mer-CURE-ee-us TRIS-ma-GIS-tus.

34. Many pronounce this name TOATH, but it may also be pronounced like THOUGHT, or even TAUGHT.

35. Walter Scott, ed. and trans., *Hermetica: The Ancient Greek and Latin Writings Which Contain Religious or Philosophic Teachings Ascribed to Hermes Trismegistus* (Boston: Shambhala Publications, 1993), 6.

tion of Aristotelian, Platonic, Stoic, and Pythagorean doctrines, interspersed with motifs from Egyptian mythology and themes of Jewish and Iranian origin."[36]

Christianity was decreed the official religion of the Roman empire in 380 CE.[37] Another decree was issued in 391 CE by Emperor Theodosius I for the purpose of eradicating all traces of paganism and allowing demolition of the remaining temples in Alexandria.[38] Acting upon that decree, Theophilus, the bishop of Alexandria, and a violent mob of his Christian followers burned the remaining Serapeum of the Library of Alexandria to the ground.[39] Fleeing persecution as heretics, many of the Hermetic philosophers migrated east into pre-Islamic Persia (modern-day Iran and Iraq) where they guardedly continued their studies. The word *alchemy* formed from the word for Egypt being Khem, or Khemet, which meant "The Black Land." This described the dark, fertile soil left by the flooding of the Nile river. Knowledge of the Egyptian sciences was called *Khemia*, or The Black Art. In Persia, the Arabic prefix *Al-* (the) was added. The word *Al-khemia*, now alchemy, came to be roughly translated as "The Black Arts of Egypt" and describes the practical application of Hermetic philosophy to both spiritual and physical evolution.[40]

Hermetic philosophy, with its Neoplatonic influences, forms the warp strings upon which the tapestry of Modern Witchcraft is woven. It is impossible to extract those threads without our entire magickal paradigm unraveling. In *The Corpus Hermeticum*, we find the foundations for a nature-based spirituality, providing the mechanics of a divine cosmos that reveals magick to not only be possible but also ubiquitous, self-evident, and the birthright of every sentient being.

The Divine Pymander: An Occult Cosmology

The Corpus Hermeticum begins with a story about the creation of the cosmos. In 1871, this story would be reprinted as *The Divine Pymander* by African American occultist

36. Florian Ebeling, *The Secret History of Hermes Trismegistus: Hermeticism from Ancient to Modern Times*, trans. David Lorton (Ithaca, NY: Cornell University Press, 2007), 9.

37. Matthias von Hellfeld, "Christianity Becomes the Religion of the Roman Empire—February 27, 380," DW, November 16, 2009. https://p.dw.com/p/JJNY.

38. Mostafa El-Abbadi, "Library of Alexandria," Encyclopedia Britannica, updated July 17, 2020, https://www.britannica.com/topic/Library-of-Alexandria.

39. El-Abbadi, "Library of Alexandria."

40. Robert Allen Bartlett, *Real Alchemy: A Primer of Practical Alchemy*, 3rd rev. ed. (Lake Worth, FL: Ibis Press, 2009), 12–13.

Paschal Beverly Randolph of the Hermetic Brotherhood of Luxor, bringing the tale into a place of prominence among the mystery schools, which would later inform Wicca.[41]

In *The Divine Pymander*, Hermes Trismegistus was said to be meditating one day when he was given a vision of the creation by the *Divine Source*, who is introduced by the name "*Poimandres [Pymander] the Mind of the Universe*."[42] Pymander shows Hermes a narrated vision of the method by which the cosmos came into form by speaking *the Word*. Which word Pymander used to create the cosmos is subject to interpretation. That word was translated as "reason" by Manly P. Hall in his work *The Secret Teachings of All Ages*. [43]

In Hall's version of the story, Pymander appears in the form of a Great Dragon, the personification of Universal Life. Hermes "beheld a figure, terrible and awe-inspiring. It was the Great Dragon, with wings stretching across the sky and light streaming in all directions from its body."[44] Hermes asks the Great Dragon to "disclose the nature of the universe and the constitution of the gods," and then Pymander's form changed into a "glorious pulsating Radiance. This Light was the spiritual nature of the Great Dragon itself."[45]

Pymander raises Hermes's consciousness into a divine radiant splendor, and shows him how the first movements of creation established a polarity. From the chaos, there was an upward movement of light, elemental fire, and air, which later comes to have a distinctly masculine vibe. Then there is a "downward moving darkness … a twisting and enfolding motion," of elemental water, and earth that later has a distinctly feminine vibe. As they separate, Hermes hears an "inarticulate cry" from the light and a "mournful echo" from the water as if it pained them to be divided.[46]

The Source, who is described in translation as hermaphroditic, containing all genders, gave birth to another Supreme Mind called *Nous* (pronounced like noose) who

---

41. William Walker Atkinson (Three Initiates), *The Kybalion: The Definitive Edition*, Philip Deslippe, ed. (New York: Jeremy P. Tarcher/Penguin, 2008), 13.

42. Manly P. Hall, *The Secret Teachings of All Ages: An Encyclopedic Outline of Masonic, Hermetic, Qabbalistic and Rosicrucian Symbolical Philosophy*, 50th anniv. ed. (Los Angeles, CA: The Philosophical Research Society, Inc, 1977), 38.

43. Hall, *The Secret Teachings of All Ages*, 38.

44. Hall, *The Secret Teachings of All Ages*, 38.

45. Hall, *The Secret Teachings of All Ages*, 38.

46. Clement Salaman et al., *The Way of Hermes: New Translations of* The Corpus Hermeticum *and* The Definitions of Hermes Trismegistus to Asclepius (Rochester, VT: Inner Traditions, 2000), 17.

is also described as all-gendered. Nous is the creator of the world who establishes the seven celestial spheres that govern destiny and sets into motion the never-ending cycles of nature. Nous then wills the seven celestial spheres to bring forth "from the downward moving elements living beings without speech." From Book 1:11 "and the air produced winged creatures, and the water swimming creatures. The earth and the water were separated from each other … and the earth brought forth from herself what she possesses, four-footed animals, reptiles, beasts; wild and tame."[47]

Nous the Creator goes on to form another deity in their own image (so, again, all-gendered) translated as *Universal Man*, who is then granted all the powers of creation. Note that there are now three stratifications of this creative force. In the original text, Source, Nous, and Universal Man are spoken of in generational terms, as though they are grandparent, child, and grandchild. Note also that the animals are referred to here as "beings without speech."

Being a Witch, I equate the creative force called *Universal Man* with the Neopagan archetype of *Father Sky,* of light, air, and fire, but with the interesting understanding that this being actually contained all potential gender. When I read "downward moving nature" of darkness, water, and earth, I find the familiar pagan archetype of *Mother Nature.* I'll paraphrase the next passage of the Pymander creation story, substituting the modern Neopagan lingo.

> Book 1:14. Father Sky then looks down from the realms of Spirit, through the harmony of the cosmos governed by the celestial spheres, and he shows to Mother Nature his energetic form. Upon seeing his beauty and power, Mother Nature "smiles with love." She recognizes Father Sky from his reflection in her waters, and from the shadow he casts upon her earth. When Father Sky beheld Mother Earth, he recognized her as "a similar form to his own" and he fell in love with her, wishing to dwell with her in the middle realm.[48]

> With the ease and speed of thought, Father Sky descends through the celestial spheres, and is cast into a "form without speech."[49] Mother

47. Salaman, et al., *The Way of Hermes*, 19.

48. Salaman et al., trans., "Book 1," in *The Way of Hermes*, 20.

49. Salaman et al, "Book 1," in *The Way of Hermes*, 20.

Nature arches to enfold him "wrapped him in her clasp, and they were mingled in one; for they were in love with one another."[50] His light, fire and air become wrapped within her darkness, waters and earth. In Divine Love they conjoined as the Two Who Move as One, as the Great God/dess, from whom all blessedness flows.

15–16. From their union, seven humans are born, each cast according to the powers of the seven celestial spheres. Humanity has dual existence as both matter and spirit, both immortal with Divine Mind's power of creation, and mortal with carnal desire for union. Having passed through the spheres of the heavens to dwell on Earth, humanity is subject to the mechanisms of celestial destiny.

17. The creation of those seven happened like this: the female earth and her potent waters, when met with his fire she brought forth fruit. "… and from the ether nature received the breath and produced the bodies" in the God/dess image. They were "beyond gender and sublime."[51]

18. At the end of the cycle, and at the beginning of the ages, the first seven hermaphroditic humans were "parted asunder" into individual forms as male and female sexes.[52] Divine Mind spoke to them the Holy Word: make love and multiply, recognize you are also endowed with my Divine Mind and therefore immortal and powerful; physical desire brings mortality; live so that you may come to "know all things that are."[53]

19. Through divine providence, all of nature made love, and the harmony of the cosmos brought forth generations of all life. Through many reincarnated lives, they came to know all things taught through the destiny of the spheres. Those who recognized their own Divine Mind, even-

---

50. Walter, Scott, ed. and trans. *Hermetica: The Ancient Greek and Latin Writings Which Contain Religious or Philosophic Teachings Ascribed to Hermes Trismegistus.* (Boston: Shambhala Publications, 1993), 123.

51. Salaman et al, "Book 1," in *The Way of Hermes*, 21, 20.

52. Salaman et al, *The Way of Hermes*, Book 1 of the *Corpus Hermeticum*, 21

53. Salaman et al, *The Way of Hermes*, Book 1 of the *Corpus Hermeticum*, 21

tually shed their mortal bodies, and ascended back through the seven
spheres, returning to their Source beyond the fixed stars. Those lost in
the material illusion of separateness, repeated their suffering through
the fear of death.

In this story, Mama and Papa didn't procreate to make a separate baby, they merged
into a single being who had all of their powers. The Source's Divine Spirit, Nous's Divine
Mind, Universal Man's powers of creation, thought (air) and will (fire), which merged
with Mother Nature's physical body (earth) and emotion (water). An all-gendered, multiform, panentheistic God/dess of nature was the result. Then, they brought forth the
seven archetypical humans.

Did you notice that gorgeous symbolism of the yin and yang in this cosmology? She
saw the God reflected in her waters. He saw the Goddess in his own image. The Two Who
Move as One—each recognized the opposite within themselves! Creation began with
the Goddess and God differentiating from a single source to establish a scale of polarity,
then *falling in love*. They were then reunited in love, giving nature and all beings within it
a dual existence as both matter and spirit. Nature is empowered by their Divine Love to
keep evolving through ongoing creation.

Note also that when Father Sky descends to join Mother Nature, the translation says
he took "a form without speech," which is the same phrasing used for the creation of
animals in the previous passage. This nods to the Wiccan mythos of the divine masculine
appearing on Earth with animal form, as the Horned God, consort of the Goddess. Like
Cernunnos, a Celtic antlered god of beasts and wilderness. Even more interesting could
be the Hermetic correlation to Pan, Greek god of nature, fertility, flocks, and herds. Pan is
described as being half male with horns, legs, and ears of a goat, who is carnal and lusty.
His father is the Greek god Hermes. *Pan* is the root word meaning "all." *Pan* also being
the root word of panentheism, "all in god."[54]

This poetic story expresses a perennial philosophy that mystics have been intuiting
for ages. Just because some ancient sage named Hermes Trismegistos told a story in
Egypt thousands of years ago doesn't have to make it the most true story for you right
now. However, it does echo the *is-ness* of human hopes and dreams that, deep down,
when we ask the question what is all this hokey pokey about? We just know the answer

---

54. "Pan," Encyclopedia Britannica, accessed March 22, 2021, https://www.britannica.com/topic/Pan
    -Greek-god.

should be *love*. We just know that the purpose of living should be reunion and experiencing carnal life to the fullest.

Seven Celestial Spheres Establish Astrology

In the cosmology of *The Pymander* the mechanisms of the cosmos that govern human destiny are laid out in detail. Within this poetry the material earth is symbolized as being the core of a nested series of celestial spheres, with each layer being governed by one of the seven wandering gods or stars, as seen from the perspective of Earth. In some translations they are called "administrators" of their celestial sphere. However, we know well enough that the planet Earth is not the center of the cosmos or the solar system. Cosmic domes do not literally encircle the planet. Think of them metaphorically like a *sphere of influence.*

These powers that govern each sphere of influence, called stars, planets, gods, or administrators, are now recognized as the other planets (and our moon) within our solar system that were visible with the naked eye, on their own orbits around our sun. Their spheres of influence extend outward from earth in order of distance to us. "In their traditional order, these were the moon, Mercury, Venus, the sun, Mars, Jupiter, Saturn."[55]

From our perspective, these wandering gods/planets/stars move in spiraling patterns against the background of the fixed outer stars, which are divided into the twelve signs of the zodiac. Imagine that our solar system is like a vast spirograph with every celestial body holding a pen and drawing a line as it moves across a vast three-dimensional canvas. As they swirl around each other in their orbits and the sun moves within the spiral arm of the Milky Way galaxy dragging along all his planets, the spirograph image that would result would look a lot like a giant mandala that flows in repeating looping, fractal patterns.

Astrology Roadmap to Personal Destiny

Each planetary sphere regulates and informs one of the seven areas of consciousness, arenas of life, divine archetypes, elements, chakra energy centers, parts of the human body, colors in the spectrum, notes in an octave, *etcetera infinitum*. Think of each sphere, with each moving planet relative to the outer zodiac, being like a cog in a giant mechanism. There is constant movement drawing a specific interrelated fractal pattern in each

---

55. John Michael Greer, *The New Encyclopedia of the Occult* (St. Paul, MN: Llewellyn Publications, 2003), 375.

moment. So, each moment of creation reflects a unique and circulating pattern. There are greater and greater patterns of the cycle that repeat infinitely throughout this mechanism: Macrocosm to microcosm. Each layer's pattern mirrors all the rest of the layer's patterns.

The same cyclical movements of the Mental and Spiritual planes reflect concretely in the Physical Plane. Meaning the energies of that fractal pattern materialize in the chemistry of plants, the biology of animals, the crystalline geometry of stones, and the geological formations of the landscape. Thus, the Hermetic axiom states: As above, so below; as below, so above.

At the moment of your birth, your spirit emerged through the astrological fractal-filter of that specific moment into your new baby form, and the die was cast. Your spirit chose that moment and that body with the strengths, weaknesses, lessons to learn and to teach, and sacred mission to fulfill based on the astrological pattern of that moment. That map is called your natal chart. Read that map and your life and sacred purpose here will become so much clearer. This is the map of your *destiny*, by which you are guided within this lifetime. Those stars deliver the divine message you left for yourself, writ large upon the heavens so big that you could see it from anywhere on Earth, whenever you were ready. Hence, the stars and planets aren't "making things happen"; they are reflecting a repeating pattern and the flow of energies throughout. The divine mechanism grinds on in a predictable manner, but divinity is *within* the mechanism, *as* the mechanism, not on the outside pulling levers arbitrarily.

The lore of the seven celestial spheres has been studied through astrology by alchemists throughout the ages. They discerned the characters of those planetary powers and archetypes and how those powers were encoded within all the materials and beings of creation, establishing tables of correspondences to their planetary and elemental powers. Every plant, stone, metal, animal, and so on would also exist concurrently within the three worlds, with an immortal spirit (alchemical mercury), a soul (alchemical sulfur), and a physical body (alchemical salt) that held the key to those specific powers here on Earth. This is sometimes called the *holy trinity of the universe*. Another clue to the *is-ness* is that most cultural paradigms, and the systems of traditional medicines they derive, have some form of these three principal parts. In astrology, they are called *mutable, cardinal, and fixed* modalities. In ayurvedic medicine from India they are called *vata, pitta, and kapha*. In physics, these are represented by the proton, neutron, and electron. In the Western alchemical tradition, they are called *philosophical mercury, sulfur, and salt.*

These terms describe the same threefold principle from the perspective of their cultural paradigm.[56]

Much of alchemy involved the refinement and use of those materials for spiritual, magickal, and medicinal purposes. This treasure trove of correspondences can be drawn upon by Witches as they create their own magickal formulary. It is from these alchemical operations that fermentation of alcoholic "spirits" (mercury, spiritual realm), the extraction of volatile essential oils (sulfur, the soul), and the preparation of herbal tinctures, botanical extracts (salt, the body) and spagyrics was developed.[57]

Alchemists also discerned how the planetary powers influence our movement through time and methods of magickal timing by zodiac period, day of the week, and hours of the day. We'll discuss that magick in further detail in chapter eleven.

The Kybalion: A Hermetic Philosophy

The Seven Hermetic Principles are often attributed to Hermes Trismegistus; however, this is not the whole story. *The Kybalion* was published in the United States in 1908, originally claiming to be written anonymously by "Three Initiates." It is now irrefutably understood to have been authored alone by William Walker Atkinson (1862–1932).[58] Atkinson was a prolific and influential voice within the New Thought Movement in the early twentieth century. He was a lawyer, a renowned occultist, a prolific author, the editor of many magazines, and a publisher through his Yogi Publication Society in Chicago.[59]

William Walker Atkinson successfully syncretized Hermeticism, Neoplatonism, transcendentalism, Spiritualism, and New Thought philosophy with the advances in subatomic physics and the emerging field of psychology.[60] During the same era, the term *panentheism* also emerged from the same transcendentalist and New Thought roots.

---

56. Catherine Beyer, "Alchemical Sulfur, Merucry and Salt in Western Occultism," Learn Religions, updated July 3, 2019, https://www.learnreligions.com/alchemical-sulfur-mercury-and-salt-96036.

57. Beyer, "Alchemical Sulfur"; Manfred M. Junius, *Spagyrics: The Alchemical Preparation of Medicinal Essences, Tinctures, and Elixirs* (Rochester, VT: Healing Arts Press, 2007), 55, 60, 57; "The Three Philosophical Principles." Organic Unity, accessed May 31, 2021, http://www.organic-unity.com/top-menu/the-three-philosophical-principles/.

58. Atkinson also wrote under the pen names Yogi Ramacharaka, Theron Q. Dumont, Magus Incognito, and others.

59. Philip Deslippe, introduction to *The Kybalion*, by William Walker Atkinson, 1–12.

60. Deslippe, introduction to *The Kybalion*, 1–44.

Atkinson's Seven Hermetic Principles became ubiquitous across the New Age movement over the next hundred years, from *Science of Mind* by Ernest Holmes to *The Secret* by Rhonda Byrne. They found their way into Modern Witchcraft via Laurie Cabot, who featured the seven Hermetic laws as "The Science of Witchcraft" in chapter 5 of her book *Power of the Witch* in 1989.[61]

Seven Hermetic Principles of *The* Kybalion:

The Kybalion proposes a Hermetic understanding of the divine order. It also gives a structure to work effectively within that order toward becoming the captains of our own destiny. *The Kybalion* offered "master keys" by which we could unlock "the many inner doors in the Temple of Mystery," then use the mysteries revealed to successfully play the game of life.[62] Following is a brief look at each of those principles, as applied to Modern Witchcraft thealogy and magickal practice.

1. *The Principle of Mentalism*

"THE ALL is MIND; The Universe is Mental."—The Kybalion.[63]

The cosmos exists in the mind of divinity, or *nous* in Greek, which is translated as *divine mind* or *supreme intelligence*. Everything in the cosmos is a thought within this Divine Mind. In Hermetics, "the ALL" is a way of referring to divinity in its largest and most inclusive aspect and the source from which all else emanates. "'The infinite mind of the ALL is the womb of Universes.'—The Kybalion."[64]

The poetry here is that all of creation is a dream held within the Divine Mind, interconnecting all of creation through thought. The God/dess is both the dreamer and the dream. Humans, as the children of the God/dess made by their template, also think divine thoughts. Separateness is the illusion, but in truth we are all one complex being. "Salvation" from the cycles of reincarnation comes from just remembering our interconnection through Divine Mind. If we realize the power of our thoughts, we can put them to good use. That power either sets us free or enslaves us.

---

61. Laurie Cabot, *Power of the Witch: The Earth, The Moon, and the Magical Path to Enlightenment*, with Tom Cowan (New York: Delta Book, 1989), 151.

62. Atkinson, *The Kybalion*, 51.

63. Atkinson, *The Kybalion*, 64.

64. Atkinson, *The Kybalion,* 92.

2. The Principle of Correspondence

"As above, so below; as below, so above."—The Kybalion.[65]

Everything at the *macrocosm* level of the Universe mirrors the *microcosm* levels of the Universe. There are repeating patterns throughout the planes of reality that correspond in harmony and agreement to one another. These three planes are defined by Hermeticism as the Physical Plane, Mental Plane, and Spiritual Plane. I correlate these planes with the Neopaganism three-world view as:

- Physical Plane = Middleworld
- Mental Plane = Underworld and astral plane
- Spiritual Plane = Upperworld and Heavens[66]

The seven celestial spheres, governed by the seven classical planets, mirror those seven areas of consciousness throughout all of existence. Seven is a magickal number no matter where you look! *The Kybalion* outlined how these "octaves" repeat infinitely through the three great planes, which are each further subdivided by seven sub-planes. On the Mental Plane of the Underworld, there are sub-planes for the mineral mind, plant mind, and animal mind, among the planes for the elemental minds and human mind. I call these the realms of plant, stone, and bone.

Every iota of the cosmos contains a map of the whole in patterns that repeat infinitely. In nature we observe *fractal scaling* where the golden ratio is seen repeating throughout natural formations, from the array of petals on flowers to swirls in seashells to patterns of coastlines. This golden ratio is represented by the pentagram! Every cell contains the DNA instructions that could recreate the whole organism. Galaxies are structured a lot like solar systems, which are structured a lot like atoms. Neurons in the brain are structured like the array of galaxies within the cosmos. These are all thoughts within the Divine Mind.

The iconic image of the Baphomet represents this principle in its posture, which Eliphas Levi calls the "sign of occultism" of one hand pointing above to the heavens, to the

---

65. Atkinson, *The Kybalion*, 65.

66. Christopher Penczak, *The Temple of Shamanic Witchcraft: Shadows, Spirits and the Healing Journey* (St. Paul, MN: Llewellyn Publications, 2005), 123–124.

white waxing moon of Chesed (mercy) on the Qabala Tree of Life, and one hand pointing below toward earth and the black waning moon of Geburah (severity).[67]

The Baphomet symbol was designed by Eliphas Levi, a nineteenth-century French occultist, as a pantheistic symbol of the "universal equilibrium" and reflects symbolically the Hermetic principles of alchemy. As pictured in *Transcendental Magic*, the Baphomet symbolism includes an upright pentagram of the microcosm on the brow of a bearded, goat-headed, hermaphroditic figure. There is a flaming torch of Divine Mind between the horns, with female breasts, the caduceus of Hermes as a phallus, and animal features of the beasts of air (wings), water (scales), and land (goat legs and hooves), which merge the four elements. Inscriptions on the arms represent the operations of alchemy: solve and coagula.[68] Levi's Baphomet symbol is often conflated with the Sabbatic Goat, Goat of Mendes, and erroneously with the Christian Devil.[69] However, Levi described it "like all monstrous idols, enigmas of antique science and its dreams, is only an innocent and even pious hieroglyph."[70]

3. The Principle of Vibration

"Nothing rests; everything moves; everything vibrates."—The Kybalion.[71]

Everything in the Universe is in a constant state of motion; nothing rests; it is all in a state of cycle and change. The only difference between states of matter, thought, energy, and spirit are their rate of vibration. The modern science of physics informs us that matter and energy are the same, just vibrating at different frequencies. The lower frequencies merely come into perceptible form, and then we start to call it matter.

---

67. Eliphas Levi, *Transcendental Magic: Its Doctrine and Ritual*, trans. A. E. Waite ((London: George Redway, 1896), 290.

68. Levi, *Transcendental Magic*, 290.

69. Levi, *Transcendental Magic*, 291.

70. Levi, *Transcendental Magic*, 290.

71. Atkinson, *The Kybalion*, 66.

4. The Principle of Polarity

"Everything is Dual; everything has poles; everything has its pair of opposites; like and unlike are the same; opposites are identical in nature, but different in degree; extremes meet; all truths are but half-truths; all paradoxes may be reconciled."—The Kybalion.[72]

Everything in the Universe exists as a blend of this spectrum between opposites and the tensions between them. In Taoism, this principle is symbolized as the yin and yang. The mystery revealed is that while there are two opposites held in cycles of swirling balance, they cannot be separated into absolutes. The dot held within each side is their strength. That dot is also the keyhole to accessing the true power of any mystery.

Figure 2: Taoist yin-yang symbol

5. The Principle of Rhythm

"Everything flows out and in; everything has its tides; all things rise and fall; the pendulum-swing manifests in everything; the measure of the swing to the right, is the measure of the swing to the left; rhythm compensates."—The Kybalion.[73]

Everything in the Universe is subject to cycles, which are in consistent balance of ebb and flow. There is a natural and equal swing between extremes, like a pendulum. All paradoxes may be reconciled. These natural rhythms repeat in a cycle on all levels: birth,

---

72. Atkinson, *The Kybalion*, 67.

73. Atkinson, *The Kybalion*, 69.

growth, maturity, attainment, decline, death, rebirth. In astrology, we break this cycle into three parts: cardinal, fixed, and mutable. The sabbats on our Wheel of the Year, the ebb and flow of the moon's cycles, the inherent balance within the projective and receptive elements all maintain this inner balance between poles.

6. The Principle of Cause and Effect

"Every Cause has its Effect; every Effect has its Cause; everything happens according to Law; Chance is but a name for Law not recognized; there are many planes of causation, but nothing escapes the Law."—The Kybalion.[74]

Every effect in the Universe was the result of a logical cause and vice versa. There is no such thing as chance. Even when that causal relationship isn't obvious to us here on the Physical Plane, likely the cause was triggered in the Mental or Spiritual plane. When we notice the repeating patterns in recurring details, we call those *synchronicities* because they are *in sync* with that Divine Mechanism that is repeating throughout the three worlds.

Moreover, within Divine Mind, all our lifetimes are considered one big path that our spirit is traveling higher as we evolve. So, the effect in this life could very well be caused by something in a previous life. It isn't so much a "karmic" thing, as that implies a judgment. This is more neutral and impersonal than that … more like shooting a game of pool. In one life you lined up a great shot and made your move. That ball is set into motion, but it might take until the next life to feel the effect of the ball slamming into that corner pocket. It's not so much a "reward" for good behavior on your part or a "punishment" for bad behavior of the other players in that game of pool, just the natural outcome of your engagement in the game.

7. The Principle of Gender

"Gender is in everything; everything has its Masculine and Feminine principles; Gender manifests on all planes."—The Kybalion.[75]

Going back to the cosmological story of *The Pymander*, everything in the Universe emerged when the Goddess and God fell in love and then merged into one manifest being. Together, their projective qualities of air (thought) and fire (will) and receptive qualities of earth (matter) and water (emotion) were passed on to all they created in varying blends.

---

74. Atkinson, *The Kybalion*, 71.

75. Atkinson, *The Kybalion*, 72.

To the ancients, projective qualities were considered masculine and receptive qualities were considered feminine. I prefer to reframe the language and put it in context to cycles:

- Projective = outpouring energy, cardinal flow to fixed peak
- Receptive = indrawing energy, mutable ebb to transmutation

Do not confuse this concept of *mental gender* with the physical sex of organic beings. Physical sex is only one way that this principle expresses on only one layer of the Physical Plane out of many, and the least important defining quality of our multiform, all-gendered, seven-sphered character. In the Pymander story, this biological division was the last consideration, and only then for the necessity of procreation.

Remember, the *Hermetic Principle of Polarity* already states that there are no either-or, toggle-switch scenarios. Think of it more like a slider bar that completely depends on relative relationship, making all the room we need for a range of possible expressions. If a being of any possible form exists in the below, there is a corresponding spiritual template mirrored above. All expressions of gender and sex are valid and equally valuable, as affirmed by this principle.

Hermeticism in Witchcraft

This brief introduction to Hermetic philosophy barely scratches the surface. Over the millennia, these mysteries directed occultists of many traditions toward that ineffable *is-ness* we seek on instinct. This Witchcraft interpretation is somewhat unique when compared to other occult traditions. However, strip away the patriarchal lens through which this philosophy was first viewed, and the procreative surge of the God/dess *in balance* is continually revealed.

The moral of this story is that the imagery and principles of Hermeticism are consistently beneficial, and so they persist. They inspire an ancestral remembering of what the ancients understood of nature and our place within that divinity. This persistent remembering through time is likely in accordance with a higher Divine Will, which continues to evolve and reveal itself. It resurged anew through Wicca in the 1900s and continues to evolve. Following are key tenets of Hermeticism today, as applied to a religion of Modern Witchcraft.

Tenets of Hermetic Modern Witchcraft

Occult Syncretism

Hermetic Witchcraft is based upon a paradigm of poetry, not to be taken literally. Through metaphor and correlation, the patterns reveal the occult mysteries. Repeating patterns found in nature, thought, and culture provide "arrows" that point in the direction of a deeper, more universal truth. Hermetic Witchcraft is therefore eclectic and syncretic. Spiritual paradox is a mystery to be understood, not denied.

Three-World Model

The cosmos is multiform; everything exists simultaneously within the Spiritual Plane, Mental Plane, and Physical Plane, which each have seven layers. Humans can access the nonphysical realms using spiritual and magickal techniques that shift their conscious awareness into their spiritual and mental interconnections.

Panentheism

Divinity is personified as the Great God/dess in cooperation, who are both immanent within nature and have transcendent consciousness. Therefore, the universe is infinitely diverse yet unified within God/dess. This panentheism recognizes a multiplicity of divinity, honoring all cultural faces and names of the gods.

Magick and Speech

The material realm (below) and spiritual and mental realms (above) are mirrors of each other and remain in equilibrium. Therefore, what happens on a spiritual level will eventually be mirrored in the material. Flip that and what happens in the material will impact the spiritual, allowing for change through sympathetic magick. If the cosmos was created by Divine Mind (nous) speaking the Word (reason) into existence, then our greatest power is our command of language. All beings with sentience who have the powers of speech are therefore co-creators within the Divine Mind. Hence, Witchcraft includes magick spells, chants, charms, and affirmations that are both written and spoken aloud.

Interconnection

There is unity within the cosmos, with sympathy and interconnection throughout our threefold being within the spiritual, mental, and physical realms. Separateness is the illusion created by the material world, but all is alive and united within an eternal God/dess. This interconnection is reflected by the *Threefold Law of Return*, which warns that the energies we direct outward, whether they be beneficial or baneful, will also return to affect our threefold Self, ultimately impacting our own thoughts, emotions, and physical condition as well.

Blessèdness

God/dess came into being by falling in love and merging as the Two Who Move as One. Their Divine Love manifests as humanity in their image. Therefore, all humans exist because of Divine Love, are made from Divine Love, with the existential purpose to explore all the facets of loving interconnection; no exclusions, no value rankings. All humans have a blessed nature with inherent capacity for benevolence and cooperation. The potential for "evil" emerges from fear and fear-driven choices to take baneful actions that impede the natural flow of Divine Love through nature's cycles.

Orthopraxy

Spiritual growth is achieved through aspiration and engaging in spiritual practices. Hermetic Witchcraft encourages spiritual curiosity through diverse study of texts and learning from wise teachers, but ultimately requires personal devotional and magickal engagement to experience God/dess firsthand. Therefore, initiation into the mysteries is attained through a direct and personal connection between the Witch and God/dess.

The Great Work of Magick

Hermetic Witchcraft engages in the Great Work of Magick as an intentional process through which we evolve in awareness of our manifest divinity toward eventual reunification with our Source. Our spirits incarnate in the physical realm to learn and grow through diversity so that when we return to our Source, we add a complex wisdom of what it means to exist. Through self-improvement, we aid the evolution of humanity as a whole.

Immortality and Reincarnation

Everything and everyone has an immortal spirit. Change is a universal constant, but spirit never perishes. Both life and death are merely perceptions, trading forms within God/dess. Humanity's evolution through the Great Work takes many lifetimes. Our destiny, as governed by the seven celestial spheres, guides our exploration through the patterns of astrological movements and the lessons they impart. The sacred mission of each lifetime is revealed by the pattern of the cosmos through which we are cast at the moment of birth.

Free Will and Personal Sovereignty

Through free will, Witches claim sovereignty over their own lives and take responsibility for their choices, thoughts, emotions, and actions. They take up benevolent stewardship of nature and society within their sphere of influence. This maxim is expressed in the last line of the "Rede of the Wiccae" poem, as "an it harm none, do what ye will."[76]

Wholeness and Sexual Liberation

Hermetic cosmology establishes a divine spectrum of gender in balance, with all material beings containing a unique blending of feminine and masculine divinity. We are all whole and complete within the Two Who Move as One. All forms of responsible sex among consenting adults are considered to be sacred expressions of Divine Love. In contrast to classical Hermeticism, Witches consider our bodies to be holy vessels of divinity, bestowed as a blessing, and we exalt the healthy enjoyment of incarnate life as an act of devotion.

Natural Religion

Hermeticism seeks connection to God/dess through the cycles of nature. To reveal the divine mysteries, Witches celebrate the cycles of birth, death, and rebirth on all levels of reality. The yearly celebration cycle is called the *Wheel of the Year*, with auspicious timing based upon astrology and earth's movement relative to the outer stars of the zodiac. The wheel includes eight seasonal tides of the sun called *sabbats* and thirteen monthly tides of the moon called *esbats*.

---

76. Robert Mathiesen and Theitic, *The Rede of the Wiccae: Adriana Porter, Gwen Thompson and the Birth of a Tradition of Witchcraft* (Providence, RI: Olympian Press, 2005), 52–53.

Balance of The Pentacle Path
Our ritual practices bring balance between the polarities as they manifest on spiritual, mental, emotional, will, and physical levels. Creating equilibrium is pivotal to empowerment and growth; therefore, Hermetic Witches embrace both light and shadow along all phases of the birth, death, rebirth cycle.

Cooperative Culture
An application of the tenets of Hermetic Witchcraft and the tools of Divine Love granted through the balance of God/dess are used to rebuild a society of cooperation and equality for the purposes of peace, fulfillment, and abundance of all their progeny in harmony with the natural order.

Establishing a Meditation Practice

Before we get much further along our Pentacle Path, a regular practice of meditation needs to be established as a first step connecting to our power within Divine Mind. The purpose of cultivating a daily meditation practice is to achieve a mind at rest. Then you are prepared to go about your regular day effectively. In every action, through every observation, you will be opened to the wonder of the revealed universe that was always right there surrounding you. The difference is that your eyes can now see, your mind can now comprehend, because it is properly prepared and opened to receive.

❧ Meditation 1: The Meditation Room Inside Your Mind ❧

Needs

Candle, any kind

Incense you like, any kind

A comfortable and supportive chair with arms, if possible

Your Book of Mirrors and a pen

Preparation

Light your candle and incense, then sit comfortably in an armchair that allows your spine to be perpendicular to the floor. Your thighs should be parallel to the floor, feet flat. Hold nothing crossed or with awkward tension.

Praxis

Close your eyes and picture a comfortable little room inside your own head. Picture your consciousness like a tiny version of your most magickal Self, sitting in your comfortable chair, in that comfortable room in your mind. Your eyes are a window on a distant wall of that room.

Look around the room. See that this is a perfect room for you, decorated just the way you like it. You are surrounded in comfort. (*Pause.*) Here you sit in a comfortable meditation chair far away from that window. Far away from the bustle of the outer world.

It is quiet and still here in the inner sanctuary of your mind. Any distracting noises or stray thoughts are merely birds flying past that distant window … release them without care.

There is a skylight above and a soft beam of white light shines down upon your head.

Begin with three deep and exaggerated breaths. Allow an audible sigh as you loosen any pent-up tension. (*Pause.*) Now, slow, deep breaths in through the nose and out through the mouth …

Feel the energy of the environment all around you. A white light of all colors shines down through that skylight, holding you gently in its beam. Light flows in on your breath, through your nose, making its way throughout your body until you glow.

Allow that energy to flow where it is needed. Just observe as you sit comfortably, breathing deeply.

On each exhale, gently release all that does not serve your highest good. Blowing it away on the breath. (*Pause.*)

Inhale the light that flows into your mental body and your mind opens. Exhale illusions that blind your eyes from the truth. Blow illusion away like smoke. (*Pause.*)

Inhale the light that flows into your emotional body, and your heart waters calm. Exhale grief and heartbreak. Blow that pain away like smoke. (*Pause.*)

Inhale the light that flows into the body of your will, and your fires are stoked. Exhale guilt that hinders right action. Blow guilt away like smoke. (*Pause.*)

Inhale the light that flows into your physical body, and you are at rest. Exhale fear that causes suffering. Blow fear away like smoke. (*Pause.*)

Inhale the light that flows into your spiritual body, and you are at ease on all levels. All baneful impediments blow away and the air clears. (*Pause.*) You are complete and rejuvenated.

Rest here and enjoy ten more minutes of quiet meditation. When ready to return to your day, move to the window and open your eyes. Stretch. Complete your journal entry for the day in your Book of Mirrors. Extinguish your candle when done.

Chapter 3
Thealogy and Ethics

From the foundational paradigm of Hermetic philosophy, we've answered a few of the existential religious questions about the creation of the cosmos and humanity. God/dess merges the four elements to become all of divine nature. All of nature being multiform, containing both light and darkness, both mortal and immortal, and subject to destiny as governed by the seven spheres of the celestial mechanism. We learn that our human purpose is to learn, unite in love, and evolve into full realization of our Divine Mind so we may someday rejoin with Source and contribute our knowledge of existence. In this chapter, we'll further explore Modern Witchcraft's paradigm with an introduction to the Witch's Jewel of Divinity, Wicca's sacred poetry, and the Thealogy of Perfection, then follow through with the ethical principles that are an extension of that thealogy as the Four Rules for Personal Sovereignty.

The Witch's Jewel of Divinity

Descriptions of divinity are just poetic reflections of the ineffable. They are arrows that point in the direction of truth, but don't confuse the arrow for the destination or you'll miss the most exciting part of the trip. My advice is to approach divinity with an open mind. Researching the various written descriptions will just get you started. When in doubt, go direct. Ask divinity to be revealed to you in a way that is obvious and understandable. Then release expectation about the outcome and trust your inner vision. Divinity will let you know.

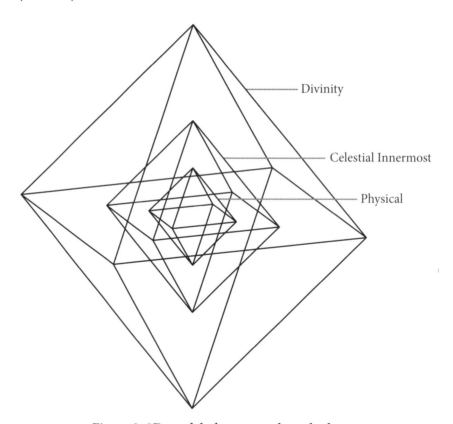

Figure 3: 3D model, three nested octahedrons

One such metaphorical "arrow" pointing toward divinity that felt most correct to me was the *Diamond of Divinity* concept proposed by Christopher Penczak in his book *Outer Temple of Witchcraft* (2004). He described spirituality as a search for this "beautiful, multifaceted, multilayered diamond reflecting the light of creation."[77] This divine jewel is a symbol for the wholeness of Divine Mind, which is being experienced from the infinite perspectives of every being in the cosmos. These beings range from deities and spiritual entities to humans, plants, stones, and animals that each contain their own spark of divinity. In this metaphor there are as many facets as there are beings experiencing it.

Applying Hermetic cosmology, I envision Penczak's symbol of the diamond in its three-dimensional form: the octahedron, an eight-sided bipyramid. The octahedron happens to be the natural formation of mineral diamonds and is the Platonic solid that ancient pagan philosophers associated with the element of air. (We'll get to that more later on.) The diamond octahedron would therefore be an appropriate symbol for a "Divine Mind."

For this symbolic approach to divinity, I nested three octahedrons inside each other, reflecting the three-world Hermetic model of the cosmos: mental, spiritual, and physical layers. Within this "multilayered, multifaceted" jewel, the light of *Source* shines in through the largest, outermost boundary. While the details are beyond the scope of this work, *The Kybalion* does go into detail about how each layer is further subdivided into layers of seven—so there could be infinite facets of possibility within each strata of this symbol.

The facets of the outermost diamond represent phases of the cycle of cosmic creation and destruction called *modalities* of cardinal (birth), fixed (life), and mutable (as death through regeneration.) Each of these modalities reflect above and below, and relate to the major archetypes of deities based on the classical planets who were said to "govern" the seven celestial spheres.

The facets of the intermediate diamond represent the seven celestial spheres of influence. These facets form the cosmic pattern of destiny, like the "die" through which Source, as raw creative power, is cast into form and character. Through these facets, Source comes into greater focus and detail as the individual deities we know by name and cultural expression. Within this celestial diamond, Spirit diversifies into smaller and more detailed facets: Angels, Fey, nature devas, ascended masters, and mythical creatures like dragons and phoenix are all possible facets on this celestial diamond.

---

77. Christopher Penczak, *The Outer Temple of Witchcraft: Circles, Spells, and Rituals* (St. Paul, MN: Llewellyn Publications, 2004), 55.

The innermost nested physical diamond at the center represents material nature, with facets bringing into focus all material beings: every physical person, animal, plant, mineral, molecule, chemical element, and atom, deeper and simpler, all the way down to the subatomic level. At the basement level of reality, we loop back around to intersect with the Plane of Forces, tapping pure creative potential as the elemental powers of earth, air, fire, and water.

How does a Witch employ this model for their magick? With a panentheistic approach to this Jewel of Divinity, a Witch could partner with the collective consciousnesses at any strata within. Mentally seek out the needed facet and see divine energy focusing that particular type of power like a laser beam into your spell. For example, I could focus on planetary Saturn to help in an issue of justice.

Or, with an animistic approach to the Jewel, every being, animate or inanimate, also has their own small facet and unique agency. Here, a Witch can connect to the spirit of a particular being and ask for aid. In that case, I could appeal to the tulip poplar tree in my backyard, which happens to be a more refined facet of planetary Saturn, whom I can physically touch.

Going the other direction, in a polytheistic way, a Witch can focus a devotional relationship through the facet of the Roman god Saturn himself. The further outward toward the wholeness of Source we expand, the more nebulous and mysterious the forces, but that would also be said for the "weird" physics we find at the subatomic levels. This symbolic progression reminds me of the blooming thousand-petaled lotus from the crown chakra often expressed in Hindu spiritual imagery.

Therein lies the greatest occult mystery: our Creative Source flows in a cosmic-sized donut, a torus energy field just like the human aura and the planetary electromagnetic field. In its entirety, divinity at its most dazzling bright, pure, and ineffable is both the outermost reaches of the jewel and the innermost core of every facet within. As above, so below; as within, so without.

When you rotate a 3D wire-frame model of our three nested octahedrons and look down at a 45° angle from a top face, the traditional sacred geometry of the hexagram comes into focus. The following figure and tables further illustrate and add correspondences to this model.

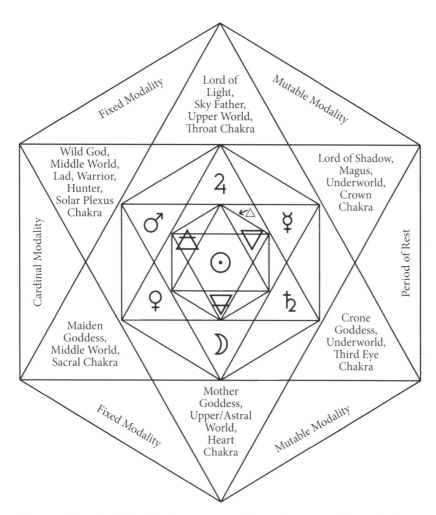

Figure 4: Jewel of Divinity hexagrams, from three nested octahedrons

	Outer: divinity hexagram	Intermediate: celestial hexagram	Inner: physical hexagram
	Modalities, Divine archetypes	Seven celestial spheres, individual deities	Middleworld, elemental Witch's Jewel of Power
Upperworld: Ascending Masculine Divinity	Chakras: Third, solar plexus: Wild God, hunter, warrior Fifth, throat: Lord of Light, Father Sky, solar Seventh, crown: Lord of Shadow, Magus	☉ Sun—center ♃ Jupiter ♂ Mars ☿ Mercury	Projective: Air: to know Fire (back side): to will Water: to dare Earth: to be silent
Underworld: Descending Feminine Divinity	Chakras: Second, sacral: Maiden Goddess Fourth, heart: Mother Goddess Sixth, third eye: Crone Goddess	♀ Venus ☽ Moon ♄ Saturn	Receptive: Air: to wonder Fire (back Side): to surrender Water: to accept Earth: to resonate

It is my experience that every individual who observes this mystical, magickal universe sees themselves and their own level of understanding mirrored back to them from this multifaceted jewel. You see what you are prepared to handle seeing, and then reality mirrors that expectation. As you walk the Pentacle Path and engage in the Great Work of Magick, you expand your awareness outward, better able to perceive and handle larger facets. With this expanded view comes a broader range of understanding about how it all corresponds and the power that flows throughout. This model can resolve the paradox of diversity vs. oneness.

In the same way that I am the individual human named Heron, I'm made up of billions of individual cells and simple organisms. Each cell serves a special purpose. I have consciousness and agency, but so does the bacterium in my gut. I also accept that my individual consciousness is part of the collective human consciousness. I can be all three at the same time. There is a synergistic effect here, where the collective spirit is greater than the sum of its individual parts. When you can harmonize all three levels at the same time, you reach your maximum potential.

Different cultures developed from different experiences of divine nature, and with that experience, we came to have differing expectations. However, the longer one endeavors to understand the complexities of our natural world, opening the mind to new possibilities, one slowly uncovers the occult mysteries beneath the obvious. Remember that in panentheism, the entirety of nature is divine, and nothing is excluded from that divinity. When you look for "god," no matter what you find, you are partially correct. We fulfill our own prophecies about what is true for us in that moment.

Sacred Poetry of Wicca

In Wiccan liturgy, there are several poems of special significance to the thealogy and ethics of Modern Witchcraft. They encode the mysteries in simple, quotable form and offer tools of the God/dess that help Witches reclaim their sovereignty and then thrive. Among these poems, the prose form of "The Charge of the Goddess" is practically scripture. It was arranged from older occult sources, such as Leland's *Aradia*, and inspired by the Greek classics, with the "White Moon Charge" penned anew by Doreen Valiente in 1957.[78] "The Charge" became part of *The Gardnerian Book of Shadows* and is cherished widely throughout the witchery.

Another crucial piece of sacred Wiccan liturgy is a twenty-six line poem first published in 1974 called the "Rede of the Wiccae." This poem was arranged by Lady Gwen Thompson (1928–1986), the founder of the New England Covens of Traditionalist Witches, and claimed to have been passed down from her grandmother, Adriana Porter. It is believed that the last couplet of the longer "Rede of the Wiccae" poem actually hearkens back to Valiente, who first spoke the lines exactly during a speech for the Witchcraft Research Association in October of 1964. "Eight words the Wiccan Rede fulfill—an it harm none, do what ye will."[79]

This famous credo of Wiccan ethics also forms the last stanza of Valiente's poem, "The Witches Creed," which says "And Do What You Will be the challenge, So be it in Love that harms none, For this is the only commandment. By Magick of old, Be it done."[80]

---

78. Ronald Hutton, "The Origins of 'The Charge of the Goddess,'" in *The Charge of the Goddess*, by Doreen Valiente, 2.

79. Mathiesen and Theitic, *The Rede of the Wiccae*, 76.

80. Valiente, *The Charge of the Goddess*, 21.

These poetic works encode the same perennial mysteries as the Hermetic paradigm, offer advice for magickal techniques, and instruct Witches on when to celebrate the auspicious tides of nature. They also offer ethical guidelines for building a successful cooperator culture founded upon the Divine Love of the God/dess.

"The Charge of the Goddess"
by Doreen Valiente

Listen to the words of the Great Mother, who was of old also called Artemis; Astarte; Diana; Melusine; Aphrodite; Cerridwen; Dana; Arianrhod; Isis; Bride; and by many other names.

Whenever you have need of anything, once in a month, and better it be when the Moon be full, then ye shall assemble in some secret place and adore the spirit of me, who am Queen of all Witcheries.[81]

There shall ye assemble, ye who are fain to learn all sorcery, yet have not yet won its deepest secrets: to these will I teach things that are yet unknown.[82] And ye shall be free from slavery; and as a sign that ye are really free, ye shall be naked in your rites; and ye shall dance, sing, feast, make music and love, all in my praise. For mine is the ecstasy of the spirit and mine also is joy on earth; for my Law is Love unto all Beings.

Keep pure your highest ideal; strive ever toward it; let naught stop you or turn you aside. For mine is the secret door which opens upon the Land of Youth; and mine is the Cup of the Wine of Life, and the Cauldron of Cerridwen, which is the holy grail of Immortality.

I am the Gracious Goddess, who gives the gift of joy unto the heart. Upon Earth, I give the knowledge of the spirit eternal; and beyond death, I give peace, and freedom, and reunion with those who have gone before. Nor do I demand sacrifice, for behold I am the Mother of All Living, and my love is poured out upon the earth.

81. "Ye" means you, but referring to a group, like "you all."

82. Fain means "would like to."

Hear ye the words of the Star Goddess, she in the dust of whose feet are the hosts of heaven; whose body encircleth the Universe; I, who am the beauty of the green earth, and the white moon among the stars, and the mystery of the waters, and the heart's desire, call unto thy soul. Arise and come unto me.

For I am the Soul of Nature, who giveth life to the universe; from me all things proceed, and unto me must all things return; and before my face, beloved of gods and mortals, thine inmost divine self shall be unfolded in the rapture of infinite joy.

Let my worship be within the heart that rejoiceth, for behold: all acts of love and pleasure are my rituals. And therefore, let there be beauty and strength, power and compassion, honor and humility, mirth and reverence within you.

And thou who thinkest to seek for me, know thy seeking and yearning shall avail thee not, unless thou know this mystery: that if that which thou seekest thou findest not within thee, thou wilt never find it without thee.[83]

For behold, I have been with thee from the beginning, and I am that which is attained at the end of desire.[84]

"Rede of the Wiccae"
(Being knowne as the counsel of the Wise Ones)
Attributed in current form to Lady Gwen Thompson

Bide the Wiccan laws ye must, in Perfect Love and Perfect Trust.
Live and let live—fairly take an fairly give.
Cast the circle thrice about to keep all evil spirits out.
To bind the spell every time, let the spell be spake in rhyme.
Soft of eye and light of touch—speak ye little, listen much.

---

83. "Avail" means to be valuable or profitable to you.

84. Doreen Valiente, "The Charge of the Goddess."

Deosil go by waxing moon, chanting out the Wiccan rune.

Widdershins go by waning moon, chanting out the baneful rune.[85]

When the Lady's Moon is new, kiss the hand to her times two.

When the Moon rides at her peak, then your heart's desire seek.

Heed the Northwind's mighty gale—lock the door and drop the sail.

When the wind comes from the South, love will kiss thee on the mouth.[86]

When the wind blows from the East, expect the new and set the feast.

When the West wind blows o'er thee, departed spirits restless be.

Nine woods in the Cauldron go—burn them quick an burn them slow.

Elder be ye Lady's tree—burn it not or cursed ye'll be.

When the Wheel begins to turn—let the Beltane fires burn.

When the Wheel has turned to Yule, light the Log and let Pan rule.

Heed ye flower, bush, an tree—by the Lady blessed be.

Where the rippling waters go, cast a stone, an truth ye'll know.

When ye have need, harken not to others greed.

With the fool no season spend or be counted as his friend.

Merry meet and merry part—bright the cheeks and warm the heart.

Mind the Threefold Law ye should—three times bad an three times good.

When misfortune is enow, wear the blue star on thy brow.

True in love ever be, unless thy lover's false to thee.[87]

Eight words the Wiccan Rede fulfill—an it harm none, do what ye will."[88]

---

85. Couplets 6 and 7 offer a variation in phrasing different from Thompson's. This version was originally printed in the periodical *Earth Religion News* by Herman Slater, volume 1, issue 3 (Spring Equinox, 1974). Discussed by Mathieson and Theitic in *The Rede of the Wiccae*, 56.

86. Thee means "you."

87. An alternate version of this line was in the versions I was taught, and can be found in numerous locations online without credit to who changed it from Thompson's and Slater's versions first published. It is more consistent with couplet 23 in regards to the Threefold Law: "True in love ever be, lest thy love be false to thee." This version's advice is to always be true in love, or your false love will return as false love back to you.

88. Mathiesen and Theitic, *The Rede of the Wiccae*, 52–53.

Thealogy of Perfection: Perfect Love and Perfect Trust

In the first line of Thompson's "The Rede of the Wicca" poem above, Witches are given the advice to "Bide the Wiccan laws ye must, in Perfect Love and Perfect Trust."[89] This line refers to the "two keys" necessary to enter the temple gate of a Witch's circle. This challenge ensures they are prepared to enter and commune with their gods and fellow Witches in good faith. "How do you enter?" the challenger asks, brandishing the ritual blade. "For it would be better to rush upon my blade and perish than to make the attempt with fear in thy heart."[90] The answer to this question is precisely where Witches are instructed on what kind of society and culture the God/dess wishes us to build. The two keys to enter the temple are answered back as "in Perfect Love and Perfect Trust."

Defining Perfection

What do Witches mean by "perfection?" This is a loaded term in our modern world. To understand this mystery, Witches reclaim the original meaning. The short version is that perfect means complete, whole, nothing excluded. This meaning is derived from the panentheistic paradigm, where the cosmos is understood to be the wholeness of the God/dess, where all matter (earth), feelings and relationships (water), thoughts and ideas (air), and actions (fire) are woven of their Divine Love. In that panentheistic cosmos, the concept of "love" goes way beyond a feeling. Divine Love would be every atom of every galaxy, the whole range of every polarity, all four seasons, all phases of the life cycle, all life-forms, light and dark, sinners and saints, *ad infinitum*. Like a "perfect circle," there are no parts missing or excluded, and that is "wholesome" love. "The good, the bad, and the ugly," as they say, are still all part of the God/dess, and their Perfect Love is unconditional. The relationship humans have with their God/dess is not transactional; there is no *quid pro quo*, no "do as I say or else," no ranking for superiority, no possible way to be abandoned.

To pledge to enter a Witch's circle in Perfect Love is an acknowledgement that we are all interconnected and sacred; and you pledge to treat others in that temple with the same benevolence of the God/dess, with equal dignity and consideration.

---

89. From Thompson's "Rede of the Wiccae," poem line 1, as printed in Mathieson, *The Rede of the Wiccae*, 52.

90. Vivianne Crowley, *Wicca: The Old Religion in the New Millennium*. (London: Thorsons, 1996), 111.

Perfect Love Is Benevolent

Why assume a God/dess of nature is benevolent? I mean, nature has river otters who snuggle and hold hands *and* volcanic eruptions snuffing whole ecosystems. Again, the answer comes from the Hermetic paradigm. Nature's cycles flow in accordance with destiny, governed by the seven celestial spheres, yes? Destiny's purpose is to evolve the manifest world into enlightened beings so our collective souls may one day re-merge with Source in bliss.

You can't focus on a "supreme good" without acknowledging a "supreme bad." Next thing you know, a "Satan" character has taken form. That is the pitfall of the *good vs. evil* battlefield paradigm so prevalent in the invasive orthodoxies. So, Witches can't think in terms like good or bad. The *Hermetic Principle of Rhythm* reminds us that God/dess must be all sides of every equation in balanced measure. The power of Divine Love is the neutrality of nature—both the rise and the fall of the pendulum swing. The cycle can feel like a blessing or a smiting but is really just the rhythm of nature.

Perfect Trust Is Reciprocal Benevolence

Therefore, this natural power that Witches channel for their magick would also begin as neutral potential. Like electricity, that power can be directed to both the hospital and the prison. According to *the choices* of a skilled electrician, that power can nurture a premature infant's life in an incubator or extinguish a life by electric chair. Similarly, a skilled Witch has a choice to direct their power toward manifesting benefits or detriments. Perfect Trust is a promise that the benevolence of Perfect Love will flow both ways, with reciprocity of mutual respect.

Perfect Trust Is Mutual Respect

Which brings us 'round to the Wiccan Rede, a guideline for magickal conduct.

As stated in Thompson's "Rede of the Wiccae": "an it harm none, do what ye will."[91] Or, the version in Valiente's poem "The Witches' Creed":

> *An Do What You Will be the challenge,*
> *So be it in Love that harms none,*
> *For this is the only commandment,*
> *By Magick of old, be it done.*

---

91. Mathiesen and Theitic, *The Rede of the Wiccae*, 52–53.

Eight words the Witches' Creed fulfill:
If it harms none, do what you will.[92]

When you pledge to enter in Perfect Love and Perfect Trust, the other Witches on that sacred ground can rest assured that their free will is respected, and no one would intentionally harm them, or anyone else, in any way: physically, mentally, emotionally, or spiritually. This promise especially applies to what magick is performed. Which begs the question: What do Witches mean by "harm"? Again, the answer is found in our foundation of Hermetic philosophy.

Harm: Divine Love vs. Fear of the Void

The *Hermetic Principle of Polarity* states that every quality in the cosmos has its opposite. If Divine Love is everything, the opposite is nothing, or *the void.* The mere notion of an absolute deprivation of Divine Love is terrifying. This is the foundational threat upon which the invasive orthodoxies extort their followers (hell, or the abyss, in their paradigm).

The void can't be perceived on its own. Like a black hole, we detect the void of Divine Love based on the surrounding effect it has. Observe nature, and the first effect of the void we detect emerges as fear. I call this a *fear of the lack of Divine Love.*

Harmful choices tend to be the next effect that flows from this fear. Harm would be any attempt to thwart the cycle of the natural order within Divine Love—to oneself or others. The results of that kind of harmful action tend to be called "evil" by our society. Which requires us to further define what this *natural order* within Divine Love would even look like in practical terms.

Nine Divine Love Conditions of the Natural Order

As revealed to me by the goddess Aphrodite, these nine Divine Love Conditions are the ways in which I believe Perfect Love and Trust would be experienced here on Earth. These Divine Love Conditions are a sacred right; deprivation of these sacred conditions would be profane. These conditions also describe the *values* or *moral imperatives* of a cooperator culture built within the God/dess's paradigm.

---

92. Valiente, *The Charge of the Goddess*, 21.

1. **Resources:** I have what I need to ensure my physical survival in comfort: clean air and water, nourishing food, safe shelter and clothing to protect me from the elements, and access to healthcare. I have no fear of suffering.

2. **Affection:** I have access to the kind of desired physical intimacy that I prefer to share with other people. I have no fear of abandonment.

3. **Free Will:** I have agency and sovereignty to pursue happiness as I see fit and am treated with dignity and respect. I have no fear of oppression.

4. **Acceptance:** I am accepted as my whole, authentic Self. I have no fear of bigotry.

5. **Security:** I have safety on all levels: boundaries are honored and privacy is respected. I have no fear of violation.

6. **Trustworthiness:** I can rest assured that those around me and my environment can be trusted not to harm me. I have no fear of duplicity.

7. **Expression:** My input is registered and honored as a valuable contributor. I have no fear of disenfranchisement.

8. **Authenticity:** The outward declaration of any circumstance is the actual truth without deception. I have no fear of exploitation.

9. **Reciprocity:** There is a two-way street of trustworthiness between myself and the world around me, with mutual care that all beings have these nine love conditions. I have no fear of betrayal.

Evil and the Wounds of Fear

When we are deprived of the Divine Love Conditions, we are wounded deep down in our souls. To be denied these basic human needs for too long creates stress and eventually trauma. That trauma causes anxiety, fearfulness, and anger. That anger festers inside us until it emerges as paranoia, hatred, abusiveness, and violence. When left unchecked for too long, that profane state may result in reactions that society deems "bad."

Witches don't trade in the currency of "good and bad." Those words are problematic and loaded with value judgments. I prefer the more precise distinctions of *beneficial* or *baneful.* The nine Divine Love Conditions are the beneficial *natural order* as intended by the God/dess. Bane, or harm, is any intentional impediment to that natural order.

Fear of a lack of Divine Love causes spiritual wounds, and it is in defense of those wounds that baneful behaviors arise. You cannot heal spiritual wounds by inflicting further wounds with further deprivation. Hope for a beneficial outcome? Only Divine Love can properly restore us and our society to our natural state of benevolence and cooperation. You can't heal the wounds of the patriarchy using their dominator weapons. Only the cooperative balm of Divine Love can heal the "evils" of that dominion.

As for the natural struggles we all face in life, here is what Aphrodite taught me when I asked her the age-old existential question: "Why do bad things happen to good people?" The health challenges and setbacks, the hurtles we must jump, the disabilities and divergences to navigate, the heartbreak and loss, the growing pains, and storms of destruction we face? Those are all lessons. They are important lessons to have in the great arching scheme of our destiny. This is especially true when we accept that the purpose of life on Earth is to be our proving ground, the University of the soul. Every lifetime of diversity is a different course in what it means to exist. Some courses are harder than others. Some subjects we like and others we loathe, but they all further us toward mastery. This is the natural order. What is *not* natural is when individual facets of this divine jewel intentionally, selfishly, abusively, profanely use their power to make life harder for others. To inflict suffering, abandonment, oppression, bigotry, violation, duplicity, disenfranchisement, exploitation, or betrayal is an evil choice. We aren't supposed to just "take it." The lesson is in how we check the bane and make changes to shift all parties back into the natural state of Divine Love.

Four Rules for Personal Sovereignty

So, how are Witches supposed to behave while putting these ideals of Divine Love into action? In answer to this question, *the Four Rules for Personal Sovereignty* emerged. They are pithy and comedic reminders but have deep foundations in witching lore. They are also interwoven ideas that continually bring us back into balance. Each has an inner and outer application as all mysteries flow with the tides.

1. Don't Burn the Witch: Self-Care and Compassion

Inner Mystery: Self-Care. Don't burn yourself on the stake of fear and self-loathing. Divine Love includes you, so give yourself a break! We have all—and I do mean *all of us* living in the patriarchy—sustained spiritual wounds or worse. That abuse is systemic and a real problem that is not our fault. It is traumatizing, and the pain and anger it causes is justified. The question becomes, what are we going to do about it? *Principles of Mentalism and Correspondence* suggest that if we remain a pulsing magnet of wounded victimhood and our thoughts create our reality, those thoughts manifest more of the same victimiza-tion. Any magick we attempt before we sort that out will only reinforce our fears instead of our dreams.

Beneficial Witchcraft helps us sever all lingering connection to what wounds us, so we can heal from the inside out. Note that I did not say "forgive and forget." Witches shift mindset from victim to victor and then act accordingly. Witches call this process *shadow work*. What is blocking Divine Love from shining through your life and casting that fear-ful shadow? Work that out so you can break the *cycle of woundings* and don the crown of personal sovereignty.

Self-care is paramount to successful magick. Establish a healthy set of priorities that attend to your health first. This way you have the necessary strength to improve the world for others. This will be the focus of our elemental magick in section three. Remember the nine Divine Love Conditions are meant to be yours too. Proper rest, nutrition, hydration, physical and mental pampering, sexual intimacy, and enjoyment of life are not rewards reserved for the most dominant. They are human rights and a witching credo. In "The Witches' Creed," Valiente states this best as "So drink the good wine to the Old Gods, And dance and make love in their praise."[93]

Outer Mystery: Compassion. Don't burn other Witches at any stakes, either. By "Witches," I mean any other incarnated being. That's the baneful patriarchal weapon that is wound-ing our society in the first place. Dwell in hate and resentment, and you're weaponizing your traumas as an excuse to further traumatize others. This is the *cycle of woundings* we have to break! I challenge you to find any "bully" or "criminal" you'd like to hex into oblivion and dig deeper into their motivations. I promise you will find a traumatized and victimized child of the God/dess who is inappropriately lashing out in defense of their wounds because they just don't know any better. But you do. However, don't confuse this *explanation* for an *excuse* to carry on their baneful behavior! Witches defend the bound-aries between benefit and bane, taking action to protect the natural order of Divine Love. Stop harmful behavior compassionately and you aid in their healing. Ethical change starts with our choices to do better to others than they did to us.

In every religion there is some form of this "golden rule" of treating other people the way you'd expect to be treated. In Thompson's poem "Rede of the Wiccae," there is an important line that says, "Merry Meet an Merry Part, bright the cheeks an warm the

93. Valiente, *The Charge of the Goddess*, 21.

heart."[94] This key instruction seems trite and is too often overlooked. It means that if you are pleasant and respectful of others, both to their faces and behind their backs, it makes everyone happier and friendlier, and those affiliations will build up a stronger, more cooperative society for everyone. When Witches gather, we greet each other by saying "Merry Meet!" as an affirmation of this promise that we won't *burn the Witch*.

2. Don't Be the Problem: Effectiveness and Ethics

Inner Mystery: Effectiveness. Many of the problematic "shadows" Witches struggle in facing are what psychologists call a traumatic stress reaction. Often those are maladaptive ways to cope with what wounds us. The traumas inflicted by the dominator culture are often subtle and insidious, but they are pervasive, and we are all forced to reconcile the tension between our natural state of Divine Love and the systemic abuses deemed "normal" by society. Our stress reactions are a natural response to an unnatural circumstance. However, not all reactions are helpful. "Maladaptive" coping techniques cause us more problems in the long run, like substance abuse, avoidance or denial of the problem, compulsive and impulsive risky behaviors (like self-harm), or projection of fears inappropriately onto others. Some are conditioned to "learned helplessness," convinced they have no control over their situation, so they take no action to change it.[95] Extreme examples become hostility, violence, or abusive inflictions of the same wounds on others in an attempt to regain control, but those are the most common weapons the patriarchy teaches. The inner mystery is not to perpetuate *the problem* for yourself.

Witchcraft practices provide more effective, resilient, and healthy coping strategies. "The Charge" tells us that what we seek we'll find within ourselves. The balm of the God/dess is affirming your wholeness and sacredness, your power and interconnection, which are unbreakable and unalienable. Grounding and mindfulness techniques, trustworthy bonding in relationships, building community support, redefining your priorities, commitment to your sacred mission, and intentional cooperation are effective coping mechanisms provided by Witchcraft.[96]

94. Mathiesen and Theitic, *The Rede of the Wiccae*, 52–53.

95. "Chapter 3: Understanding the Impact of Trauma," in *Trauma-Informed Care in Behavioral Health Services*, Treatment Improvement Protocol (TIP) Series 57, HHS Publication No. (SMA) 13-4801, Rockville, MD: Substance Abuse and Mental Health Services Administration, 2014, https://www.ncbi.nlm.nih.gov/books/NBK207191/.

96. "Chapter 3: Understanding the Impact of Trauma."

Outer Mystery: Ethics. Too often, traumatic wounds are inflicted through maladaptive reactions to personal trauma, which then damage our interconnected web unintentionally. Sadly, other times they are intentionally weaponized; people become *the problem* for others. The question becomes, is it you? In any conflict, somebody is banefully overstepping a boundary.

What even is a boundary? Any damage to nature itself or infringement upon the natural order defined through the nine Divine Love conditions violates a boundary. Boundary disputes are a normal part of life. Humans have a choice to be part of the problem or part of the solution. "The Witches' Creed" states "An Do What You Will be the challenge, So be it in Love that harms none…"[97] Think of any example of conflict and figure out which one of those Divine Love Conditions it violated. Then it is usually clear who (or what) is harming whom. Again, discretion is key; there are no absolutes.

The application of any ethic to a situation requires the sorting through of consequences, because the exact same action in one scenario makes you a hero and in another makes you the villain. Example: euthanasia vs. murder by poison. The second line of "The Rede of the Wiccae" poem says, "Live an let live—fairly take an fairly give."[98] What does fair mean in this context? The more sentient we are, the more responsibility we must take for all our interactions. The goal is to remain a beneficial contributor within our sphere of influence.

The *Threefold Law of Return* is also mentioned in "The Rede of the Wiccae" poem: "Mind the Threefold Law you should—three times bad an three times good."[99] This refers to the *Hermetic Principle of Cause and Effect*. This Threefold Law of Return is a natural system of consequence inherent in the cosmos, relating to the exchange of energy. This system is in effect at all times regardless of your awareness or acceptance of it. Simply put, whatever energies you put out into the world, whether those be thoughts, feelings, magickal workings, or physical actions, will return to affect you in kind but mirrored throughout all three realms: physical, mental, and spiritual. That last part refers back to the *Hermetic Principle of Correspondence*: As above, so below. Be beneficial, receive benefits. Be detrimental, receive detriments.

The *Hermetic Principle of Vibration* also kicks in; what you do in this world causes ripples throughout the web of existence, and what you emanate acts like a magnet. Both

97. Valiente, *The Charge of the Goddess*, 21.

98. Mathiesen and Theitic, *The Rede of the Wiccae*, 52–53

99. Mathiesen and Theitic, *The Rede of the Wiccae*, 53.

bliss and misery love company. This system is holistic; the effects you cause will ultimately change you on all levels: your mental, emotional, physical, and spiritual health will all be improved or destroyed by your choices. *Don't be the problem.*

3. Don't Be the Weak Link: Sovereignty and Responsibility

Inner Mystery: Sovereignty. The panentheist cosmos is often described as a web or woven tapestry. But as Aphrodite illustrated this rule to me in a vision, the interconnections were revealed as more like a metal cloth of chainmail, like the knights of old used to wear into battle. The metaphor is that each being, both physical and nonphysical, became their own circle link in this chainmail. Chainmail is made of metal links which are pliable, but their strength comes from the pattern of their interconnections! These links are flexible enough to have free will and strong enough on their own, but together … *together*, they can do so much more! Which hearkens back to Eisler's Cultural Transformation theory, defining a partnership (cooperator) culture of the God/dess based on *linking* affiliations rather than *ranking* for dominance.[100]

Like links, all the bright spirits of the cosmos are interconnected as though standing arm in arm, mind to mind, heart to heart, etc., forming an intricate pattern above and below, seen and unseen; if all the links remain strong of character, beginning and ending every interaction in alignment with their moral compass; if they take up their personal sovereignty and choose to use their power to create a responsible world within their sphere of influence, then together they can all coexist in harmony to enormous, reverberating benefit.

Outer Mystery: Responsibility. However, if even one link weakens, sees themselves as a straight line pointing only to their own ego, *burns* themselves through self-loathing or projects that fear onto others as distrust; if they become the problematic jerk who wields their own wound as a weapon to wound other people, through this weakness of character they betray the bonds of the surrounding links. If they selfishly or neglectfully damage the natural environment or disrupt their relationship to the Divine by harming each other, then that hole in the chainmail grows and ruins things exponentially.

If we let fear turn us against each other, the chainmail becomes a battlefield of reactionary, vengeful, fearful people. The horrors spread like an apocalyptic plague. This is

---

100. Eisler, *The Chalice and the Blade*, xvii.

your *Threefold Law of Return* demonstrated! We can be beneficial and build the world or destructive and destroy the world, but we are all in this together. If we work with unity, for unity, all of Divine creation flows with us. It is so simple. It only takes one weak link to ruin the "armor" of harmonious existence for everyone. *Don't be the weak link.*

4. Must Be Present to Win: Mindfulness and Activism

Inner Mystery: Mindfulness. Witches are called to wake up from the illusion of separateness. Each exquisite moment of life is a gift not to be squandered. Witches are charged to live fully present through every swing of the pendulum, through all cycles of nature, through both the joy and the pain, the abundance and the loss, even the love and the *fear of a lack of love*. The lessons learned will hone our wisdom and propel us to betterment as we adapt and evolve.

The Pentacle Path of Modern Witchcraft demands that you keep showing up for yourself every day, on all levels, for the rest of your life. Get up off your couch, stop wishing, stop bitching, stop turning a blind eye to atrocity, stop bending over and taking that beating. You want this wisdom? This power? It's not available by mail order; there will be no remote third-party download. No one else holds the keys to your gateway to the God/dess. Get thee to the crossroads and *do the work*. Now do it again … and again, with every breath, in full engagement in the dance. The minute you project the locus of your control onto anyone or anything outside of yourself, you might as well hand in your pointy hat, because you lose.

Outer Mysteries: Activism. Witchcraft is *not* pacifism; it is activism. It can be peaceful and cooperative, but neither does it "turn the other cheek."[101] *Must be present to win* is our calling to show up in person, to pay full attention, to listen carefully and speak up thoughtfully. It is also a Witch's commission as a warrior of Divine Love, but in a cooperator culture, that warrior is a civil servant, advocate, peacekeeper, and defender of the boundaries between benefit and bane, ensuring justice and liberty for all. Witches of Divine Love know when to stand up to the bullies of the world and nullify their harms. The "Rede of the Wiccae" poem also states: "With the fool no season spend or be counted as his friend."[102] If you do nothing to check hatefulness, or abide alongside injustices

---

101. Matthew 5:39.

102. Mathiesen and Theitic, *The Rede of the Wiccae*, 52–53.

within your reach, then you are guilty by association. We *must be present to win.* This is the paradox of personal sovereignty, which we'll discuss more in a later chapter. With great power comes great responsibility. *Do as ye will*, yes, but since we are spiritually interdependent, we make sure to *harm none*, including ourselves. Which loops us back around to the first rule: *don't burn the Witch.*

The thealogy, values, and ethical guidelines we've discussed here attempt to describe a holistic system of cooperation, wherein each individual Witch is in full possession of their sovereignty, well-balanced, and empowered. We do not yet live in a cooperator society that shares these values. However, if we begin with ourselves, our choices, and our behaviors, then at least our lives and relationships will be enriched. By extension, the world may be reenchanted one life at a time until together we make big changes. That describes the Great Work of Magick that Witches enact through our Wheel of the Year, which we'll discuss in chapter 4.

✤ Meditation 2: Pranic Breathing Relaxation ✤

This method of intentional breathing is inspired by practices from the East that focus on the relationship between the body and the breath. Pranic breathing is often referred to in yogic practices. As a means to shift our thinking, we'll integrate a spoken magickal charm, an affirmation version of the two keys and Four Rules for Personal Sovereignty.

Needs

Candle, any kind

Incense, any kind

A comfortable and supportive chair with arms, if possible

A veil or hood that can be lowered over your eyes

Your Book of Mirrors and a pen

Written affirmations from the end of this meditation, where you can easily read them

Preparation

Light your candle and incense, then sit comfortably in your armchair in the same manner introduced in meditation 1: The Meditation Room Inside Your Mind.

Praxis

Place a veil or hood over your eyes if that helps you block out the world for a time. Close your eyes and sit comfortably. Your spine is perpendicular to the earth, like a lightning rod. Your hands lay gently resting in your lap or on the arms of the chair.

Return to the meditation room inside your mind, remembering the skylight over your head and the soft white light of all the colors shining down from above.

Turn your focus inward and downward. Breathe in through the nose and out through the mouth. Take three dramatic breaths, filling your lungs completely, and exhaling with an audible sigh.

Shake out any tension in your jaw. Blow a big raspberry with your lips, loosen up.

Breathing more normally now, welcome your breath to flow deeply into the center of your being.

Filling first your belly like a bellows, then expanding upward into your chest. Exhale in reverse, letting the chest fall first, and then the belly. (*Long pause.*)

See your breath entering your nose as a soft white light, which then flows wherever it is needed in your body. This energy flows in like liquid Divine Love, pooling where it is needed to relax you. This light is the energy that sustains your spirit and your health.

Breathe the light into your physical body from toes to scalp. Wherever the light touches, your muscles relax, becoming heavier now. Your physical body is healed and at ease. (*Pause.*)

Breathe the light into your belly; the light fires the furnace of your will. Wherever the light touches, you feel alive and powerful. The body of your will is invigorated and at ease. (*Pause.*)

Breathe the light into your heart; your feelings flow freely. Wherever the light touches, you feel loved and accepted. Your emotional body is nurtured and at ease. (*Pause.*)

This nurturing liquid light bubbles up to fill your mind, flows through your thoughts. Wherever the light touches, you feel serene and alert. Your mental body is receptive and at ease. (*Pause.*)

Thought patterns slow as you sink into deeper states of restful awareness. (*Pause.*)

You are one with your breath as the liquid light flows in to fill you completely. Wherever the light touches, you are at ease. (*Pause for three long breaths.*)

The light now overflows, and you are wrapped in a comforting sphere of light, surrounding you, softly glowing, fully sustained and invigorated now. Breathe in the healing light to strengthen yourself on all levels. (Pause for three long breaths.)

Descending again, deeper and deeper into your center, find at your core the shining Jewel of Divinity, your facet within the Divine Light of Creation. (*Pause.*) The Divine Light of Creation shines brightly from your center. You are a dazzling Jewel of Divinity.

You are a being of light in a world made of light. You are a being of thought in a world made of thought. You are a being of love in a world made of love. You are one with Divinity, and you may go anywhere you desire with the speed of imagination. Your dreams create the world. (*Long pause.*)

Repeat the two keys to the temple of Witchcraft and the Four Rules for Personal Sovereignty in their affirmation form:

> *I am whole and complete within Divine Love.*
> *I am trustworthy in thought and deed.*
> *I am compassionate to myself and all others.*
> *I am beneficial in my life and society.*
> *I am sovereign within my sphere of influence.*
> *I am mindfully engaged within Divinity.*
> *I am a perfect child of the God/dess.*
> *I am loving; I am lovable; I am love.*
> *Blessèd be.*

Rest in quiet meditation for twenty minutes or so before gently returning to waking consciousness. Reflect on the meditation in your Book of Mirrors.

Chapter 4
Astrological Timing and the Great Work of Magick

In "The Charge of the Goddess" poem, Witches are tasked to "Keep pure your highest ideal; strive ever towards it; let naught stop you or turn you aside."[103] One's highest ideal would align with their values and personal aspirations and would therefore be personal. However, there are some common ideals to a religion of Hermetic Witchcraft. Doreen Valiente once wrote of the Great Work that "The dances, festivals, and rituals of the old religion were intended to further … the harmonizing of humanity with the life-force of

---

103. Valiente, *The Charge of the Goddess*, 12.

the Universe … the union of the microcosm, the human being, with the macrocosm, the Universe."[104]

The Hermetic charge in *The Pymander* was to remember that we think within the Divine Mind to evolve in personal attainment and come to "know all things that are" so that all of humanity may eventually transcend the cycles of reincarnation and destiny to go bliss out with our Source among the outer stars.[105] Striving for pure, golden enlightenment came to be known as the Great Work of Magick by the alchemists who refined these natural philosophes into a laboratory science.

For Witches, that magick of personal attainment is enacted throughout our year-long cycle of seasonal celebrations known as the Wheel of the Year. Our Great Work of Magick takes daring forms through meditation and devotional work, rituals, and magickal techniques, which keep us successfully flowing with our starry destiny, on track to accomplishing our sacred mission. Each person works in their own unique way, on their own little piece of the puzzle. Collectively, Witches create great changes to the interconnected web of existence within which we can all thrive. Or, at least, that is the idea.

The Pentacle Path: Microcosm and Macrocosm

When I syncretize the Hermetic Great Work with Modern Witchcraft practices, I call it the *Pentacle Path* because it focuses on balancing and healing all the layers of oneself in a holistic, fivefold way. This way the Witch may enjoy a happy, healthy life here on Earth. This alchemical process of refinement and attainment takes place simultaneously on the inner and outer planes of existence. Every mystery is revealed in two parts: the inner and outer lesson, which reconcile a paradox. We do the inner work to improve our own lives here in the microcosm, and the outer work of evolving the macrocosm mirrors naturally. Let's further refine what we mean by the microcosm and macrocosm levels of the Great Work.

Microcosm: Inner Magick for the Individual. Each Witch levels up to a greater state of awareness on their own journey of self-realization within the greater flow of an unfolding nature. We are also in a process of unfolding, like the blooming of a flower, into our most beautiful, true, divine selves.

104. Doreen Valiente, *Witchcraft for Tomorrow* (Custer, WA: Phoenix Publishing Inc., 1987), 133.

105. Salaman, et al., *The Way of Hermes*, 21.

Another goal of the Great Work is discovering our True Will, or Divine Will, and then attaining that goal, attaining mastery of all the lessons presented by life on Earth.[106] The goal of one's True Will for this lifetime is also referred to as one's *sacred mission*. In Hermeticism, the long game would be to eventually transcend incarnation and join the Mighty Dead as an ancestor of spirit who guides others along the path, until all humanity has rejoined with Source beyond the outer stars.

As a Witch, escaping incarnation doesn't much interest me. Witches are of this world. Rather than "deny the flesh," we Witches are encouraged to "dance, sing, feast, make music and love" as praise.[107] Rather than striving to reach a distant "heaven," a witching focus tends to be sideways into the Middleworld: and the shenanigans we can get up to at this party right now. However, a healthier and more cooperative humanity would certainly be a lot more fun for everyone! This is the high ideal for which I strive.

Macrocosm: Outer Magick for the World. Helping all of humanity to level-up in awareness. Nature itself is also unfolding in a process of self-realization on the Path of Return back to its Divine Source. Collective human consciousness is still in the process of awakening, and the state of the material world exists according to the average ability we have to perceive it. Thus, as our collective human minds evolve beyond the current level, so will follow all of creation.

The larger goal of the Great Work is to further humanity's awakening so that the consensus reality we all perceive advances into a more enjoyable and wonderous state. The point of the Great Work is that we are in a continual process of self-improvement. We work individually within the wholeness of Divine Mind, but ultimately, we are all one being. We progress in awareness because we all uplink to a collective consciousness. The theory is that at some point the species reaches a critical mass of understanding, and then suddenly even the most ignorant stragglers are awakened. These are the nefarious mysteries of the witching agenda: do innovative, compassionate, beautiful things for so long and so well, by so many of us, until humanity fully awakens into enchantment. Then maybe we can fully realize our paradise here on Earth.

---

106. Bartlett, *Real Alchemy*, 170–171.

107. Valiente, *The Charge of the Goddess*, 12–13.

Defining Magick

First things first, we need to define what Witches mean by "magick," because this word has little to do with Hollywood depictions. The infamous magus Aleister Crowley, founder of the magickal tradition known as Thelema, defined it as such: "Magick is the Science and Art of causing Change to occur in conformity with Will."[108] Crowley was also the first to propose the spelling of religious magick with the "k," as a distinction from parlor tricks and illusions of stage magic performances.

I'd go further to define magick as the co-creative partnership that occurs easily (and almost effortlessly) when the five layers of the Self are in balance and harmony with nature, creating a conduit of power. The power of nature is neutral. That power may be formed by intentions, directed by will, manifested through physical actions, and empowered by emotions within Divine Love. Then voila!

Modern Witchcraft provides one such method for balanced alignment. To align ourselves holistically, we use energetic work to connect to divinity and the elemental forces of nature. This brings balance through our own mental body (air), emotional body (water), body of our will (fire), physical body (earth), and spiritual body (God/dess). Our Witchcraft rituals and magickal workings help us to twist each layer of ourselves into an open and balanced position. It's like a channel lock mechanism: aligning the tumblers of each Self opens the free-flowing conduit of power to course through us from root to crown, above to below.[109] These five aspects of nature and the Self are symbolized by the perfectly equal and interwoven strokes of the pentagram. This symbol of a five-pointed star has been associated with power and protection since antiquity.

As long as the magick we make is in alignment with Divine Will and flowing in accord with nature, then change is relatively simple and easy. This is because we are interconnected with nature, on all levels, all the time. All the other trappings of spells and ceremonial magick are busywork to keep our focus and enhance our will through partnerships in the realms of plant, stone, bone, and spirit.

---

108. Aleister Crowley, *Magick in Theory and Practice* (New York: Castle Books, 1929), 8.

109. I first heard this "channel lock" analogy for opening your chakras in a workshop with author Wendy Joy as she discussed her book *Clear Channel: A Guide for the Newly Awakening* (Balboa Press, 2011).

Auspicious Timing Through Astrology

Astrological timing is precise to movements of the cosmos, reflecting the is-ness of truth on planet earth, which transcends any religion. This science is called archaeoastronomy.[110] Ancient megalith builders, like Stonehenge in Britain and the pyramids in Egypt and across Mesoamerica, all precisely pinpointed the equinoxes, solstices, and cross quarters of the year according to our relative position among the stars. Astrological timing also predates recorded history and all of the invasive orthodoxies. By contrast, the typical Gregorian wall calendar was installed in 1582 by Pope Gregory XIII for the purpose of planning Catholic holidays and has little to do with the cosmic tides of nature's power.[111]

Witches strive to perceive every moment in its flow of natural magick; every thought and action we take can either engage effectively with that flow or fruitlessly against it. The trick to Witchcraft is in knowing which actions to take and when they will be most effective. This is the distinction of auspicious timing.

Here is the secret to magick: it's all relative. It is relative to your vantage point right now and your position within this divine mechanism of the cosmos. Per the Hermetic paradigm, astrology describes the mechanics of the divine cosmos from our relative perspective on Earth. It also precisely measures the cycles of each player in our solar system and the relative relationships between those players through time. The Great Work system built upon astrological timing works consistently from the macrocosm down to the microcosm. I share this system as a starting place for you. Your job is to adjust your Witchcraft practices to be effective and consistent with your perspective and needs.

We'll be integrating the tides of elemental, lunar, solar, and astrological cycles, thus laying out a year-long map of energetic tides. We'll then plan magickal workings within the Wheel of the Year. The astrology part can seem technical and complicated at first. However, I promise that if you live by the tides of nature long enough, it ceases to be academic. This Witchcraft becomes a reflex as easy as breathing. As an instinct, you begin to project and receive by these tides, just as surely as all the sailboats in the harbor rise with the water. After a while, the Wheel of the Year becomes the undeniable is-ness in syncopation with your spirit.

---

110. For exact astrological dates of Neopagan solar holidays see https://www.archaeoastronomy.com/.

111. "Gregorian Calendar," Encyclopedia Britannica, n.d., https://www.britannica.com/topic/Gregorian
-calendar.

Figure 5: Great Work Wheel of the Year system by Heron Michelle

The Wheel of the Year

The Great Work of Magick forms the bones of my Witchcraft practice, but that skeleton is fleshed out through the celebratory cycle known as the Wheel of the Year. This is a system for year-round spiritual work that spirals us inward, deeper, and more refined with every turning. With this system, we can learn to effectively ride the waves of power experienced in nature. The Wheel of the Year maps the cycles that are mirrored throughout the three realms: physical, mental, and spiritual. This map helps us navigate our journey along the Pentacle Path between who we are now and who we choose to become.

Like all occult symbols, the integrated graphic provided above is packed with correspondences and lore, all of which inspire a yearly practice, working from the outer elemental ring to the center solar ring, layer by spiraling layer.

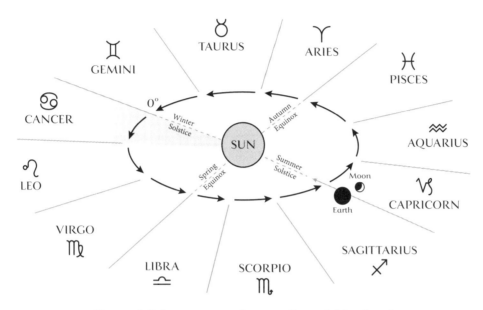

Figure 6: Solar system and our zodiac neighborhood

Stellar Cycles: Zodiac Stars

Our stellar neighborhood is known as the zodiac. It is the backdrop of fixed stars we see surrounding the earth. We divide the zodiac into twelve sections, or signs, of 30 degrees each, making 360 degrees of a perfect circle. Each sign expresses the qualities of a classical element and a phase of the cycle, known as a modality. There are four sets of three signs that flow in their own cycle of birth, growth, and death corresponding to our seasons. The following table shows the modalities of a cycle and their corresponding zodiac signs by element.

Modality	Earth	Fire	Water	Air
Cardinal	Capricorn	Aries	Cancer	Libra
Fixed	Taurus	Leo	Scorpio	Aquarius
Mutable	Virgo	Sagittarius	Pisces	Gemini

Modalities: Cardinal, Fixed, and Mutable

Remember the *Hermetic Principle of Rhythm*: "Everything flows out and in; everything has its tides; all things rise and fall; the pendulum-swing manifests in everything."[112] Cardinal energies initiate a cycle. The pendulum swings out and so boldly starts something new. Fixed energies maintain a cycle. The momentum of the pendulum crests mid-swing at the peak and hangs before turning to head back. Mutable energies conclude the cycle then transmute in preparation of a new cycle. The pendulum hangs that second on the other side of full ebb, then shifts again as it prepares for the next swing.

Solar Cycles: Sabbats of the Sun

We can apply the three modes of a cycle to Earth's orbital path around the sun through the twelve zodiac signs. Each season is equivalent to one pendulum swing. In the Wheel of the Year graphic (figure 5), the central petals depict the wave form of the seasonal cycle, with the point of each season's petal at the midpoint, or crest, of that tide. Along Earth's orbit, Witches celebrate eight equally spaced solar holidays that explore the *yang* side of divine polarity and the mythos and mysteries of masculine divinity within nature.

Cardinal Zodiac Signs begin each season at the equinoxes and solstices. When we enter a cardinal sign, we celebrate a Lesser Sabbat, or quarter day, and kick off the new season. Cardinal signs are the "flow" of seasonal tides.

Fixed Zodiac Signs will peak the energies of that season. At 15 degrees of the fixed sign, we celebrate a Grand Sabbat, or cross-quarter day. These holy days have many names, cultural and modern, depending on your tradition's preferences. For general

---

112. Atkinson, *The Kybalion*, 145.

purposes, we can call them High Spring, High Summer, etc. to remind us that they hold the peak of seasonal tides.

Mutable Zodiac Signs will resolve the energies of the season. Mutable energy destroys, integrates, and concludes each season as we shift into a new one. This is the "ebb" of seasonal tides.

Modalities and Elemental Powers Through the Zodiac Signs

In his book *Practical Astrology for Witches and Pagans*, Ivo Dominguez Jr. describes the modalities and their relationship to the four elements of earth, air, fire, and water that are expressed through the zodiac signs:

> The Modalities have transcendent qualities as well as immanent qualities that become visible through the behavior of the Elements. They exist separate from each other, but they also arise from each other. You may think of the Modalities as operating both above and below the Elements, and as the context and environment within which the Elements exist.[113]

The twelve zodiac signs reflect twelve basic personality types, which exhibit the twelve unique combinations of element and modality. Thus, $3 \times 4 = 12$. Fire and air signs are considered extroverted, projective signs that have a yang (positive) polarity. Water and earth signs are considered introverted, receptive signs that have a yin (negative) polarity.

There are six pairings of signs, which lie opposite each other across the wheel of the zodiac and naturally balance the virtues and vices of each element and sign. Notice in the chart below that the air and fire signs are always paired, and the water and earth signs are always paired. This zodiac and elemental system of balance can also aid us along our Pentacle Path to balance, especially as we celebrate lunar cycles.

The following table shows the six zodiacal pairings with their element, polarity, and modality. At full moons, when the sun is the sign of the first column, the moon will be in the sign of the second column. For the dark half of the year, the cycle repeats, but with sun and moon in opposite signs of that pairing.

---

113. Ivo Dominguez Jr., *Practical Astrology for Witches and Pagans: Using the Planets and the Stars for Effective Spellwork, Rituals, and Magickal Work* (San Francisco, CA: Weiser Books, 2016), 40.

Zodiac Pairings with Element, Polarity, Modality		
1	Aries (Fire, Yang, Cardinal)	Libra (Air, Yang, Cardinal)
2	Taurus (Earth, Yin, Fixed)	Scorpio (Water, Yin, Fixed)
3	Gemini (Air, Yang, Mutable)	Sagittarius (Fire, Yang, Mutable)
4	Cancer (Water, Yin, Cardinal)	Capricorn (Earth, Yin, Cardinal)
5	Leo (Fire, Yang, Fixed)	Aquarius (Fire, Yang, Fixed)
6	Virgo (Earth, Yin, Mutable)	Pisces (Water, Yin, Mutable)

Deosil and Widdershins Cycles:

In similar parlance to the modalities of a cycle, in Wicca the directional flow of power is referred to as either a *deosil spiral* or a *widdershins spiral*.[114]

Deosil Spiral: Pronounced like *jeh-shel*. Means "sunwise" and spirals clockwise, as does the relative appearance of the sun moving around the earth from east to west as seen from earth. This movement symbolizes projective energies and a positive energetic charge. It corresponds to the cardinal modality and the waxing, or growing, phase of a cycle. Deosil spiraling movements are used magickally to increase and build things.

Widdershins Spiral: Pronounced like *weh-der-shins*. Means "moonwise" and spirals counterclockwise, as does the revolution of the moon around the earth. This movement symbolizes receptive energies and a negative energetic charge. It corresponds to the mutable modality and the waning, or decreasing, phase of a cycle. Widdershins spiraling movements are used magickally to decrease and deconstruct things.

Unfortunately, because Witches honor the Goddess during lunar cycles, often associating her with the darkness of nighttime, persecution from the invasive orthodoxies also lumped the Goddess with "evil" forces as an excuse for misogynistic abuses of women and religious persecution through "Witch trials." Pay heed not to lump either of these

---

114. Timothy Roderick, *Dark Moon Mysteries: Wisdom, Power and Magic of the Shadow World* (St. Paul, MN: Llewellyn Publications, 1996), 79.

spirals into categories of judgment like "good or bad," "cursing or blessing," or even "benefit or bane." Effective witchery does not impose a false dichotomy of either "white or black" magick or a "light or dark" path, as this language is highly problematic (steeped in colonialism and racism) and inaccurate. Both the solar and lunar cycles have both light (growing) and dark (waning) halves of their cycles. By extension, the God and the Goddess, the wholeness of whose power Witches explore throughout the Wheel of the Year, each have aspects of growing through life and decreasing until death and rebirth. Both are necessary for a balanced and healthy life and are entirely separate considerations from any judgment over ethics. For example, for a beneficial cure of cancer, I'd work widdershins to "curse" those baneful cells into oblivion, but it would be compassionate, ethical, and effective medicine to destroy that bane to restore overall health.

Elemental Cycles: Pentacle Paths

The Great Work of the Witch is to evolve through a healthy balance between all areas of consciousness. Those are most easily observed through the four physical elements below: air, fire, water, and earth. We observe them within nature, and then we extrapolate their spiritual lessons above. In chapter 6, we'll further organize these mysteries into the Witch's Jewel of Power and then fully explore them in section three.

The *Hermetic Principles of Polarity and Gender* inform us that each element would teach us both a receptive (inner, widdershins) lesson and projective (outer, deosil) lesson, which are a reflection of each other along a range of polarity.[115] Our elemental work is to reconcile the paradox this polarity creates so that they are brought into harmonious balance within ourselves.

Therefore, there are four receptive and four projective elemental expressions through which we ebb and flow. Over the course of the year, these lessons are interwoven between the sabbats, spanning the tides between solar holidays. This allows for a full sabbat cycle of exploration of each elemental mystery each year but offers a counterpoint: As we flow with the seasonal tide, we ebb with the receptive elemental tide. Then as we ebb with the seasonal tide, we flow with the projective elemental tide. See figure 7.

---

115. Roderick, *Dark Moon Mysteries*, 79.

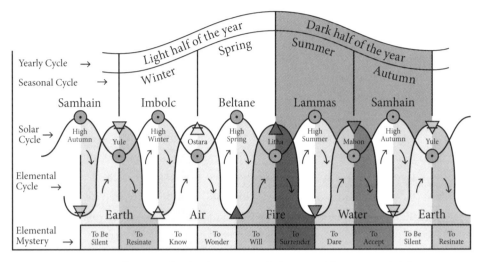

Figure 7: Elemental tides in counterbalance with seasonal tides

Like the five strokes necessary to draw a five-pointed star, the Pentacle Path of Elemental Witchcraft takes five legs of a journey. The legs of this journey are mapped to the seasons throughout the Wheel of the Year. A solar year spans between Spring Equinoxes. Within that solar year there are roughly fifty-two weeks, in which we have four seasons. Fifty-two weeks divided by four seasons comes to thirteen weeks per season, revealing the magickal number thirteen of Witchcraft on Earth! There are also thirteen full moons during blue moon years. Each elemental tide spans the thirteen weeks between midpoints of each season, with the inner and outer elemental mystery each given half that time. The elemental paths are explored during these timeframes, which I name as tides that conclude with their sabbat:

Earth: The Path of Sovereignty
Yuletide: Samhain until Yule—earth's projective mysteries of silence
Imbolctide: Yule until Imbolc—earth's receptive mysteries of resonance

Air: The Path of Truth
Ostaratide: Imbolc until Ostara—air's projective mysteries of knowing
Beltanetide: Ostara until Beltane—air's receptive mysteries of wonderment

Fire: The Path of the Power
Lithatide: Beltane until Litha—fire's projective mysteries of the will
Lammastide: Litha until Lammas—fire's receptive mysteries of surrender

Water: The Path of Love
Mabontide: Lammas until Mabon—water's projective mysteries of daring
Samhaintide: Mabon until Samhain—water's receptive mysteries of acceptance

Spirit: The Path of Completion as Goddess and God
The lessons of Spirit are typically addressed all year long: our God connections made through sabbats and Goddess connections made through esbats. Their mysteries of union are explored specifically at Beltane. For our purposes this year, after wrapping up the water mysteries at Samhain, continue the path of completion lessons with God/dess for as long as you need.

Lunar Cycles: Esbats of the Moon

Witches celebrate the Great Goddess throughout the 29.5–day cycle of the moon as she orbits the earth, known as a lunation. Esbats of both the waxing and waning lunar tides explore the *yin* side of divine polarity, and the mythos and mysteries of feminine divinity within nature.

The moon is the most important player in the magick of Witchcraft as practiced on Earth. It is the closest to us of all the celestial players in our solar system and has the most dramatic effect on earthly life. There are twelve to thirteen lunations, during the Wheel of the Year. During each of the twelve zodiac signs, there will be at least one full moon to celebrate, maybe even two. Every 2.5 years we have a "blue moon," when two full moons peak within the same zodiac sign.

Just like the Grand Sabbats are the peak of a seasonal tide, the full moon is the peak of the lunar tide. From new moon, celebrated as the first sighting of a new sliver of cresent, through waxing tide is the cardinal phase of the cycle, like a Maiden Goddess. The full moon is the fixed phase of the cycle, like a Mother Goddess. The waning tide through dark moon, celebrated as the total absence of moonlight, is the mutable phase of the cycle, like a Crone Goddess. Like the Lesser Sabbats, the dark moon ends one cycle while transmuting into the next one. Full moons occur when sun and moon are in opposite zodiac signs from each other. Dark moons occur when sun and moon are conjunct in the same sign.

Again, either balancing or reinforcing the elemental influences of those tides at another octave of the cosmic mechanism.

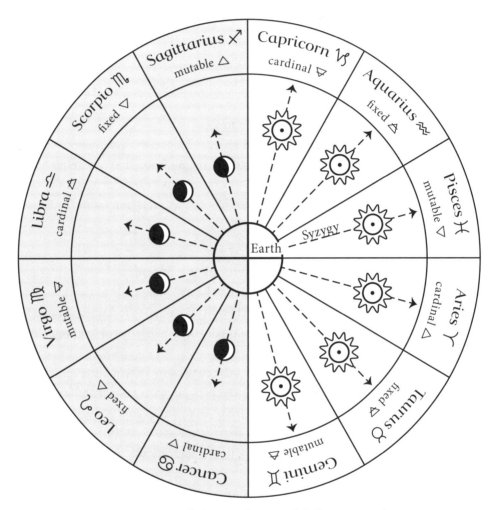

**Figure 8: Syzygy balance of sun and full moon trading
places during light and dark halves of the year**

The cycle of *cardinal* (create, begin), *fixed* (change, maintain), and *mutable* (transmute, end) is part of all the things we experience in the world. This pattern recurs throughout your day, your life, the month, the seasons, the overall year, and the longer spanning epochs beyond. The *Hermetic Principle of Correspondence* describes how the pattern also mirrors through all levels of reality: physical, mental, and spiritual. This is the pattern of the pendulum swing referred to in the *Hermetic Principle of Rhythm*. The good news to be found in this cosmic truth is that no matter how bleak and cold your "winters of discontent" may be, there will inevitably be a glorious summer right around the corner.[116] There is balance within the cycle, as "rhythm compensates."[117]

Turning the Wheel of the Year

Keeping an eye on the Wheel of the Year graphic in figure 5, let's flow through an example of Elemental Witchcraft working as they are marked by the seasons and sabbats.

New cycles always begin in the darkness, in the period of rest and transmutation preceding the emergence into being. So it is with the Wheel of the Year in the still darkness of descent following Samhain (*SOW-wen*) when the sun reaches 15° Scorpio and the midpoint of autumn. After Samhain, which is the end of last year's cycle, is when we rest, cease striving, and hold the space. Here we learn from the projective powers of elemental earth: to be silent in reflection over the previous year's work.

At Winter Solstice, the transmutation side of the mutable season of winter begins. Our Yule sabbat rites kick off the new Great Work cycle while we shift down into the receptive powers of earth: to resonate. Here we use various means of meditation and divination to open our perception to divine inspiration to hear what our next Great Work intention should be. Like striking the cosmic gong to set the tone and vibration of our next area of becoming. We turn our inner eye toward the future to begin a new vision.

The most important aspect of the winter season is this time of darkness needed to refocus. Just as when one sits in the dark backyard when there is no moon nor glare of artificial light and your eyes can relax into the low light. Perception expands and deepens, and points of starlight, previously imperceptible, now come into our view; the patterns of the stars take on new clarity and meaning. Without fail, as soon as I broadcast to the cosmos at Yule that I am again actively listening for their messages, the synchronicity, signs, symbols, and omens blaze and sizzle into awareness like fireworks. It becomes almost comically clear what threads I'm meant to begin weaving anew into the tapestry of my evolving consciousness. As the "Rede of the Wiccae" poem so wisely advises: "speak little, listen

---

116. The phrase "winter of discontent" was first coined by William Shakespeare in his play *Richard III*: "Now is the winter of our discontent / Made glorious summer by this sun [or son] of York."

117. Atkinson, *The Kybalion*, 145.

much."[118] Between Winter Solstice and the peak of High Winter at Imbolc, we formulate our new dedication. All those strands of data form a pattern, like a big arrow pointing in a direction that we can discern, but it is for the best that we still withhold judgment and just begin that journey with the first step, since there are no guarantees to be had anyway.

We then make the magickal dedication in the pursuit of that goal at the High Winter sabbat, also known as Imbolc (*im-molk*). To use an agricultural metaphor, Imbolc dedications are like planting the seeds of this new potential. After High Winter, we attune ourselves to the projective elemental mysteries of air: to know. We do academic research to investigate what it is we think we already know about the subject. What did the ancients believe? How have my contemporaries answered this question? As the cardinal season dawns with the Spring Equinox sabbat, also known as Ostara (*oh-STAR-ah*), we fertilize those seeds of intention. Then we switch to the receptive lessons of air: to wonder. This is the most important part of the entire process. We release what we thought we knew and ask big, new questions, open our minds to new possibilities, and ask Divinity to reveal the truth that would be for our highest good at that time.

When High Spring sabbat peaks, also known as Beltane (*bell-tayn*), we apply our fires to empower the Great Work as the elemental pendulum swings back into the projective lessons of fire: to will. This is where we throw our backs into the work and physically do whatever things the journey requires. While the spring season winds down, this toil cultivates the Great Work we've been growing.

With Summer Solstice sabbat, also known as Litha (*LEE-thah*), the fixed summer season revs into high gear, but elemental lessons ebb back into the receptive mysteries of fire: to surrender. We release our ego-attachment to what we thought we wanted, allowing any hindrance to achieving our goals to be transmuted into the light we need to see clearly. We get the energy boost needed to keep up the good work until the peak of the High Summer Sabbat, also known as Lammas (*LAH-mahs*) or Lughnassadh (*loo-NAH-sah*). At Lammas, we arrive at the midpoint of the summer season. Now we can celebrate the first harvest and make the necessary offerings of toil to reap the rewards of the coming harvest. After the Grand Sabbat of High Summer, the summer season winds down, but the elemental cycle shifts into the projective mysteries of water: to dare. Daring to reap the changes to ourselves and the world, like a fast-rising tide we flow over all obstacles and carve out a new terrain as the summer cycle concludes.

---

118. Mathiesen and Theitic, *The Rede of the Wiccae*, 52–53.

The autumnal equinox sabbat, also known as Mabon (*MAH-bon*) begins the integration phase of the mutable season of the year. As autumn tides grow, we open our harvest baskets and receive the fruits of our labors. Meanwhile, the elemental cycle swings back to the receptive powers of water: to accept. As the solar year wanes toward the sabbat of High Autumn, also known as Samhain (*SOW-wen*), we allow ourselves to be molded into new form by our new awareness, applying and integrating the lessons learned throughout the Great Work. At the last harvest of Samhain, like a funeral, we lay to rest our former selves and all aspects of our lives that no longer serve our highest good in light of the new developments.

With Samhain we complete the Great Work of Magick for that turning of the wheel. As the mutable season of autumn wanes into darkness, elemental tides shift back into the projective earthy lessons of silence and reflection once again. Approaching the Winter Solstice sabbat, also known as Yule (*yewl*), we turn the inner eye backward in review of that turning of the wheel. We tie all loose ends into a bow, and in the dark quiet, draw our conclusions. The waning Yuletide is a time of rest and reflection. As though looking out from beyond the grave, we seek the necessary objective distance from the work. From this deeper vantage point, we take it all in, like reading an epic poem that we've written with our lives. Which loops us back to the beginning of the next turning of the wheel once more…

Truth be told, even if I have an idea where Spirit is leading me at Imbolc, I'm always amazed by the unexpected journey around the wheel. I never end up where I expected, but it is always exactly where I need to be. I would call that trust in the witching process a kind of faith that our destiny flows beneficially along to a better state of being eventually—even when that ultimate destination is shrouded and difficult to see in the moment.

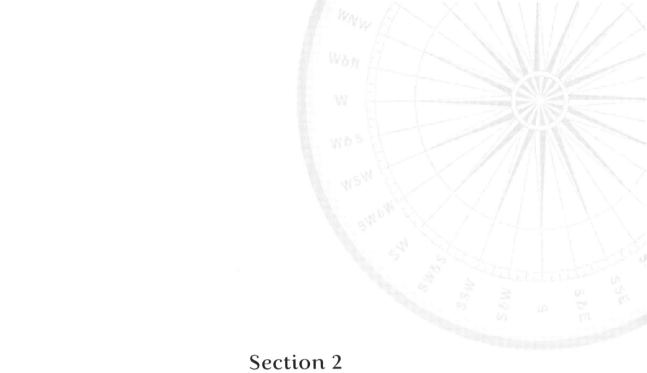

Section 2

ELEMENTAL MAGICK AND THE FIVEFOLD SELF

In section two, we'll discuss the foundations of elemental magick inherited by Wicca and how the powers of earth, air, fire, and water are symbolized by the Witch's Jewel of Power. We'll map these powers onto the human energy system to align the fivefold Self, interlacing with Hindu chakra systems. Then we'll shift into practical applications of elemental power in Wiccan ritual techniques, including the elemental tools, laying and consecrating an altar, casting an energetic temple, opening the elemental gateways, and evoking the God/dess.

Chapter 5
Elemental Basics

The cosmology story in *The Corpus Hermeticum* illustrated the role of the four elemental powers in the creation of the cosmos and all the beings that came from the God/dess to dwell within the natural world. It is from this Hermetic philosophy, and the study of alchemy that furthered that philosophy, that the elemental powers of earth, water, air, and fire took their place of prominence in Western esoterism and magick. However, elemental ideas similar to these are found in ancient religions and magickal systems from all over the world, suggesting a root truth. In this chapter, we'll follow that root from ancient Greece and the occult lore about the Plane of Forces, the elemental beings who regulate their power in the Middleworld, and how these map to the three realms.

Elemental Forces of Nature

A fellow named Empedocles is credited with formulating the philosophy of the four essential ingredients that compose matter. A philosopher, poet, religious teacher, and statesman, Empedocles was born around 490 BCE in Sicily and died in Greece around 430 BCE. For historical context, he was a contemporary of the philosopher Socrates (470–399 BCE). Two years prior to his death, Plato (428–348 BCE) was born.[119]

Empedocles's work *Tetrasomia* (Doctrine of the Four Elements) introduced the elemental forces of air, fire, water, and earth not just as physical building blocks but as spiritual essences. He believed that nothing could be created or destroyed; they just changed form depending on the blending and ratio of the four elements within. He stated that these four elements were all equal and have their own individual characteristics. Different mixtures of these elements produced the different natures of things. The concept of elemental energies went on to influence the Platonic philosophies and ultimately the Hermetic philosophers in Alexandria, Egypt. Empedocles's concepts of the elements of creation found their way into Western esoteric magick via the Renaissance-era studies of alchemy.

The most influential alchemist was renowned Renaissance-era physician and occultist Philippus Aureolus Paracelsus. He was born in Switzerland as Theophrastus Bombastus von Hohenheim and lived from 1493 to 1541. Paracelsus traveled extensively through Europe and Britain, as far east as central Asia, and as far south as Egypt.[120] His work is referenced by later occult writers, such as Eliphas Levi and Manly P. Hall, regarding the spiritual essence of the *elements* and the *elemental beings* that Witches and ceremonial magicians now partner with in ritual circles and magick.

The *four classical elements* refer to the collective spiritual energy that is of a similar character to the very real materials after which they are named: earth, air, water, and fire. If, according to the Hermetic axiom "as above, so below," everything in the *below* of matter has a mirror image in the *above* of spirit, then elemental energies are the pure spiritual essence that interweaves the material world. Each elemental energy has an essential quality required for the operation and formation of nature. In modern science, the four classical elements correlate to both a state of matter and one of the four fundamental forces

---

119. "Empedocles," Encyclopedia Britannica, updated March 7, 2021, https://www.britannica.com/biography/Empedocles.

120. Greer, *The New Encyclopedia of the Occult*, 361.

governing the activity of everything in the cosmos.[121] The following chart collates the alchemical, scientific, and psychological associations with the four classical elements.[122]

Element/ Alchemical Class	State of Matter	Fundamental Force	Qualities	Alchemical Properties	Aspect of Self
Earth—Celestial Salt	Solid	Gravitational force	Stability, rest, inertia, strength, solidity	Dry and cold	Physical human body
Air—Celestial Niter	Gas	Electromagnetic force	Penetrating, diffuse, moveable,	Wet and hot	Self-conscious mind
Fire—Celestial Niter	Plasma	Strong nuclear force	Radiance, expansion, warmth, light	Hot and dry	Supercon-scious mind
Water—Celestial Salt	Liquid	Weak nuclear force	Coolness, contraction, mutability, change	Wet and cold	Subconscious mind

Here in the Middleworld of matter, Hermetic magicians understand that our physical reality is created and sustained when the elements interact, combine, and emerge. Life depends on it. We literally need air molecules to breathe, water molecules to drink, the vitamins, minerals, and matter of earth to eat, and warmth and light of the sun's fire to even exist on planet earth. However, when we call on these forces to aid our magick, we are not calling the literal air, water, etc. We are tapping the original source and weaving together the collective *spirit* of the elements in order to manifest change. You have a body, soul, and spirit. So does every iota of gas, fluid, solid, or plasma.

It was Paracelsus who taught that these elements were twofold in nature; they had both a "subtle, vaporous principle" ("above," in the realms of spirit) and a "gross corporeal substance" ("below," in the world of matter).[123] Each element was both "visible and invisible,

121. Bartlett, *Real Alchemy*, 22.

122. Table information drawn from Paracelsus as referenced by Hall, *Secret Teachings*, 105, and Bartlett, *Real Alchemy*, 21.

123. Hall, *Secret Teachings*, 105.

discernible and indiscernible."[124] As such, air was described as both "tangible atmosphere and an intangible, volatile substratum which may be termed *spiritual air*" that is pervading and mediating.[125] Fire is a "spiritual, ethereal flame manifesting through a material, substantial flame" that is active, energizing, and transforming. Water is both a dense fluid and "a potential essence of a fluidic nature": receptive and responsive. Earth has a lower being that is "fixed, terreous, immobile" that is stable and enduring, and a higher being that is "rarefied, mobile, and virtual."[126]

All the minerals, plants, and animals of the material world are made from various combinations of the physical components of these elements. However, these physical components of which everything is made are fed by purely spiritual dimensions made of the elemental essences—the spiritual ethers that create through each physical element.

In "the above," or subtle spiritual layers of things that are beyond perception by our five senses, there is an energy we may direct and spiritual beings within that element with which we may partner to create the changes that we desire. Best yet, those elements aren't just potential "things." They also govern all the other layers of consciousness: thoughts, emotions, passions, and the intangible aspects of life.

Plane of Forces

The elemental forces exist in their pure, spiritual state in what we call their *elemental realms*. Collectively these are known as the *Plane of Forces*.[127] The elemental realms are layers of energetic vibration in a spectrum that are at once right here existing concurrently with all of reality, intersecting with the material world, weaving it all together, yet remaining pure. The elemental realms exist within the same space as matter, just slightly off-phase from each other. The elemental realms are distinct dimensions within a multilayered universe, and we exist concurrently within all of them. In our Witch's Jewel of Divinity model discussed in chapter 3, I place these realms in the innermost octahedron as the final energetic filter that casts into form all the material beings within it.

124. Hall, *Secret Teachings*, 105.

125. Greer, *The New Encyclopedia of the Occult*, 151.

126. Hall, *Secret Teachings*, 105.

127. Penczak, *Outer Temple of Witchcraft*, 93.

Elemental Beings

The elemental realms are populated by a host of beings Paracelsus called *elementals*.[128] Elementals are pure energy, pure consciousness in the essence of the element. They embody that element and regulate its function in the physical world. The lore of elementals and their rulers are Persian and Indian in origin, taught to Paracelsus when he studied in Constantinople, Turkey.[129] He divided these beings by elemental kingdom and called them gnomes, undines, sylphs, and salamanders. Paracelsus describes the elementals as entities with limited intelligence, who resembled humans somewhat, had families, and had their own societies and political struggles.

In *Transcendental Magic*, Eliphas Levi wrote that elemental beings may successfully be evoked for magick by a magus who has mastered that elemental force through ordeals out in nature, and as mastery over our own spiritual natures.[130] Levi says "a shallow and capricious mind will never rule the Sylphs; an irresolute, cold and fickle nature will never master the Undines; passion irritates the Salamanders; and avaricious greed makes its slaves the sport of Gnomes … in a word, we must overcome them in their strength without ever being overcome by their weaknesses."[131] Levi advises that once we achieve inner balance within the elemental natures, our magick can accomplish anything.

The elementals are envisioned in folklore from many ancient cultures. The higher-order elementals were called *daemon* by the Greeks and may have been worshipped like gods.[132] It is thought that perhaps the twelve Muses were actually elemental beings of air who inspired humans. It is because they are a single element, that elementals can have an unbalancing effect on the psyche of those who make contact. For example, the "absent-minded professor" stereotype is what we may today call what Hall described as the "peculiar qualities common to men of genius are supposedly the result of the cooperation of sylphs, whose aid also brings with it the sylphic inconsistency."[133]

The following descriptions of elemental beings are derived from the works of Paracelsus as referenced by Manly P. Hall in *The Secret Teachings of All Ages*:[134]

---

128. Greer, *The New Encyclopedia of the Occult*, 151.

129. Hall, *Secret Teachings*, 150–151.

130. Levi, *Transcendental Magic*, 215, 222–223.

131. Levi, *Transcendental Magic*, 222–223.

132. Hall, *Secret Teachings*, 105.

133. Hall, *Secret Teachings*, 108.

134. Paracelsus, Hall, *Secret Teachings*, 105.

Earth: Gnomes

Envisioned very close in vibratory nature as the material earth and plants themselves, clothed in stone, plant, or fur-like garments that grow with them. Often pictured in folklore as wee, bearded, in red-pointed hats, or as goblins, dwarves, brownies, etc. Melancholy, gloomy, despondent, with insatiable appetites.

Air: Sylphs

Envisioned like winged mothlike creatures. Aerial, usually very delicate, associated with highest mountainous reaches. "Mirthful, changeable and eccentric."[135] Air elementals came to be confused in folklore with fairies or pixies, but this is not accurate.

Water: Undines

Envisioned in folklore as mer-people. Seen as flowing and fishlike, with humanlike features, beautiful, abounding in symmetry and grace. Very emotional beings, prone to jealousy, treachery, and rage, like a storm at sea.

Fire: Salamanders

Pictured as tiny red lizards that exist in the heart of every flame; also shown in folklore as firedrakes and some dragons. Lower order elementals are seen as fiery balls of light or larger lizard-like figures. Higher order elementals are seen as high-flaming giants in flowing robes or fiery armor.

Perceiving Elemental Beings

Human literature and folklore is full of references to elemental beings, as perceived by different cultures and authors; Antoine Galland's vision of Aladdin's genie in *The Thousand and One Nights*, J. M. Barrie's Tinkerbell in *Peter Pan*, and Hans Christian Andersen's *The Little Mermaid* are just a few well-known examples. I'd argue that J. R. R. Tolkien modeled the races of Middle-earth in his *Lord of the Rings* books on elemental beings.

How humans perceive these entities is subjective, influenced by our culture, preconceived ideas and personal experiences. The elemental beings I perceive are purely energetic, more a node of instinct within their Plane of Force. In my mind's eye, and with my physical eyes when they choose to reveal themselves to me, they take on more abstract

---

135. Hall, *Secret Teachings*, 330.

forms. The "feminine" elements of water and earth appear curvilinear and swirly, like the Art Nouveau style. "Masculine" elements take on an angular and linear form, with an Art Deco style. However, those are the symbol sets that mean something to me, as I have training in art history. How your subconscious perceives these beings will rely on your own awareness and symbol sets.

Elemental beings have a distinct function in the grand scheme, driven by a sole purpose to create. They are like a specialized simple organism within our human bodies. There is a spark of consciousness there, to be sure, but as they are of only one, pure essence, I do not perceive higher functions of agency there. In much the same way I might take a probiotic to introduce the necessary bacterium into my digestive tract to restore a state of good health, I can call the various elemental beings into a magickal circle to aid, build, or even dismantle according to my direction as a means of restoring balance on some level: physical, mental, emotional, etc.

Elemental Sovereigns

There is a collective consciousness of every genus, species, and variety of bright spirit in all three kingdoms of plant, bone, and stone. The theory of morphogenetic resonance by biologist Rupert Sheldrake, PhD, supports this occult principle![136] Just as there is a transcendent consciousness of humans called *akasha* and of the gods called *Divine Mind*, there is also a transcendent, collective consciousness of the elemental beings who have an agency of their own.[137] These rulers serve as the regulators of their essences into the Middleworld. Witches may seek an alliance with these beings, who may present themselves and communicate in a semi-humanoid manner. The elemental beings and their rulers are our partners within creation and have long been allies of magickal practitioners of all kinds.

While Wiccan texts often refer to the rulers as *Elemental Kings*, Eliphas Levi refers to them simply as *sovereigns*, which is preferable to me, as that is a gender-neutral term.

Their names and rulership according to Paracelsus and Levi:[138]

---

136. Rupert Sheldrake, "Morphic Resonance and Morphic Fields—An Introduction," Rupert Sheldrake, accessed June 4, 2021, https://www.sheldrake.org/research/morphic-resonance/introduction.

137. Greer, *The New Encyclopedia of the Occult*, 151.

138. Levi, *Transcendental Magic*, 220–221; Hall, *Secret Teachings*, 330.

- **Paralda** governs the essence of air and sylphs, influencing the bilious temperament of humans. Guards the Eastern kingdom of creation, or quarter.

- **Djin** governs the essence of fire and salamanders, influencing the sanguine temperament of humans. Guards the Southern quarter.

- **Nicksa (Necksa)** governs the essence of water and undines, influencing the phlegmatic temperament of humans. Guards the Western quarter.

- **Ghob (Gob)** governs the essence of earth and gnomes, influencing the melancholy temperament of humans. Guards the Northern quarter.

A Rainbow Spectrum of Gender Expression

Regarding the gender of these rulers all being male, I beg to differ. I strive to remove the patriarchal bias found in foundational Wicca from the twentieth century. This is not an issue of biological sex because elemental essences have no biology, rendering that notion ridiculous; mental gender is an entirely different concept. The entirety of Hermetic philosophy is built upon the waters and earth being an aspect of the goddess, with a primary mental gender as feminine. So, rulership by a *king* is inconsistent. In folklore, watery beings exhibit the essence of maximum femininity, both receptive and terrifying, fierce and alluring. The other element that alchemists associated with receptive, feminine energy is earth. In folklore, the name Ghob is the root of *goblins*, and they are typically portrayed as stout and bulky. I've explored this curiosity with each of the sovereigns directly. My experience reveals Ghob to be what modern folks call *gender fluid*, expressing themself however they choose in that moment. The rulers of earth and water present themselves to me as some seriously tough queens but in different ways. This personal gnosis holds an internal consistency: feminine element, feminine ruler.

The same range of gender expression is equally true for the traditionally masculine, or projective, elements of air and fire. In accounts in the old texts, the salamanders of fire and their sovereign, Djin, typically appear as towering flame, as great dragons, or just pure energy, but they are distinctly masculine. Djin is a powerhouse, dangerous, and aggressive. However, the airy sylphs and their sovereign, Paralda, have a far more subtle, gentle, graceful gender fluidity. I encourage you to arrive with an open mind to ask them directly yourself. We have sacred permission to shine a new light onto old lore and allow these evolving spiritual beings to be recognized with fresh eyes.

Elemental Gateways

Within the ritual circle, Witches call upon the four elemental powers. In Wiccan parlance, this is typically called "calling the quarters." I prefer to call it "opening the gateways." Through these elemental gateways, Witches draw in the flow of pure elemental essence and invite the guardian beings to regulate that flow safely.[139] The guardians can then direct their essence in becoming whatever it is we're working to change. The gateways become anchors in the sacred circle that support the temple like giant girders made of the elemental forces. As the elemental realms exist between the worlds, so does the Witch's circle; therefore, we need energies of *the between* to stabilize that energy construct.

The Four Sacred Directions

The elemental realms have long been associated with the four sacred directions, which correspond to the cardinal points of the compass. The first known philosopher to make the association between elemental essences and the quarters of the zodiacal circle is a fifth century BCE Pythagorean named Philolaos. However, the placement of which element into which quarter did change over the 2,500 years since Philolaos. A third century CE alchemist named Zosimos of Panopolis assigned the elements to the cardinal directions in his work *Upon the Letter Omega* as "Fire in the east, Air in the South, Water in the west and Earth in the north."[140] This pairing of fire in the east and air in the south remained consistent until the mid-nineteenth century.[141]

The directions assigned to air and fire were reassigned in the writings of Eliphas Levi, the French occultist and master of the Qabala, in his book *Transcendental Magic*. Levi wrote specifically about the elemental powers in a symbolic form he referred to as the *Powers of the Sphinx*. He traded the directions to air in the east, and fire in the south.[142] Aleister Crowley focused heavily on Levi's writings, later claiming to be his reincarnation![143] Therefore, the east/air and south/fire attribution became part of the practices of

139. Penczak, *Outer Temple of Witchcraft*, 99.

140. Sorita d'Este and David Rankine, *Practical Elemental Magick: Working the Magick of the Four Elements in the Western Mystery Tradition* (London: Avalonia, 2008), 20.

141. D'Este and Rankine, *Practical Elemental Magick*, 20.

142. Levi, *Transcendental Magic*, 220–221.

143. Aleister Crowley, chapter 151, in *Liber Aleph vel CXI: The Book of Wisdom or Folly [...]* (York Beach, ME: S. Weister, 1991).

the Ordo Templi Orientis and Thelema.[144] From there it became the standard directional association among many occult traditions, including the Wicca of Gerald Gardner.[145]

Does it matter so much which cardinal direction one is facing? The elemental realms aren't literally *over there*. They are all *right here*, but in another dimension of frequency. However, there is a lot of magickal power built into these traditions over time. When the same symbol, thought, idea, or vision is held focused in the mind of many and fed power for a long time, this becomes its own powerful thought form called an *egregore*. This egregore is a shared energetic construct among a group of people who agree upon its function.

After a while, an egregore takes on a power of its own apart from its originators. The cosmos arranges itself to meet the expectations of its observers. Eventually, it takes on an agency of its own too. This egregore of power may eventually be tapped by anyone, even if they don't know what it is supposed to mean, simply by calling upon it by using that same symbol or image. "Magick words" act in a similar way. I think of an egregore like tapping a keg that others filled for me: even if I don't know what beer does, if I wander in and drink the beer, I'm going to get drunk the way it was intended by the maker. To that end, it does matter how these practices have been done by magicians over time.

As long as you have all four elements and can keep it straight in a logical manner in your own mind, your magick will likely work out just fine. Just know why your placement makes sense on all levels of your thealogy and praxis. Does this placement have internal consistency to the rest of what you do? Then do it that way every time; consistency of practice is also a key to building power in your rituals. The repetition of your method over time will build your own egregore of power.

That being said, on this question of compass directions of air and fire, the praxis throughout this book taps the egregore placement of Paracelsus, Levi, Hall, and ultimately Gerald Gardner. This placement has elemental air in the east in alignment with the dawning of spring and the morning and beginnings of all kinds. Elemental fire follows clockwise around the compass to be found in the south in alignment with midday and the hot summer and apexes of all kinds.

144. Crowley, chapter 151, *Liber Aleph*.

145. D'Este and Rankine, *Practical Elemental Magick*, 20.

Figure 9: Witch's pentacle with alchemical symbols

Pentacle: The Witch's Star

In Modern Witchcraft, the most widely used symbol for elemental balance is the *pentacle*, an encircled five-pointed star, which is also known as the *Witch's star*. The five points of the star are created by interweaving five lines that cross in the golden ratio, which we will define in a moment. For Witches this symbol represents the pattern of creation—weaving together of earth, air, fire, water, and ether (aether) of spirit to create the cosmos in perfect balance and wholeness. The star itself is a *pentagram*, a word derived from the Greek *pentagrammon*, meaning roughly "five-lined."

The pentagram is a persistent and potent symbol through history, used by many cultures for all kinds of meanings. This symbol has been found as far back as the first millennium BCE on Babylonian clay tablets, where it had magical associations with Venus/Ishtar, tracing the symbol the planet appears to draw in her movements across the sky. In Greece, the pentagram was used by Neoplatonists and Pythagoras representing harmony between physical and mental health. In medieval Europe, Christians used it to represent the five wounds of Christ. The pentagram famously appeared on the shield of Gawain, a knight of King Arthur's round table. The pentagram as the "blazing star" can be found upon the eastern wall of Masonic lodges.[146] Paracelsus called it the "seal of the microcosm," and as such Eliphas Levi emblazoned the forehead of his Baphomet image with an

---

146. Greer, *The New Encyclopedia of the Occult*, 367.

upward-pointing pentagram. He states that this placement of the pentagram between the horns represents human intelligence, and beneath the flaming torch represents divine revelation.[147]

In the Renaissance, Heinrich Cornelius Agrippa (1486–1535) published his *De Occulta Philosophia Libri Tres* in which he associated the pentagram to the four classical elements, and as a geometric figure that is powerful in magick, and "with the virtue of the number five hath a very great command over evil spirits."[148] Book 2 included a figure of man standing with hands, feet, and head touching the five points of a pentagram to illustrate that the human body was a "microcosm" reflection of the divine harmony of the macrocosm, containing in himself the four classical elements.[149] This image is similar to Leonardo DaVinci's sketch of the Vitruvian man, who likely influenced Agrippa's work.[150]

Eliphas Levi described the pentagram symbol as a "sign of intellectual omnipotence and autocracy."[151] As a Judeo-Christian Qabalist, it is no wonder that Levi used the emblem of the pentagram for "domination of the mind over the elements," saying that the elemental beings were "enchained by this sign."[152] As such, the magickal pentagram found its way into the Hermetic Order of the Golden Dawn, founded in 1888. From there it was adopted as a primary symbol of Wicca and Modern Witchcraft.[153] Witches today also see the pentagram as representing a microcosm of the cosmos and our fivefold selves; however, our ritual usage of the pentagram is used for cooperative partnership with elemental beings rather than domination.

---

147. Levi, *Transcendental Magic*, description of figure IX (page xxii) of the Sabbatic Goat, the Baphomet of Mendes, which appears on page 174.

148. Henry Cornelius Agrippa of Nettesheim, *Three Books of Occult Philosophy: The Foundation Book of Western Occultism*, ed. Donald Tyson, trans. James Freake (St. Paul, MN: Llewellyn Publications, 1993), 331.

149. Agrippa, *Three Books of Occult Philosophy*, 347.

150. Frank Zöllner, "Agrippa, Leonardo and the Codex Huygens." *Journal of the Warburg and Courtauld Institutes* 48 (1985): 229–234, accessed June 6, 2021, https://doi.org/10.2307/751218.

151. Levi, *Transcendental Magic*, 224.

152. Levi, *Transcendental Magic*, 60.

153. Greer, *The New Encyclopedia of the Occult*, 367.

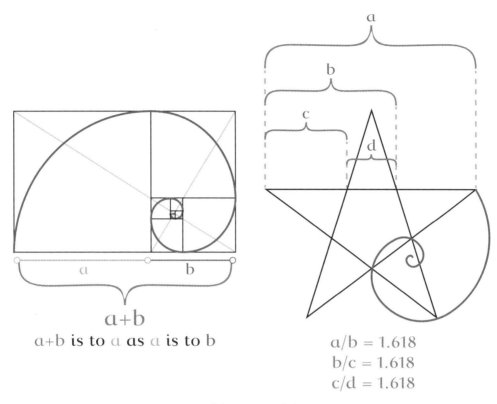

a+b is to a as a is to b

a/b = 1.618
b/c = 1.618
c/d = 1.618

Figure 10: Golden ratio of the pentagram

Golden Ratio of the Pentagram

What makes the pentagram so symbolically interesting is that each line crosses the next line with the *golden ratio*, which is thought to be a fundamental characteristic of the Universe and called the *divine proportion*.[154] The golden ratio is a fingerprint of that divine order, which repeats from macrocosm to microcosm. It describes the relationship between two measurements "such that the smaller relates to the larger in the same ratio as the larger to the sum of both."[155] The golden ratio is an irrational mathematical constant, approximately 1.6180339887. This number is represented by the Greek letter phi. If you draw a pentagram inside of a pentagon, the relationship between the sides

---

154. Greer, *The New Encyclopedia of the Occult*, 367–368.

155. Greer, *The New Encyclopedia of the Occult*, 205.

of the pentagram and pentagon will also be in golden ratio.[156] This golden ratio also describes the relative distribution of flower petals and leaves, and the spiraling seeds in a sunflower.[157] This same proportional pattern can be found throughout the cosmos, from spiral galaxies to hurricane clouds to the design of animal bodies to the organization of honeybee hives. Even the dimensions of the DNA double-helix spiral have a ratio that comes extremely close to phi. Therefore, the pentagram as a symbol made by this golden ratio represents the balance of divinity within matter.

Witches encircle the pentagram, creating a *pentacle*. The pentacle symbolizes our panentheistic paradigm: the circle is the transcendent Great Spirit, the unbroken wholeness of the universe, and the cycles of life, death, and rebirth. The star is the inherent spirit integrated within the four elements of earth, air, fire and water. The fifth element of spirit (ether or quintessence) is represented with the top point of the pentacle most of the time. However, as far as Wiccans and Witches are concerned, regardless of the direction the star is turned, it would not signify evil at any time.

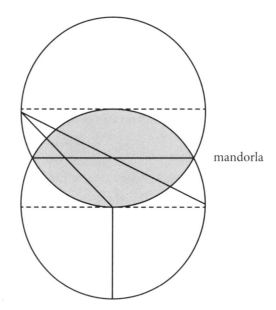

mandorla

Figure 11: Vesica pisces

156. Greer, *The New Encyclopedia of the Occult*, 205.

157. Greer, *The New Encyclopedia of the Occult*, 205–206.

Witches often wear the pentacle symbol to represent their own spiritual harmony. Considering "evil" actions result from any imbalance within the flow of Divine Love, the pentacle is also considered a protective amulet against all baneful energies and harms. The symbol of the pentacle is drawn in magickally significant patterns as a key to invoking and banishing the various elemental essences, which we will further explore in chapter 10.

Mapping the Elements Within the Three Worlds

This vesica pisces symbol is often used as a diagram of a three-world model that is common throughout pagan cultures with a shamanic or animistic paradigm.[158] This sacred geometry goes back to Euclid, born in 300 BCE in Alexandria, Egypt, who presented the vesica pisces in his work *Elements*.[159]

The vesica pisces is formed by the intersection of two circles of equal radius and arranged such that the midpoint of one circle lies on the perimeter of the other circle. The two circles symbolize divine union of *the Two Who Move as One* and the creation that flows from that union. It is basically a Venn diagram. The center shape, which is formed by the overlap, is sometimes called *the mandorla*, forming a Yoni, or birth canal, as it is through this intersecting "gate" that material creation is born. The vesica pisces appears in much sacred art and architecture. For example, the modern cover of the Chalice Well in Glastonbury is adorned with the vesica pisces symbol.

From a Hermetic viewpoint, this Venn diagram represents what happened in the creation story of *The Pymander*. When "Father Sky" with his air and fire descended through the celestial spheres to be enwrapped in the love of "Mother Nature" and her water and earth. From that loving union, every material being was formed.

The Upperworld—Spiritual Realm

The Upperworld, or Overworld, is best known as *the heavens*. This realm is considered a higher frequency of energy than matter. Matter being merely a lower frequency of energy to take on a density we may perceive with the five senses. In the Hermetic three-world model, this is the Spiritual realm: lofty, intellectual, a distant, heightened awareness. The Upperworld is often associated with the white light reported by people who've had near-death experiences.[160] Yet we remember that white light contains the entire visible spectrum

158. Penczak, *The Temple of Shamanic Witchcraft*, 88.

159. Bartel Leendert van der Waerden and Christian Marinus Taisbak, "Euclid," Encyclopedia Britannica, updated January 5, 2021. https://www.britannica.com/biography/Euclid-greek-mathematician.

160. Penczak, *The Temple of Shamanic Witchcraft*, 89.

of colors. The Upperworld is associated with the projective and volatile characteristics of spirit, or as alchemists would call "Celestial Niter." In many ways, this Upperworld realm is distant and detached, objective and impersonal. When I seek angelic presence, ascended masters, or any of the God/desses known for intellect and action, when I seek Divine Mind and Divine Will to access my superconscious mind, I cast my mind's eye into the Upperworld to seek insight. If you need to get the lay of the land and find the larger patterns of the forest you're in, the Upperworld is where you may retrieve that information in a very straightforward manner. This realm contributes the elements of air and fire to the Middleworld mix, and so elemental beings of air and fire may also be found there. The Upperworld is the realm of the Great God, day forces, and is symbolized by the sun.

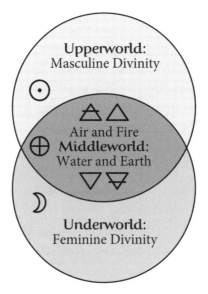

Figure 12: Three worlds Venn diagram

The Underworld—Mental Realm

The lower circle represents the Underworld and receptive and fixed characteristics of Spirit. The Underworld is often associated with darkness, like black pigment, which is also made with all the colors of the spectrum. This is the Hermetic Mental realm, or as alchemists would call "Celestial Mercury." The Underworld is the astral realm of dream, symbols and shadows, the subconscious and psychism—the realm of emotion and healing. The elements of water and earth are closest here. Like the Greek realm ruled by

Hades, or the Wiccan Summerlands, the Underworld is where you'd find the spirits of the dead on their layover between incarnations. Spiritual beings with direct links to nature are also associated with the Underworld: devas, Faery, spirit animals, plant spirits, stone spirits, water and earth elementals all may be encountered on a journey to the Underworld. This is a primordial realm, home of the chthonic God/desses of creation. It is also a realm of challenge, where fears are mirrored back to us so we may face them.[161] The Underworld is primarily the domain of the Great Goddess as both the womb and tomb, night forces and darkness, and is governed by the moon.

The Middleworld—Physical Realm

The "eye," "yoni," or mandorla where the Upperworld and Underworlds overlap is the Middleworld of matter. This is the realm we all live in and know the best. The Hermeticists call this the Physical Realm, and folks tend to agree that it is substantially real because our five senses perceive it in similar ways. This creates a consensus reality. The Middleworld is the 3D construct of energy created when the two Divine Forces intersect. Their divinity passes through the elemental Plane of Forces like a focusing lens, through the "die" of the celestial spheres, which sets form and destiny into being. The illusion of our physical separation is cast like a sculpture made of subtle energy and dense matter. The Middleworld is subject to linear time.

Axis Mundi

In many indigenous mythologies with a three-world paradigm, there is often a great world tree or another vertical connector between the three worlds, like a mountain, ladder, pole, or obelisk of some kind. This vertical construct is known as the axis mundi, and it lies at the center of one's cosmic map. This construct acts as a pathway between these three worlds. The Norse world tree is a giant ash called Yggdrasil.[162] In Hermetic Qabala, it is known as the Tree of Life. The Mayan Tree of Life is a ceiba tree named Ya'axche.[163]

---

161. Penczak, *The Temple of Shamanic Witchcraft*, 89.

162. "Yggdrasill," Encyclopedia Britannica, updated February 7, 2018, https://www.britannica.com/topic/Yggdrasill.

163. "La Ceiba: The Sacred Tree of Life," Na'atik Instituto De Lenguas Culturas, accessed June 6, 2021, https://www.naatikmexico.org/ceiba-tree/.

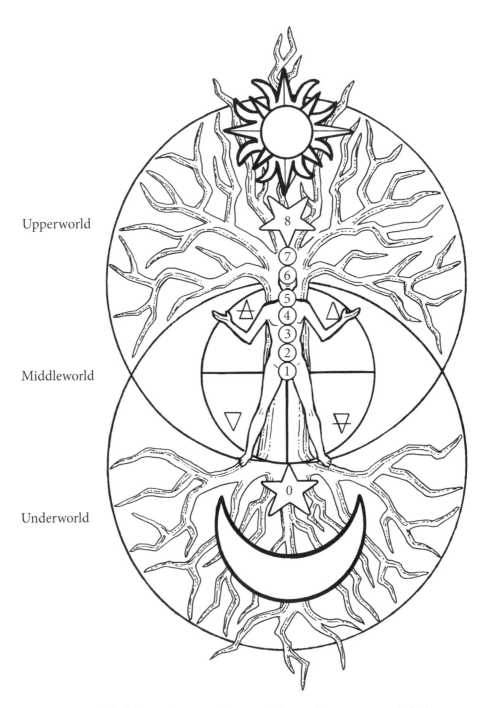

Upperworld

Middleworld

Underworld

Figure 13: World tree, human, three worlds, and interpersonal chakras

The axis mundi holds in relationship the sky and earth where the four compass directions intersect with spirit. World tree imagery holds the underworld in the roots and the heavens in the branches. Which makes the Middleworld the strong trunk in this metaphor. In the Middleworld, the trunk of a tree is the sturdy support system, but it is also the living conduit that carries the water and minerals up from the roots and carries down the carbon dioxide gas and energy from the sun that was absorbed through the leaves.

This symbolic map works on the macro level and the micro. In our axis mundi metaphor, humans also have a trunk with our spine connecting us on all levels. We have subtle roots that connect us to the Underworld and a subtle crown of branches connecting us to the heavens. The Hindu chakra system also maps the human body as an interconnected microcosm reflection of our macrocosm.

Remember that there are no value judgments based on location within these cosmic maps. Higher is not better. Under is not a punishment. There is nary a whiff of brimstone to be found. They are all sanctuaries within the temple of Divine Love. "Up" and "down" aren't objectively real, either. The danger would be in hyper-focusing on any one particular part of this complex world to the detriment of the others. The Pentacle Path requires us to continually check in and rebalance on all levels so that we can remain centered, connected, and effective.

If we were to hyper-focus on the Middleworld of the flesh, we might trip into the pitfall of self-destructive hedonism or greed. If we were to take a page from the invasive orthodoxies—"denying the flesh" to live solely for heavenly admission—we'd miss out on all the fun (and the entire purpose) of being embodied. Hyper-focus on "the light" and you're ensnared by "toxic positivity." Too much baking in the bright "sun" of the day is exhausting and will burn you out. By the same token, Witches sometimes hyper-focus on the restful dark shadows of the Underworld, dwelling overlong on death and spirit work, solely seeking their ancestors, or trying to resurrect a long-dead culture in memorial. Preferring the mystical, macabre dark of the chthonic goddess, they may neglect the bright fires of their projective side and lose themselves in dreams, drowning in their own psychic and emotional depths. To be fair, this is the witching aesthetic and plays an important counterpoint within the dominator over-culture. However, they, too, would be well-served to come above ground and enjoy a sunbeam every now and again. If for no other reason than to make some vitamin D! This is why a healthy practice of Witchcraft dances to the beats of earthly elemental magick, lunar magick of the dark night, and solar magick of the bright day. All are sacred and necessary in balance.

So, this three-world, great-tree, axis-mundi, vertical map makes for a handy visualization because it mirrors life on a planet that has gravity! Plus, Witches and trees are old pals. Within a cosmos where everything is divine, remember that it is whole and complete. It is all necessary and in perfect balance between the full range of possibilities. The three-worlds paradigm and the world tree metaphor are a symbolic system of organization that may be used like a cosmic map when you spiritually journey beyond the veil of illusion.

Just like yourself, where each cell has your DNA with complete instructions on how to make a whole new you, every system of the cosmos contains an observable pattern that repeats infinitely. You also carry within you the axis mundi, that access point to all worlds through your own body. The sacred crossroads of the cosmos are right there inside you. Your center, deep in your guts and your soul, is the 0, 0, 0 crossroads of your own compass rose. If you navigate by your own center, you'll never get lost. To follow the Pentacle Path of the Witch and engage in the Great Work of Magick is to ultimately make the path of completion … arriving within yourself, fully present and living your best life.

Chapter 6
The Witch's Jewel of Power

So far, we've outlined how the elemental forces of earth, air, fire, and water create the Middleworld, governing obvious material things like rocks, water, atmosphere, and fiery sunlight. They also regulate consciousness and our experience of existence in the Middleworld: how we deal with physical needs, emotions and relationships, our thoughts and attitudes, and our passions and actions. The practice of magick deals with areas of consciousness, which then mirror into substance. This brings us to a study of the occult wisdom gleaned from an observation of the elemental forces. These forces provide "tools" with which to implement their powers for an effective life.

Up until the 1990s in Western esoterism, there were four elemental axioms that formed the cornerstones of magick. They are often repeated among magi as *to know, to will, to dare, to be silent.* Throughout occult texts since the 1800s these outer mysteries appear in varying symbolic orders and sometimes with conflicting details. However, these steps only reflect the outer mysteries—the deosil spiral—of elemental power and therefore only reflect half the necessary tools to be fully effective in life. To reconstruct the missing inner mysteries, Wiccan author Timothy Roderick synthesized his knowledge of Jungian psychology and his professional practice as a psychoanalyst with his training in English Traditional Wicca. From this synthesis, he offered the "widdershins spiral" of elemental powers: *to wonder, to surrender, to accept, and to resonate.*[164] These were first introduced in his book *Dark Moon Mysteries* (1996) and furthered in his subsequent works *Apprentice to Power* (2000) and *Wicca: A Year and a Day* (2005). In this chapter, we'll lay out a brief history of this lore, with both the projective and receptive mysteries, organized into a new symbol, which I call the Witch's Jewel of Power.

Levi's Four Powers of the Sphinx

These elemental maxims were first presented by French occultist Eliphas Levi with his book *Transcendental Magic*, originally published in two volumes (1854–1856). Levi called these four axioms of magick the *four powers of the sphinx.* Levi describes the sphinx as a symbol which is made of four Kerubic creatures. These creatures are based on an order of Angels called the Kerubim (the strong ones), which are described as having four heads of beasts and three sets of wings each. The four heads represent the four fixed astrological signs and their elemental powers. The fixed signs occur during the four cross-quarter points in the year when Witches celebrate the Grand Sabbats and the peak of seasonal power. Though there was some confusion between the late-nineteenth-century grimoires and the Golden Dawn and Thelemic practices later on; ultimately Aleister Crowley corrected two of the attributions. The Kerubic beasts, their powers and elemental associations became:[165]

- **Air:** The water-bearing man of Aquarius, to know
- **Fire:** The lion of Leo, to will
- **Water:** The eagle of Scorpio, to dare
- **Earth:** The bull of Taurus, to keep silence

---

164. Roderick, *Dark Moon Mysteries*, 79.

165. Michael Osiris Snuffin, Hermetic Library, "On the Powers of the Sphinx: Part 2: Aleister Crowley," 2002, accessed June 6, 2021. https://hermetic.com/osiris/onthepowersofthesphinx2.

If you read the tarot, you've seen these four Kerubic symbols on many of the cards. The Thoth deck designed by Crowley heavily employs these animals in illustrating the mastery of the elemental essences along the path of the Magus to elevate themselves.

In the words of Eliphas Levi from *Transcendental Magic*:

> To attain … the knowledge and power of the Magi, there are four indispensable conditions—an intelligence illuminated by study, an intrepidity which nothing can check, a will which nothing can break, and a discretion which nothing can corrupt and nothing intoxicate. TO KNOW, TO DARE, TO WILL, TO KEEP SILENCE—such are the four words of the magus, inscribed upon the four symbolical forms of the sphinx.[166]

In order to successfully work elemental magick, you must first balance your own disposition as evenly as possible between the four elemental natures. Once more, this brings us back to a Pentacle Path of Witchcraft, where the wise Witch first strengthens themselves as an interwoven being in five aspects. Our fivefold Self must first be healed of the wounds that weaken us. Once you've attended to your balance life gets much easier.

Witch's Pyramid: Yang

The symbolic construct for the powers of the sphinx morphed again within Modern Witchcraft in America. This lore came to be arranged into a "Witch's Pyramid" and included in Christopher Penczak's book *The Inner Temple of Witchcraft*. The four powers of the sphinx described by Levi became the four cornerstones and sides of this pyramid symbolism. This symbol is useful, being a 3D solid built from a square base with four equal, triangular sides, much like the triangular alchemical symbols for earth, air, fire, and water. Typically, the Witch's Pyramid stands alone, upward pointing as pyramids tend to do. Wiccan thealogy assigns the meaning of the top point to spirit, or the quintessence of ether (meaning fifth element), and the guiding principle known as the Wiccan Rede: "an it harm none, do what ye will."[167]

Though Timothy Roderick never mentions a pyramid, he suggested that these traditional elemental powers spoken of by Levi were just one side of the divine coin. Like all

---

166. Levi, *Transcendental Magic*, 30.
167. Mathiesen and Theitic, *The Rede of the Wiccae*, 53.

other natural cycles, the elemental mysteries also have both sides of the pendulum swing, both an ebb and flow of power. Roderick flipped the traditional pyramid to include the inner, receptive, feminine, "widdershins spiral" of elemental powers.[168] The receptive side of the polarity holds the keys to true power within a Witch's magick. These keys are the gift of the Goddess.

The *Hermetic Principle of Polarity* informs us that everything in the universe has an inherent balance throughout the range of its spectrum. The Taoist yin-yang symbol reminds that while there may be a dominant attribute, there must also be that spot of its flip side and vice versa. That is the *occult mystery;* its hidden wisdom, and that "spot" that some might view as a weakness, is actually the keyhole to unlock its power.

The *Hermetic Principle of Gender* takes this idea of polarity one step further and states that everything in the universe also has masculine and feminine attributes. Masculine attributes include *projective qualities* and are actualized through air and fire. Feminine attributes include *receptive qualities* and are actualized through earth and water. Just like polarity, gender cannot be an either-or situation, but an infinite rainbow range of possibility. Each side held in that cosmic dance of tension.

That lesson of gender is true for the elemental forces too. Though earth, air, fire, and water may express a dominant mental gender, the key to their true power comes from the occult wisdom that they also express through their flip side. This is the key lesson that will keep us in balance so that we don't fall into madness and self-destruction.

The traditional occult powers of the sphinx and upward-pointing pyramid embodied the dominant and active power of the four elements but also focused on the qualities prized within the typical patriarchal, dominator culture. The upward pointing triangle of the hexagram of Solomon represents the masculine phallus of god rising up like a blade and is used to represent the two masculine elements of air and fire (see figure 14). However, for the *Hermetic Principle of Polarity and Gender* to be fulfilled, there would also have to be the downward-pointing triangle of the feminine womb that receives and is used to represent the two feminine elements of water and earth.

The traditional pyramid is more or less a 3D model of the phallus, and its lessons do speak to the *me me me, what I want to do for myself* projective side of magickal improvement. Valid. So, the magickal directive of the top point, from the masculine ethers of god, would certainly speak to what Witches should do about fulfilling their personal desires.

---

168. Roderick, *Dark Moon Mysteries*, 79; Timothy Roderick, *Wicca, A Year and a Day: 366 Days of Spiritual Practice in the Craft of the Wise* (St. Paul, MN: Llewellyn Publications, 2005), 160, 167, 178, 183.

What do I do to help *numero uno*? I'll do as I will, harming none. Very good, but where is my goddess's chalice?

Witch's Inverted Pyramid: Yin

In exploring the receptive, goddess side of the elemental forces, we add a flipped pyramid and receive four inverse elemental maxims: to wonder, to surrender, to accept, to resonate. As I worked in depth with these mysteries, I asked the Goddess directly what her downward-pointing, feminine etheric message for the Witch would be. The Goddess affirmed for me that the projective yang pyramid symbolism expresses the dominant mystery lesson regarding personal improvement and responsible independence, as the Wiccan Rede: "an it harm none, do what ye will."[169] However, the receptive yin pyramid symbolism expresses the cooperative mystery lesson regarding societal improvement and responsible interdependence as the two keys to the temple: "Perfect Love and Perfect Trust." The following table outlines the two sides of this mystery teaching in comparison and introduces the elemental mystery lessons, which we will further unpack throughout the exercises in section three.

	Yang Pyramid: Projective		Yin Pyramid: Receptive	
Divine Polarity	The Great God		The Great Goddess	
Direction	Upward pointing		Downward pointing	
Altar Tool	The Athame, or Ritual Blade		The Chalice, or Cauldron	
Symbolizes	Phallus		Womb	
Relationship	Self-Improvement, Personal		Societal-Improvement, Interpersonal	
Tide	Projective Elemental Mysteries		Receptive Elemental Mysteries	
Air: knowledge and awareness	To know	Communicating clear intention; awakening.	To wonder	Open-mindedness, Releasing preconceived ideas, questioning, inspiration.
Fire: passions and drives	To will	Discipline, Physical action taken to manifest desires; Mastery.	To surrender	Humility. Releasing fears to be tempered by Divine Will; Allowing change.

---

169. Mathiesen and Theitic, *The Rede of the Wiccae*, 52–53.

Tide	Projective Elemental Mysteries		Receptive Elemental Mysteries	
Water: dreams and emotions	To dare	Dare to transcend outmoded conventions, which inhibit personal enlightenment and evolution.	To accept	Defining and honoring boundaries; allowing true circumstances to mold a new state of being.
Earth: practical, physical needs	To be silent	Stillness of Nonstriving. Observing without judgment. Releasing attachment and expectation. Holding the space of possibility.	To resonate	Spontaneity of striving. Setting new frequency of intention, initiating new expectations.
Ether: Directive of Spirit	Wiccan Rede: An it harm none, do what ye will.[170]	Sovereignty. Responsible and benevolent personal liberty and independence.	Two Keys: Perfect Love and Perfect Trust	Wholeness. Responsible and benevolent interdependence within society and environment.

Within the persistent illusion of our separateness here in the Middleworld, the yang pyramid speaks to us as individuals. The traditional cornerstones to achieving the empowerment of the magus, was to discover the "Holy Kingdom" within oneself. To both remember that you are the incarnation of divinity on Earth and then to empower yourself as a sovereign within your kingdom.

However, when the occult mages of the nineteenth and twentieth centuries stopped at just the masculine mysteries of the yang pyramid, they opened themselves up to an imbalance of spirit, which only dug the pitfalls of our dominator culture even deeper. So deep, in fact, that many of them fell right in and would eventually die destitute, mad, addicted, or worse.[171] Even those early Wiccans who paid lip service to a reemergence of the mother goddess, if they continued to exclusively utilize the patriarchal tools of a dominator culture in her name, they were still doomed to repeat the mistakes of their oppressors. Modern Witchcraft restores the full complement of tools to our magickal toolbox so we may attain true mastery as humans, forsaking neither god or goddess, and

---

170. Mathiesen and Theitic, *The Rede of the Wiccae*, 76.

171. For the gory details, see the biographies of Alex Sanders, Aleister Crowley, and Robert Cochrane.

reconciling the tensions between the chalice and the blade that have dogged our culture since the Neolithic era. This becomes the Great Work of transformational magick Modern Witchcraft is ideally suited to achieve.

The Knife Goes in the Cup

Long ago, I asked Wiccan author Miles Batty, who wrote *Teaching Witchcraft*, to give me the nutshell teaching of British Wicca—to boil it down for me. He looked across the dinner table and said, "The knife goes in the cup." He was referring to the Wiccan *Symbolic Great Rite ceremony* where the athame blade, as symbolic of the projective vital energy of the God, is dipped into a chalice of wine as a blessing. The chalice is symbolic of the receptive womb of the Goddess, which brings matter into form. The yang and yin pyramids are poetry to express both the projective god and receptive goddess held in balance within each of us, just like the Hermetic cosmology story in *The Pymander* told: all who were created from their merging were made in their image and inherently all-gendered.

Wicca began as a fertility religion, and on one metaphorical level, it still is. The sexual metaphors in the old pagan rites that inspire our modern practice may seem a bit crude for today's sensibilities. Sure, they can be especially hetero-centric if you aren't careful. Yet, there remains both a biological and poetic truth: Creation flows from union. Unions of all kinds, among all beings, to create all sorts of beautiful love—not just babies or crops or livestock, as our ancient ancestors so desperately needed to survive.

Anima and animus, sexual and contra-sexual sides must be balanced within ourselves and united on all levels in order to take full possession of our being. The path of completion is revealed in these mysteries we knew as the Witch's Pyramids. They seek to merge and harmonize the yin and the yang within each of us, regardless of our sex or primary gender identity. This harmony will inevitably affirm and heal the entire rainbow of human expression: spiritual, mental, emotional, will, and physical. It is in the Witch's Jewel of Power we uncover the cooperator tools that can restore balance to the *Force*.

The Witch's Jewel of Power

I've worked with this construct of the Witch's *Pyramid*, both yin and yang, and viewed these mysteries from different angles for many years now. Traditional occultism and fertility cults from all over the world persistently symbolize male and female divinity intersecting in sexy union to create the world. Obviously. And, obviously, these symbols are based on the Goddess and God being separate and at a distance—I mean, to *get together* assumes at some point you were *apart*. As if Mom and Dad sleep in separate beds down the hall from each other and only occasionally get their act together on date night.

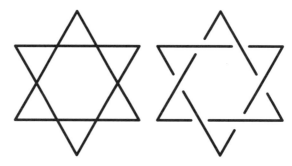

Figure 14: Star of David (left), Seal of Solomon (right)

Consider that the Seal of Solomon has two triangles pointing toward each other to intersect; if there are two pyramids to symbolize those powers, then having them approach each other to merge echoes the Wiccan sentiment of "the knife goes in the cup." This notion is true enough in the Middleworld. It certainly keeps biological life interesting!

However, the binary separation of the sexes and genders is a Middleworld *illusion* in the same way that *linear time* and *contiguous space* are Middleworld illusions. Right? I know I'm way out there on some cosmic trip with this one, but hang with me here while I lay this out…

Flip the whole script. Come back to the Hermetic idea of Source in *The Pymander* cosmology. This Divine Light that illuminates the Jewel of Divinity is a *mirror image* of the material world below—as above, so below—the Two Who Move as One, are a God/dess who are *both sides of a reflection*.

Rather than their divine union envisioned as a 3D model of the Seal of Solomon, wouldn't a mirror image be more consistent with the Hermetic philosophy upon which all of this elemental magick is based? A mirror image is equal: expressing polarity, but not in opposition, in reflection. Rather than arranging the pyramids to approach each other, like a knife entering a cup, place them base to base, like a mirror reflection of the sun upon the water.

Mother Nature, chthonic goddess of the earth, moon and Underworld; a force that descends. Father Sky, celestial god of the sun and stars, lord of light and shadow, wild god of nature and animals; a force that ascends.

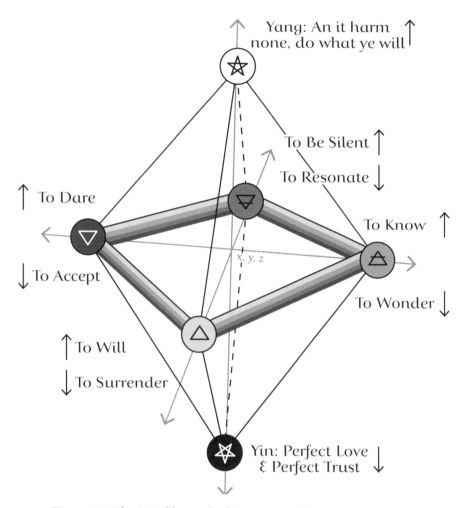

Figure 15: The Witch's Jewel of Power as a Platonic Octahedron

When you place two pyramids base to base, this bipyramid has a new name in sacred geometry: the octahedron. The octahedron is one of five Platonic solids, defined by Greek philosopher Plato of Athens. The octahedron represents elemental air, which seems fitting for a representation of Divine Mind. It has eight faces made of equilateral triangles, which echo the alchemical sigils of the four elements, with twice the faces for inner and outer mysteries. Octahedrons form what we typically call the "diamond shape," and diamond gemstones naturally form into octahedrons as do the crystal formations of fluorite.

If you're into tabletop roleplaying games, the octahedron solid is one of the more common polyhedral dice, known as a "d8."

I call this new construct of elemental balance the *Witch's Jewel of Power*. It symbolically maps the five projective elemental mysteries and five receptive elemental mysteries onto this octahedron solid, and places it at the center of the larger Jewel of Divinity construct we discussed in chapter 3. Within this symbol, I see the four corners still anchored by the elemental mysteries with a rainbow ribbon of four Plane of Forces joining the two pyramids, forming that lens of material creation through which the Goddess and God interlace into form. The downward point, like the black dot in the Taoist yin-yang symbol, represents a message from the Goddess for responsible interdependence in "Perfect Love and trust." The upward point, like the white dot, represents a message from the God for responsible independence as "an it harm none, do what ye will."[172]

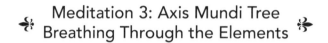

Meditation 3: Axis Mundi Tree Breathing Through the Elements

Needs

Candle, any kind

Incense, any kind

A comfortable and supportive chair with arms, if possible

Your Book of Mirrors and a pen

Preparation

Light your candle and incense then sit comfortably in an armchair that allows your spine to be perpendicular to the floor. Your thighs should be parallel to the floor, feet flat. Hold nothing crossed or with awkward tension.

Praxis

Close your eyes and picture a comfortable room inside your head. Picture your consciousness like a tiny version of your most magickal Self, sitting in your comfortable chair. Your eyes are a window on a distant wall of that room from you now.

---

172. Mathiesen and Theitic, *The Rede of the Wiccae*, 76.

Look around the room. See that this is a perfect room for you, decorated just the way you like it. You are surrounded in comfort. (*Pause.*) Here you sit far away from that window. Far away from the bustle of the outer world.

It is quiet and still here in the inner sanctuary of your mind. Any distracting noises or stray thoughts are merely birds flying past that distant window … release them without care.

There is a skylight above, and a soft beam of white light shines down upon your head.

Begin with three deep breaths. Allow an audible sigh as you loosen any pent-up tension; slow, deep breaths in through the nose and out through the mouth. (*Pause.*)

You notice that there is an intriguing trapdoor in the floor nearby, and so you move closer to see it more clearly. This is a beautiful, ornate door to your own private gateway of adventure. (*Pause.*)

Beyond this door, the path beyond can lead anywhere that you wish to go in the three realms of Upperworld, Middleworld, and Underworld.

Say aloud: *I invite my guides, gods, and ancestors to join me on this journey, keep me safe, show me the way. I ask that the visions be clear and your messages be understandable and gentle. May all that I do be for the highest good of all involved, harming none. Blessèd be.*

Open that ornate door in the floor, finding the spiral staircase descending beyond. With each exhale, step down, deeper and deeper into your meditative state. With each breath, with each step, your mind relaxes, thoughts easing, breath deepening.

Take a step down; deeper and deeper you sink into your subconscious mind. Twelve steps down, around and 'round you tread the spiral staircase, knowing that at the bottom of these steps you arrive at your own center. (*Pause.*)

You step off that bottom step and arrive at the crossroads within yourself. Behind your navel, you are connected like a silver umbilical cord to the astral realm.

Before you is a looking glass, a screen of your deepest mind, and the gateway to the silver cord leading you outward into the astral realms where all things are possible by a mere thought. Your imagination can change this vista to anywhere you'd like to go. Visualize a great world tree through the looking glass now. On the count of three, you will step through and begin your adventure … One, two, three, step through!

You arrive on the vast field of the astral plane. Approach the world tree whose wide branches hold the cosmos and all the heavens and whose deep roots hold the planet and all the Underworld. You step onto its roots like knobby knees and lay your hands on the broad trunk, which is the Middleworld. Feel the pulse of creation, like a heartbeat of the cosmos. Your heartbeat. You and the tree are one energy, so you push straight through the bark and merge with the tree. Feel your tree-ish connections through roots and branches. (*Pause.*)

Your consciousness now finds its way down to the Underworld held in your roots. As you breathe deeply and slowly, allow your attention to sink down into your roots, down into the earth itself. Deep, deep into the earth you find that stability of the stones themselves. Sink your roots into the elemental essence of earth, finding a green light. Breathe that light up through your roots as the color green. Here you find stillness, solidity. Feel that heavy foundation keeping you rooted. Your roots draw in sustenance. As you breathe up the green light, all that you need flows inward to sustain your body. Hold the space in silent receptiveness. (*Pause.*)

Push your roots even further down until you find the water table. There is water flowing as a blue light. Dip into this water and feel the refreshing blue light flowing up through your roots. Breathe up this blue light, filling you completely. The water of Divine Love flows freely wherever it needs to go, overcoming all obstacles. Breathe up the blue light and accept all the love needed to nurture your heart. Receive the love in peace. (*Pause.*)

Push even further into the depths of the planetary core, finding a luminescence of the Great Goddess. She is the cool darkness of midnight. She is the dot of black pigment in the yang, holding all potential within her dark shadow, and the sun's light illuminates her moon against the night sky. Breathe up her luminescence and rest in ease within her embrace. Receive her unconditional acceptance. (*Pause.*)

Inhale up the powers of goddess, earth, and water throughout the trunk of your tree and your body. Shifting attention upward, from your crown, feel your branches holding the heavens. Move higher and higher now, into the atmosphere, into the breezy air like the sky at yellow dawning. The yellow light of wisdom blows through your mind. Breathe down the yellow light into your mind, opened with wonderment. Receive air's inspiration. (*Pause.*)

Push up through your branches once more, further and further, your leaves turned toward the fiery sun. Breathe down the red light of fire through your leaves, down into your belly, igniting the furnace of your power. Receive the fiery fuel of invigoration, and feed to the fires all that does not serve your highest good … allow those hindrances to burn away. (*Pause.*)

Push out once more, further and further beyond the atmosphere, to find the sun itself. Father Sky, the Great God, white light of all colors, all possibilities, radiating life and warmth. Breathe down this rainbow of white light. He is the dot of white in the yin as he seeks out her moon in the darkness. She is the black void of space through which he burns. Breathe down his sunlight, and rest in confidence within his protection. Receive his unconditional acceptance. (*Pause.*)

Return back through your crown, back into the trunk of your tree, down the axis mundi. Cycle your breath as the tree inhales: breathe up the waters, minerals, and the moonlight. As your tree exhales, breathe down the wind, energy, and sunlight. They swirl throughout your body, entwining at your heart, swirling as the yin and yang. Inhale the goddess. Exhale the god. (*Pause for three cycles.*) Where the Two Who Move as One conjoin, all blessedness flows. (*Pause.*)

When you are ready to return to the waking world, rejuvenated and empowered, simply pull back your roots just enough … Pull back your branches just enough. Step out from the world tree to stand upon the astral plane.

See an image of yourself on the looking glass once more. Knowing that the silver umbilical cord back into your center follows just three steps beyond: one, two, three, step through! You arrive back at the center of your being.

Take the spiral staircase up into waking consciousness … higher and higher you take twelve steps upward into your waking mind. Until you emerge in the little meditation room in your mind, closing the trap door behind you with gratitude for the journey. Stretch your muscles, and when ready, move to the window and open your eyes. Take time to journal about this experience in your Book of Mirrors.

Chapter 7
Energy Body and the Pentacle Self

Along the Pentacle Path of Elemental Witchcraft, we will explore the pentacle as a map of the microcosm. On this level, the pentacle represents the fivefold nature of the human being as having a physical body, mental body, body of the will, emotional body, and spiritual body. Before we can successfully engage with the elemental forces for our magick, let's explore this symbolism and how the essences of the classical elements are thought to emerge into physical form to become a person like us. We'll define terms for our energy body systems learned from Hinduism and how our *aura* and *chakras* both create our human experience and, in reverse, serve as our human access points to the elemental Plane of Forces and the three worlds.

I used to think of myself as a spirit temporarily wearing this physical meat suit. I let my eyes deceive me into thinking that my skin was my outer edge and everything that distinguished "me" was encased by that meat. Then I began studying Modern Witchcraft and attuned as a Reiki energy healer.[173] Truth is that our anatomy extends far beyond our skin. Rather than a little spirit driving an organic machine, I'm more like spiritual cotton candy floss spun into form around a body cone. The material body is just a relatively solid core of a vast energetic being; the body is the end result of consciousness materializing at a vibration slow enough to be perceived here in the Middleworld. We are huge, multidimensional beings of energy with all these layers of Self, vibrating at a range of frequencies. The biofield generated by my heart is a torus, a rotating spiral like a ring-shaped doughnut, just like the planet's electromagnetic field. That field is also called the *aura*.

The Pentacle Path to Balance: A Five-Pointed Plan

The purpose of the Pentacle Path is to return to our natural state of being, which is whole and balanced, whereby we are able to enjoy our lives most effectively. To do that, we must figure out how to de-stress, heal our emotional wounds, set and accomplish goals, and build healthy relationships so that we may enjoy the ease and balance that we might call spiritual fulfillment.

A holistic approach to balance seeks wholeness. Wholeness is based upon the interconnections between consciousness and the body. A magickal approach to empowerment works for a harmonic balance between the many subtle layers of the Self. The noncorporeal parts of us, or the mental, emotional, will, and spiritual bodies, form a lens through which we experience our physical body and vice versa. *As above, so below.*

In fact, we are mostly nonphysical. I'd go so far as saying that this meat suit isn't even the most important part of a person! Yet sadly, many folks get stuck at the body level—fretting and discriminating over the most trivial aspects of material appearance, like height, hair texture, cellulite, or their quantity of melanin. We are so much more than our skin, folks! Our physical bodies are merely the density formed from an interference pattern created as our very important bodies of heart, mind, will, and spirit intersect. Your body is like a beautiful, blooming flower as your consciousness creates physical reality. Exploring diversity is the entire purpose of the veil of illusion; the veil is not meant to be a blindfold!

---

173. A Reiki attunement is similar to a ritual of initiation, opening the spiritual connection between the healer and ki. Attunements typically occur in three stages of preparation.

When all these layers of Self are in balance with each other, we feel at *ease.* When there is a disruption, we feel *dis-ease.* That dis-ease will eventually be mirrored throughout our many layers of Self if we don't correct the issue in a timely fashion. Abiding stress, frustration, anger, worry, anxiety, and even seasonal blues are forms of dis-ease that should not be discounted. Otherwise, they may manifest as more serious forms of physical illness or misfortune.

Figure 16: Pentacle Path of Witchcraft

The greater part of the practice of Witchcraft is about conquering our *fear of a lack of love* and knowing ourselves within and without. Maintaining balance comes first. So, we work on the fivefold path of aligning ourselves within divinity. Follow along the symbol of the pentacle in figure 16.[174] All begins in spirit, which we symbolize as the top point. As we are born, spirit is drawn down through the celestial spheres to the earth point—which is symbolized as drawing the line down to the lower right point—and elemental earth. Spirit blooms into the Middleworld and our spark emerges as a baby. Then follow the remaining strokes around clockwise, or deosil.

Now that we're born, first things first: we have to figure how out to drive the meat suit—taking care of our physical needs until we are independent and self-sufficient. The earthy *path of sovereignty* establishes our independent physical lives. As adults, sovereignty enables our pleasurable pursuit of fulfillment on all the other levels.

Next up is our education. The airy *path of truth* aligns our mental bodies and thoughts within the Divine Mind. We study and develop critical thinking skills. We experience life, honing raw data into complex understanding of our interconnection.

Then we get to work. The fiery *path of power* aligns the body of will, our little ego, and passions and drives with the Divine Will that is our sacred mission or personal destiny. We activate, work hard, and accomplish what we were sent to earth to do.

In time, we rise in leadership and relationship. The watery *path of love* aligns our emotional bodies, feelings, intuitions, and relationships within Divine Love. We seek out partnership and engage meaningfully with other people. Love and reunion are the whole purpose of life. On this path of love, we realize the importance of our interconnections and our interdependence, then we engage compassionately and ethically with our beloveds for mutual benefit.

The *path of completion* balances and integrates the god and goddess within ourselves. Both anima and animus, projective and receptive sides, Underworld and Upperworld are eventually harmonized, so we find peace and wholeness as a fully realized human being on Earth.

---

174. Note that the point assignments in the Pentacle Path system are rearranged from the traditional order arranged by alchemical density, which flows as spirit, fire, air, water, earth. When re-mapping the points as a spiritual journey corresponding to the Wheel of the Year, the Elemental Mysteries flow from spirit at top to earth at lower right, then deosil to air, fire, and water.

Ultimately, the wholeness we attain allows a transcendent view along the *path of return*. We discover that all began in spirit, all returns to spirit, and that path brings us home to ourselves. God/dess is "that which is attained at the end of desire."[175] All of these efforts open us like a channel lock between all three worlds, with our lives as the conduit. This open channel becomes our source of divine empowerment.

When we are open, balanced, and flowing freely through all worlds, this allows us to respond to any challenges effectively rather than remaining slaves to our reactions. The Witchcraft praxis offers us the handy framework to consider the idea of balance through the five points of the pentacle and the five elements.

Note how many times I've used the words "open" or "ease." The occult lessons presented again and again are that in order to receive the bounty of Divine Love like we are intended, we must first be opened, cleared, and ready to take it all in. You have to relax! Stressed-out anxiety is the clenched opposite, and yet that is the major problem of modern life we all must overcome. When we are at *ease*, we've relaxed the tension held along each polarity; we've reconciled the paradox. A mother laboring to deliver a baby will tell you that if you clench up in fear, try to avoid the unavoidable pain, cramp up your muscles and mind, the baby will not move. It will hurt more! We must release, soften, lean in, accept the occasional rapids, and float like a leaf upon the river of our destiny. The Goddess taught me this lesson directly while I labored with my first child. If we keep breathing and open fully to the challenge, the pain then falls away. If we are really doing it right, the pain transmutes into ecstasy.

The same wisdom applies for all the other layers of being. If we tightly guard our hearts against the potential pain of heartbreak, there is no space left to receive the potential joy of love that would heal that wound. If we go through life with a clenched fist and greedy with our resources, that hand will never open to receive true spiritual abundance. If we lock down our minds in fearful fundamentalism, we will never experience the eureka of a fresh and liberating perspective. If we freeze up from fear of failure, never doing what needs to be done, we'll never know the thrill of victory. If we only ever see our spirits as locked within the particular nationality, race, sex, or style of meat suit we happen to be

---

175. Valiente, *The Charge of the Goddess*, 13.

wearing, then we may never strip off the bindings and go skinny-dipping in the boundless sea of Divine Love.

Open Channel: Five Bodies

As a general overview of the magickal process of the Pentacle Path of Elemental Witchcraft, let's follow through the analogy of creating an open channel of divine power through the five bodies of the Self.

Mental Lock

We begin the magickal process by figuring out how we fit into this Divine Universe. Get the creative juices flowing to delete old programming and connect our individual minds to our Divine Mind. Learn the thealogy and paradigm of Witchcraft and learn the science and lore of how magick works. I call this step *screwing our heads on straight*—understanding the mechanics of magick, the why and logic of how the metaphysical systems work. This should destroy the need for "blind faith" and "superstition." Superstition is based in fearful ignorance, driving us to take irrational actions that can become harmful to ourselves and others. With true Witchcraft we conquer our fears through knowledge. The elemental lessons of air—to know and to wonder—are the keys to the mental lock.

Lock of the Will

Next on the witching agenda is to freely align our personal will and little ego with Divine Will. We figure out our sacred mission and then put to work our passions and energies to fulfill that mission. After the engine of your will is fired by the fuel of the divine cosmos, anything you set your mind to becomes possible. Then we back up our intentions by practical action—by the fire in our belly and the engine that powers our muscles, our passion for charging into whatever "battle" is required to accomplish the work we were born to do. The elemental lessons of fire—to will and to surrender—are the keys to opening the lock of the will.

Emotional Lock

Next, we heal our hearts through a connection to Divine Love. It takes a colossal effort to face our shadowy fears, forgive ourselves, and release those who wounded us. This over-culture is hostile to the spiritual and receptive nature of Witches, so no matter what you look like or where you came from, we arrive at the crossroads of the God/dess with at least a few wounds to tend. Accepting our whole, beautiful selves, all shadow and light, grit and squish, hunger and disgust is our challenge. To open the emotional lock requires deep inner journey work, courageously undertaken. Before we work magick for external change, we must shift our own vibration from wounded consciousness into a state of Perfect Love and trustworthiness of ourselves. The elemental lessons of water—to dare and to accept—are the keys to opening the emotional lock.

Physical Lock

Opening the lock of our physical bodies is another unique challenge to Witchcraft. Truly, it is the first lock we should attend to, but until we know *why*, it's hard to know *what* to do. The physical realm is where Witchcraft finds its distinction, where we thrive. Witches glory in our bodies, fully engaged in the physical actions of rituals, the selection of just the right *stuff* from our partners in the realms of plant, stone, and bone, crafting talismans and amulets, digging our hands into the black earth. When I finish a rite, I'm dirty and smell of exotic smoke, salt, and mystery, or I get back in there until I've done it right!

But more importantly: self-care. In order to become the conduit to divine power in the world, Witches have to strengthen and nourish our physical vessels. Casual devotions don't require much beyond general health. You owe your indwelling spirit a standard of minimal care. However, to become a magus, spiritual medium, or energy healer of any kind, that takes far more rigorous care of your physical body. Proper exercise, rest, purification, eating natural foods, and drinking plenty of water are a bare minimum. Avoidance of addictions to alcohol, tobacco, and unnecessary drugs are the healthy lifestyle choices that will be inevitably necessary for the higher-vibrational workings. You can attempt to channel that power through a toxic vessel, but you will burn your temple to the ground. Trust me; I learned this lesson the stupid way and have the neurology bills to prove it. Conveniently, the more progressed your awareness within spirit develops, the greater your natural bliss, and you simply lose your desire for baneful things.

Remember that your body is the temple of the God/dess. Your flesh is divine flesh. Into what quality vessel do you invite the gods? Put the same high-quality reverent care into yourself as you do your altar table, magickal tools, and offerings. If you eat trash, drink and breathe poison, and carelessly neglect yourself, what good have your devotions to an indwelling divinity accomplished? Just think about it carefully, and then *don't burn the Witch*, starting with yourself. The elemental lessons of earth—to be silent and to resonate—are the keys to opening the physical lock.

Spiritual Lock

By the time we've attended to the four elemental locks, we're likely most of the way toward realizing our inner divinity and opening our spirit as a conduit of divine power. We intentionally tap our personal spirit into the Great Spirit, like logging onto the divine server through a continuous spiritual uplink. Meditation practices establish this uplink. A personal relationship between God/dess and Self is reconciled. The circuit is now open and complete, above and below, within and without; we become an open channel of enormous power.

Once Witches find their power, the little things of life are able to be enjoyed easily and effectively. I believe that Witches, as a vocation, are called to be caretakers, starting with ourselves. Once we figure out our own lives, we can help protect nature and elevate society, becoming the voice for the voiceless, the defender of the defenseless.

The Five Bodies: Mental, Will, Emotional, Physical, Spiritual

It is the Eastern traditions that inform Modern Witchcraft about the anatomy of our energy bodies and the role that elemental essences play in the experience of our lives. The similarities between Hindu and Taoist paradigms to Hermetic Witchcraft are due to their purposeful syncretism. In this Hermetic Witchcraft, we might describe God/dess as our Source of divine energy, which is cast through the four elemental planes. That divine energy is then organized into various forms by the astrological patterns (celestial spheres) guiding our destiny. Similarly, in Taoism, philosophers and alchemists as early as the fifth century BCE described that vital life force energy as *qi* (pronounced *chee*), thought to emanate from "the Great Ultimate (taiji)," through "the dynamic ordering pattern (*li*)."[176] That qi, or chi, is manifest through an interplay between active (*yang*) and passive (*yin*) modes, which define the cosmos through their five-element system of wood, metal, earth, water, and fire.[177] In Chinese, qi, chi, or ch'i translates as "breath," "vital force," or "organic material energy" and refers to the "psychophysical energies that permeate the universe."[178]

In Japanese systems of energy healing such as *Reiki*, this universal life force energy is called *ki* (pronounced *key*). In Hawaiian spirituality, it is called *mana*.[179] This concept was introduced to many of us in the West through the fictional Jedi religion in *Star Wars* movies, which called it *the Force*. In Hindu systems of India, this energy is called *prana*, which means "life force" in Sanskrit and is central to the practices of yoga. All these terms refer to a spiritual energy that is within all things, including plants and animals, the air we breathe, the food, minerals, and water we consume—everything. Metaphorically, I describe this energy as the Divine Love of the God/dess, both manifesting as humans and interconnecting all of humanity through the collective consciousness we call Divine Mind.

The Auras, Chakras, and Our Fivefold Self

As both a Witch and Reiki healer, I utilize techniques from both Eastern and Western traditions. However, I was constantly translating the Eastern vocabulary and the systems derived from Hinduism to match my Western Witchcraft. For ease in this work, let's define those terms and systems, then correspond the two systems for our use in Elemental Witchcraft.

The Aura

From Hinduism we learn about the *aura*, which is a psycho-electric field that interpenetrates and surrounds the physical body to an extent that is typically just beyond our reach in all directions. The aura is generated through the interaction of your physical

---

176. Specifically, the Song dynasty (960–1279); "Qi: Chinese Philosophy," Encyclopedia Britannica, updated May 7, 2020, https://www.britannica.com/topic/qi-Chinese-philosophy.

177. "Qi," Encyclopedia Britannica.

178. "Qi," Encyclopedia Britannica.

179. Christopher Penczak, *Magick of Reiki: Focused Energy for Healing, Ritual & Spiritual Development* (Woodbury, MN: Llewellyn Publications, 2009), 2.

body's energy with our subtle bodies of energy. This field is in the donut shape of the torus around us—same as planet earth's electromagnetic field—and is made of divine consciousness.

Our own thoughts and intentions directly influence the auric field. The more conscious you become of this interaction, the greater your control over well-being. The auric field acts a lot like a spiritual magnet. Remember the *Hermetic Principle of Vibration*: like vibrations attract like vibrations. So, your auric field is tuned to the frequency of your core thoughts and feelings.

The auric field has multiple layers of various densities, which are referred to collectively as the subtle bodies. Those layers take a variety of names across traditions. We'll return to name them in a moment.

The Chakras

Within a layer of the auric field close to our skin, we also have energy organs called *chakras*. Just as we have physical organs and circulatory systems that regulate the flow of blood, hormones, and digestion throughout our biology, we also have energy organs that regulate the flow of elemental energy from the *above of our subtle bodies* into the *below of our physical body*.

Chakra is a Sanskrit word that means *wheel or vortex*. There are seven main chakras, which swirl like a whirlpool between the subtle bodies and our matter. Our chakra energy organs also connect us to all three realms. From the crown chakra (7) at the top of our heads connecting us to the Upperworld down the trunk of our bodies to the root chakra at the base of the torso (1) connecting us to the Underworld. There are additional chakras within the auric field and at various points on our extremities. For our purposes along the Pentacle Path, we'll also access the earth star chakra (0) and the soul star chakra (8). The earth star chakra is located near the base of our egg-shaped auric field, just below the feet, and connects us to planetary feminine divinity below. The soul star chakra is located just above our heads and is our connection to the cosmic masculine divinity above, which flows down through the *stellar gateway* at the topmost limit of our aura.[180] Refer to figures 13 and 17.

---

180. Penczak, *Magick of Reiki*, 32–33.

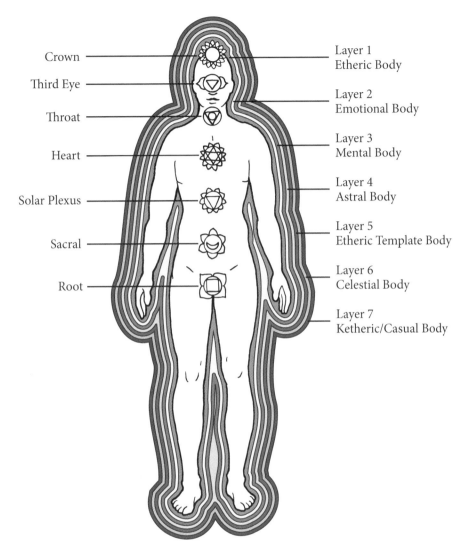

Crown
Third Eye
Throat
Heart
Solar Plexus
Sacral
Root

Layer 1
Etheric Body

Layer 2
Emotional Body

Layer 3
Mental Body

Layer 4
Astral Body

Layer 5
Etheric Template Body

Layer 6
Celestial Body

Layer 7
Ketheric/Casual Body

Figure 17: The chakras

Chakras function like valves and regulate the way spiritual energy ebbs and flows between Spirit and all our subtle layers down to our flesh and bones.[181] Just as the aura is made of consciousness, so are the chakras, but the chakras are slightly denser and can be perceived by a sensitive touch once you know what you're looking for. Each of the

181. Energy being called many things by many cultures: ki, chi, prana, Divine Light, archaeus, the Force…

seven main chakras is the energy organ interacting with one of the endocrine glands and a nerve bundle called a *plexus*. Therefore, the chakras regulate spiritual energy to their corresponding physical systems and the related organs in the body. For example, heart chakra governs the thymus gland and the cardiac plexus and thus impacts the health of the circulatory and immune systems. Chakras also correspond with the seven colors of the visible light spectrum and seven notes in the octave. These connections inspire modalities of energy healing using colored light, sound, and the crystals that amplify the corresponding vibrations. See the table below ("Mapping Chakras to The Pentacle Paths, Bodies, and Divine Love Conditions") for specifics of each chakra and their corresponding areas of consciousness.

Aspects of Consciousness

The *Hermetic Principle of Mentalism* reminds us that everything in the cosmos is interconnected through divine consciousness. Therefore, our individual consciousness is also interconnected to every cell in our bodies. Through this interconnection, we can not only communicate throughout time and space with divine beings, past lives, spirit animals, and so on, we can also communicate with every organ, cell, and organism within our own bodies. It all begins in the consciousness of the Divine Mind. Then like light through a prism, that spirit further expresses into the rainbow spectrum of colors through our chakras so that we also experience our full spectrum of selfhood.

To recap this system in context to the Hermetic paradigm we've already outlined: the divine light of Spirit shines through the fractal pattern created by astrology and the twelve zodiac signs of the outer stars that regulate the elemental Plane of Forces, which then emerge through your chakras to become your physical body, also impacting endocrine glands and nerve bundles to create the 3D experience of your physical reality. Your body is an embodied pentacle—a perfect balance of spirit, flesh, emotion, mind, and will.

The following table of correspondences maps the pentacle points to states of matter, body, chakra, and path.

Element	Earth	Air	Fire	Water	Spirit
State of Matter	Solid	Gaseous	Plasma	Liquid	Etheric
Body	Physical Body	Mental Body	Body of the Will	Emotional Body	Spiritual Body
Chakra	Root and Sacral	Throat and Third Eye	Solar Plexus	Heart	Crown, Soul Star, Earth Star
Path	Sovereignty	Truth	Power	Love	Completion

The Fivefold Self

Just like the pentacle symbolizes, human beings have an interwoven fivefold Self. The physical body is just the solid core at the center of your wholeness and is easily corresponded to elemental earth. Across traditions, there are many names for the layers of subtle bodies that extend outward from your skin, forming your auric field. For our Pentacle Path of balance, we'll call those subtle bodies our mental body (elemental air), emotional body (elemental water), body of the will (elemental fire), and spiritual body (quintessence).

These subtle layers cannot always be seen, but they can be felt. Humans are certainly aware of them subconsciously, as our language and idioms reflect. For example, when suffering emotional loss, we call that "heartbreak," and we feel that pain in our chests despite the fact that the heart muscle is there to pump blood and not emotions. However, the heart chakra *does* pump emotional energy from the emotional body into the physical body, and it also is located mid-chest. When our feelings are hurt, the chakra contracts and in turn creates a tight, aching sensation in our chest; hence, a broken heart.

The following table maps the Hindu chakra system correspondences to the Pentacle Paths of Witchcraft, the five bodies, and the elemental forces that empower them. I've correlated these to the nine Divine Love Conditions from chapter 3 and a charm of affirmation introduced in the meditation at the end of this chapter.

Mapping Chakras to The Pentacle Paths, Bodies, and Nine Divine Love Conditions

	The Physical Body: Earth		Body of the Will: Fire	Emotional Body: Water	Mental Body: Air		Spiritual Body: Ether
Pentacle Path	Sovereignty		Power	Love	Truth		Completion
Chakra	Root Chakra	Sacral Chakra	Solar Plexus Chakra	Heart Chakra	Throat Chakra	Third Eye Chakra	The Crown Chakra
Sanskrit Name	Muladhara	Svadhisthana	Manipura	Anahata	Visuddhi	Ajna	Sahasrara
Physical Location	Base of Torso, Perineum	Between pelvic bone and naval	Diaphragm	Sternum	Base of Throat	Brow, Center Forehead	Top of Head, Fontanel
Color of Light	Red	Orange	Yellow	Green	Blue	Indigo	Violet
Endocrine Gland	Ovaries, testicles	Pancreas	Adrenal	Thymus	Thyroid	Pineal	Pituitary
Physical Systems	Excretory, Lower Digestive, Sexual Function	Kidney, Bladder, Reproductive	Upper Digestive, musculature	Heart, Circulatory, Immune	Respiratory	Eye, Ear, Brain, Nervous	Nervous, Endocrine
Governs	Physical Survival	Pleasure	Free Will	Love	Truth	Insight	Cosmic spirit
Blocked By	Fear	Guilt	Shame	Grief	Deception	Illusion	Ego Attachment
Divine Love Condition	Resources	Affection	Acceptance and Sovereignty	Security and Trustworthiness	Expression	Authenticity	Reciprocity

Wounded by	Fear of Suffering	Fear of Abandonment	Fears of Bigotry and Oppression	Fears of Violation, Deception	Fears of Disenfranchisement	Fears of Exploitation	Fears of Betrayal
Auric Layer	Etheric Body	Emotional Body	Mental Body	Astral Body	Etheric Template	Celestial Body	Ketheric/Causal Body
Consciousness	Physical identity, self-preservation; foundation, survival instincts, grounding and connection to our physical reality	Emotional identity, self-gratification; sexuality, desire, sensation, procreation, reproduction, creativity, intimacy, enjoyment	Ego identity, self-definition and strength; personal power, autonomy, metabolism, action, spontaneity, and power; gut instincts	Social identity, self-acceptance, emotions, relationships, compassion; integrator of opposites: mind and body, anima and animus, ego and unity	Creative identity, self-expression, communication, engagement, creativity, vibration, language, expression, artistry	Archetypal identity, self-reflection, clairvoyance and mental perception, psychism; spiritual wisdom and enlightenment	Universal identity, self-knowledge, pure awareness, wisdom, understanding, and bliss; connection to Divine Mind, Will, and Love
Affirmation Charm	By elemental powers five, I have all I need to survive and thrive.	By the powers of earth and sea, I share desired intimacy.	By the powers of fire and bone; I am who I am, and do what must be done.	By the powers of water and air, I am safe from all harm; I can trust in my care.	By the powers of air and fire, my voice is strong, my truth admired.	By the One Who Moves as Two, my vision is clear and divinely imbued.	By the Two Who Move as One, I am complete through interconnection. Open channel, flowing free, blessed on all levels, so mote it be!

Consciousness Creates Reality

Divine consciousness flowing through the subtle bodies of our aura create our physical body. The physical body is just the end result in a divine process of becoming. When you feel tension, or a lack of ease, you first feel it in the chakra associated with that part of your own consciousness under duress. Then that tension transfers to the parts of the physical body connected to that chakra. Where you feel the discomfort depends on why the situation makes you uncomfortable. The pinching closed of the chakra impedes energy flow to the nerves of the associated plexus, which then effects the body parts controlled by those nerves. If that tension lasts a while or is intense, a physical ailment can develop.

For healing and balance, if we can change our minds, we can change our physical reality. A shift of consciousness tunes our auric field to a different frequency. Then the frequency of our auric field is mirrored as a change in our physical body. As above, so below.

❄ Meditation 4: Chakra Balancing Through Pentacle Powers ❄

In addition to this guided visualization and energy working, we'll affirm our balance by speaking aloud the lines of the charm included in the table above, taking advice from the "Rede of the Wiccae": "To bind the spell every time, let the spell be spake in rhyme." [182]

Needs

Candle, any kind

Incense, any kind

A comfortable and supportive chair with arms, if possible

Words to the chakra affirmation from the table above, for easy reference

Your Book of Mirrors and a pen

Preparation

Light your candle and incense then sit comfortably in an armchair that allows your spine to be perpendicular to the floor. Your thighs should be parallel to the floor, feet flat. Hold nothing crossed or with awkward tension. While meditating, allow the power of each

---

182. Mathiesen and Theitic, *The Rede of the Wiccae*, 52.

chakra's elemental energy to pulse through the cadence of the words. Repeat the lines with power as many times as you need to feel them sealed. Visualize the written words themselves blaze within your mind's eye in the colored light associated with that chakra.

Praxis

Begin with the pranic breathing relaxation in meditation 2 in chapter 3. When fully relaxed, visualize yourself in the meditation room in your mind, and then head down the trapdoor in the floor and down the spiral staircase to your center as taught in meditation 3. At the looking glass, envision the great world tree on the astral plane beyond and step through.

Step up to the great world tree, your axis mundi, connecting you above and below, infinitely linked within the cosmos. Lay your hands upon the tree and feel the energy of life pulsing through. You and the tree are one energy, so you push straight through the bark and merge with the tree swaying gently in the breeze.

Remember your tree-ish connections through your roots to the bedrock, the water table, and the planetary core and goddess. Remember your branches, connecting to the atmosphere, the fires of the sun, the God, and the cosmos beyond.

Spend a few moments tree-breathing: inhale up from the earth, exhale down from the cosmos. Where the Two Who Move as One connect at your heart, all of creation flows. (*Pause for at least three long, circulating breaths.*)

There is connection between your physical Self and the world of consciousness. Shift your attention now to your taproot, to where the Underworld meets the trunk of your tree and physical body. This root chakra at the base of your being, your perineum, and the base of your spine, connects your physical body to consciousness. The root chakra now spins open like a red flower, and a red light flows upward from earth into your body, nourishing, stabilizing, grounding you in physical reality. As you inhale red light, think of your need for material resources. (*Pause.*)

Note how you feel. Is there some fear of suffering causing an obstacle to the flow? (*Pause.*)

Now visualize the resources needed for fulfillment and balance coming to you now. (*Pause.*)

Chant aloud: *By elemental powers five, I have all that I need to survive and thrive.* (*Pause.*)

On the breath, draw the light into your belly below the navel. Inhale an orange light, the sacral chakra spins open like a flower, and a liquid enjoyment flows throughout your body, bringing pleasure, sensuality, satisfaction. As you inhale the orange light, think of your needs for affection and intimacy. (*Pause.*)

Note how you feel. Is there a fear of deprivation causing an obstacle to the flow? (*Pause.*)

Now visualize the loving interactions needed for fulfillment and balance opening for you now. (*Pause.*)

Chant aloud: *By the powers of earth and sea, I share desired intimacy.* (*Pause.*)

Draw that light up into the sternum, turning yellow. Your solar plexus burns with fires of your will, your personal engine, your muscles, and your energy. The solar plexus spins open like the door to a furnace. As you inhale the yellow light, think of your sovereign right to free will. (*Pause.*)

Note how you feel. Is there a fear of oppression causing an obstacle to the flow? Is there fear of bigotry? (*Pause.*)

Now visualize the liberty and acceptance you need for fulfillment and balance realized for you now. (*Pause.*)

Chant aloud: *By the powers of fire and bone, I am who I am and do what must be done.* (*Pause.*)

Draw that light up once more to the heart as the green light of Divine Love. In the heart you find the love of yourself, family and friends, love of your planet, love of the world. The heart chakra spins open like a green flower, and compassion flows throughout your body and beyond you into your relationships. As you inhale the green light, think of your sense of security in those connections, your need for trustworthiness. (*Pause.*)

Note how you feel. Is there a fear of violation or deception causing an obstacle to the flow? (*Pause.*)

Now visualize the Perfect Love and Trust needed for fulfillment and balance offered to you now.

Chant aloud: *By the powers of water and air, I am safe from all harm; I can trust in my care.* (*Pause.*)

Draw the light up once more to the base of the throat. The throat chakra swirls open like a blue flower. Blue light of easy expression fills your body honestly and genuinely. In the blue light you find acceptance and mutual respect. You are seen, and your contributions are heard. (*Pause.*)

As you inhale the blue light, think of your own expressions. (*Pause.*)

Note how you feel. Is there a fear of disenfranchisement? A fear of not being heard or respected causing an obstacle to the flow? (*Pause.*)

Now visualize living your truth out loud and fulfillment and balance your reality now.

Chant aloud: *By the powers of air and fire, my voice is strong, my truth is admired.* (*Pause.*)

Draw up the light to the middle of your brow to the third-eye chakra, which spins open like an indigo lotus flower. In the indigo light your intuition awakens from the illusion of your separateness. Through the indigo light, peer beyond the veil to your interconnection with all things, all times, all dimensions. Look deeply. As you inhale the indigo light, think of the world of illusion around you. (*Pause.*)

Note how you feel. Is there a fear of exploitation causing an obstacle to the flow? What disillusionment impedes your sight? (*Pause.*)

Now visualize an authentic world of mutual truth shared with you now. (*Pause.*)

Chant aloud: *By the One who Moves as Two, my vision is clear and divinely imbued.* (*Pause.*)

Draw the light once more to the very top of your head. Your crown chakra spins open like a violet flower, connecting you to a dazzling divine light. As you inhale the violet light into your spirit body, expand into connection with the Divine Mind. You are complete within God/dess. Think of your need for reciprocity, for your trustworthiness to be returned. (*Pause.*)

Note how you feel. Is there a fear of betrayal causing an obstacle to the flow? (*Pause.*)

Now visualize the interconnected web of existence glowing violet, flowing freely, whole and complete without impediment or interruption.

Chant aloud: *By the Two Who Move as One, I am complete through interconnection.* (*Pause.*)

Shift your awareness outward once more, remembering yourself as the great world tree, the axis mundi. You are interconnected through your roots and branches. Your trunk now a rainbow of light, flowing above to below, below to above. You are rejuvenated and healed on all levels.

Take a few moments to tree-breathe: inhaling up from goddess and exhaling down from god, creating a circuit throughout your body that merges at your heart chakra. Dwell within this heart space of Divine Love for at least three long, circulating breaths.

Chant three times aloud: *Open channel, flowing free, blessed on all levels, so mote it be!*

When you are ready to return, simply imagine yourself pushing outward from the trunk of the tree, separating yourself again. Return to the looking glass, seeing yourself. In three steps, find your way back to the waking world.

One, two, three, step through! Take the spiral stairs, rising higher and higher to the little room inside your head, closing the trapdoor behind you. Find your way to the window of your eyes, and when ready, open them.

Journal Reflection

Spend some time journaling about your meditation experience in your Book of Mirrors.

Chapter 8
Elemental Tools

The *stuff* of Witchcraft is purposefully romantic, aesthetically intriguing, and iconic. Witches, cauldrons, and brooms go together like Halloween and pumpkins! Because Witches embrace our Middleworld existence, beauty, form, function, and the symbolic poetry of our tools are all important to our sacred purpose. They become an extension of our physical bodies, assisting us by channeling the elemental essences. They help us focus and direct with natural energy, constructing our temples and then all the magick we create. With each of the elemental journeys we take in section three, we'll seek guidance on what our individual tools should be and where to find them. Until then, let's explore the traditional choices and their occult meanings and uses within a typical Modern Witchcraft practice. In section three, you'll find a ritual for tool consecration to perform after you've both found the perfect elemental tools and established the connections necessary to properly charge them to their purpose.

The short story is that a Witch's tools function like a key that unlocks each gate to an elemental realm and then directs that power into Middleworld reality. While not strictly necessary, the physical tools do help the energetic work, and there are valid psychological reasons that these items continue to fascinate our culture: they work. Plus, these iconic symbols add nuance, drama, and shared visual cues that always makes group magick more effective. I recommend making an effort to properly collect and consecrate your own tools of the Craft eventually. That being said, they do not have to be acquired all at once, so you can take your time.

For an Elemental Witchcraft practice grounded in the eight mysteries of the Witch's Jewel of Power, eight magickal tools are consecrated to embody their elemental force, anchor their elemental mystery lesson in our consciousness, and defend one of the eight qualities of ritual worship given to us by the Goddess in "The Charge" in this passage:

> Let my worship be within the heart that rejoiceth, for behold: all acts of love and pleasure are my rituals. And therefore, let there be *beauty and strength, power and compassion, honour and humility, mirth and reverence* within you.[183]

There are four *grand tools* that anchor the elemental gateways at the boundary between worlds, working magick of interconnection, so they anchor the *receptive* elemental energies of the Witch's Jewel of Power. Then there are four *altar tools*, which empower and focus our personal will, so they anchor the *projective* mysteries. As we go through each tool, those associations are included.

Tools of Elemental Earth

The altar itself is one of the grand tools of earth. Any tools meant to embody, hold, and direct elemental earth are best to be made of anything that grew up out of the earth. The obvious choices are items made of stone, metal, crystal, clay, wood, or other natural materials that grow. If your choice still pulses with the life of earth when you tap into it, then it is the correct tool of earth for you.

---

183. Valiente, *The Charge of the Goddess*, 13; italics added.

Altar Tool of Earth: The Paten, Peyton, or Pentacle

Traditional altar tools of earth are the *paten*, or *peyton*, which is a flat disk or plate with the pentacle symbol fashioned into the material in some way. In occult parlance, it is called the shield. The pentacle being a symbol that represents all the interwoven elements of the physical earth.

- Infuse with earth's projective **power of silence**.
- Charge to manifest your magick **empowered** by nature's balance.

One of my first Wiccan teachers, Spanish Moss, called the altar pentacle a "magickal hotplate" because it focuses elemental energy into manifestation. If you want to charge an object, set it on your pentacle on the altar overnight. This is a gateway to all the realms and so forms a focus of power there.

I prefer a ceramic or glass dish with a slightly raised lip, with the pentacle painted or in relief. The dish can potentially hold things, like items to be consecrated. I often use mine to hold the altar cakes or offerings. My pentacle paten often serves as a little stage for my spellworkings. It conveniently holds herbs, powders, and assorted mysterious fluids neatly and can later be easily washed.

Grand Tool: Besom

The grand tool of earth is the besom (*bey-sum*) or the Witch's broom. The besom, when made with proper intent, is another fertility symbol and image of creation.

- Infuse with earth's receptive **power of resonance**.
- Defends sovereignty through Perfect Divine Trust and the God/dess's charge of **reverence**.

The besom is often used to clear the sacred space with a ritual gesture of sweeping out baneful psychic energies. The handle represents the phallus of the god, and the triangular shape of the broomcorn bristles represent the yoni of the goddess. The traditional method for construction would include an acorn nestled in the bristles, just where the handle embeds, and is then kept snug by the woven bindings. This symbolic tool represents the pagan three-world model that is like the big *vesica pisces*: Father Sky intersects with the

Mother Earth, and where they are conjoined, the manifest world of nature is born of their seed. Ash or birch are traditional woods, but again, I'm no slave to convention.

The *flying broom* is a very liminal notion—flying through the mystical between spaces of astral, so the broom is often used in ritual to represent a boundary. By jumping over the broom, you arrive in another stage of life or another realm. This is why after the speaking of vows the newly handfasted couple and newly initiated Witches "jump the broom," landing in their new lives.

For tools of earth, I recommend a monthlong cleansing by one of the earthy cleansing techniques prior to the ritual of consecration. Earth techniques always take the longest, and considering the intimate connection between earth and lunar cycles, I think a full lunation gives it time to do the job properly.

Earth Cleansing Techniques

- **Shallow grave:** Bury the object about six to twelve inches down in the soft earth, like in a flower bed or at the base of a tree. Have them pointing down in the earth. This only works right if the object cannot be harmed by exposure to the damp ground, but this is especially helpful with stones and crystals. Make sure to clearly mark your burial place, or you may lose it.

- **Herb bath:** In a wide, flat bowl create a bed of dried plant materials that correspond to purification and lay the object on top of them in a place that won't be disturbed. Examples: cedar, sage, juniper, lavender, vervain, or mugwort.

- **Salt or stone bath:** Same as the last option but in a dish of large crystal sea salt and other small stones. Examples: selenite and black tourmaline are my go-to stones for clearing.

Tools of Elemental Air

Tools of air are typically made of wooden branches of specific trees, chosen for their magickal associations. However, they can also be long, pointy crystals or feathers bound at the quill with a bit of leather or metal wire. Tools of air are often used to summon spiritual energies and then direct them in the casting of enchantment, so something with a comfortable grip in your hand and a directional dimension for "pointing" will serve you well.

Altar Tool of Air: The Wand

The traditional altar tools of air vary from tradition to tradition. Much of the Wiccan-based praxis uses the wand for air. Yet still others choose the blade, and there are valid reasons for both choices. My altar tool for air has always been the wand. When I visualize air, I think of the trees with their branches high in the sky, blowing in the breeze, and forming perches for birds. Branches that support the green leaves are each a wee factory for transmuting the gases of carbon dioxide into oxygen as a living lung of the ecosystem.

- Infuse with air's projective **power of knowledge**.
- Charge to inspirit your magick, casting enchantment with **mirth**.

I encourage any Witch to make their wand with their own hands, from a tree with whom they have a kinship. There are many correspondences and mythologies surrounding trees and their wood for magickal purposes. Just be mindful of the lore and magick of the wood you choose and do so with reverence and intention.

Go meditate near a tree with whom you might like to partner. Trees are known to be the priests of the plant realm, and if a tree-priest gifts you a branch (essentially one of their bones) of their own free will and agrees to partner with you in your magick with elemental air, well, that is a very powerful and special partnership. It can be an already fallen branch or one you harvest.

Should you choose to harvest a living branch, please do so with reverence and permission. Bring an offering of fresh water along and some sharp garden sheers. After the trimming, offer thanks to the tree, pour out the water, and spend some time with your hand over the snip, sending healing energies. To do so, tap into the natural magick of the area as done in meditation 3: Axis Mundi Tree Breathing Through the Elements. Then direct that energy through your own heart chakra, through your hands, into the tree for a few minutes.

Cut your branch to length by bending your arm at the elbow and resting the larger end of the branch inside the crook of your arm. Measure the length to the tip of your middle finger. Wand diameter at the base works well if it is at least as thick as your thumb. This is a traditional measure; but your wand, your rules.

Grand Tool: The Staff

The staff is a larger version of the wand, typically made of a wooded branch of a tree that has been selected based on spiritual powers and personal relationship with the Witch. Do some research concerning the magick of trees and then select accordingly.

- Infuse the staff with air's power of **wonderment**.
- Charge to create within the Divine Mind, defending your sovereignty with **strength**.

A staff stands shoulder height or less and is comfortable to hold in the hand, like a walking stick. The staff may be carved, finished, or decorated in any meaningful way. Often, stones or crystals are embedded in the head to further magnify powers of the mind and communications with spirit. The grand tool of air amplifies and directs wonderment and creative thinking into manifestation. I chose the charge of *strength* for the staff based on my own love of *Lord of the Rings* and the wizard character of Gandalf the Grey. In much the same way, to wield the Witch's staff with wonderment requires a courage and strength to overcome the beasts of convention.

Air Cleansing Techniques

- **Wind:** After you've completed your wand or staff, hang it from the branches of a tree and allow it to blow in the breeze for a complete day/night cycle during the waxing moon.
- **Smoke:** Build a fire outdoors in a firepit and throw handfuls of air cleansing herbs or resin, such as copal, on the fire and pass the wand or staff through the billowing smoke for as long as supplies last.
- **Oil:** Blend a wood sealant of walnut oil with a few drops of an essential oil that corresponds to elemental air, such as lavender or clary sage. With a soft, clean cloth rub the sealent into the wood with widdershins (counterclockwise) motions.
- See the air formulary in chapter 13 for options of herbs, oils, and stones of air.

Tools of Elemental Fire

Tools of fire are typically forged blades of iron or steel. Of course, some traditions mirror the tarot and other occult systems, which use the wand for a tool of fire. If that is your preference, refer back to the wand selection section. In my own choice about which tool best represents fiery energies, I think of the blacksmith's forge. A blade is made in the hottest fires until it is so hot it glows red, then pounded through sheer strength, muscle, and iron until it surrenders into an exalted form. The fires temper the metals, burning away all impurities, which makes the steel stronger and sharper. The artistry and skill of the blacksmith, as an act of their own will, transforms the materials into a weapon of exquisite beauty, power, and precision. The metal is transmuted through this fiery process from something base to something finely honed and balanced. The knife is born of fire for the purpose of establishing our boundaries and defending our sovereignty with the fires of our will. These are all the lessons of elemental fire, and so the blade is the easy choice as my tool of fire, because of all the elements, fire is the most projective, aggressive, and wild. The steel knife aids me in wrangling and channeling these forces in the most masculine way. I feel powerful when holding my athame, like a warrior prepared for any challenge. In occult parlance, the altar tools were called "weapons." For the others, I don't see it, but for fire, that is exactly what is called for!

Altar Tool of Fire: Athame

The traditional altar tool of fire is the athame (*ah-THAW-may* or *ATH-a-may*). Doreen Valiente included *ath-AY-me* as pronunciation in *Witchcraft for Tomorrow*.[184] The athame is typically a double-edged, black-handled knife.

- Infuse the athame with fire's projective **power of the will.**
- Charge to empower your magick, banishing fear with **humility**.

The athame is used for directing spiritual energy toward a purpose, "cutting" or "carving" energetically, and banishing enchantment. I know of many beautiful athames made of horn, bone, and stone, but for this last purpose of banishing enchantment, I have found it very important that the tool of fire be constructed of steel or contain iron in some manner.

---

184. Valiente, *Witchcraft for Tomorrow*, 78.

The blade of the athame has long been regarded as a tool of the God—specifically masculine divinity. Whereas the wand was of the Goddess—specifically the feminine divine. I also find the balance there to be interesting: the "masculine" elements have a feminine side, seen in air and expressed through the gentler wand. And the "feminine" elements of water and earth have a masculine side, seen in earth and expressed through the "shield" or pentacle paten.

Grand Tool of Fire: Sword

The grand tool of fire is the sword, another double-edged blade, for the same fiery reasons. The sword is seen as a representation of the God and can be the tool to summon him. Covens often use the sword in carving a magickal circle between worlds.

- Infuse the sword with fire's receptive **power of surrender**.
- Charge to empower Divine Will, defending your sovereignty with **honor**.

The sword may also be used for the challenge at the gate of our group circles whereupon each Witch is stopped and questioned if they enter into this rite of their own free will, understanding the dangers. Then they pledge to enter of their own accord and with a promise of perfect, unconditional love and trustworthiness. The sword may then be laid across the eastern gateway to represent that liminal boundary and protect it further. The sword is seen as a collective link to the elemental energies of fire and the collective purpose of the coven.

I regard the sword as a symbol of our ethics being in alignment with Divine Will and the courage it takes to practice Witchcraft without fear as our true selves. The sword holds surrender, remembering knighting ceremonies where the warrior kneels to accept his solemn duty of service.

Cleansing and Preparing Ceremonial Blades

- **Lodestone:** Traditionally, Witches would magnetize the blade by rubbing the edge with a lodestone so that it attracts energies efficiently.
- **Flame:** When purifying by flame, you hold the blade in or near the fire and then visualize the elemental essence as red light surrounding and infusing the blade with its power.

• **Sunlight:** Bathe the tool in direct sunlight for a few hours prior to your consecration rite.

Tools of Elemental Water

Magickal tools of water tend to be vessels made of natural materials that symbolize the womb of the Goddess and the Divine Love from which all of creation emerges.

Altar Tool of Water: Chalice

The chalice is a drinking vessel, typically a cup on a stemmed base like a goblet.

- Infuse the chalice with water's projective **powers of daring**.
- Charge as a fountain of **beauty**, which flows through your magick.

The chalice is often made of silver, as that is the metal of the Goddess and the moon, but it truly can be made of any natural material so long as it is easily washable and hygienic. Beware drinking alcohol from pewter vessels unless you know it is lead-free. Avoid aluminum vessels altogether for similar health safety concerns. Ceramics, crystal, and glass are all perfectly acceptable if they feel correct to you.

Grand Tool of Water: Cauldron

The cauldron is the grand tool of water. Typically, the cauldron is a vessel made of metal, preferably cast iron, with three little feet holding it off the ground so fires may be lit underneath and a handle for lifting it. The three feet are said to be the support given by the triple goddess in all our magick.

- Infuse the cauldron with water's receptive **power of acceptance**.
- Charge as a fountain of Perfect Divine Love, defending sovereignty with **compassion**.

A cauldron can serve many magickal purposes. Stoke a fire underneath and it can be used to boil up a brew. Build the fire inside it and it can serve much like a firepit. Layer some sand in a small cauldron and burn incense and other spell materials safely indoors.

Cleansing and Preparing Tools of Water

- **Stream:** Find a natural stream where the water flows clean and clear and hold the vessel in the water such that the stream flows into the chalice and overflows. If possible, secure it and leave it there to be cleansed for a full day/night cycle under a full moon.

- **Herbs:** Fill the vessel with pure water and add herbs and flowers of water like chamomile, jasmine, or gardenia blossoms. Leave outdoors for a full day/night cycle during the full moon to absorb the moon's power.

- **Stones:** Similarly, and if leaving water in the vessel for too long is not advised, add to the vessel stones of water, like moonstone, and allow to charge in a window that receives the moonlight throughout a waxing lunar cycle.

- See formulary section in chapter 15 for herb and stone options.

Preparation of Elemental Tools

The dedication of your tools begins in those first moments you choose them. Ask them whether they are willing to work with you and in what way. The purpose of dedication is to have the two of you coordinating your energies and focusing them on a single purpose. Make sure you have consent from this object to take the job. That may sound silly to some, but if you connect to any material thing deeply on a spirit level and you get a feeling of dis-ease, tightening, or any "nope" feelings at all, then you really don't want to force that issue; it will be coercive and a waste of your precious energy.

Cleanse any object before setting it to use in your magick, as materials are imprinted with the energies of all those beings and places where it has been previously. When anything—people, places, objects, spirits—shift up a gear to a purer vibration, anything less pure is canceled or removed. Witches use the powers of the five elements to cleanse because that creates a resonance with the pure elemental energy, which then entrains the vibration of the object as they syncopate.

Consecrating a Witch's Elemental Tools

After you have found or made your tools to channel the four classical elemental powers, they need to be ritually consecrated to clear and imbue them with their divine purpose. A ritual of consecration for your tools serves three purposes: it clears the material object of all previous energies, sets the intention for their use, and then imbues the tool with the necessary elemental power. That tool then anchors the flow of that power in the Middle-world for you so you can then shift your attention to other aspects of the working. By wielding the tool, you can easily tap that power and direct it for use later on. Magickal tools are like your keys to that realm, but they aren't just a skeleton key that, if lying around, any ol' body could pick up and use to the same effect. They are keyed to *your* spirit because this is a consensual partnership, not ownership. Your magickal tools will quickly unlock the door to that realm for *you* alone. A ritual of consecration is provided in chapter 16.

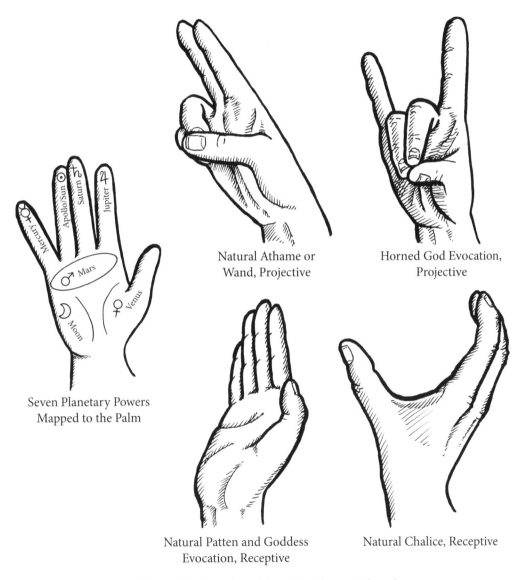

Seven Planetary Powers
Mapped to the Palm

Natural Athame or
Wand, Projective

Horned God Evocation,
Projective

Natural Patten and Goddess
Evocation, Receptive

Natural Chalice, Receptive

**Figure 18: Hand positions for elemental tools
and evocations with planetary sigils**

The Hand as a Natural Tool

As we begin our ritual practices, we'll only need our bodies for magickal work, starting with the building and consecration of our altars. In section three we will journey to each elemental realm to seek out guidance on the perfect tools for you and where to find them. As you receive that information, begin gathering or crafting them. The cleansing processes described in this chapter can take time, so attend to those as we continue along.

In the coming chapters we'll introduce altar preparation, consecration, and ritual techniques for circlecasting. You may begin practicing these techniques with just your body as a fundamental tool to channel and direct divine power. From the art of palmistry, or chiromancy, we learn that each finger and areas of the palm are associated with a classical planet and the deities they represent. See figure 18.

Base of Thumb	Index Finger	Middle Finger	Ring Finger	Pinky Finger	Palm
Venus	Jupiter	Saturn	Sun/Apollo	Mercury	Moon/Luna and Mars

Your hand can channel all four elements, just like all four altar tools. The receptive hand is typically the left, or nondominant hand. The projective hand is typically the right, or dominant hand. This can vary among individuals. The five fingers of your receptive hand are a pentacle of earth, so anything held in your palm will focus the elemental power to physical objects. A natural chalice is formed with the thumb and index finger of the receptive hand held sideways and opened to the moon like a cup. A natural athame or wand is formed by pointing the index and middle finger of your projective hand, with your thumb holding your other fingers to your palm. Similarly, the Goddess is channeled through both upward-cupped palms. The Horned God is channeled by both hands held at head height holding the middle and ring finger down with the thumb and pointing the index and pinky finger like horns.

Journal Reflection

Practice the hand postures from figure 18, mindful of the planetary powers that are connected through the placement of your fingers. Note in your Book of Mirrors how each posture feels for you.

Chapter 9
Sacred Space, Sacred Life

Now that we've laid the foundations of the paradigm, how the elemental forces fit into the cosmic scheme of things, and the tools that channel those forces, let's shift focus into basic ritual techniques needed for our Elemental Witchcraft. It all begins within your fivefold Self and is built outwardly in layers from there. The first outward piece of magick is the creation of one's personal altar at home, laid out with purpose and beauty to suit your needs. We'll begin by adding the consecration elements and exploring the techniques necessary for purifying and consecrating the altar, ourselves, and eventually the circle round.

The Witch's Altar

An altar is symbolic of the divine cosmos it represents. Begin by carving out the sacred space you'll need within your busy modern life. Integrating our spiritual lives into our material lives is part and parcel to a witching life. What we make space for in our homes sets it as a priority, and that priority will mirror up through the other four aspects of ourselves. If you carve out a sacred space in your home, you announce to divinity that spirituality is important to you.

Unlike a formal altar in a public temple, which is shared by a group and more permanently installed, a Witch's *personal altar* can be far less formal or structured. A personal altar becomes an adaptable and mobile workplace that can be flexibly set up and rearranged anywhere in your home or out in nature, wherever you choose to cast circle in that moment, for whatever purpose you need. Altars are just as holy on a kitchen table or a picnic blanket in the woods as they would be on the altar stone of an ancient monolith circle. Spirit is within everything.

Your altar becomes your miniature theater of props and players that is flexible enough to host all manner of productions. The Witch is the director of those plays. Magick is then the cosmic poetry enacted upon that stage, and that becomes an art form. The key component is the creativity that ignites the senses and imagination to be in alignment with inherent divinity. Every choice after that is yours to make; there are no other universal requirements.

An altar can be placed just about anywhere in your home and is typically a functional piece of furniture made of a natural material like wood, stone, or metal, as it is another grand tool of elemental earth. A tabletop, desk, or dresser with drawers, one shelf in a bookcase, or the mantelpiece are all nice possibilities. An easily launderable and sturdy altar cloth is nice for easy cleanup of incense ashes or spilled wax, as is likely to happen on occasion. The color or symbolism of that cloth (sometimes I just use a placemat) can be selected intentionally for the season or purpose of the current working. Black is standard, as the color black absorbs and holds all the energies that are called into it. Every other aesthetic consideration can reflect the style and practice of the individual Witch.

Typically, a Witch's altar will need to be large enough to hold the consecration tools of water, salt, candles, incense, stones, etc. It also holds the symbols that represent deity and the spirits that guide you. Those could be in the form of statuary, candles, or both. As you collect them, your elemental altar tools of athame, chalice, wand, and pentacle paten will also find their home here.

Working Altar Layout

For the magick we'll enact in section three, you'll want to set up an even more specialized type of *working altar*. The only difference being that it includes an easily accessible work surface from a nearby place to sit, like a desk, that has some extra space for writing and crafting your magickal supplies. If possible, choose a place that is out of the way and can be left set up all the time. Ideally, this could include a comfortable chair that allows you to sit upright, with your feet flat on the floor, and your spine more or less perpendicular to the earth. I prefer arms, as this relieves pressure on my shoulders. Or, if seated on a floor cushion, a coffee table could work too

The workspace should be accessible because the workings will include the use of candles, incense, and recording thoughts in your Book of Mirrors. During the rituals you will stand and move about to cast your circles, but also sit comfortably to meditate as you access your astral temple and the Plane of Forces through inner journey work.

The altar is your place of witchy business, so organize it in any way that makes sense to you. For the elemental mysteries explored through the Witch's Jewel of Power, I find it helpful to lay out a working altar with the projective elements associated with the God on the right and the receptive elements associated with the Goddess on the left. As you face the altar, this corresponds to how energy flows through most human bodies. Typically, energy projects through the right side and receives energy on your left side. This division also mirrors two of the pillars within the Hermetic Qabala (Cabala) Tree of Life: the Pillar of Mercy on the right having divine father associations, and the Pillar of Severity on the left having divine mother associations.[185] However, in some folks, especially those who are left-hand dominant, you may find energy flows the opposite direction for you. Experiment and adjust to what feels natural for you.

---

185. Greer, *The New Encyclopedia of the Occult*, "Tree of Life," 491, "Binah," 65, "Chokmah," 100.

Personal Altar: Layout by Gender

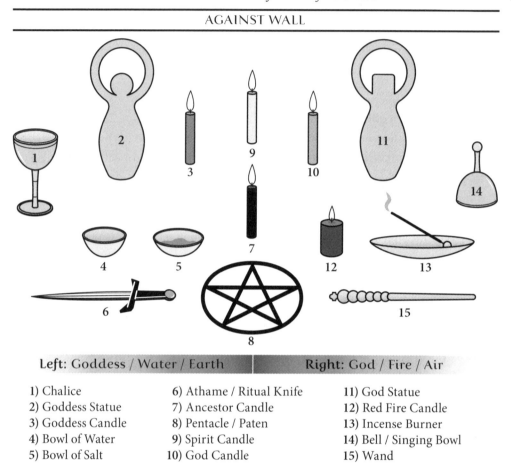

AGAINST WALL

Left: Goddess / Water / Earth   Right: God / Fire / Air

1) Chalice
2) Goddess Statue
3) Goddess Candle
4) Bowl of Water
5) Bowl of Salt

6) Athame / Ritual Knife
7) Ancestor Candle
8) Pentacle / Paten
9) Spirit Candle
10) God Candle

11) God Statue
12) Red Fire Candle
13) Incense Burner
14) Bell / Singing Bowl
15) Wand

Figure 19: Diagram of an altar layout by projective/receptive sides

Consecration Elements: Salt, Water, Candle, Incense

The first things to add to your new working altar will be the consecration elements. Consecration elements are used for clearing all baneful energies, grounding in the body, igniting the spiritual flame, and focusing our attention for magickal work. The standard Wiccan consecration elements include some kind of burning incense from a plant material in a censer or other incense holder, a small bowl of sea salt, a small bowl of purified water, and a candle to burn in a fire-safe holder. The following table provides further details about the gear and materials for elemental consecration.

Consecration Elements		
Bowl of salt	Earth	Salt is a receptive, fixed element used to cleanse and purify. Typically combined with water in ritual to make saltwater for consecrating the circle.
Censer	Air	A censer is an incense burner used during ritual. Some have small legs to keep the hot bottom off of the ground. I use a five-inch diameter iron cauldron filled almost to the top with sand. I can then jab in stick incense, rest cones directly on the sand, or burn charcoal tablets and loose incense on top. Then I just stir in the ash and it self-replenishes and gains a collected power of all the incense burned there previously.
Incense	Air	Incense is chosen depending on its magical properties. Composed of a combination of plants, oils, and resins, they are used for purification and meditation. All-natural products are best. The point isn't the "smell" of the incense; it is the releasing of that plant's energy to aid your work. No plant, no aid. Synthetic incense may be cheap, but it is a waste of your time.
Bowl of water	Water	Water is a receptive, fixed element and serves to cleanse and purify when combined with salt. The water itself should be the purest water you can get: filtered or spring water.
Candles	Fire	Candles are an essential tool for illumination, a representation of fire element, and an offering of combustion to fire elementals. Candles should be snuffed out, never blown out. The traditional lore informs me that this is so that the elementals are not offended by fire being conquered by air. Candles embody all four states of matter and so can be the single player on your altar's stage, if necessary: the wax is solid for earth; the flame is obviously fire, then it melts the wax to liquid for water, and it consumes oxygen in the air. The perfect tool of elemental magick!

Why are these consecration materials necessary for Elemental Witchcraft? As a courtesy to the elemental beings we'll be inviting to our circle and who function at a vibrational rate higher than their earthly substance. They cannot exist in our dimension without the gross form of their element present. If you plan to open the elemental gateways and invite elemental beings to the party, put out the snacks they like. The consecration elements also serve as an offering to entice those beings to help you out. Much like humans must have atmosphere and fish must have water to survive, so must elementals have their element to dwell within your circle.

For the most part providing the necessary sustenance is easy to achieve without many supplies at all. The air we breathe is always there for the sylphs (unless you plan to cast circle in the vacuum of outer space.) There is likely at least a little humidity present for the undines, but at minimum the moisture of your own breath may suffice, though you will find yourself extremely thirsty by the end. The ground you're standing on can support the gnomes, but salamanders are most definitely going to require something to be burning if you want them to actually help you. (Note the speed with which you'll burn out incandescent lightbulbs, otherwise.)

For many other aspects of Witchcraft, I would remind the Witch again and again that we work with symbols and metaphors—that we are writing poetry with our lives. Each tradition and culture chooses their own metaphors through which they engage in the natural magick around them, but those metaphors are merely arrows that point to an ineffable truth. *Not in this case.*

I now understand that my altar candle provides the literal fuel to feed the beings of fire that I've called upon to aid my magick.

Consider the possibility that these elemental beings and their sovereigns are objectively real. They are living spirits with agency, personalities, and a job to do within the grand cosmic schema. They also have physical requirements that are only polite for you to supply when you summon them into your temple. I would also caution you that these beings, while mostly helpful and benevolent, also exhibit both the virtue and the vice of the element from which they are made, and it is unwise to neglect them. It is romantic to think of the spirits of the babbling brook or the mossy knoll. However, they can be just as present in your plumbing and foundation stones. This warning goes doubly so for any being of fire. If they need fire to survive and you have not provided for them a living flame, they may take it upon themselves to provide their own, and you may not like their choice. Don't let the fire candle extinguish during a windy rite. Remember the first rule of Witchcraft is *don't burn the Witch!* How did I come by this notion? The stupid way. The expensive way, wherein plumbers, electricians, and a new stove top were required.

Consecrating Your Altar

If the altar is a stage and all the items are the players, then you are the director of this production. You will need to awaken the spirit within each item, imbue it with your intention by giving them their part in the script, and then weave them all together as your cast. The powers of above, below, and between will be channeled through you and held by them.

These items are both the spiritual anchors of the elemental energies in your magickal space and the conduits to keep everything open, flowing, and fed while there.

More important than *what* is on a Witch's altar is *how* you activate their powers and then utilize them. With a consecration and awakening ritual, the Witch becomes the catalyst that transmutes a table full of arcane tchotchke into a microcosm of empowerment.

Figure 20: Basic banishing pentagram

Basic Banishing Pentacle

For the following altar consecration rituals, you'll use a basic banishing pentagram as a magickal means to clear any spiritual or energetic imbalance or impurity from the physical materials then the altar itself. We use the traditional banishing pattern of elemental earth—because we are clearing "earthy" physical materials. The trick to this magickal gesture is in the order and direction of how you draw the lines and points. This pattern taps into the egregore of power built by occultists since the Hermetic Order of the Golden Dawn, and follows the organization of the points by alchemical density: spirit, fire, air, water, earth.[186]

For now, practice drawing a five-pointed star in this particular pattern: Begin in the lower left point of earth and draw upward toward the top point of spirit. Follow along clockwise from there, drawing down to the lower right point, up and across to left point, across to right point, back down to complete the star at the lower left point of earth, ending where we started. Visualize the pentagram drawn in a black, absorbing pigment or a void of light through which all baneful influences are being sent back to the nonphysical realms from whence they originated.

---

186. Greer, *The New Encyclopedia of the Occult*, 368.

Drawing the banishing pentagram of earth is like throwing an unwanted energetic guest out the door and then putting a specific key in the lock behind them that engages the tumblers in the correct order. Finish by encircling the pentagram in a widdershins spiral, like twisting that key, and throwing the dead bolt lock. A widdershins circle locks the door between realms. I add this extra circling, which now turns this pentagram into a *pentacle*. A banishing pentacle can be drawn to clear all kinds of unwanted energies and for general protection. We'll discuss use of the elemental pentagrams in further detail in chapter 10.

Ritual Postures to Open the Divine Channel:

When physical movements and postures accompany our visualizations and magickal language, they help a Witch to fully engage their bodies in the work at hand. Plus, it keeps our hands busy so our minds can concentrate. Do the same movements and postures every time, and your other senses drop into the magickal frame of mind more easily and effectively each time. In the ritual for altar consecration below, we'll flow through three body postures: pentacle, God/dess branches, God/dess roots, and then stand to flow energy through our hands. Take a moment to practice shifting between these movements until they feel natural. Refer to figure 21 as you practice these ritual body postures to open your body as a creative channel.

Pentacle posture: Stand in power, imagining a pentacle star around you with your head at the top spirit point, chin held high. Open arms wide at shoulder height, hands held palms up, at top left and right points of the pentacle. Feet spread shoulder-width apart, standing at lower left and right points like the image of Leonardo da Vinci's "Vitruvian Man." Imagine your balanced, interwoven fivefold Self at peace.

God/dess branches posture: Shift slightly from pentacle posture, gazing upward toward the sky, hands cupped and raised above your head in a straight-armed "V" before you. Imagine yourself like a tree, hands like leaves absorbing air and sunlight, drawing down "Father Sky." Cross your arms over your chest to pull god energies into your heart chakra. In perfect balance, this posture is typically called "goddess position" and is also used to draw down the moon and evoke the Goddess.

1: Branches Heavens
Receptive

2: Osiris Standing

3: Roots Underworld
Receptive

4: Osiris Kneeling

5: Open Channel,
Above to Below

6: Projective

**Figure 21: Ritual body postures to open the creative channel:
God/dess branches, God/dess roots, and open channel**

God/dess roots posture: Kneel on one knee and place both palms (or fingertips) flat on the ground in front of you. Imaging the roots of your tree reaching deep into the planet, absorbing water and minerals, drawing up "Mother Earth." Cross your arms over your chest to pull goddess energies into your heart chakra. In perfect balance, notice that you are in a posture reminiscent of a seated, four-footed animal mythologically associated with the Animal Lord, or Horned God.

Open channel of creation: Envision the divine forces blending in your heart like the yin-yang energies swirling together, as the Perfect Love of the Two Who Move as One flows through your body. Stand in power again, right hand's natural athame pointed above, left hand's natural athame pointed below. Feel the power coursing through you from head to foot, flowing through your arms (see figure 21). Clap your hands three times, and vigorously rub them together until you feel an electrifying, tingling sensation in your palms. Hold them about six inches apart, and you'll feel the power flowing like a tingling and slight tension. You are now opened and prepared to direct chi as Divine Love energy through your hands. When ready to close the channel, shake your hands loose at the wrist a moment to sever the flow, and then place the palms together, fingers pointing up, in front of the heart. Release and dismiss the connection with gratitude. *Blessèd be.*

❧ Ritual 1: Building a Personal Altar with Consecration ❧

Prepare your altar to your style and comfort level. If you already have altar tools, add them also. However, those tools aren't strictly necessary, and I encourage you not to let that hinder a beginning of your magickal practice. Note that this altar consecration does not go so far as to open the elemental gateways or to invite the guardian elemental beings, but it does prepare the consecration items with which we will anchor their presence in future rituals. This is why there is no need to "release" the elemental energies at the end. For now, we'll practice these techniques and enjoy the benefits of their clearing and grounding power for ourselves.

Needs

A white candle in a firesafe holder to represent the ever-present Spirit of divinity

A red candle to represent elemental fire in a firesafe holder

Matches or a lighter

Any incense you like, in a safe incense holder

A small bowl of water, filtered or distilled is preferable

A small bowl of sea salt

A bell, chime, or singing bowl that may be rung to make a pleasant frequency of sound

Anything that helps you to be mindful of divinity within nature and the four elements: deity images, stones or crystals, shells, living houseplants, feathers, etc.

A reference image of the basic earth banishing pentacle from figure 20

Your Book of Mirrors and a pen

Preparation

Arrange your altar with reverence and intention, as beautifully or simply as you desire. Make sure the space is physically clean and well-organized. Consider performing this ritual consecration with your feet bare and your hair unbound, wearing loose and comfortably fitting clothing that helps you feel magickal, or nude if you prefer.

Praxis

Chime the bell three times and allow the tone to ring naturally until diminished.

Light the white candle. Face the altar and stand in pentacle posture.

Say: *Welcome, Spirit who is ever-present within and without!*

Stand in God/dess branches posture. Remember that you are like a tree whose branches reach up through the atmosphere, touching air and the fires of the sun. Tap into Father Sky and the heavens above.

Draw down that power, crossing your arms over your chest, feeling how that power flows through you reaching all the way through the soles of your feet. Say: *Hail and welcome, Great God!*

Remember that like the tree, your roots also reach deep below into the earth and water to Mother Nature, as earth, moon, and all the Underworld below.

Kneel into God/dess roots posture. Draw up the earth energy to cross arms over your chest again. Say: *Hail and welcome, Great Goddess!*

Feel the flows from above and below meeting and anchoring at your heart chakra—you are an open channel of their Divine Love.

Stand as an open channel as creative power flows through your heart and down through your hands. Clap them three times and rub vigorously together; feel them pulse with power. Say: *Hail and welcome to the Two Who Move as One! Flow through me as perfect Divine Love.*

Hold the incense in your dominant hand, say: *I charge this incense as a being of air.* Visualize yellow light from the atmosphere imbuing the incense, awakening it to its purpose.

Light the incense from the spirit candle. While drawing a banishing pentagram over the altar with the incense, then encircling the altar widdershins, or counterclockwise, say: *Powers of air, blow free any impurity from this sacred space.* Visualize a yellow energy imbuing the altar.

Hold the red candle in your dominant hand.

Say: *I charge this candle as a being of fire.* Visualize red light from the fires of the sun and stars imbuing the candle, awakening it to its purpose.

Light the fire candle from the spirit candle. While drawing a banishing pentagram over the altar with the candle, encircling the space widdershins, counterclockwise, say: *Powers of fire, burn free any impurity from this sacred space.*

Visualize a red energy imbuing the altar.

Hold the bowl of salt in your receptive hand. Visualize green light drawn up from the earth itself to imbue the salt, awakening it to its purpose.

Say: *I charge this salt as a being of earth.* Draw a banishing pentacle in the salt with your finger (or athame, when you have one).

Say: *Powers of earth, ground free any impurity from this sacred space.* Sprinkle three pinches of salt over the altar. Visualize a green energy imbuing the altar.

Hold the bowl of water in your receptive hand. Say: *I charge this water as a being of water and cast out all impurity.* Visualize blue light drawing up from the water table to imbue the water, awakening it to its purpose. With fingers (or scooping with the athame when you have one), add three pinches of consecrated salt to the water. Stir by drawing the banishing pentacle in the water with your finger or athame.

Say: *Powers of water, wash free any impurity from this sacred space.* Sprinkle the water over the altar three times. Visualize a blue energy imbuing the altar.

Now that the elements have been awakened and the altar cleansed, we begin charging. With your hands or wand, stir the air around the altar in a clockwise, deosil, spiral five turns, saying: *As above, so below; as below, so above; macrocosm to microcosm. Spirit! Indwell within this altar in sacred harmony between all worlds. Blessèd be.*

Visualize a white light containing all colors now awakening the altar to its sacred purpose.

Chime the bell three times and mindfully listen as the tone naturally diminishes.

Your altar is now consecrated and would be ready for further magickal spellwork or ritual.

Purify, or hallow, your own fivefold body with these elements:

- Waft the incense in your auric field; as you smell the scent, see a yellow light clearing and balancing your mind.
- Anoint your heart with a drop of water and see a blue light healing and balancing your emotions.
- Feel the warmth from the fire candle and see a red light stoking your fires to clear and balance your motivations.
- Taste a grain of salt and see a green light nourishing and balancing your physical health.

Take twenty minutes or so for your daily meditation, repeating any of the affirmations or charms from previous exercises that you like.

Journal Reflection

Reflect about this experience in your Book of Mirrors.

When finished, thank Spirit for their continuous flow of Divine Love throughout your life, saying: *Hail and farewell, Great Spirit!* as you extinguish the candles. End by saying: *Blessèd be!*

Chapter 10
The Witching Temple

The altar functions like the heart of a Witch's temple. Now that you've awakened and consecrated your altar, those energies can be expanded outward to form a larger temple—large enough to share with other Witches, to dance around enacting ritual theater and creating magick. The witching temple is an energetic sphere constructed at the crossroads of creation. It is constructed from the same energy (chi, ki, prana, the Force) that is running through our chakras and creating our bodies. I prefer to think of this energy as the Divine Love of the God/dess. When Witches cast our circle, we create a miniature, symbolic cosmos. Then we invite the powers-that-be to partner with us in our cosmic nursery. Whatever we create symbolically here in *the below* will be given an energetic template in *the above*. Then the first half of the Hermetic axiom kicks back in: "As above, so below." To keep the balance, the cosmic nursery manifests a physical reality to match, because that is what the astral mirror is here to do. This is how Wiccan ritual magick works. In this chapter, we'll explore the ritual techniques, postures, and language you may use to create a witching temple for yourself.

The Circle Cross

The witching temple is symbolized as *the circle cross*, which represents the intersection of the five elements and the three worlds, forming a liminal place betwixt and between where gods and mortals can meet. When Witches cast a circle, we also activate the same crossroads of divinity within our fivefold Self. The circle cross is the astrological symbol for the planet Earth and the sigil associated with the Wiccan first degree initiation.[187] In our mapping analogy, think of the circle cross as the "X" that marks the spot of where to begin and end your witching journey on your cosmic map. No matter the need or the question you need answering, get thee to the crossroads.

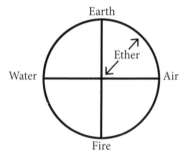

Figure 22: Circle cross and planetary earth sigil

In some traditions, you literally meet where three roads cross to work your magick. This goes back to Greek and Roman devotion of Diana Trivia (Diana of the Three Ways) and the triple goddess Hecate, both goddesses of the moon and Witchcraft.[188] When Witches cast a circle, we carve out that sacred place, then we open the gates to the four elemental realms and evoke divinity from the center. This connects the Upperworld and Underworld to join us on consecrated ground here in the Middleworld.

---

187. Vivianne Crowley, *Wicca*, 119–120.

188. Doreen Valiente, *An ABC of Witchcraft Past and Present* (Custer, WA: Phoenix Publishing Inc., 1973), 73.

Ritual Techniques for Building the Witching Temple

Building a witching temple is called *casting the circle*. We can cast the circle anywhere at any time, and then we deconstruct it when the rite is done. Here we celebrate the seasonal festivals of sabbats and esbats of the moon, perform magickal and devotional work, raise and direct energy for healing or rebalancing, and conduct rites of passage. A ritual is any predetermined set of actions meant to accomplish a goal. Within Wiccan-esque Witchcraft, rituals are a devotion that enacts the divine dance between goddess and god at the microcosm reflection within ourselves. Ritual is a devotional expression of liberation from the illusion of separateness from God/dess.[189]

Circle Basics

Anyone, no matter their magickal experience, can cast a circle. The only Witches who can't are the ones who never gave it a shot that first time. Yes, your skills grow stronger with time, but you have to start somewhere, and now is your moment.

In Wiccan ritual, the "circle" can be any shape that fits the working and the space. It does not have to be perfectly round. The circle can be any size necessary, but traditional Wiccan circles were nine feet in diameter.[190] Nine is a magickal number that represents spiritual attainment. It is the sum of three multiplied by itself, and three is sacred to the triple goddess. Unless it is just you and maybe a few others, that is going to be tight. I like to move! For group circles consider eighteen feet in diameter, so a nine-foot radius.[191] As a visual reminder, the circumferance of the circle can be marked on the ground by scratching it into the dirt outside, or drawing it with chalk powder, flour, cornmeal, salt, etc. Alternately, after casting a small circle energetically, you can mentally "push" the edges to the extents of the room, building, or property so you can wander about as the inspiration moves you, without worry about where the edge is this time.

After the sphere of your temple is cast, it can be attuned to any purpose you designate. It will respond to thoughts and words, and can be used as a *filter*, *magnifying lens*, or an *amplifier*. It is a collector of energy but not necessarily a container. The circle is spiritually permeable so that energies and spirits we invite may enter and exit freely. The circle

---

189. Paraphrase of a teaching given at a workshop with friend and Wiccan priest Spanish Moss.

190. Raymond Buckland, *The Witch Book: The Encyclopedia of Witchcraft, Wicca, and Neo-paganism* (Detroit: Visible Ink Press, 2002), 91.

191. Buckland, *The Witch Book*, 91.

focuses your will like a lens, directing it into a laser beam of intention. By itself, the circle will not necessarily keep out unwanted influences or spirits, making one neither safer nor more vulnerable from spiritual entities. The circle does heighten your spiritual sensitivity and helps one to establish boundaries and rules of engagement with those spiritual entities. You set the rules in your temple, like programming your home security system.

Leaving and Reentering Circle

Despite some superstitious lore, the perimeter of a circle may be crossed if necessary. Simply be mindful of your passage through, much like gently pressing a finger into a soap bubble. It will re-form around you. Approach the boundary and remember that you are an energetic being—your auric bubble merges with the circle's bubble. You are now of one energy. Move through, and now you are separate energies again, passing through to the other side and resealing behind you. However, I would caution you to reconsider any old lore that suggests "cutting a door" with your athame. The iron of an athame is there to banish enchantment and carve between realms. In my experience, jabbing pointy iron unnecessarily into an energy bubble defeats its purpose.

You Are the Magick

Try not to get sidetracked by the minutiae of this ceremonial magick stuff; that will only distract you from your genuine work. Yes, these techniques are important, and with them you can boost your effectiveness. As long as your intentions are pure and you give it your best shot, the cosmos will flow with you. Just remember that *you are the magick*. The whole cosmos is magick. Everything in your life is a spiritual event. Moreover, your aura is a built-in, personal temple. So, every mundane chore you did today from making coffee to moving your bowels was a spiritual event done in your temple. The rest of this technique is a matter of just pushing that boundary out a little further and heightening awareness that your bubble is interconnected with the larger divine bubble for a while.

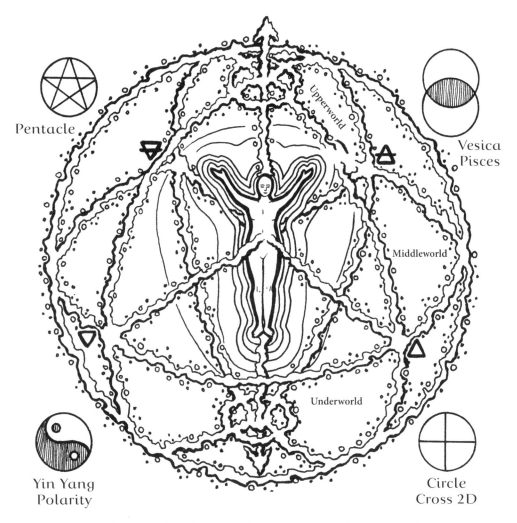

Pentacle

Vesica
Pisces

Middleworld

Upperworld

Underworld

Yin Yang
Polarity

Circle
Cross 2D

Figure 23: Witches' temple as a sphere at the crossroads

Figure 23 illustrates how I picture a Witches' temple, with gateways and girders as
a sphere. Note that it creates a 3D construct embodying the mysteries of the pentacle,
awakening all five essences through our chakra and aura connections. The "circle" is
actually a sphere, which models the vesica pisces and the three-world model. The yin-
yang of divine polarity is envoked through the center, as anchored by the axis mundi
within ourselves, and the Middleworld. A cross section through the middle of the sphere
is the land itself and forms the circle cross symbol of planet Earth that also intersects at

our own centers. The x, y, z axis at your own center is the midpoint of the cast circle. I feel it around my navel: where the physical umbilical cord once connected me to my mother, and the spiritual energy cord still connects me to the Mother Goddess. This intersection is your internal crossroads.

The occult mystery of the circle is this: in order to expand into the greatness of cosmic-level divinity, you'll first have to take the deep dive to open these connections within your-self. In our journeys throughout section three, we'll establish relationships with the ele-mental essences and the beings who dwell there. But first, let's practice the ritual techniques needed to get started.

❧ Ritual 2: Building a Witch's Temple ❧

The ritual of building your temple gets easier and more effective the more you do it. The ritual exercise below will walk you through the steps, both outward movements and inner visualizations. At first it might just seem like you're going through the motions. However, there is a deep egregore of power to be tapped here by enacting this praxis and saying these words as so many Witches have done before. Just lean into this with your whole heart. Be sincere and focused as you begin. Trust your intuition.

Remember that anyone can rattle off the "magick words." That is not where elemental power is found. The power is tapped *through your earth*; your very bones should rattle in answer to your call. The words suggested below work to tune your own consciousness into the appropriate frequency, which opens the gateway. Which words you say aren't nearly as important as how they affect your state of mind.

Needs

A white candle in a firesafe holder to represent the ever-present Spirit of divinity

A red candle to represent elemental fire in a firesafe holder

Matches or a lighter

Any incense you like in a safe incense holder

A small bowl of water, filtered or distilled is preferable

A small bowl of sea salt

A bell, chime, or singing bowl that may be rung

A reference image from figure 24 of the four elemental invoking and banishing pentagrams

Preparation

Before casting the temple sphere, begin with a physical cleaning and organizing of the space and your altar. Bathe and dress in fresh, comfortable clothing, preferably barefoot with hair unbound, or nude as you prefer.

Praxis

Begin the ritual of temple creation by lighting your spirit candle and tapping into the power of nature above and below with the physical postures of the *pentacle, god/dess branches and roots.*

Awakening the Altar

Direct the power of nature through your hands to awaken and consecrate your altar, as previously taught in ritual 1. That rite includes purifying and grounding yourself through the elements.

This spiritual cleansing is called *hallowing.* Remember that *like attracts like.* If you enter the circle in Perfect Love and Trustworthiness, then that is what you will attract to your circle. The same is true of those with baneful intent. Which is why we do a thorough grounding and clearing prior to any magick. Don't go into ritual angry or you might not accomplish what your mouth said; rather, you'll get what your anger was screaming deep down in your subconscious.

Hallowing the Temple

Once you are hallowed, you can hallow the ground upon which your temple will be constructed. We hallow *before* we cast the temple so that we aren't inadvertently trapping unwanted energies within our sphere. The hallowing of the circle's perimeter begins the process of laying down energies at the perimeter of the circle, which will later be raised and enclosed during the casting.[192] We begin in the east like the rising of the morning sun and proceed deosil around in all building movements.

- **Air hallowing:** Pick up your censer with smoking incense and carry it to the eastern quarter. Presenting the incense aloft to the east, saying with power in

---

192. This hallowing technique is adapted from a public rite created by Doug Helvie and Anna Meadows Helvie and enacted by the Eternal Harvest Tradition of Wicca of New Bern, NC.

the voice: *I consecrate this circle by the powers of air!* Walk the perimeter deosil, wafting the burning incense while repeating the chant. As an energy builder, slightly increase your volume as you chant. When you arrive back in the east, present the incense to the quarter again and say: *As your Witch of air, I greet you with air and ask that you blow free any baneful energies from this circle tonight. So mote it be!* Return to your altar.

- **Fire hallowing:** Pick up your red fire candle and repeat the same process at the southern quarter. Present it to the quarter first, saying: *I consecrate this circle by the powers of fire!* Then walk the perimeter deosil with the burning candle while repeating the chant. Present to the southern quarter again and say: *As your Witch of fire, I greet you with fire and ask that you burn free any baneful energies from this circle tonight. So mote it be!* Return to your altar.

- **Water hallowing:** Pick up your bowl of salted water and repeat the same process at the western quarter. Present it to the quarter first, saying: *I consecrate this circle by the powers of water!* Then walk deosil, sprinkling the water with your fingers while repeating the chant. Present again and say: *As your Witch of water, I greet you with water and ask that you wash free any baneful energies from this circle tonight. So mote it be!* Return to your altar.

- **Earth hallowing:** Pick up your bowl of consecrated salt and repeat the same process at the northern quarter. Present it to the quarter first, saying: *I consecrate this circle by the powers of earth!* Then walk deosil, sprinkling the salt with your fingers while repeating the chant. Present again and say: *As your Witch of earth, I greet you with earth and ask that you ground free any baneful energies from this circle tonight. So mote it be!* Return to your altar.

Casting a Circle

To cast a circle, you must first raise energy, then direct that energy into a spherical shape. The hallowing started building that energy. Continue to visualize nature's power of Divine Love flowing into your roots, branches, and breath, and then direct that energy with your heart, thoughts, and physical actions. This step is important, lest you accidentally try to build your whole temple with just your personal chi.

Raising a Cone of Power: Awen Chant

My favorite power-raising technique is to chant *Awen*, the Welsh word for divine inspiration. *Awen* was the gift of the goddess Cerridwen, given through three drops of the greal potion from her cauldron. To honor those three drops and the mysteries of wisdom, power, and love they convey, it is magickally pronounced in three syllables: *Aa-oo-wen*.[193] We also make three laps, to "Cast the Circle thrice about to keep all evil spirits out." as advised in the "Rede of the Wiccae."[194]

Move to the eastern quarter of your circle's perimeter. Hold your receptive hand over the earth to draw in power. As you chant the Awen, walk slowly deosil around, pointing the "natural athame" of your projective hand's index and middle finger to draw a spiral cone of white light up from the perimeter (refer to figure 18). As you chant the Awen, start low and slow, singing the energies in; draw from above and below and direct them with the notes: *Aa-oo-wen-aa-oo-wen-aa-oo-wen*… Slowly, with each repeat of the word as long as a breath, raise a half note up the scale. Take a breath when needed. Meanwhile, with a dramatic posture, spiral the circle thrice about, raising your hands from pointing at the ground level, drawing a dome upward to the center point of the heavens above. Increase in pitch and speed, and by the third lap, stamp your feet—make a wild ruckus! Summon and mold this cone of inspired power, drawing it upward on your fingertips. When you feel the energy is peaking (believe me, you'll know; it's a lot like an orgasm), throw both your hands all the way heavenward, shouting, *Awen!*

This cone is just the raw power, which now needs to be shaped into a sphere. With downward sweeping motions with the arms, pulling the heavens down to earth, saying *I call down the heavens to these crossroads*. Then continue the sweeping gesture downward, scooping from circle's edge downward, enclosing the bottom of the sphere, saying, *I call up the Underworld to these crossroads!* Repeat the sweeping gesture back all the way up to the top, then resume the pentacle posture.

Say: *I stand at these crossroads in Perfect Love and Perfect Trust in a temple of my own making. In this time out of time, in this place between the worlds, this temple serves as a magnifier of my will, an amplifier of my power, and a protection from all bane. May all magick wrought here serve the highest good of all involved, harming none. Naught but love will enter in, and naught but love will emerge. So mote it be!*

---

193. Christopher Penczak, *The Three Rays of Witchcraft: Power, Love and Wisdom in the Garden of the Gods* (Salem, NH: Copper Cauldron Publishing, 2010), 21.

194. Mathiesen and Theitic, *The Rede of the Wiccae*, 52–53.

Figure 24: Invoking and banishing pentagram
diagrams for all four elements

Opening Elemental Gateways to the Four Quarters

Now that we are safely within this containment field, we cut portals to let in the four elemental essences, giving our spherical temple a support structure. Some refer to this action as "calling the quarters." I see this ritual action more as *opening the gateways.* Because you can call all night long, but unless you open the door, they aren't getting in. We open the gate by drawing an invoking pentagram in that particular elemental pattern, which cuts a portal between the dimensions. That pattern begins at the point *before* the specific element and draws *toward* it on the first stroke, then follows on around deosil to close the star. We then encircle the star with a deosil spiral to "open the lock." See figure 24 for those patterns.

Opening the elemental gateways feels like turning on a faucet of pure energy to flow into and fill the temple. When done effectively, there is a tangible shift to the energy of the circle once the elements are flowing and mixing. They need the circle to contain them. For safety, only open the elemental gateways into a fully erected energetic temple.

Once you've magickally opened a gateway to the elemental realms and called the elemental beings to be present, *never forget* to send them back and close that door when you are finished. Release and seal that gateway with a banishing pentagram of that element, encircled widdershins to lock the gate. This action is like turning off the faucet or flipping the breaker to stop the flow of electricity completely.

When we open the elemental gateways, we also awaken all aspects of ourselves that are nurtured by those realms: our physical, mental, emotional, and spiritual bodies. We are twisting each of our "locks" into the open position so that the energy of nature flows freely through an open channel, above to below.

Symbols and the Psyche

The language of a "quarter call" is poetically descriptive for valid psychological reasons. When we make contact with elemental beings and visualize the forces we mean to draw in, that symbol is activated within our psyche. Jungian psychologist Vivianne Crowley called this magickal technique "an act of passive clairvoyance."[195] Later, when we deliberately visualize that symbol, we are brought into contact with the force behind that symbol; we focus our minds on their power as a means to activate the psyche in reverse.[196] As a form of active magic, Witches evoke the elemental essences by name out loud, painting verbal pictures that describe them symbolically. It doesn't much matter what that symbol is so long as it activates your psyche and gets the powers flowing. This process works in both directions. To some degree, the psyche will provide its own notion of what the elementals look like and then fulfill that prophecy. For this reason, if sylphs show up in your imagination as the twee, sparkling "fairies" you once saw in a children's cartoon, so be it. Just release your attachment to the notion that they look like that to anyone else. No matter what image your subconscious conjures, it is correct for you at that time.

You may also stand in particular elemental postures while opening and closing the gateways. These postures are an adapted technique described in Scott Cunningham's Ritual of Gestures in his book *Wicca: A Guide for the Solitary Practitioner.*[197] Refer to figure 25 for images of those elemental postures, and they'll be described below. The

---

195. Vivianne Crowley, *Wicca*, 47.

196. Vivianne Crowley, *Wicca,* 47.

197. Scott Cunningham, *Wicca: A Guide for the Solitary Practitioner* (St. Paul, MN: Llewellyn Publications, 1989), 44.

receptive hand takes a posture ready to receive the elemental essence through the gate. The projective hand takes the "natural athame" posture to cut the portal using the invoking pentagrams.

Air   Fire

Water   Earth

Figure 25: Elemental postures

East/Air:

- Face east. Stand in a posture of air: Feet at shoulder width apart, stand tall, chin up, shoulders back. Receptive hand at chest height with palm facing away, fingers splayed like branches of a tree. Visualize yellow and sense movement like the wind. Projective hand in natural athame raised in salute to the quarter.

- Remember your connections in the three realms, like the axis mundi tree. Shift your conscious connection to your branches in the wind. Vibrate as that wind. Breathe down that power as yellow light. See the light beaming from your fingers or athame. Your receptive hand is prepared to receive the inflowing energy.

- As you speak the words of the call, do so with volume and authority from the diaphragm. Allow the voice to vibrate through the atmosphere and rattle the timbers. Summoning the wild essence of nature and the elementals is instinctual. They respond to like vibrations. Speak from the marrow of your bones!

- Call: *Powers of the east! Essence of air! I summon you to this sacred place! Sylphs! Sovereign Paralda of the windy reaches! Be with me now and lend your powers of wisdom, imagination, and communication. Open my mind! Awaken your power of knowing and wonderment within me. Come wings of flight and mountain height; come golden dawning, breezes light and laughter lifting to focus and inspire this magick.*

- Draw the invoking pentagram of air. See the star glowing with yellow light in the air of the eastern quarter. Encircle the pentagram deosil (clockwise), unlocking.

- Draw the power in with your natural athame, like pulling a yellow streamer of light, to kiss your fingers. The portal opens, the circle is flooded with elemental energy, and the yellow girder encircles your sphere.

- Place your dominant hand on your heart and bow to the east. Say: *I welcome you with gratitude. Hail and welcome!*

South/Fire

- Face south. Stand in a posture of fire evocation: Receptive hand at hip height balled into a tight fist, thumb outside your fingers, like holding a hammer at a forge. Visualize red and a raging fire. Projective hand with natural athame raised in salute.

- Shift your conscious connection to where your leaves absorb the blazing fires of the sun. Vibrate as that fire. Breathe down that power as red light. See the light beaming from your fingers.

- Call: *Powers of the south! Essence of fire! I summon you to this sacred place! Salamanders! Sovereign Djin of the burning inferno! Be with me now and lend your powers of courage and transformation. Awaken your powers of will and surrender within me. Come glowing ember and fiery sun; come heat of summer noon and blazing passion to temper and empower this magick.*

- Draw the invoking pentagram of fire. See the star glowing with red light in the air of the southern quarter. Encircle the pentagram deosil, unlocking.

- Draw the energy inward. Kiss your fingers. The portal opens; the circle is flooded with elemental energy, and the red girder encircles your sphere.

- Hand over heart, bowing. Say: *I welcome you with gratitude. Hail and welcome!*

West/Water

- Face west. Stand in water posture: Receptive hand at head height, hand sideways with thumb and index fingers forming a crescent moon, like a cup opening upward. Visualize blue and fluidity of the ocean waves. Projective hand with natural athame raised in salute.

- Shift your conscious connection to your roots dipping into the water table. Vibrate as that still water. Breathe up that power as blue light. See the light beaming from your natural athame.

- Call: *Powers of the west! Essence of water! I summon you to this sacred place! Undines! Sovereign Nicksa of the ocean depths! Be with me now and lend your powers of intuition and emotion. Open my heart! Awaken your power of daring and acceptance within me. Come crashing wave and foggy dusk; come glistening dew and river rapids to buoy and carve the way for this magick.*

- Draw the invoking pentagram of water. See the star glowing with blue light in the air of the western quarter. Encircle the pentagram deosil, unlocking.

- Draw the power inward. Kiss the fingers, drawing in the essence of water. The portal opens, the circle is flooded with elemental energy, and the blue girder encircles your sphere.

- Hand over heart, bowing. Say: *Water, I welcome you with gratitude. Hail and welcome!*

North/Earth

- Face the north. Stand in earth posture, with receptive hand open, flat like the horizon at hip-height before you. Projective hand raised as natural athame in salute.

- Shift to consciousness of your roots deep in the earth; draw power from the bedrock. Inhale as green light. Exhale and see the light beaming through your natural athame.

- Call: *Powers of the north! Essence of earth! I summon you to this sacred place! Gnomes, Sovereign Ghob of the realm of earth! Be with me now and lend your powers of manifestation, stability, and sovereignty. Strengthen my body for the work at hand! Awaken your lessons of silence and resonance within me. Come dark cave and moss-covered stones; come growing green from rich, fertile soil; come root and seed and arching canopy to nourish and manifest this magick.*

- Draw the invoking pentagram of earth. See the star glowing with green light in the air of the northern quarter. Encircle the pentagram deosil, unlocking.

- Draw in the power; kiss the fingers. The circle is flooded with that elemental energy. A green girder now encircles your temple in the north.

- Hand over heart, bowing. Say: *I welcome you with gratitude. Hail and welcome!*

Center: Evocation

Now we need the central divine support columns of our temple. We evoke our deities, spiritual guides, and ancestors of land, blood, and spirit to join us on this consecrated ground. That action opens a portal at the bottom and top of the sphere, connecting our axis mundi tree to touch both Upperworld and Underworld. An *evocation* is an invitation of a spiritual entity to join you. At this stage, we'll use a simple evocation. Stand in the posture of God/dess branches from figure 21.

Call: *Great Mother Goddess! Great Father God! I call upon your Divine Love as the Two Who Move as One! I honor your presence in this sacred place. Join me in these rites. Hail and welcome.*

Welcoming the Ancestors of Land, Blood, and Spirit

We welcome the ancestors of land, which are spiritual entities native to your location. There are also the collective spirits of place known as *genius loci* in Latin.[198] Ancestors of the blood are your own blood relatives who continue to watch over and guide you. Ancestors of spirit are any other spiritual entities who protect you: angels or ascended masters, for example.[199]

Call: *Ancestors of the land!* Stamp your foot on the ground in a double heartbeat pattern three times. Example: stamp, stamp (pause) stamp, stamp (pause) stamp, stamp (pause).

Call: *Ancestors of the blood!* With dominant fist, beat your chest in a double heartbeat pattern three times.

Call: *Ancestors of spirit!* Clap your hands in the air above your head in a double heartbeat pattern three times.

Call: *All beings of good will who guard, guide, and inspire my spiritual journey, be welcomed in this sacred space. Aid my magick for the highest good of all involved, harming none. Hail and welcome! The temple is made!*

Ritual Body

After the temple is constructed, the statement of intention is made. Then the body of the ritual or magickal working is enacted, including inner work like meditations, journey work, and prayerful calls for aid to fulfill goals, empower, protect, balance, and heal. Outer sympathetic magick will actualize those energies by creatively engaging with symbols, plants, stones, and animals through ritualized actions and craftings. Power is then raised and directed to manifest your intention through all kinds of creative and ecstatic ways: breathwork, dancing, chanting, sex, drumming, etc.

Simple Feast

When all the magickal work is complete, typically a "Simple Feast" of cakes and ale, or wine, concludes the ritual and helps get the Witch grounded back into their physical body. This small snack serves both a symbolic and practical purpose. When magickal

---

198. "Genius," Encyclopedia Britannica, updated January 16, 2012, https://www.britannica.com/topic /genius-Roman-religion.

199. This Ancestor calling technique is adapted from a public rite I first saw enacted by Doug Helvie and Anna Meadows Helvie of The Eternal Harvest tradition of Wicca in New Bern, NC.

work is done properly, it will burn calories and require significant hydration for the vessel of your flesh to channel that much divine energy. Magick can leave you very hungry and thirsty! Most importantly, during the Simple Feast we share in pleasurable physical sensations, and so I feel strongly that whatever you feast upon should be delicious, spiritually intoxicating, and emotionally satisfying. During group rites, I'm known to quip that chocolate chip cookies are how the God/dess says "I love you." However, this rite holds very serious magickal symbolism. As preparation for enacting that rite during the journey to Spirit, we'll explore the deeper mysteries of this ceremonial blessing magick in chapter 16.

Deconstructing the Temple

The temple is released in the opposite order than it was created, and movements switch to widdershins (counterclockwise), spirals of dissolution.

Releasing the Center

- Call: *Ancestors of Spirit!* Clap your hand in the air above your head in a double heartbeat pattern three times.

- Call: *Ancestors of the Blood!* Beat your chest in a double heartbeat pattern three times.

- Call: *Ancestors of the Land!* Stamp your foot on the ground in a double heartbeat pattern three times.

- Say: *Thank you for your guidance and protection throughout this rite and ever onward along my spiritual journey. I release you now. Stay if you will, go if you must. Depart in peace. Hail and farewell.*

- Face the altar and stand in God/dess branches pose.

- Call: *Great Mother Goddess! Great Father God! The Two Who Move as One! Thank you for your loving presence in this sacred place and your continued guidance along the path ahead. Stay if you will; go if you must. Depart in peace. Hail and farewell!*

Closing the Elemental Gateways

In closing the elemental gateways to the four cardinal directions, we begin with the last quarter opened (in this example, the north) and then close them in widdershins, counterclockwise, order.

North/Earth

- Face the north in the posture of earth, natural athame raised in salute.
- Call: *Powers of north! Essence of earth! Gnomes and Sovereign Ghob! I am grateful for your lessons of silence and resonance. Continue to strengthen my body and Great Work along the path of sovereignty. For now, I release you to your fair and earthy realms. Hail and farewell!*
- See the green girder and all powers receding back through the gateway of your circle. Draw the banishing earth pentagram with your athame or fingers like a key in the lock. As you encircle the star widdershins see the portal closing and locking.
- Once more kiss your athame, but this time follow through like a fencer with a thrusting gesture toward the quarter with fierce resolve, directing any remaining energy outward to their realm. Bow.

West/Water

- Face the west in the posture of water, natural athame raised in salute.
- Call: *Powers of west! Essence of water! Undine and Nicksa! I am grateful for your lessons of daring and acceptance. Continue to nuture my heart and Great Work along the path of love. I release you now to your fair and fluid realms. Hail and farewell!*
- See the blue girder and all powers receding back through the gateway. Draw the banishing pentagram. As you encircle the star widdershins, see the portal locking.
- Kiss your athame; follow through with a thrusting gesture toward the quarter, directing any remaining energy outward to their realm. Bow.

South/Fire

- Facing the south in the posture of fire, natural athame raised in salute.

- Call: *Powers of the south! Essence of fire! Salamanders and Djin! I am grateful for your lessons of will and surrender. Continue to empower my will and Great Work along the path of power. I release you now to your fair and fiery realms! Hail and farewell!*

- See the red girder and all powers receding back through the gateway. Draw the banishing pentagram of fire. Encircle the star widdershins; see the portal locking.

- Kiss your athame; follow through with a thrusting gesture toward the quarter, directing any remaining energy outward to their realm. Bow.

East/Air

- Face the east in the posture of air, natural athame raised in salute.

- Call: *Powers of the east! Essence of air! Sylph and Sovereign Paralda! I am grateful for your lessons of knowing and wonderment. Continue to inspire my thoughts and Great Work along the path of truth. I release you now to your fair and breezy realms. Hail and farewell!*

- See the yellow girder receding back through the portal.

- Draw the banishing pentagram of air with your natural athame. As you encircle the star widdershins, see the portal closing and locking.

- Kiss your athame; follow through with a thrusting gesture toward the quarter, directing any remaining energy outward to their realm. Bow.

Releasing the Sphere: Jump Shot

To release the sphere, move to the north with your natural athame first pointed to the top of the sphere. Walk a widdershins lap around the circle, spiraling the sphere inward, smaller and smaller, as you move back to the central altar. Visualize the remaining energy like a ball of light between your hands, glowing brightly and held over your altar.

Say: *I charge this sphere of Divine Love to be a guiding beacon of light upon the path that leads from this sacred place. Light my way home to these crossroads again.*

Throw the sphere upward toward the heavens like a basketball jump shot, and clap your hands three times to break the temple completely.

Say: *May the circle be open but never broken. Merry meet, and merry part, and merry meet again! Blessèd be!*

As you clean up, extinguish all the candles by snuffing. Carry the consecrated water dish and any food offerings made during ritual outside to the edge of a natural place. This can be the boundary of your property or a hedge at the edge of the parking lot. Pour out the water, and leave the food offerings on the ground, but take care not to leave behind any garbage or foods that would be toxic to animals, like chocolate. Turn and walk away without looking back or trying to discover which aspect of divinity showed up to enjoy your offering.

❧ Journal Reflection: Temple Creation ❧

In your next Book of Mirrors journal entry, reflect on your experiences with temple creation. How do you feel when engaging in the postures and gestures for each elemental energy? Did you experience any shift of perception as you spoke the calls or while opening or closing the portals? Do these techniques feel effective for you? Experiment with adaptations and follow your intuition as you continue to practice these temple building techniques. Throughout the exercises in section three you will have many opportunities to customize your techniques so that they feel most natural to you.

Chapter 11
Magickal Preparations

Alrighty then! Now that we know the *why* of Elemental Witchcraft, *where* it comes from, and *what* we need to do, let's talk about *how* to put this besom into high gear and go for a ride… a ride of discovering *who* we are. In this chapter we'll shift into the magickal preparations needed for the spiritual workings of section three. Remember, Witchcraft is an ortho*praxy*. What matters is what you do with these mysteries so that you can live an enjoyable and effective life. It is a lifelong process, and the Pentacle Path never ends. I've been working the system presented in section three for nigh on a decade. Each spiral hones a Witch's understanding of these mysteries more sharply with each repetition.

Magick requires nuanced timing, and so our first task is to grab a calendar and plan out the Great Work through the next turning of the Wheel of the Year. We'll also begin collecting specific materials for our rituals. The material aids we'll make throughout our Elemental Witchcraft include loaded and charged candles, incense blends, anointing oils, lotions, potions, and more. These physical keys help unlock the doors between worlds and facilitate partnerships with the spirits of plant, stone, and bone. In this chapter we'll cover some basics of crafting formulary and technique, then prepare for the dedication rite you'll perform, kicking off your Great Work of Elemental Witchcraft at the sabbat of Samhain. Then section three begins with the elemental lessons of earth.

Planning Your Great Work of Elemental Witchcraft

The following course of magickal study is integrated into the seasonal tides of power Witches call the *Wheel of the Year*. Referring back to the integrated wheel graphic in figure 5, you'll find that the elemental lessons of the outer ring unfold in a logical progression, aligned by the sabbats. They correspond to the inner ring of seasonal "petals." The elemental workings and seasonal tides then blossom together, revealing a new layer of truth with each petal. This is why it is important to experience them in order and by sabbat.

☀ Exercise 1: Planning Your Year of Study ☀

Below is a table which can help you plan your elemental magick studies by astrological timing, showing Sabbat cycle and the Jewel of Power mystery we'll explore during that time.

Needs

A calendar for the years you'll engage in this magick that includes astrological information. One such resource is the *Witches' Datebook* published by Llewellyn. There are many websites and smartphone apps that offer the same information.

Praxis

Find the specific dates of the astrological sabbats for you in the coming year and fill in the table. These will be the most auspicious times to celebrate each sabbat during that Wheel of the Year. These dates establish the time frames for the waxing and waning solar tides throughout the year. Note on the table below the waning solar tides are gray and the waxing solar tides are white.

For the time frames below, note that the time period is named for the sabbat that will conclude the cycle. For example, the Yule cycle *begins* immediately following your Samhain celebrations at 15° Scorpio and ends with your celebration of Yule at 0° Capricorn, during which we'll focus on the earthy lessons of silence. During that 6.5 weeks between sabbats, you'll do the readings, meditations, and craftings for the projective earth lessons, then begin the Great Work cycle anew after the celebration of Yule. Then we turn into the Imbolctide and shift focus to the receptive lessons of resonance and the rituals of magick along the path of sovereignty.

Determine the date you'll complete your dedication rite. This rite is best held at the full moon closest to Samhain. Depending on the year, this moon could fall slightly before or after Samhain. Also, depending on your hemisphere, the sun will either be in Scorpio (Northern) or Taurus (Southern), with the full moon in the opposite sign. Example: Witches in the Northern Hemisphere, figure out the date that the sun is in Scorpio, and the exact day that the Full moon peaks, it will be in Taurus. (Vice versa for Southern Hemisphere.)

Fill in the dates for the rest of the full moons during this Wheel of the Year. Record them by which solar tide (and elemental lesson) they'll fall within. Note that there are twelve to thirteen moons each Wheel of the Year, but I've provided space for up to two moons per tide. Usually there is only one full moon per zodiac period; however, every third *wheel* there will fall a second full moon within a zodiac sign, which is a "blue moon" of special power.

6.5 Week Solar tide leading to Sabbat	Element and Polarity	Mystery Teaching	Astrological Beginning Date	Calendar Beginning Date	Astrological Ending Date	Calendar Ending Date
Date of Dedication Rite	Full Moon closest to Samhain (Scorpio/Taurus):					
Yuletide (Waning)	Earth Projective	To Be Silent	15° Scorpio		0° Capricorn	
Dates of Full Moons						

6.5 Week Solar tide leading to Sabbat	Element and Polarity	Mystery Teaching	Astrological Beginning Date	Calendar Beginning Date	Astrological Ending Date	Calendar Ending Date
Imbolctide (Waxing)	Earth Receptive	To Resonate	0° Capricorn		15° Aquarius	
Dates of Full Moons						
Ostaratide (Waning)	Air Projective	To Know	15° Aquarius		0° Aries	
Dates of Full Moons						
Beltanetide (Waxing)	Air Receptive	To Wonder	0° Aries		15° Taurus	
Dates of Full Moons						
Lithatide (Waning)	Fire Projective	To Will	15° Taurus		0° Cancer	
Dates of Full Moons						
Lammastide (Waxing)	Fire Receptive	To Surrender	0° Cancer		15° Leo	
Dates of Full Moons						
Mabontide (Waning)	Water Projective	To Dare	15° Leo		0° Libra	
Dates of Full Moons						
Samhaintide (Waxing)	Water Receptive	To Accept	0° Libra		15° Scorpio	
Dates of Full Moons						

Auspicious Timing Throughout Section Three

A main lesson learned through the Great Work system presented in section three will hopefully bring a greater awareness of the interlocking astrological cycles of sun, moon, and the elemental energies filtered through each zodiac sign. With the handy Wheel of the Year graphic from figure 5, notice that each elemental cycle between Grand Sabbats is to be experienced while the sun/earth passes through at least half of four different zodiac signs, which provide all four elemental filters for the sun. This span of time is roughly three calendar months with roughly three lunations and at least three full moons, by which you may time three main magickal workings presented in each chapter. Meanwhile, the moon is orbiting the earth, passing through the entire zodiac at the rapid pace of a new sign/elemental energy filter every 2.5 days. That makes for a lot of chances to work while the moon is in the elemental energy of that lesson.

As you work through the chapters, you'll find notes on the auspicious timing recommended for each magickal working, with emphasis on what sign the moon is in or the ideal corresponding day of the week. Chances are good that it won't work out perfectly to hit each mark *and* your personal schedule, so just do the best you can. Having an astrological calendar or Witches' datebook for the year will greatly aid your Elemental Witchcraft planning.

For general planning purposes, during the first lunation of the elemental cycle, read and prepare your formulary. During the second lunation, ideally shortly after the Lesser Sabbat passes and you shift into the receptive mysteries, enact the main ritual journey to the elemental realm. During the third lunation, find your elemental tool and enact the spells for balancing and improvement along that path.

Astrological Timing for Formulary Creations

Now that you know *when* you'll perform your dedication rite, there are materials you'll need to prepare in advance. Before we get to the specific recipes, we'll begin with some basics you'll need to know prior to any adventures with magickal herbalism.

Once magickal blends are created, they hold the specific astrological imprint of that moment; they have their own natal chart and "destiny" to fulfill, as governed by the seven celestial spheres. You then further charge them with the desired elemental or divine energies. These magickal blends become focused powers in a bottle, which can later be released to good use whenever you need them.

In section one, we discussed how each of those seven celestial spheres are ruled by one of the seven classical "planets" that also govern elemental forces. These planets were thought to be "wandering gods" by the ancients, and so there are archetypes full of deities associated with each planetary sphere of influence. It is from the Norse and Roman deity names for each planet and god that we derive the names for the seven days of the week.

The Chaldean Order: Planetary Days

The order of the days of the week was derived from the classical Greek astrological system known as the *Chaldean order*. This system was derived from the Babylonians, who established the seven-day week and named the days after the seven classical planets. This system was later copied by the Roman Empire. The weekly pattern became: the sun (Sunday), the moon (Monday), Mars (Tyr, Tuesday), Mercury (Woden, Wednesday), Jupiter (Thor, Thursday), Venus (Frigg, Friday), Saturn (Saturn, Saturday).[200]

Each day is "ruled" or influenced by that planet, and so that day is a good time to work spells for the needs within that sphere of influence. However, a planetary "day" is not based on the mundane calendar or clock. As with most magickal and Neopagan religious observances, we celebrate the flowing and ebbing energies felt with the rising and setting of the sun throughout one full rotation of the earth. Planetary days run from the precise moment of sunrise until the following sunrise.

The following table introduces the planet, deities, day of the week they govern, elemental correspondences, and their sphere of influence for use in planning spells with planetary magick.

Symbol	Planet	Day	Deity/Archetype	Sphere of Influence	Magickal Aid
☉	Sun	Sunday	Sun's day. Apollo, divine youth, Solar deities.	Power of growth. Life. Upperworld, elemental fire.	Health, success, career, goals, ambition, personal finances, advancement, drama, social status, authority figures, crops, promotion, men's mysteries.

---

200. "Week." Encyclopedia Britannica, updated April 20, 2020, https://www.britannica.com/science/week.

Symbol	Planet	Day	Deity/Archetype	Sphere of Influence	Magickal Aid
☽	Moon	Monday	Moon's day. Luna, Artemis, lunar deities.	All magickal power. Underworld, astral realm, emotional, elemental water.	Psychic pursuits, dreams/astral travel, women's mysteries, reincarnation, domestic concerns, emotions, all things pertaining to water, initiation, shapeshifting.
♂	Mars	Tuesday	Tyr's day. Mars, Ares, warrior, protector, battle deities.	Power to project. Will, elemental fire.	Action, passion, sex, aggression, energy, strife, courage, physical energy, athletics, weapons, confrontation, mechanics, hunting, battle.
☿	Mercury	Wednesday	Woden's day. Mercury, Hermes, Thoth, messenger, magician, scribe, psychopomp deities.	Power of the mind. Mental, elemental air.	Travel, communication, wisdom, healing, communication, intelligence, memory, education, messages, merchants, writing, contracts, visual arts, languages.
♃	Jupiter	Thursday	Thor's day, Jupiter, Zeus, sky and storm deities.	Power of expansion. Highest Self, elemental air.	Business, gambling, political power, material wealth, education, religion, philosophy, expansion, luck, charity, self-improvement, research, study.
♀	Venus	Friday	Frigg/Freya's day. Venus, Aphrodite, love, fertility and ocean deities.	Power of love and attraction. Physical body, elemental earth and water.	Romantic love, friendships, beauty, performance art, harmony, peace, relationships, grace, luxury, social activity, marriage, creativity.

Symbol	Planet	Day	Deity/ Archetype	Sphere of Influence	Magickal Aid
♄	Saturn	Saturday	Saturn's day, Chronus, death and rebirth, grain deities, Grim Reaper.	Power of contrac- tion. Death, elemental earth.	Binding, protection, karma, death, rebirth, structure, discipline, toil, the law, justice, boundaries, obstacles, endurance, sacrifice, separation, trans- formation, breaking habits, accepting responsibility.

The Chaldean Order: Planetary Hours

The Chaldean order also describes the cycle of all seven planetary powers throughout the "hours" of that daily rotation. Depending on your location and latitude, as the seasons change, the relative lengths of daylight and darkness shift. However, the Chaldean plan- etary "hours" remain an equal twelve periods of daylight and twelve periods of darkness, which cycle in rulership through the seven planets in a spiral pattern.[201] Near equinoxes, the span of daylight and darkness are close to "equal," and so those "hours" will each be close to 60 minutes long on your clock. However, close to Winter Solstice the span of darkness is longest, and at Summer Solstice the span of daylight is longest depending on your latitude, making day and night hours variable in length.

For example, this Winter Solstice where I live in North Carolina, when the sun enters the earthy sign of Capricorn, between sunrise and sunset we have 585 minutes of day- light. Divide by twelve parts into "daylight hours" of roughly 49 minutes each. From sunset to the following sunrise, we'll have 856 minutes of darkness. Divide by twelve into "darkness hours" of roughly 71 minutes each. The rulership of each planetary day also rules the first planetary hour starting at dawn and then flows from there in Chaldean order. The order for planetary hours is different from those of planetary days. The ruler- ship of hours is organized from slowest to fastest moving, as observed from Earth.[202] This

---

201. Maria Kay Simms, "Planetary Hours: The Method and the Magick for Quick Timing Decisions," Llewellyn, October 30, 2003, https://www.llewellyn.com/journal/article/534.

202. Simms, "Planetary Hours."

Chaldean order also follows the Hermetic model of celestial, or planetary, spheres from outermost to innermost sphere: Saturn, Jupiter, Mars, sun, Venus, Mercury, moon.[203]

This Winter Solstice falls on a Monday, ruled by the moon, which is a great time for elemental water workings, for psychic and emotional healing magick. My handy *Farmers' Almanac* website tells me that sunrise is 7:15 a.m. So, from 7:15 a.m. (lasting 49 minutes) until 8:04 a.m. is a time that is doubly ruled by the moon and so a doubly powerful time for lunar magick. However, if that day I need a quick hit of the fires of Mars to boost my emotional work, I could wait until the second "hour" from 8:04 a.m. to 8:53 a.m.— day of moon, hour of Mars. The elegance of this system is that the following dawning we cycle to the hour ruled by the next planet in the sequence.

The following tables are a quick reference for the Chaldean cycle of hourly rulership. However, there are many great websites and apps for your mobile device that can quickly and easily calculate these times and powers for you based on your GPS location and the date. Some apps will provide alarms to notify you when the planetary energies shift throughout the day, revealing remarkable synchronicities to affirm the power of this system. It has never been easier for Witches to practice successful planetary magick!

Planetary Hours of Daylight							
Hours	Sunday	Monday	Tuesday	Wednesday	Thursday	Friday	Saturday
1	Sun	Moon	Mars	Mercury	Jupiter	Venus	Saturn
2	Venus	Saturn	Sun	Moon	Mars	Mercury	Jupiter
3	Mercury	Jupiter	Venus	Saturn	Sun	Moon	Mars
4	Moon	Mars	Mercury	Jupiter	Venus	Saturn	Sun
5	Saturn	Sun	Moon	Mars	Mercury	Jupiter	Venus
6	Jupiter	Venus	Saturn	Sun	Moon	Mars	Mercury
7	Mars	Mercury	Jupiter	Venus	Saturn	Sun	Moon
8	Sun	Moon	Mars	Mercury	Jupiter	Venus	Saturn
9	Venus	Saturn	Sun	Moon	Mars	Mercury	Jupiter

203. Denis Labouré, "The Seven Bodies of Man in Hermetic Astrology," trans. Michael Edwards, *The Traditional Astrologer* 4 (1994): https://www.skyscript.co.uk/7bodies.html.

Hours	Sunday	Monday	Tuesday	Wednesday	Thursday	Friday	Saturday
10	Mercury	Jupiter	Venus	Saturn	Sun	Moon	Mars
11	Moon	Mars	Mercury	Jupiter	Venus	Saturn	Sun
12	Saturn	Sun	Moon	Mars	Mercury	Jupiter	Venus

Planetary Hours of Darkness

Hours	Sunday	Monday	Tuesday	Wednesday	Thursday	Friday	Saturday
1	Jupiter	Venus	Saturn	Sun	Moon	Mars	Mercury
2	Mars	Mercury	Jupiter	Venus	Saturn	Sun	Moon
3	Sun	Moon	Mars	Mercury	Jupiter	Venus	Saturn
4	Venus	Saturn	Sun	Moon	Mars	Mercury	Jupiter
5	Mercury	Jupiter	Venus	Saturn	Sun	Moon	Mars
6	Moon	Mars	Mercury	Jupiter	Venus	Saturn	Sun
7	Saturn	Sun	Moon	Mars	Mercury	Jupiter	Venus
8	Jupiter	Venus	Saturn	Sun	Moon	Mars	Mercury
9	Mars	Mercury	Jupiter	Venus	Saturn	Sun	Moon
10	Sun	Moon	Mars	Mercury	Jupiter	Venus	Saturn
11	Venus	Saturn	Sun	Moon	Mars	Mercury	Jupiter
12	Mercury	Jupiter	Venus	Saturn	Sun	Moon	Mars

Hermetic Foundations for a Witch's Spellwork

As divinity descends through the celestial spheres to become any kind of new matter—whether that be animal, vegetable, or mineral matter—it is cast into form with its own consciousness, spirit, and unique powers to eventually manifest on Earth as a multiform being. The moment that being is born, its destiny, personality, strengths, and weaknesses are set into motion. It was upon this foundation that the laboratory practices of alchemists were built. They exhaustively studied and rarified the essences of plants and minerals into both magickal and physical medicines.

The *doctrine of signatures* was one early system that claimed that by observing plants carefully, the "signature of divinity" would describe the qualities that plant offered. A famous example is that the leaves of lungwort are lung-shaped and contain compounds helpful for respiratory health. The results of alchemical experimentation are still used widely today in the healing usage of essential oils and tinctures, the fermentation of "spirits," medicinal herbalism, and crystal healing. It is this lore linking planet, to zodiac sign, to aspect of God/dess governing an area of consciousness, to the days of the week, to element, to power, which founds all of a Witch's tables of magickal correspondences. For example, sphere of planet Venus ➡ Libra and Taurus ➡ God/desses of love (Astarte, Ishtar, Venus, Aphrodite, Freya, Frigg) ➡ Friday (Frigg's Day) ➡ elemental earth and water ➡ aids in romance, beauty, grace, creativity, sensuality, sexuality, relationship, pleasures ➡ roses, rose quartz, copper, dove, etc.

When planning a spell by auspicious timing, start with the appropriate planetary power, then the ingredients for the spell become clear! Then partner with the spirits within these material beings and their elemental essences, and your vibration further attunes to that frequency. Now you'll draw more of the same power because "like attracts like." Enact that spell during an auspicious time ruled by that planet and your desires further syncopate with the flow of nature, and magick becomes even easier to manifest.

How to design your spell, partnering with these powers to change your life, becomes your artform … be creative. All the spells and formulary I've provided in section three of this book are just a starting place. I created them based on my knowledge of these mechanics and trial and error to see what worked for me. You may do the same.

Magickal Technique Basics

In addition to the seven Hermetic principles we discussed in chapter 2, there is perennial wisdom within many magickal systems throughout history, codified into "laws" of magick.

Law of Sympathy: Items that are similar or associated in some way can be linked through ritual intent to be in "sympathy" with each other, which then mirror the symbol into reality between the three realms. Ritual magick is smaller symbolic representations of what we wish to manifest.

Law of Contagion: If two things touch, then they continue to influence each other even at a distance. Physics even calls this "quantum entanglement." Contagion is why in spells witches add "taglocks" like hair or fingernails or something previously worn by the subject of the spell, like clothing or jewelry, to "lock" the spell's affects to the person "tagged." Also, any powers held by something are contagious, so that power is spread to anything it touches. So, if a single drop of water holds a blessing, pour it into a larger bowl of water, and that blessing is transferred to all of the water. Contagion is also why a sprinkle of a charged herbal blend or a drop of charged oil can transfer that power to a whole charm, amulet, or talisman, and why a new candle, when lit from a previously charged candle, will transfer that power to the new wax.

Law of Triplicity: Witchcraft is stronger in threes. "Mind the threefold law you should …"[204] Thrice chanted, thrice done, and add multiples of three items to impact the three realms of mental, spiritual, and physical. Thrice done for cardinal, fixed, and mutable phases, and for the God/dess in three aspects: Underworld, Middleworld, and Upperworld.

Formulary Basics: Magickal Herbalism

Witchcraft has a unique history of using *stuff* for magick. Here's the ironic thing: You don't need expensive stuff to lead an effective witching life. Not really. While very enriching, the "things" are luxuries, not necessities. With or without material things, you are the magick. Start with you and find your connection to the Spiritual Source. Going direct, mind to mind, and spirit to spirit costs you nothing. That being said, Elemental Witchcraft is specifically about digging into this material world and figuring out how to thrive in partnership here alongside all these persons of flora, fauna, and mineral. Plus, it can be both spiritually satisfying and fun. However, if do-it-yourself magickal herbalism isn't your favorite thing, seek out and make a fair trade with a magickal craftsperson whose practices and integrity can be trusted.

Conscientious Material Magick

I encourage you to take a bioregional and sustainable approach to your magick. Much has changed since the formularies in old grimoires were written. Simple, sustainable, inexpensive, and locally available materials are always preferable. Consider the source of your materials as the first step. Support your locally owned retailers when at all possible (please and thank you.) Aim for goods that are natural, sustainably grown and harvested, and respectful of the cultures and ecosystems from which they are derived.

---

204. Mathiesen and Theitic, *The Rede of the Wiccae*, 53.

Magick with plants, stones, or animal parts is a co-creative alliance with the spirit inherent to those materials. However, beneficial Witchcraft isn't *materialistic*. It isn't supposed to be the commodification of "stuff" to "get what you want." Remember, domination and exploitation are the creeping bane of the patriarchal over-culture we're trying to transform through partnership and cooperation. What kind of magick do you aim to make? Deceitful and exploitative? Or authentic and beneficial? These are your choices. Conscientious magick should work to preserve the interconnected web of existence within which we are all sacred and worthy of safety and abundance, including the beings within the realms of plant, stone, and bone. Develop respectful relationships with your allies, and you'll find that your magick becomes far more effective.

Spiritual Authenticity and Discernment

Spell ingredients are chosen for their inherent spiritual attributes. A panentheistic paradigm would regard these beings as part of the God/dess family. Therefore, respect and responsible stewardship of nature are nonnegotiable. The DNA within a plant or animal acts as a spiritual uplink to the collective consciousness and power of that species.[205] Therefore, only the real deal will do. The same applies for stones whose crystalline structures resonate at a particular frequency within consciousness. Those structures can dial you into that "station" within consciousness like a knob on a radio. If it isn't the actual plant, animal, or stone you intended, it won't tune you into anything beyond what the placebo effect can provide. In other words, *dyed howlite* is lovely, but it won't tap you into the authentic spirit of *turquoise*, even if they look alike. These material friends provide a specific key to open their specific doors of power.

Sometimes it is difficult to tell the difference between unscrupulously marketed fakes and the real material. Good thing you're a Witch and you have *ways*. Practice discerning the power of a natural ingredient just by touching it, smelling it, connecting through consciousness to this material's consciousness, and asking it directly: *Hello friend, tell me about yourself.* If it's a synthetic, petroleum-based piece of garbage, the feeling I get in my guts is sickening—it has a dead, poisonous feeling. If it is natural but just misidentified, pay attention to what your intuition tells you about the powers it can authentically lend. Start by asking which elemental essence it magnifies, and see what images pop into your mind's eye or where in your body you feel its vibration. Intuit from there.

---

205. Sheldrake, "Morphic Resonance and Morphic Fields."

Candle Burning Basics

Candle burning is a Witch's magickal sweet spot. The kind of candles you'll need for the Witchcraft in section three are seven-day sanctuary candles in a glass jar. They are typically 2.25 x 8 inches tall and take refill insert candles no more than 2 inches wide. These candles are commonly available at local Witchcraft and metaphysical stores. For a sustainable alternative to the typical paraffin wax candle, seek out beeswax. They burn twice as long, clean the air as they burn, naturally smell great, support bees, which are sacred to the God/dess, and help the environment.

Spell candles are loaded and charged as a physical symbol of your intended changes and represent the partnerships you have with allies in all realms. The plants, stones, images, and sigils are keys that help to open that particular door for you. Your energies invested into this symbol merely anchor your Divine power here on Earth. It helps broadcast that power into the world to create change in *accordance with your will*. However, you are the source of this power, which is only actualized through the candle. Unless *you* charge that candle with magickal purpose, it might as well be a crayon.

Loose Incense Basics

For my incense blends, I use a pretty simple formula. The ratio is 1:1:1 of base wood: resin: herb plant material and assorted bits.[206] The essential oils are optional, and do add a rich aroma, but aren't strictly necessary. In the following exercises I've included my recipes based on materials that I can easily obtain at a reasonable cost where I live. You may cater your blends to what is local to you. The old grimoire recipes were written in another time and likely on a distant patch of earth from where you are now. They were likely using ingredients that grew in their backyards! Consult the correspondence tables included in each elemental chapter's formulary section for other options and substitutions. Experiment to create something unique for yourself.

You may make as little or as much incense as you'll need by using different sized measures as "1 part." For personal use, I recommend using a tablespoon as a measure. This way you'll end up with 7 tablespoons, which will last you at least 7 burnings. This will easily get you through this year's lessons. After blending and charging, move your incense to a small, sealable glass jar. Darker colored glass provides longer shelf life. Label with the appropriate

---

206. As taught to me by Witch and herbalist Courtney Varnadoe.

alchemical and astrological sigils and the date of creation to keep charging via the Law of Contagion.

Anointing Oil Basics

Anointing oil blends are a major part of most magickal traditions. Do not use most essential oils without dilution in a carrier oil. Carrier oils can be any vegetable oil, but they will eventually go rancid, with varying shelf lives. Jojoba oil is preferred because it is a liquid vegetable wax. It is fantastically nourishing for the skin and has an incredibly long shelf-life.[207]

Essential Oil Cautions:

- Do not use undiluted essential oils directly on the skin unless directed by a certified aromatherapist. Some can cause chemical burns if not used properly.
- Do not use essential oils on anyone under the age of twelve unless guided by certified professionals, and never on an infant. Many essential oils should be avoided during pregnancy.
- Many essential oils are toxic to pets, and even when used in an oil diffuser, they settle on surfaces potentially causing medical harm.
- Do not ingest essential oils.

Don't bother substituting pure essential oils with synthetic fragrance oils. For example, the spirit of a rose is present because that drop of essential oil is the "soul" extracted alchemically from real roses. Rose "fragrance oil" may smell rosy, and it certainly would be easier on your wallet, but it is a chemical cocktail of fakery and not a replacement. Better to go pick an actual rose (organically grown) and include a dried petal in your oil blend or select a substitute with similar Venusian powers.

Stone, Crystal, and Metal Basics

Stones, crystals, and metals are the bones of the earth herself and long studied by alchemists. These mineral friends have a natural ability to focus and regulate the flow of power, including chi energy. The crystalline structure and molecular content of each stone variety

---

207. Amy Blackthorn, *Blackthorn's Botanical Magic: The Green Witch's Guide to Essential Oils for Spellcraft, Ritual, and Healing* (Newburyport, MA: Weiser, 2018) 23.

are especially capable of amplifying their unique characteristics into whatever or whomever they come into contact. They only need to be within the subtle bodies of an auric field to begin attuning that field into resonance with their sphere of consciousness. That is why it is important to know by which classical planet(s) a material is governed and which zodiac sign(s) to figure out which elements and modalities they magnify. From there, they can be mapped to which chakra they'd balance and which magickal intentions they'd aid. Because these materials have complex components and typically resonate in multiple spheres of influence, their strengths and correspondences are rarely simple. Example: moonstone ➡ moon ➡ Cancer ➡ cardinal ➡ water ➡ receptive (yin) ➡ heart chakra ➡ aids affection, psychic ability, compassion, creativity, love, pregnancy and childbirth, moon magick, etc.

Stones are typically available in many forms to serve different needs. They don't have to be huge or expensive to be helpful. Stones are everywhere, and you can choose what is local to you and sustainably derived. Magick doesn't have to include exotic, rare, toxic, or endangered materials to work for you; make substitutions for what is available and least harmful to all involved.

Tumbled and raw stones work equally well regardless of if they are in their raw form or have been tumbled into a smooth polish. One inch or smaller are easier to add to charm bags or slip under a pillow or into a spiritual bath.

Stone chips are very tiny gemstones typically sold in little jars—easy to fit into a small oil bottle or herbal blend.

Warnings: Do not ingest stones or crystals directly; do not put them in your mouth. Some gemstones react dangerously to stomach acid or are hazardous when particles are inhaled. Take care which gemstones are added to charge waters for consumption (sometimes called crystal elixirs) as some stones dissolve in water. Be especially careful using stones to charge waters that may come in contact with your skin, like spiritual baths and ritual waters. Many stones contain components that are toxic to human health if breathed or ingested, such as copper, asbestos, aluminum, lead, zinc, and arsenic. In most stones, they can be safe to handle but toxic when wet or inhaled. For example, malachite, a rich green stone high in copper, is wonderous for planetary Venus, heart chakra, and love magick, but can make you sick if ingested or inhaled.

Stone sands are available and wonderfully easy to use in herbal blends, but they are also dusty and should be carefully selected if they could be inhaled or later burned. Just choose carefully and do your research. For reference, the International Gem Society website maintains a Gemstone Toxicity Table of over 280 minerals.[208] The following table is a quick reference for more commonly used minerals for magick and energy healing, rating their toxicity risk based on ingestion or inhalation of particles, not necessarily for just holding them or general usage. However, for higher-risk varieties, tumbled or polished stones are preferable to raw stones to limit exposure to dust.

Element	No Known Toxicity	Low or Medium Risk	High Risk (if ingested or dust is inhaled)
Air	angelite, calcite (clear, yellow), celestite, howlite, iolite, moldavite, sodalite, aragonite	agate (tree), black onyx, chalcedony, opal, tektite	apatite, clear quartz, ametrine, aventurine (green quartz)
Fire	beryl, calcite (red, orange), diamond, danburite, garnet, ruby, serpentine, sunstone, topaz, tourmaline (red)	agate, bloodstone, carnelian, hematite, jasper (red), obsidian, opal (fire), rhodochrosite, rhodonite, zircon (red)	amber, ametrine, citrine, pyrite, quartz, tiger's-eye
Water	alexandrite, angelite, aquamarine, beryl, calcite (blue), fluorite, kyanite (blue), labradorite, lepidolite, larimar, moonstone, morganite, sapphire, sodalite, topaz (blue), tourmaline (blue)	agate (blue lace), chrysocolla, jasper (ocean), lapis lazuli (medium risk), obsidian (gold sheen), opal, turquoise	amethyst, ametrine, azurite, dioptase, rose quartz, coral, any kind of pearl
Earth	alexandrite, calcite (green), diopside, emerald, fluorite, peridot, tourmaline (black, pink, green)	agate, amazonite, chrysocolla, hematite, chrysoprase, jasper (green moss), turquoise	amber, apatite, jet, smoky quartz, malachite

208. Addison Rice, "Gemstone Toxicity Table," International Gem Society, n.d., https://www.gemsociety
.org/article/gemstone-toxicity-table/.

Preparing for Dedication to the Great Work

The Great Work is a year-long magickal endeavor that spirals deeper into the mysteries each turning of the wheel. Each year, Witches can choose to dedicate to a particular path of study. Your dedication this year will be to explore the Pentacle Path of Elemental Witchcraft program outlined in the following chapters.

In preparation of that dedication rite, you'll craft a candle to serve as your guiding light in your rituals. The purpose of this dedication candle is an evocation of divinity to your altar and a reminder of your goal during all your workings. Once made, it will live on your personal altar and serve as the "spirit" candle that is lit first through every ritual and working.

I recommend your magickal dedication candle to be the seven-day sanctuary variety in a reusable glass jar. Separate candle inserts are typically available for use as a refill and can be refreshed for all your future workings. Simply light the new insert from the last flames of the old, and the magick is transferred through the Law of Contagion. These candles are an investment and lay a foundation of ritual practice that can be used for years to come.

❀ Exercise 2: Crafting Your Dedication Sanctuary Candle ❀

This dedication candle is to be lit every time you are meditating, reading, journaling, doing exercises, or performing the rituals and magickal spells all year.

Needs

Book of Mirrors and a good pen

A rectangle of lightweight paper that is 7.5 inches square

Any art supplies needed to decorate the paper as a candle wrap

1 seven-day sanctuary candle, in white or natural, in a reusable glass jar. They are typically 2.25 x 8 inches tall. Separate 2-inch pillar candle inserts are then available for use as a refill, so your candle can be refreshed as needed.

Flat head screwdriver, or electric drill with a large bit

Three drops of olive oil

Chopstick or toothpick

3 resin tears each of frankincense and myrrh

3 tiny chips each of the following stones (or find a substitute in the formulary charts for each elemental chapter in section three)

> Black tourmaline (earth)
>
> Citrine or clear quartz (air)
>
> Hematite (fire)
>
> Moonstone (water)

13-inch length of ribbon or cord to affix your intention paper to your candle

Preparation

In your Book of Mirrors, write out your intention statement for the year. Here is an example template:

> *I [your name] come to these sacred crossroads to dedicate to the Great Work of Magick during this turning of the Wheel of the Year [name the year]. I devote myself to a study of Elemental Witchcraft as I walk the Pentacle Paths of sovereignty, truth, will, love, and completion. Return me to balance, ease, and empowerment on all levels. I call upon my guides, gods, and ancestors to aid and protect me upon this journey. May this magick serve the highest good of all involved, harming none. So mote it be!*

Copy your intention statement onto one side of your candle wrap paper.

Decorate the other side of the paper to be a "vision board" of what you want to achieve this turning of the wheel. Include images, symbols, and sigils of your intention. For the Pentacle Path, it would represent the healthy balance of all five elements in your life. A pentacle and the alchemical sigils for the elements would be appropriate, the yin-yang, the world tree, and three worlds vesica pisces would all be meaningful images to focus your mind whenever it is lit. Perhaps copy and color figures 13 or 16. You may be as creative and artistic or simple as you wish.

To load a glass sanctuary candle that is already poured directly into the glass, take a flat head screwdriver (or an electric drill with large bit) and twist out three holes in the wax an inch or more down. Just pretend you are screwing something in while burrowing down into the wax about an inch. Occasionally pull out and dump the wax shreds aside for reuse in a later step.

Awaken each material ingredient to its purpose before you add it to the candle. Tap upon, gently blow over, and talk to these items. Allies in the plant and mineral realms are much happier to work with us if we gain their cooperation first.

Hold the frankincense and myrrh resin tears in your palm; tap, blow over them, say: *Awake, awake, awaken to your power of Spiritual balance.* With a chopstick or toothpick, poke into the three holes one each of the tears.

Hold the stone chips in your palm one variety at a time. Tap, blow over them, say: *Awake, awake, awaken [stone] to your power of [element].* Into each of the three holes poke one stone chip each of the black tourmaline (earth), citrine or clear quartz (air), hematite (fire), and moonstone (water). (Or other substitutes.)

You want most of the flammable botanical stuff deep in the wax or pushed away from the wick so you don't accidentally ignite the plants or resins before the wax has begun to melt. Pack the wax shreds back into the holes, as possible.

Drip three drops of olive oil onto the top of the candle and rub it in deosil with the index finger of your projective hand. Imagine a tiny bit of your personal energy flowing through your finger into the candle. This adds your "fingerprint" as well as a touch of your DNA through shed skin cells to claim this working as your own.

Wrap the paper around the candle and tie with the ribbon or cord to affix. Do not light it until instructed to do so during the dedication ritual.

Ritual 3: Dedication Rite to the Pentacle Path and Building an Astral Temple

This is an interactive journey into the astral realm to build your astral temple and then dedicate to the Pentacle Path of Elemental Witchcraft as your Great Work of Magick this year. This ritual has parts that are done within the mind's eye in a typical meditation. But when prompted, you will also complete ceremonial actions like lighting your dedication candle and reading your intention statement. Witchcraft requires that you use your body, move around and perform ritual actions, while also in light meditative state. Ideally, you'll be able to maintain the inner envisioning while your eyes are open in soft focus, tending your altar. This takes practice, so just jump in and do your best.

Auspicious Timing

The following dedication rite is best timed during the full moon closest to the Grand Sabbat of Samhain, or High Autumn. Continue your daily meditation practice, journal regularly, and celebrate the seasons and lunar tides as they turn until then.

Needs

Consecration elements and necessary gear: salt, red candle, incense, and water

Prepared dedication candle

Your Book of Mirrors and a pen, turned to the page with your written dedication from exercise 2

A lighter or box of matches

Preparation

Dress your altar creatively to reflect your intentions for the coming year's Elemental Witchcraft. Complete the altar awakening and consecration and hallow yourself as outlined in ritual 1 in chapter 9.

Hallow the circle's edge with the four elements, cast your temple with an awen cone of power, and close the sphere as instructed in ritual 2 in chapter 10.

Praxis

Sit down and close your eyes; take a few deep breaths. Picture that comfortable little room inside your own head and your consciousness like a tiny version of your most magickal Self, sitting in your comfortable chair. Your eyes are a window on a distant wall of that room from you now.

You are surrounded in comfort. (*Pause.*) You sit far away from that window. Far away from the bustle of the outer world. Any distracting noises or stray thoughts are merely birds flying past that distant window … release them without care.

There is a skylight above, and a soft beam of white light shines down upon your head.

Find the familiar trapdoor in the floor nearby, remembering the spiral stairs and the path beyond can lead anywhere that you wish to go in the three realms.

Say aloud: *I invite my guides, gods, and ancestors to join me on this journey. Keep me safe; show me the way. I ask that the visions be clear and your messages be understandable and gentle. May all that I do be for the highest good of all involved, harming none. Blessèd be.*

Open that ornate door in the floor, finding the spiral staircase descending beyond. With each exhale, step down, deeper and deeper into your meditative state. With each breath, with each step, your mind relaxes, thoughts easing, breath deepening. Twelve steps down, around and 'round you tread the spiral staircase, deeper into your subconscious mind, knowing that at the bottom of these steps you arrive at your own center.

Step off that bottom step and arrive at the crossroads within yourself. Behind your navel, you are connected like a silver umbilical cord to the astral realm.

See a looking glass before you, a screen of your deepest mind, and the gateway to the astral realm. Upon the looking glass, an image is beginning to form; it is a great temple that matches your personal path and preferences perfectly.

It is your intention to step into a time between times and a place between the worlds to form an astral temple of your own making. You will create a sacred space where you may commune with the God/dess and all of their beings of spirit. That which you seek lies within yourself, and so you journey now to that sacred place within. (*Pause.*)

Closer to the looking glass now, and you realize that your spirit is of the same substance as the astral realms beyond. On the count of three you pass easily beyond this portal onto the path that leads to your temple. One, two, three, step through! (*Pause.*)

You are on the astral plane. In the distance, you see the world tree, your axis mundi. Beyond the world tree is a path leading to your temple. Follow the path … (*Pause.*)

Your astral temple can be anything you wish it to be, anywhere, in any natural place, in any architectural style … or none at all.

You arrive in a landscape of your own choosing. Look around; where are you? What do you see? (*Pause.*)

Your temple comes into focus now. Notice the style, the details … does it remind you of anything you've seen before? (*Pause.*)

Closer now, you stand at the entry of your personal astral temple. What does this entry look like? What does it represent for you? (*Pause.*)

Now enter the temple of your making. Perhaps it is fully formed already. Perhaps it is a blank slate. You may add or change anything you wish with a mere thought. (*Pause.*)

First, find your place of fire. See the blaze of light and warmth. Is it a hearth? An open firepit? There is a sacred flame that you tend here. What does it look like? There is illumination enough to easily see, and it warms you. You are reminded of your own fiery will and that your sovereignty is sacred. (*Pause.*)

Find your way to your place of water. (*Pause.*) Follow the feel of the cool mist; hear the tinkling as it flows gently through the temple. Is it a fountain? A cascading pool? These are the purest waters of life. Find them now. You can touch it, drink it if you choose. Purify yourself in this outpouring of Divine Love. You are reminded of your own emotions and that your love is sacred. (*Pause.*)

Find your way to your place of air. (*Pause.*) Follow the scent of incense burning and the feel of the breeze against your skin, keeping the temple fresh and vibrant. From where does the wind of inspiration blow? A window? A garden beyond? (*Pause.*) What does that look like for you? This is the Divine Mind of innovation, allowed to move freely. You are reminded of your own ideas and that your thoughts are sacred. (*Pause.*)

Find your place of earth, which is the altar itself, at the heart of your temple. (*Pause.*) Follow your intuition to find a great earthy altar. It is large, perhaps natural stone, crystal, salt, or wood. What does your altar look like? Take in all the details. (*Pause.*) This altar is the center of the manifest world for you. It is here in your sacred place where you may enact your natural magick. (*Pause.*) Gaze upon your altar. Is there anything upon it already? (*Pause.*)

Spirit surrounds you. It is the earthen foundation, the moonlight, sunlight, and the starry heavens above. Spirit as the Great God/dess was here "from the beginning," and is that which is "attained at the end of desire."[209] Spirit awakened into attention when you arrived and goes ever with you, wherever you roam. Invite *the Two Who Move as One* to dwell with you in this sacred place. Say aloud: *Welcome, Spirit!*

Hold your dedication candle in your hands. Feel your connections to the natural environment flowing in through your crown above and up from your roots below. Direct this power through your heart and down through your hands. Envision in your mind's eye that power glowing like light and saturating the candle.

Blow gently over the top of the candle, and say aloud: *Awake, awake, awaken quintessence. Be my guiding light along the Pentacle Path.*

Set the candle on your altar. From your Book of Mirrors, read the dedication statement your wrote in exercise 2. Speak it aloud with power in the voice. You are addressing the entirety of the cosmos … so chin up, shoulders back, and project your voice from your diaphragm. Announce yourself with authority to all realms. You are a god/dess, so make sure all those who hear your dedication know that you know it!

(*Pause for reading of dedication.*) Light your candle! Say: *So mote it be!*

---

209. Valiente, *The Charge of the Goddess*, 13.

Take some time exploring and designing your temple and communing with spirit.

You will return to your temple for each of the Pentacle Paths and any time you need solace or assistance. When ready to return for now, leave through the door of your temple, taking the path back … back the way you came. (*Pause.*)

Pass the world tree in the distance, finding the looking glass once more.

Seeing your own image upon the glass, take three steps to return to your own belly. One, two, three, step through!

You arrive back at the center of your being, at the foot of the spiral stair. Ascend the stairs, taking each step back up, returning to waking consciousness. Begin to stretch your muscles; until at last you reach the top, closing the trapdoor behind you. Say aloud: *To my guides, gods, and ancestors: I am grateful for your guiding presence in my life and for your aid and protection along my journey today. Blessèd be.*

Make your way to the window, and when you are ready to return to the waking world, open your eyes. Extinguish your candles by snuffing.

⚜ Journal Reflection: Intention Statement ⚜

Reflect on this ritual experience and the details of your astral temple. Include feelings, expectations, fears, hopes, dreams. Perhaps you can sketch an image of what you saw. Write a letter to the *you* that will eventually conclude this Great Work of Elemental Witchcraft and speak to that future Self. What do you hope to accomplish by the end of this magickal year? Who do you wish to become? Next year, you can reflect over the year's work by rereading this journal. That way you can see how far you've progressed and determine what more needs working through on the next lap around the Wheel of the Year.

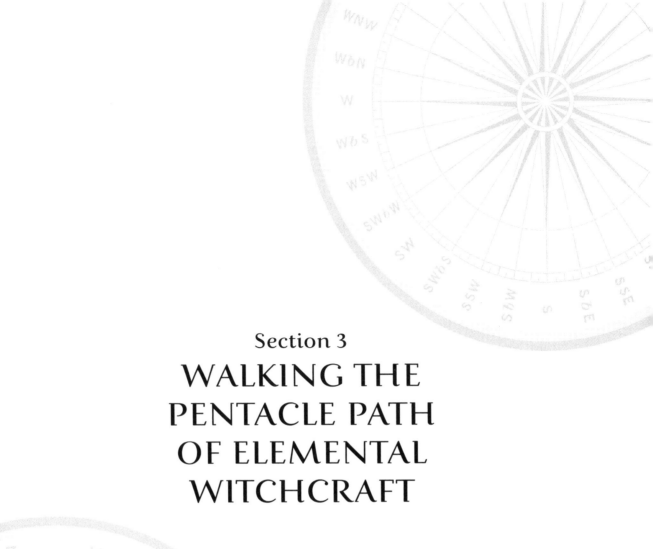

Section 3

WALKING THE PENTACLE PATH OF ELEMENTAL WITCHCRAFT

The witching life can be intense and will not be suitable for everyone. Any book or teacher who says otherwise is likely selling something that you don't want. In order to succeed at the more advanced and glamorous *spiritual* skills of Witchcraft, you'll need to be well-balanced on the more down-to-earth levels first. If you don't begin at the very roots of your existence to figure out humanhood and adulthood, to nurture and fortify yourself from the ground up, you'll literally *blow your mind* once you get into the really mystical edges up top. Witchcraft deals with the wholeness of life. Remember that there are no exclusions within the perfection of Divine Love, no separation between the sacred and the mundane; it's all magick. So, the first work of a Pentacle Path of Elemental Witchcraft set before you right now is very practical.

Life is a process of becoming. Every turning of the wheel you become a little bit more authentically *yourself*. If you didn't have work to do to achieve your goals, there'd be no reason to bother with Witchcraft. So, give yourself a break, accept where you begin, and plot a course to where you want to be. As we turn the Wheel of the Year, start in the darkness before the dawn. We begin with the elemental lessons of earth where all life emerges: the root chakra.

Chapter 12
Element of Earth and the Path of Sovereignty

We begin our Elemental Witchcraft practices in the dark waning of the Yuletide season, exploring the path of sovereignty through the elemental earth mysteries. This chapter's lessons are divided into two parts: During the 6.5 weeks of the waning Yuletide, we'll explore the projective elemental mystery *to be silent*. During the 6.5 weeks of the waxing Imbolctide, we'll explore the receptive elemental mystery *to resonate*.

The Great Work: Wheel of the Year

As we tread the path of sovereignty, there are three ritual workings to complete, which may be timed to the three lunar tides that crest within this solar period:

1. Crafting formulary materials for earth rituals and spells.

2. Taking a ritual journey to the realms of elemental earth.

3. Performing a spell with planetary earth, Venus, and Saturn for holistic balancing of your physical needs and strengthening your personal sovereignty.

Yuletide: Samhain until Yule

From Samhain to Yule is a time of rest and reflection. During this time, check in with the earth's projective mysteries of silence. Read your old journals, reflect on what you've learned over the last year. This period of waning into the darkness is when the lessons of the previous harvest are integrated, and we find conclusion to what the year taught. Nurture yourself: rest, dream, dine, divine, pamper your body. Practice active silence. Ask questions, then listen carefully without interruption or judgment. Pray in open dialogue with your guides, then pay attention to signs, omens, synchronicities in your daily life, following the intuitive breadcrumbs as they land. Read the chapter's lessons, and then when the next waxing moon is in an earth sign, prepare your earth magick sanctuary candle and the formulary blends for the incense, anointing oils, and other goodies you'll need for the rituals and spells of earth to follow.

Imbolctide: Yule until Imbolc

From Yule until Imbolc, switch into the receptive lessons of *resonance*. Look to the birth of the new cycle and ask the cosmos, "What's next?" If you practice a form of divination like tarot card reading, seek guidance for the new wheel. Try the Jewel of Power tarot spread provided in exercise 17. While the waxing moon is in an earth sign, take the ritual journey to the realms of earth, seeking alliance with gnomes and Sovereign Ghob. It is during this journey that you'll seek guidance about the correct tool of earth for you. Then, you'll find or craft that tool for yourself as a continuation of your magick. During the final lunation before Imbolc, set the new tone for the coming year's magick through the exercises of building sovereignty and character by working the "I Am the Magick" spell for rebalancing your earth in sovereignty.

The Pentacle Path of Sovereignty and the Physical Body		
Chakra	Root chakra	Sacral chakra
Regulates	Survival, evolution	Pleasure, fertility
Opened by	Personal sovereignty	Sexual freedom
Blocked by	Fear	Guilt
Witchcraft Goal	Establishing independence	Setting your moral compass
Love Conditions	Resources vs. fear of suffering	Affection vs. a fear of abandonment
Charm of Affirmation	By elemental powers five, I have all I need to survive and thrive.	By the powers of earth and sea, I share desired intimacy.

Mysteries of Elemental Earth

Earth is an elemental energy representing the diversity of forms and physical existence. Earth energy also aids our awareness of practicality, physical pleasure, and resources. Earth rules the sense of touch, of simply being present in our bodies and sustaining them. In Hermetic alchemy, elemental earth is thought to have a dry, cold nature and primarily feminine mental gender; however, in my experience, earth holds a multifaceted gender fluidity.

The planet Earth is far more than just a home; we are made of earth, and the energetic expression of earth is embodiment. In "The Charge of the Goddess," Witches are instructed that "all acts of love and pleasure are my rituals."[210] To revel in physical pleasure is valid communion with the God/dess; to be fully present within our flesh and bones is our prayer.

It is called *grounding* when we tap into elemental earth to soothe our subtle bodies. It is an especially useful practice when we are out of balance and experiencing anxiety, agitation, or absentmindedness. Practical forms of grounding include rest, eating nourishing food and drinking enough water, working up a sweat with physical exercise, having sex, or masterbating. Making bare-skinned contact with the literal ground is helpful, like lying on the earth, bear-hugging a friendly tree, holding a stone, walking barefoot outside, and extending our energetic roots deeply to find stability in the bedrock.

---

210. Valiente, *The Charge of the Goddess*, 12–13.

Elemental earth energy is our way of linking with our natural environment as a part of the ecosystem. Earth resides in the north so it is also associated with winter's darkness, midnight, the void, and potential. Earth is an element of paradoxes, seemingly so solid and immovable; yet atoms are mostly empty space made of orbiting particles in constant motion.[211]

Earth Through the Zodiac

Earth's powers emerge through the life cycle and zodiac first through fixed Taurus as a human baby exploring the lessons of "I have." Taurus can teach others that love is patience while learning that love is forgiveness. Later, earth emerges as mutable Virgo and the responsible human adult exploring the lessons of "I analyze." Virgo can teach others that love is pure while learning that love can bring fulfillment. Finally, as the cardinal Capricorn, earth explores the lessons of "I use." Capricorn can teach others that love is wisdom while learning that love is selfless.[212]

Witch's Jewel of Power: Earth		
	Yang: projective	Yin: receptive
Mystery Teaching	To be silent	To resonate
Wheel of Year	Samhain through Yule	Yule through Imbolc
Planetary Sphere	Saturn	Venus

Witch's Jewel of Power: To Be Silent

To be silent is the projective expression of elemental earth. Silence is an energy of stillness. Through silence, the body, mind, and spirit deepen and expand to make space for what is to come next. So, this power of silence is also the void, the secret and subatomic emptiness within all things. Paradoxically, the energy of emptiness is also one of potential; the void is eternally ready to manifest as new forms. At the basement level of reality, beneath the subatomic level, is a sea of pure information and ultimate energy, there for

---

211. Roderick, *Wicca: A Year and a Day*, 180.

212. Linda Goodman, *Linda Goodman's Love Signs: A New Approach to the Human Heart* (New York: Harper Collins Publishers, HarperPerennial edition, 1992), 13.

the seeking. So, in a sense, *emptiness* is also *fullness*; *nothingness* is also *everythingness*. This shift of perception is key to the magick of physical manifestation.

The expression of earthy silence rules material gain, prosperity, work, strength, fortitude, honesty, practicality, pleasure, comfort, and the arts. Rather than the term *silence*, which is too often confused with secrecy, I prefer the phrase, *to hold the space*. In our society it is hard not to fill an empty space with idle chatter or pointless tchotchkes. When was the last time you had a free minute and didn't passively grab your phone to scan the social media feeds?

Holding open a space is the active part of patiently doing nothing, yet remaining present in the moment. In our *go-go-go* society, this may be the hardest lesson of all. Yet, from the funeral at Samhain to the rebirth of Yule, we are tasked to rest, just like the God/dess taking a layover in the Underworld. Once the dusk of Samhain falls and the lessons of silence are upon us, it is time to pay attention to what effects are coming into being as a result of our previous actions. We hold the space open, like a mold, to give those manifestations a place to form.

The *Hermetic Principle of Cause and Effect* informs me that everything in my life is the effect of a cause that I can affect, even if that source isn't obvious down here on the Physical Plane. If this reality is not one that I'd like to continue, what might I change to manifest a different experience of life? This assessment is the first step of the magickal process.

Witch's Jewel of Power: To Resonate

To resonate is the inward, receptive expression of earth, the energy that emerges from silence where we are connected to the vibrational potential that underlies all things. It represents the interconnectedness of all reality, widening one's perspective to understand that there is no division between you and everything else, so all resources are within your reach. In moments of stillness, we can feel the pulse of life. It is in the receptive mystery of earth that we gain an awesome tool of cooperation, because in resonance, the electron shifts from finite appearance as a particle to infinite possibility as a wave of potential.[213] When you tap into resonance, the denseness of earth renders itself luminous, weightless, and effortless … an inexhaustible resource enough for everyone.

---

213. Glenn Stark, "Light," Encyclopedia Britannica, updated October 29, 2020, https://www.britannica
    .com/science/light.

Earth: To Resonate	Air: To Know	Air: To Wonder	Fire: To Will	Fire: To Surrender	Water: To Dare	Water: To Accept	Earth: To Be Silent

⟶ Wheel of the Year ⟶

Figure 26: Wheel of the Year elemental mysteries, linear form

On our Wheel of the Year system, we split these earthy mysteries into two parts to bookend the process. We start the new year's work with the receptive mysteries of earth—to resonate in the fertile womb. Resonance is the first stage, which sets the frequency and tone of what is to come, like striking the cosmic gong to see what vibration is next for us. From the rebirth at Yule to the re-dedication to the Great Work at Imbolc, we shift to resonance, set a new intention, and come up with a new plan of action moving forward.

First, put it out to the cosmos that you'd like a new "baby" to come down that birth canal at the end of the Great Work. The "due date" will fall when we circle back to silence again. By Imbolc, you figure out what to name the baby. The rest of the year you do whatever it takes to get every layer of yourself resonating in harmonic balance with that intention—physical, mental, emotional, will, and spirit bodies must all be engaged. The sabbat cycle celebrates the gestation period of nurturing and growing that baby intention all year. This ritual cycle is how we twist the gears on that channel lock of our subtle bodies, which must be in alignment, creating an open conduit between your personal will and the source of power through Divine Will. Like a midwife, once the earthy silence period rolls back around after Samhain, you can then actively attend the void and simply receive it as your new reality emerges. Just open your arms and catch the "baby." We begin in resonance; we end in silence.

Cooperative Tools of the Goddess

To resonate is the receptive (goddess) power of elemental earth and so holds the cooperative lessons needed to progress our culture toward a more abundant future. In resonance one takes an active role in creating our collective reality. Rather than mutely tolerating whatever belief or tyranny is imposed upon citizens from outside authorities, resonance grants the individual self-determination. Cooperative cultures would employ resonance through democratic means, granting voice to individuals in the public forum of free speech, shared participation in government, freedom to protest, freedom of and from religion, and an equal vote for all that actually counts. In short, earthy resonance is expressed as the civil liberties that are protected by the US Bill of Rights but fully extended to all members of a society without systemic racism, classism, sexism, or homophobia.

The Path of Sovereignty

Along the Pentacle Path, this lap through the earthy mysteries is called the path of sovereignty. Sovereignty means simply that you are the authority over your own mind, heart, body, and spirit, with free will to determine your own course in life. To be sovereign is to calibrate your own moral compass according to your own values and then navigate your own path by that compass with conviction.

In "The Charge of the Goddess," a sovereign Witch is tasked to define their "highest ideals" for themselves, then in sovereignty make choices that "strive ever toward" those ideals, keeping them "pure," or uncompromised, letting nothing "turn them aside" from their goals.[214] Affirming personal sovereignty claims one's *independence*. No pressure, right? Sounds lonely. Which leads us to the paradox that the elemental mysteries help to reconcile.

The Sovereignty Paradox: Independence vs. Interdependence

While sovereignty in that definition above may seem like a solitary, every-Witch-for-themselves pursuit, the mystery teaching cannot stop there. Such radical independence might isolate a Witch with the lonely assumption that we are separate, abandoned to fend for ourselves. The paradox is that Witches also affirm our *interdependence* within God/dess, the matrix weaving us together. While manifested on Earth, we are tasked to govern our personal patch of that matrix.

Yet, as the old adage reminds us all, "With great power comes great responsibility." The key to the personal sovereignty paradox is that we are interconnected through Divine Love of the God/dess, which is perfect and fulfills the nine Divine Love Conditions for everyone as our sacred rights. Through the Witchcraft praxis of union, we discover that separateness is the illusion. Me, my neighbor, that tree, the dirt, the ocean, the air, and all the creatures who dwell within the three worlds are all fundamentally interdependent

---

214. Valiente, *The Charge of the Goddess*, 12–13.

aspects within the wholeness of God/dess. After that realization, sovereignty becomes the easy choice to fully participate in that wholeness as stewards of Divine Love; this is our God/dess's commission.

Interdependent sovereignty means there are no excuses for harmful behavior, including self-harm, or by participating in the injustices of a dominator society. The paradigm of Divine Love has no scapegoats and no elite "chosen people." Once you take possession of your rightful crown, *you internalize your source of control* and then put that control to beneficial use. Think about interdependent sovereignty like this: We are all here to make this bed we are sleeping in together. The more comfortable the bed we all make, the better we all sleep.

Root Chakra: Establishing Independence

The elemental essence of earth is regulated through the root chakra at the base of the torso. Just like a taproot on a tree, we also tap into the elemental earth through our root chakra.

From the root up, we slowly establish our independence. When we are first conceived, we are completely dependent on our mother's body to support our life. Our growth steadily prepares us to emerge from our mother's womb and exist as a separate body. Through birth itself, we pass through our mother's root chakra, which corresponds to the perineum area of the body between the vaginal and anal openings.

Root chakra consciousness corresponds to the life stage of human infancy. During our infancy, we are still completely dependent on the care and nurturing of others. This stage is when wee new humans have to figure out that we are once again incarnated into the illusion of a separate body. This could explain all the crying. Infants work through the lessons of "I am."[215] Through toddlerhood, we realize there are things we need and things we want, and figure out what is ours. Toddlers figure out the "I have" lessons.[216] All of this is the initial establishment of our sovereignty: this is my separate body, these are my things, these are my parameters within the material world.

Throughout our childhoods we grow out of that place of powerlessness. By necessity, the source of our control, security, and authority are located outside of ourselves. We are dependent upon our caregivers to provide for our education (air) and emotional (water)

---

215. Goodman, *Linda Goodman's Love Signs,* 13.

216. Goodman, *Linda Goodman's Love Signs,* 13.

needs. Our parents or caregivers provide all our physical needs (earth) and keep us safe with external structures by making rules (Saturn) and enforcing them, whether we like it (will) or not. However, as we transition to adulthood, we naturally individuate and separate from our parents until we are sufficiently able to internalize control over our lives and derive our own authority from within ourselves. Through a life of trustworthy experience, we grow in self-esteem and self-confidence, eventually internalizing our sense of security as we mature.

Boil down the entirety of Witchcraft thealogy, purpose, and praxis, and what sets it so radically apart from the invasive orthodoxies, is the requirement for individuals to have personal sovereignty. It is much harder to control or exploit fully empowered people! Personal sovereignty speaks to the full embrace of our adult maturity, taking leadership and responsibility within your sphere of influence.

❧ Exercise 3: Sovereignty Mapping ❧

Along the path of sovereignty, ask yourself the tough questions about your current physical circumstances. Resolving every question will not happen overnight, but you can start by *getting real* about what is real. In what condition, with what parameters, resources, strengths, and needs do you begin this journey of sovereignty? *Must be present to win.*

Consider the following questions that start at the "root" of the issue: Are you as physically healthy, secure, abundant, financially independent as you'd like to be? Do you know what you need to know to do what you'd like to do, provide for your needs, and accomplish your sacred mission? Are you expressing your beautiful diversity, in your way, within the quality of relationships that you desire? Are you having any fun yet? If the answer is *not really*, then the first magickal work laid out on the path before you would be to achieve those goals.

Witchcraft is rooted in partnership, in mutually beneficial relationships with beings in both seen and unseen realms. Ideally, we're all supported within the network formed by our village, friends, family, or partner(s) of our choice, and with our gods, ancestors, and spiritual guides. However, these relationships should be consensual and mutually beneficial. Meaning they empower you to become your most fulfilled Self. In turn, you support the sovereignty of everyone else in the network. Effective personal sovereignty is the key to transmuting the dominator culture of the invasive orthodoxies into the cooperator culture of the God/dess.

Here is the stickiest and most important thing to consider: If the relationships that support your physical survival also entrap, oppress, abuse, deprive, or belittle you, that is the opposite of sovereignty; that is enslavement. If the people you depend upon manipulate your presence through a *fear of suffering or abandonment* or attempt to oppress your will to become your most authentic Self in any way, you have serious witching work to do, and it won't be easy. The Witchcraft set before you first is to remove yourself from their control. Prudently seek out different support structures and relationships that will nurture the fullness of your unique needs over time. This is a lifelong process, requiring creative diplomacy and gradual development. For now, set goals for your ideal state of sovereignty and then carefully "strive ever toward it."[217]

Consider the questions above and write out all the ways your physical needs are currently provided for and your goals for filling any needs. This is like dropping the little pin on your GPS map of destiny. Find point A on your map: *you are here*. Now, where do you want to end up? That is point B. Now, draw a line between them of the incremental tasks needed to achieve that goal. This is your witching plan. Now that you *know* what you need, you can employ both mundane and magickal techniques to fulfill that plan.

Sacral Chakra: Setting Your Moral Compass

The Hindu chakra system associates the sacral chakra with the element of water. However, along the Pentacle Path, I include these needs with earth's elemental mysteries. Pleasure is a higher octave of earth's resources, wherein we aren't just surviving, we're thriving. Through the sacral chakra we enjoy the pleasures of our incarnate life; we enjoy chocolate cake, not just simple bread. Sacral chakra really touches all of the five bodies. So much of human existence is wrapped up in our sexual needs and the drive to procreate. The sacral chakra is also associated with the human need of physical touch (earth), emotional intimacy (water), our primal lusts and desires (fire), and our identity and self-expression (air.) In a paradigm based in Divine Love, sacral chakra even touches on our spiritual mission as Witches. For ease and proximity, these sacral lessons also balance our physical bodies and elemental earth.

The Divine Love condition for affection and this sacral chakra need for intimacy is wounded by deprivation of touch and the *fear of abandonment*. The term for this lack is *touch starved* and so many people suffer from the psychological detriments of not having

---

217. Valiente, *The Charge of the Goddess*, 12–13.

safe, platonic touch. Handshakes, hugs, pats on the back, dancing, a cuddle—this need for affection is much bigger than just sexual intimacy. The wounds caused by abandonment, isolation, and social rejection, and the terrors that can result from those wounds, may be avoided by the loving support of Witchcraft's cooperative partnership culture that accepts and affirms sexuality as sacred in a healthy, balanced, and consensual way.

❧ Exercise 4: Building Strong Character ❧

The goal of most esoteric philosophies is to "know thyself." For a balancing of our earthy natures, discover what gives you pleasure, what you like, and what you don't like. These are the earthy boundaries that sovereignty asks us to establish and then defend. The point to this exercise within Witchcraft begins with the notion that it is sacred and necessary to enjoy your life; your consent is paramount, and that includes careful, deliberate cultivation of your character.

Character emerges from a fully explored, enjoyed, challenged, and experienced life. Wholeness on all levels results in making beneficial choices. But, before your character can gain *strength*, it needs to be *cultivated*. That cultivation is another benefit of the Witch's Great Work of Magick and is key to internalizing our sense of *authority*. Authority is confidence in your character and what you stand for so you can trust your gut intuition to make sound decisions for yourself. Otherwise, we remain infantilized and vulnerable to exploitation.

Step 1: Ask Questions

For this exercise, consider the following questions about what is pleasurable for you: What kind of food do you like to eat? What type of home, clothing, music, entertainment brings you joy? What kinds of recreation or hobbies spark you? Just as importantly, what do you *not* like?

What about sexual preferences? It is holy to love and be loved the way you desire, to touch and be touched. We have every right to seek out consensual affection among other adults, or not, as we prefer. (The operative words here being *consensual* and *adults*.) What do you desire? In what sensual activities do you *not* consent to participate?

What about social issues? Passivity is hardly a witching trait; explore social, philosophical, and political ideas across the spectrum so you can define where you stand on important issues well beyond just your own backyard. What is sacrosanct to you?

Remember that there are no puritanical taboos to enslave Witches. No "deny the flesh" dominator extortion for us to feel ashamed about. In Doreen Valiente's poem "The Witch's Creed" we're tasked to "…drink the good wine to the Old Gods, And dance and make love in their praise…"[218] However, it takes some time and effort to reprogram those deeply ingrained fears and learn to enjoy our lives intentionally and in a healthy balance.

Step 2: Write Your "I am" List

In your Book of Mirrors, start a list of *I am*'s. We spend so much of our lives defining who we are *not*: I *am not* a child; I *am not* my parent's religion; I *am not* a victim; I *am not* (insert whatever box someone tried to shove you into). The "am not" phase is necessary for differentiation from our upbringing, but a sovereign Witch eventually crosses to the other side and starts living in the *"I am…"* I *am* an adult; I *am* a Witch; I *am* a survivor; I *am* (whatever beautiful identity is true for you).

Step 3: Go Do the Things

It is never too late to become your most fulfilled and authentic Self. Remember the fourth Rule for Personal Sovereignty is *must be present to win*. Beyond just *knowing thyself*, how will you fully *become thyself* unless you get in there and start doing the important things? Based on the questions and affirmations above, make a list of all kinds of things you'd like to try, learn, explore, or get involved with, and then go do those things as an act of magick.

Here are a few earthy ideas to get you started: Explore your sexuality, and if sex is something you enjoy, learn to be a good lover (requiring both careful listening, and just the right resonance). Explore the art, music, foods, and dancing from other cultures that you've never tried before. Develop your personal fashion or interior decorating style. Read all kinds of literature, not just the books you already agree with. Travel somewhere totally outside your comfort zone. Volunteer in local political campaigns or other forms of local aid and social activism.

Step 4: Cultivate Relationships

Most importantly, as you walk the earth path, remember your interconnections and cultivate friendships. Ultimately, Witchcraft practices are about building relationships that

---

218. Valiente, *The Charge of the Goddess*, 19–21.

have healthy boundaries. We have to get along nicely with both seen and unseen powers if we are to create a better world. "Merry meet an merry part—bright the cheeks an warm the heart."[219] Think about it. If you can't work well with human people, what chance do you have at working well with the wild spirits of nature? The powers of elemental earth can help.

Figure 27: Candle wrap image for earth by Heron Michelle

---

219. Mathiesen and Theitic, *The Rede of the Wiccae*, 52–53.

Formulary for Elemental Earth

As Yuletide wanes toward the Winter Solstice, there are magickal craftings and preparations to be made. For the magick ahead, you'll need some supplies. Pick an auspicious time to craft your incense, oil, and earth candle. Reference the table below for the elemental correspondences of earth, and make substitutions as needed to suit what materials are regionally available and affordable for you.[220]

Elemental Correspondences of Earth	
Alchemical Symbol	▽
Color	Green
State of Matter	Solid
Direction	North
Time of Day	Midnight
Phase of Life	Decline/death
Season	Winter
Alchemical Qualities	Cold and dry
Mental Gender	Yin, female, gender-fluid
Governs	Physical body: practicality, stillness, contemplation
Projective Power	The power to be silent
Receptive Power	The power to resonate
Elemental Beings	Gnomes
Elemental Sovereign	Ghob/Gob
Magickal Tool	Pentacle paten, altar, besom, open hand, human body
Consecration	Salt
Planetary	Earth, Saturn ♄, Venus ♀
Day of the Week	Saturday for Saturn, Friday for Venus

---

220. I assembled these element correspondence charts from many sources, but a good reference is *Llewellyn's Complete Book of Correspondences* by Sandra Kynes.

Elemental Correspondences of Earth	
Astrological Signs	Cardinal: Capricorn; fixed: Taurus; mutable: Virgo
Stone	Alexandrite, amazonite, green calcite, chrysocolla, emerald, fluorite, jade, petrified wood, smoky quartz, tourmaline (black, pink, or green), diopside, peridot, jasper (green moss).
Metals	Lead (use with caution!)
Herbs	Comfrey, ivy, patchouli, pine needle, honeysuckle, vervain, cinquefoil, grains, High John (morning glory) root
Trees/Woods/Barks	Ash, cedar, elm, elder, juniper, magnolia, maple, oak, pine, fir
Resins	Pine, Maple
Creatures	Bull, stag, goat, bear, beetle, buffalo, deer, dog, elephant, turtle, badger, boar, groundhog

❧ Exercise 5: Earth Formulary Crafting ❧

Auspicious Timing

Waxing lunar cycle, preferably while the moon is in an earth sign of Taurus, Virgo, or Capricorn, and/or on the days/hours of Venus (Friday) or Saturn (Saturday.) Look at the time you have left until Winter Solstice and pick an auspicious moment to "birth" these materials into their blended forms. Once complete, they'll fulfill the destiny of the stars under which they were made.

Needs

See the recipes below for specific materials and equipment for each recipe.

Formulary crafting really puts the "working" into a *working altar*, so make sure you have enough surface area to spread out, make a merry mess, and be artistically creative.

Consecration elements, including a charcoal in a censer to test your incense, once made. Add anything that aids your connection to earth energies: crystals, living plants, etc.

Preparation

Awaken and consecrate your altar with ritual 1 in chapter 9.

Call upon your spiritual guides to be present and inspire your magickal creations.

For charging any earth-drawing materials, chant this charm based on "Flags, Flax, Fodder, and Frig," a traditional East Anglian blessing wishing physical comforts of a safe home, enough food, comfortable clothing, and pleasurable companionship in life![221]

Earth Blessing Charm

> *Powers of earth, of Ghob and gnomes,*
> *Flax, fodder, Frigg, foundation stones.*
> *Come powers of growth and sovereignty,*
> *As I will, so mote it be!*

Elemental Earth Incense—Planetary Earth Magick

This incense recipe is effective for any journeys and spells where the elemental power of earth would aid in manifesting your intention—brings silence, resonance, grounding, stability, prosperity, growth, and good health.

Needs

Mortar and pestle to grind and blend dry ingredients

2 parts base wood—elm, cedar, or pine bark powders (earth)

2 parts resin—pine resin or pitch

½ part herb—patchouli (Saturn)

1 part herb—pine needles (earth)

1 part honeysuckle blossoms (earth)

(optional) essential oils—9 drops each of patchouli, pine

2 parts vegetable glycerin to bind

9 stone chips of black tourmaline (or substitute)

Dark-colored jar with lid and opening large enough for your incense spoon; green glass is ideal

---

221. Valiente, *Witchcraft for Tomorrow*, 65.

Praxis

In your mortar and pestle, grind with a deosil motion all plant ingredients until relatively fine. As you add each ingredient, invite their spirits to aid your earthy work and thank them. Add the essential oil (optional) and glycerin, stir to combine and bind. Add stone chips. With the Saturn finger (middle) of your projective hand, draw the alchemical sigil of earth in the incense. Transfer the blend to the jar, then hold it in your hands.

Chant the earth blessing charm three times and charge with the powers of earth by picturing a beautiful earthly paradise of lush greenery. Visualize the natural energy of that landscape glowing in a greenish light. Now direct that light through your mind, through your hands, into the blend. Envision the blend glowing green.

Label the jar, including the date and the sigils of earth—Saturn and Venus—to keep charging. Burn some on your charcoal to test the scent and deepen the earthy energies while you keep working.

❧ Elemental Earth Anointing Oil ❧

This oil may be used to anoint candles, yourself, or other magickal objects to bring them into sympathy with physical goals.

Needs

Dark-colored 1-dram bottle

Mix 3 drops each of essential oils of patchouli and pine

3 stone chips of black tourmaline (or substitute)

Eye dropper

Fill to top with jojoba oil for longer shelf-life, or other carrier oil for short-term use

Praxis

As you add each ingredient, tap on the oil bottles and the chips and awaken them to their powers of earth, growth, stability, and abundance. Invite their spirits to be part of your magickal team and thank them for all the manifesting they will help you achieve. When all are assembled in the bottle, cap it and swirl the oils together deosil. Charge and seal it with the visualization above, chanting the earth blessing charm three times. Label it with the name, date, and sigils of earth to continue charging. Anoint your root chakra (at your tailbone) and sacral chakra (lower belly) with the oil to continue aligning your body with earth energies while you keep working.

❧ Elemental Earth Candle ☙

In the same style you prepared your dedication candle, prepare a seven-day glass-jarred sanctuary candle to channel powers of elemental earth.

Needs

Green seven-day sanctuary candle in glass jar. They are typically 2.25 x 8 inches tall, and take refill insert candles no more than 2 inches wide.

The 7-inch square image from figure 27 can be copied and colored to create a candle wrap or you may creatively decorate your own piece of lightweight paper.

13-inch length of green cord or ribbon

Flat head screwdriver or a power drill with large bit

½ teaspoon prepared earth incense

3 drops prepared earth anointing oil

3 tiny chips of black tourmaline or other stone variety (see table for options)

Praxis

On the blank side of the 7-inch square candle wrap paper, write an earth gateway opening call. Compose your own or reference the calls provided in ritual 2. If you're not using the image provided in figure 27, decorate the outside of the wrapper with images of elemental earth such as mountains, the pentacle, gnomes, coins, alchemical earth glyph, the circle cross, Saturn ♄, and Venus ♀, etc.

With the screwdriver or drill bore out three holes in the wax about an inch deep. Load the candle by poking a bit of earth incense into the holes with a chopstick. Top with a stone chip in each hole. Then anoint with three drops of earth oil and rub it around the wax deosil with a bare finger.

Wrap the paper wrapper to the jar and tie down with the green cord or ribbon. The charging of this candle will take place during the ritual journey to elemental earth later on.

Journey to Realms of Earth

This interactive ritual merges the performance of ritual actions in the outer temple with a meditative journey within your astral temple, imagined within the mind's eye. The guided meditation in the beginning helps the Witch to achieve a "high alpha" state of consciousness. This is the brainwave state of 7–13 Hz that we all experience when daydreaming. We pass through this state in the twilight of falling asleep. Author Christopher Penczak calls this "ritual consciousness," a functional meditative state where you "go deeper into your inner experience … remaining calm, relaxed, and aware, yet still being able to walk around, light candles, speak, and so forth."[222] When prompted, you'll intone or speak aloud, light candles, throw incense on the coals, etc. With practice, you'll learn to maintain the inner envisioning while your eyes are open in soft focus and performing the rite. The ritualized journey is best enacted by listening to a recording of the meditation or as someone reads it aloud for you.

☘ Ritual 4: Elemental Earth Temple ☘

We begin our ritual cycle by calling the essence of elemental earth from the northern quarter and then taking a guided journey through your astral temple to the elemental earth plane. The goal is to seek partnership with gnomes and Sovereign Ghob and receive insights about the magickal tools of earth and which allies of stone, crystal, or metal may best aid your sovereignty.

Unlike complete temple creation, this temple is opened solely for elemental earth. Elemental journeys are most impactful when done outside in nature, close to where the element is naturally occurring and uninterrupted. A hike or camping trip into the woods would be a perfect setting for these rites. However, you may perform this rite anywhere.

Auspicious Timing

During the second lunar cycle closest to the Winter Solstice, during a waxing lunar phase when the moon is in an earth sign: Taurus, Virgo, or Capricorn.

---

222. Penczak, *Inner Temple of Witchcraft*, 87.

Needs

Consecration element: bowl of sea salt as an offering to elemental beings

Add any items to your altar that evoke earth for you: green tablecloth, stones and crystals, a growing plant, flowers, etc.

An incense censer with sand, hookah charcoal tab, tongs, small spoon, and lighter or box of matches

Earth herbal incense blend

Earth anointing oil

Dedication candle for Spirit

Prepared green earth candle with green cord or ribbon

At least one crystal of earth to hold: a smoky quartz, black tourmaline, or a substitution

Your Book of Mirrors and a pen

Diagrams of earth invoking and banishing pentagrams for easy reference. See figure 24.

An athame if you already have one or just your "natural athame" of the index and middle fingers of your projective hand. Middle finger directs Saturn's power.

Device for playing a recording of the guided journey

Preparation

Begin with a physical cleaning and organizing of the ritual space and your altar. Bathe and dress in fresh, comfortable clothing, preferably barefoot with hair unbound, or nude as you prefer.

Lay your working altar accessibly before you, arranged such that you can meditate comfortably and still reach everything easily.

Anoint yourself with earth oil between your root and sacral chakra, near the top of your pubis bone.

Light your dedication candle to welcome Spirit, who is ever-present.

Light the charcoal and place in the censer in preparation for loose incense burning.

Praxis

Altar Consecration: Awaken your altar for the element of earth. Shift consciousness into your roots deep in the bedrock. Breathe deeply and establish the flow of power connecting you to the three realms. Inhale that power as green light; exhale it through your projective hand. Hold the bowl of salt in that hand. Visualize green light drawn up from the earth itself to imbue the salt. Say: *I charge this salt as a being of earth.* Draw a banishing pentacle in the salt with your projective middle finger.

Say: *Powers of earth, ground free any impurity from this sacred space.* Sprinkle three pinches of salt over the altar. Envision a green energy imbuing the altar.

Hallowing: Walk the perimeter of your circle with the bowl of salt, sprinkling and chanting, *I consecrate this circle by the powers of earth.* Present the salt to the northern quarter and say, *As your Witch of earth, I greet you with earth and ask that you ground free any baneful energies from this circle tonight. So mote it be!*

Temple: Cast your circle with the awen cone of power as taught in ritual 2; close the sphere above and below.

Open the Northern Gate: As taught in ritual 2, face the north. Stand in a posture of earth evocation. Exhale and see the green light of earth beaming from your projective hand. Your receptive hand is prepared to receive the inflowing energy. Stand tall, chin up, shoulders back; speak with authority from the diaphragm.

Say: *Powers of the north! Essence of earth! I summon you to this sacred place! Gnome, Sovereign Ghob of the realm of earth! Be with me now and lend your powers of manifestation, stability, and sovereignty. Strengthen my body for the work at hand! Awaken your lessons of silence and resonance within me. Spirit of dark cave and moss-covered stones, come growing green from rich, fertile soil, come root and seed and arching canopy to nourish and manifest this magick. I welcome you with gratitude. Hail and welcome.*

Draw the invoking pentagram of earth with the natural athame of your projective hand. See the star glowing with green light in the air of the northern quarter. Encircle the pentagram deosil, turning the lock to open. Draw your fingers toward your lips, pulling in a streamer of elemental earth. Kiss your fingers, then with hand over your heart, bow to that direction. A green girder now encircles your temple in the north.

Sit down and prepare for meditation. Begin the recording of this guided journey.

❧ Meditation 5: Guided Journey to the Realms of Earth ❧

Close your eyes; take a deep breath. Picture your most magickal Self sitting in a comfortable chair in comfortable room inside your mind. It is quiet and still in your mental sanctuary. Your eyes are now a window on a distant wall of that room. Any distracting noises or stray thoughts are merely birds flying past that distant window … release them without care. (*Pause.*)

There is a skylight above you, and a soft beam of divine light shines down upon your crown chakra. Breathe down the light with three deep breaths. Inhale through the nose and exhale through the mouth … releasing all tension. (*Pause for three breaths.*) You are at perfect ease on all levels. (*Pause.*)

There is a beautiful, ornate door in the floor of your meditation room, a door leading to all possibility. Open that door, finding a spiral staircase descending beyond. With each exhale of your breath, step down, deeper and deeper, descending into your subconscious mind, and deep into your own belly. At the foot of the stairs, you'll arrive at your inner crossroads. Twelve steps down, around and 'round you tread the spiral staircase.

Before you there hangs a looking glass, a portal outward to the astral realms where all things are possible by a mere thought. Picture your Astral Temple upon the glass. (*Pause.*)

Say aloud: *My intention is to journey to my astral temple to the elemental plane of earth to learn the mysteries of silence and resonance. I tread the path of sovereignty, seeking a relationship with the beings who govern the essence of earth known as gnomes and their sovereign, Ghob. I wish to receive my tool of earth and allies of stone to aid my physical balance. I call upon my guides, gods, and ancestors to keep me safe and show me the way. Blessèd be.* (*Pause.*)

On the count of three, step through the portal and arrive on the path to your temple. One, two, three, step through!

You arrive on the astral plane; the great world tree looms large in the distance. This time, take the temple path that lies before you. Down, down, down the path you tread, seeing the glowing light of your temple ahead. Smell the sweet scent of the temple incense burning, enticing you home.

You arrive at the door of your astral temple and enter. This sacred place is perfectly suited to your needs. The pure waters of Divine Love flow cool and refreshing from your place of water. The breeze of divine inspiration blows gently through, sweet and fresh, from your place of air. The sacred flames of your Divine Will glow brightly from your place of fire. Find your way now to the heart of your temple, the earthen altar itself, broad and stable. Stand before your altar in strength.

On the altar several things are spread before you: a green candle, a pot of herbal incense, and a censer with hot coals prepared for your ceremony. Onto that hot coal, sprinkle some incense to call earth. As the smoke billows, aromas deepen your earthy connections.

Say aloud: *Welcome, plant spirits of elm and pine, copal and patchouli, honeysuckle … Open the way to the realms of earth. Aid me now with your powers!*

Upon the altar is a crystal or a stone. Pick up this stone and hold it in your receptive hand. Shift your attention to the surface of the stone in your hand and the way it feels against your skin. Sense the solidity of the stone. Note how cool or warm it is. How smooth or rough. Feel its structure. Feel its unyielding weight. Listen now as the stone teaches you its lessons of solidity and silence. (*Long pause.*)

There is no such thing as matter, only energy so dense as to be perceived. (*Pause.*) You are also made of energy; there is no difference between you and the edge of that stone. Tune your frequency to match the stone. Now, sink your mind deeply into the stone itself; push through the surface into the stone's crystalline structure; it sings a vibration. (*Pause.*)

Find the spaces between the matrix and push deeper into its molecules. Observe the pattern and order of this matrix. (*Pause.*)

Push deeper now into its atoms. Find vast open space. Find the pulse and the rhythm in the revolving of the electrons like a solar system. Deep, deep within find movement and infinite potential. (*Pause.*) Push deeper now, finding pure information. Deep, deep into the resonance of the stone. Everything vibrates. Listen now as the stone teaches you its lessons of vibration and resonance. (*Pause.*)

Pull your attention back now, back the way you came, through electron, atom, molecule, matrix, back to feel the edge of the stone against your fingers—separate once more. Lay the stone back upon your altar.

Now, pick up your green candle and hold it in your projective hand. Remember that connection to the material realm all around you. Channel that earthy power through your hands into the candle to awaken the earth of that wax to its power. Tap upon the glass three times until you see it glowing green in your mind's eye. Now light the green candle.

The light of the temple deepens; shadows play against dappled light like a forest floor. The very marrow of your bones awakens; your vision lengthens as you sense a shift; the powers of the earth are rumbling nearby.

In your mind's eye face the northern quarter of your temple. Hold your open palms parallel to the ground, sturdy as the bedrock.

With power in the voice, say aloud: *Powers of earth! You who are toil, resistance, and form. I call upon your elemental beings called gnomes and seek to know your sovereign, Ghob! Stabilize and give me substance. Grant me entrance into your earthy realms! Open the portal and show me the way!*

A gateway in the north appears. See it clearly as you approach the gate; symbols or images adorn the frame. Remember them. (*Pause.*)

You hear the sounds of a living forest or jungle beyond the gate. Growing, scurrying life teeming, the damp of moist soil, of decay and blossom. (*Pause.*)

Shimmering green energy pours through the gateway and fills your auric field. Crystalline facets form around the edge of your aura. You are protected like a miner's safety gear. Your density shifts with your auric vibration as it resonates with essence of earth.

Touch the gateway and it shimmers open. Step forward through the portal to land gently on a soft dirt path in a dark woodland. Take in the details of this lush environment. Hear the buzz and click of hidden insects, the scratch and chirp of creatures among the rustling foliage, the creak and timbre of trees in the breeze. The vitality of the earth infuses you in silence and awe. (*Pause.*)

The crystalline edge of your aura forms a lens. Through this lens you now see the interconnections within this ecosystem: behold the matrix of all life. Looking closer now, you also see the creatures of elemental earth—beings known as gnomes are drawing around you now. They peek from behind the rocks and leaves. How do they present themselves to you? (*Pause.*)

These keepers of essential earth show you how every being of this ecosystem works together. Illustrating the story of how the light of the sun, air, minerals, and waters are passed as energy to create all life here on Earth. Receive the vision. (*Long pause.*)

Follow the gnomes down the path deeper into their realm and experience the interweaving... in perfect balance of birth, growth, procreation, death, decay, and rebirth. Follow them now... (*Long pause.*)

The gnomes bring you to the mouth of an opening in the earth. This opening takes you deep into their underground realms, where their sovereign, Ghob, will meet you in an audience chamber. The way downward is lit with a phosphorescence so that it is easy to see. With the gnomes as your guides, you are safe. Follow them down the phosphorescent path deep into the cool, dark rock. (*Pause.*)

There is a sparkle all about, and the shining veins of gold, silver, and copper lead you into a large open cavern. Look around … there are structures of shimmering crystals, majestic stone formations. What do they look like? (*Pause.*)

By singing aloud an intonation of Ghob's name, we set a resonant vibration by which to summon the sovereign to their chamber. In a deep tone, sing "Ghob" on three long, sustained breaths. Take a deep breath in … Chant aloud: *Ghob … Ghob … Ghob …* (*Pause.*)

The collective consciousness of earthy essence gathers from the surrounding rock and coalesces as the sovereign of earth. Ghob appears before you. Introduce yourself. Remember all the details of their appearance for you. (*Pause.*)

You ask aloud: *Ghob! I seek your guidance along my path of personal sovereignty in life!* Ghob shares their wisdom with you now … (*Long pause.*)

You ask aloud: *Ghob, please teach me your lessons of silence. How best should I hold the space of mindful presence in my life?*

Ghob invites you on a journey to learn their power of silence. (*Long pause.*)

You ask aloud: *Ghob, please teach me the lessons of resonance. How best do I set a frequency within the void of potential? What should I manifest next for my highest good?*

Ghob invites you on a journey to learn the power of resonance … (*Long pause.*)

You ask aloud: *Ghob, will you partner with me in my magick?* (*Pause.*)

If yes, you ask Ghob aloud: *Which altar tool of earth would best summon the powers of gnomes and elemental earth to my Great Work? Perhaps a pentacle, paten, or besom?* Ghob now presents you with that tool. Take in the details of this tool very carefully. (*Pause.*) You are shown where and how you might obtain this tool in the Middleworld. Receive the vision. (*Pause.*)

You ask Ghob: *Which stone, crystal, or metal will best aid my balance of sovereignty?* Ghob presents you with this gift and gives you a vision to help identify it clearly. (*Pause.*)

Accept these gifts and visions with gratitude as you bid Ghob farewell. Ghob dematerializes and is gone.

The gnomes now lead you back to the surface the way you came. Higher and higher, you follow that phosphorescent path. Back to the cave opening, back into the forest. Bid the gnomes farewell, and they, too, camouflage once again and are obscured from your sight.

Back to the gate, returning to your temple, step back through that portal, and the green crystalline shield is shed behind you, reabsorbed by the realms of earth. Your vibration shifts and lightens to your normal state.

Step back to your altar. Placing your gifts of tool and stone upon the altar, you remember the lessons with perfect clarity. Take a moment to reflect on all that you've learned, remembering that you can return to your temple and the gates of earth whenever you wish.

Now it is time to return to the Middleworld. Leaving through the temple door, following the path back. Back, back the way you came, seeking out the looking glass, that portal back into your body. See your body through the looking glass. When you pass through this portal you will once more follow the umbilical cord back into your own belly. In three steps, three, two, one, step through!

From those crossroads in your center, ascend the spiral stairway, rising higher and higher, twelve steps to waking consciousness. Emerging back into the meditation room in your mind and closing the ornate door in the floor behind you.

Say aloud: *I am grateful to my guides, gods, and ancestors—all those who kept me safe and showed me the way. Blessèd Be.* Stretch your muscles. Move to the window of your eyes, and then open them to find your outer temple awaiting.

Journal Reflection

In your Book of Mirrors, record the messages from your allies, draw your visions, and explore your thoughts and feelings about the experience. When finished, deconstruct your temple.

Deconstructing the Temple

Close the elemental gateway, by standing to face the north in the posture of earth, natural athame raised in salute.

Say aloud: *Powers of the north! Essence of earth! Gnomes and Sovereign Ghob! I am grateful for your sturdy presence and aid in these rites. Continue to strengthen my body and Great Work along the path of sovereignty. For now, I release you to your fair and earthy realms. Hail and farewell!*

See the green girder and all powers receding back through the gateway of your circle. Draw the banishing earth pentagram with your natural athame, like a key in the lock. As you encircle the star widdershins, see the portal closing and locking.

Once more kiss your athame or fingers, but this time follow through like a fencer with a thrusting gesture toward the quarter, brandishing your blade with fierce resolve. Direct any remaining energy outward to their realm.

Release the circle by gathering the sphere into your hands, smaller and smaller until it is imagined like a glowing ball over the altar. Charge the ball to further light your way along the Pentacle Path. Shout, *Release!* as you toss the sphere upward to the cosmos, clapping your hands, and say, *The circle is open, but never broken, Merry meet, merry part, and merry meet again.*

Magick of Sovereignty

With your newly made alliances with elemental earth, plan a holistic abundance and success spell to help you attain your physical goals and sovereignty. This ritual awakens your connection to the vast source of cosmic power already flowing through you. The end result of this magick is a shifting of perspective from the finite material illusion to the infinite resonance of potential. Through this spell, claim your phenomenal powers and tap into earthy abundance and pleasure as you create your ideal sovereign life.

✤ Spell 1: I Am the Magick ✤

This spell of sovereign abundance creates a charm pouch you'll wear to harmonize the seven chakras and the five bodies as aligned with the elements. Be mindful to select small enough materials that they will all fit in the bag you choose. It doesn't take much, substitute as needed.

Planetary Influences
Earth, Saturn, and Venus

Auspicious Timing
On a Friday or Saturday during a waxing moon phase close to full in Taurus, Virgo, or Capricorn.

Needs
Bowl of salt, earth oil, earth incense with censer, charcoal round, and tools

Dedication and elemental earth candles

A small, lightweight leather pouch or bag to hold all your ingredients with a draw-string top that can be easily worn with you daily

3 inches x 9 inches square of paper

A pen in black, brown, or green ink

For the charm bag, you need 9 items total, one for each of the 9 main chakras feeding the Witch's Jewel of Power

Spirit Body

   Goddess, earth star chakra: jet (earth, Saturn)

   God, soul star chakra: wooden matchstick (fire)

   Crown Chakra: clear quartz or amethyst (spirit)

Physical Body

   Root Chakra: acorn from an oak tree (earth, Jupiter, sun)

   Sacral Chakra: copper penny (Venus, water)

Body of the Will

   Solar Plexus Chakra: small iron or steel nail or hematite stone

Emotional Body

   Heart Chakra: rose quartz or rose petals (Venus, water)

Mental Body

   Throat Chakra: star anise pod (air, Jupiter)

   Third Eye Chakra: lapis lazuli (Venus, air)

A small stick match. This spark of fire brings the other ingredients "to life" as a talismanic entity. Author Orion Foxwood first introduced me to this Southern Conjure technique. Like Dr. Frankenstein assembling parts of his creation, when he throws that switch of electricity, that is when his creation comes to magickal life.

Praxis

Set, awaken, and consecrate your altar. Hallow yourself by the four elements as taught in ritual 1. Anoint your seven chakras with the earth oil.

Cast your circle. Open the gateway to elemental earth and call upon Ghob and gnomes to help build your sovereignty through material resources.

Invite to be present your guides, ancestors, and spirit. Calling the goddess Venus and god Saturn are appropriate if you are comfortable doing so. Ask for their aid in building your orderly, disciplined, and pleasurable life in the Middleworld.

On the paper, write a statement of intention in black, brown, or green ink.

For example: *I [your name] call upon the God/dess to aid my sovereign abundance and balance, to source my control, authority, and security from within my divine interconnections. Powers of Earth, Venus and Saturn, manifest my goals of [list your goals]. For the highest good of all involved, harming none. So mote it be!* Add the glyphs of earth, Venus, and Saturn. With your middle finger (Saturn), dab a drop of earth oil on each corner of the paper while chanting the following charm:

> *Source below to source above,*
> *Wills aligned with Perfect Love,*
> *My needs are met abundantly.*
> *By Venus's ease and Saturn's authority,*
> *I claim my personal sovereignty.*
> *Open channel, earth flow through me,*
> *I am the magick, so mote it be!*

At each step of the spell to follow, hold the material and shift your consciousness into it, just like you connected to the stone during the earth journey meditation. Repeat the affirmations in sets of three. Build a cadence and power in the voice. Sing them if that feels right. When the connection feels complete, end with "I am the magick" stated with authority, then drop the item into the pouch.

Connect to the jet and say: *Through the Goddess, I grow compassionately.* (x3) *I am the magick.*

Connect to the acorn and say: *Through earth, I grow abundantly.* (x3) *I am the magick.*

Connect to the copper and say: *Through Venus, I live pleasurably.* (x3) *I am the magick.*

Connect to the iron or hematite and say: *Through fire, I act with integrity.* (x3) *I am the magick.*

Connect to the rose quartz or petals and say: *Through water, I love unconditionally.* (x3) *I am the magick.*

Connect to the star anise and say: *Through air, I speak authentically.* (x3) *I am the magick.*

Connect to the lapis lazuli and say: *Through spirit, I perceive with clarity.* (x3) *I am the magick.*

Connect to the clear quartz or amethyst and say: *Through Saturn, I'm crowned in sovereignty.* (x3) *I am the magick.*

Carefully hold your pouch open with your thumb and pointer finger in a ring around its top, but do not grasp the bag with your remaining fingers or you could get burned in this tricky next part.

Connect to the wooden match and say: *By the God's celestial fires, ignite…* (x3)

Lighting it by your spirit candle, as it flares into light, say with authority: *I am the magick!*

With a dramatic flourish, jam the match entirely into the bag and pinch the top of the bag shut to snuff it out. (This is part of why I prefer leather spell bags—less flammable.) Leave the matchstick in the bag.

Roll the intention paper tightly and add it to the pouch.

Draw the strings closed, holding the mouth of the bag near your own lips, blowing your breath into the bag; chant: *I am the magick!* repeating many times as a power-raising mantra until you feel it is completely done and all the powers are soaked into the pouch. Use the volume of your voice to build power, whispering at first, getting louder, then softening the volume back to a whisper again.

Knot the bag's drawstring closed with nine knots, each time chanting: *By my sovereign authority, as I so will, so mote it be!*

Regularly add a drop of elemental earth oil to the top of the bag to feed it.

Tuck the pouch near your heart. Putting it on a long cord so that it is worn around the neck is my preferred way to carry such things or tucked into a bra or pocket, as Witches do.

Deconstruct your temple widdershins as previously instructed, closing the earth gateway and bidding farewell to God/dess and spiritual allies; charge and release the temple sphere to light your path. Clean up and know the work is done. Release all expectation of the outcome while remaining open to infinite possibility.

❧ Journal Reflection: The Path of Sovereignty ❧

After you wrap up the work with the powers of earth, take time to complete the elemental reflection below in your Book of Mirrors. Remember that there are no wrong answers in a journal entry. The point is to think about things deeply and record those thoughts and feelings for your future Self to find. The following framework for critical thinking is based on the Witch's Jewel of Power mysteries and can spark your process, giving you sacred permission to question everything you've learned. If it works for you, apply this framework to all your journal reflections.

From Air: To Know and to Wonder

- What impactful thing have you learned from this lesson?
- What do you still wonder about that needs further exploration?

From Fire: To Will and to Surrender

- How did you apply your will to these exercises? Did you adapt them to make them your own? What worked or didn't work well for you?
- Was there any expectation, assumption, or fear that needs to be surrendered?

From Water: To Dare and to Accept

- What gut emotional reactions came up for you?
- What surprised you? Which were easy to accept?
- Which do you dare to challenge or overcome?

From Earth: To Be Silent and to Resonate

- Now that the work is done, pay attention to what is going on in your life. How has this work affected your perceptions, actions, dreams? What patterns emerge?
- In what practical ways will you resonate your new awareness into reality?

Chapter 13
Element of Air and the Path of Truth

We continue our Elemental Witchcraft practices after the Sabbat of Imbolc, exploring the path of truth through the elemental air mysteries. This chapter's lessons are divided into two parts: During the 6.5 weeks of the waning Ostaratide, we'll explore the projective elemental mystery *to know*. During the 6.5 weeks of the waxing Beltanetide, we'll explore the receptive elemental mystery *to wonder*.

The Great Work: Wheel of the Year

While we tread the path of truth, there are three ritual workings to complete, which may be timed to the three lunar tides that crest within this solar period:

1. Crafting formulary materials for air rituals and spells.

2. Taking a ritual journey to the realms of elemental air.

3. Performing a two-part spell with planetary Saturn and Mercury for expression of your personal truths.

Ostaratide: Imbolc to Ostara

From Imbolc to Ostara, begin the airy mental investigation of your Elemental Witchcraft dedication for this year. Build upon your earthy foundation laid in the last chapter, and use that stability to explore the intellectual world, shifting into air's projective mysteries of *knowing*. This is a good time to dive deeply into complimentary texts on subjects that may have sparked your interest along the way. Check out my suggestions for further reading at the end of the book. Do more research about what is already known, thought, and believed to be true about Elemental Witchcraft. Ask a lot of questions and seek out established answers. Read the chapter's lessons, do the exercises, and then prepare your air magick sanctuary candle and the formulary goodies needed for the rituals ahead.

Beltanetide: Ostara to Beltane

From Ostara until Beltane, throw open the mental windows and let in the receptive breeze of airy *wonderment*. All those facts you just researched? Don't take everything at face value! The very definition of "occult" is that there are hidden meanings beneath the surface of the obvious. Question "the way things have always been" in your Witchcraft, beliefs, or life in general, and seek a fresh perspective based on all that you've learned. This is the time for experimentation. Shortly after Ostara, while the waxing moon is in an air sign, take the ritual journey to the realms of air, seeking alliance with the sylphs and Sovereign Paralda, guidance about the correct tool of air for you, and a plant spirit guide to aid your mental balance. Then as before, you'll seek out or begin crafting your tool of air to continue your magick. Apply what you've learned to enact the two-part spells of Saturn's reckoning and Mercury's truth.

The Pentacle Path of Truth and the Mental Body		
Chakras	Throat chakra	Third eye chakra
Regulates	Communication	Perception

The Pentacle Path of Truth and the Mental Body		
Opened by	Divine Mind	Divine Mind
Blocked by	Deception	Illusion, delusion
Witchcraft Goal	Expressing personal truth	Discerning individual belief
Love Conditions	Expression vs. fear of disenfranchisement	Authenticity vs. fear of exploitation
Charm of Affirmation	By the powers of air and fire, my voice is strong, my truth admired.	By the One Who Moves as Two, my vision is clear and divinely imbued.

Mysteries of Elemental Air

Elemental air forms our mental body and governs thought, communication, and knowledge. It is associated with education, language, speech, analysis, and philosophy. Air rules the sense of *smell*, which is one reason elemental air is engaged with incense smoke. In Hermetic alchemy, elemental air is thought to have a hot and wet nature and a primarily masculine mental gender; however, along this polarity's relative spectrum, air holds a gentler, gender fluidity.

Air Through the Zodiac

In relation to the life cycle and zodiac, air's power is expressed through mutable Gemini as the inquisitive human child, continuously turning over every rock, testing every boundary, asking a thousand times why and how? Gemini expresses as the lessons of "I think." They are here to teach others that love is about awareness while learning that love is feeling. Later, air emerges through cardinal Libra, expresses as the lessons of "I balance" by exploring partnerships. Libra is here to teach others that love is beautiful while learning that love is harmonious. Finally, the fixed Aquarius expresses the lessons of "I know" through an exploration of idealism. Aquarius is here to teach others that love is tolerant while learning that love is about unity.[223]

---

223. Goodman, *Linda Goodman's Love Signs*, 13.

Witch's Jewel of Power: Air		
	Yang: projective	**Yin: receptive**
Mystery Teaching	To know	To wonder
Wheel of Year	Imbolc through Ostara	Ostara through Beltane
Planetary Sphere	Jupiter	Mercury

Witch's Jewel of Power: To Know

To know is the projective power of elemental air. Knowing represents the acquisition of rational understanding of the world around you. The first step to solving any problem is to know what the problem is. It is the same with the magick of personal transformation. People who get stuck on whatever it is *they think they know* may become too rigid and fearful to even consider an alternate possibility.

From our Hermetic paradigm, if the cosmos is created from Divine Mind (Nous) and is primarily mental, knowing takes on unique significance. It is within the mysteries of knowing that we must collect data, discern what is true, and analyze our beliefs based on those truths so as to remove the blinders that limit how we perceive our reality. For this reason, it is critical that magickal practitioners study the science, philosophy, and thealogy that form the underpinnings of their magick. Without knowing the possibilities and how things actually work, we are left with blind faith, superstition, and empty religiosity. These leave us powerless, vulnerable, and dependent on an outside authority.

Witch's Jewel of Power: To Wonder

To wonder is the receptive power of elemental air, and the polar opposite of knowing. Wonder is the relinquishing of preconceived ideas with an open mind. It is experiencing the wisdom that emerges when you release caring about the opinions and the judgments of outsiders and smash the dusty altars of convention to adapt and evolve. In wonderment we can discover a revealed and personal truth.

Wonderment allows one to think "outside the box," which threatens to stagnate creativity. It is wonderment that compels advancement both personally and societally, sparking ingenuity and innovation. These are where invention begins. The receptive air of curiosity is what precedes a scientific inquiry and provides the necessary inspiration to even attempt magick for change. Perhaps the nine Greek muses actually are airy elementals of wonder!

In our society, those people who were most tapped into wonderment are the heroes we laud today. Many of them are well-known because they were persecuted, arrested, or murdered as heretics by the fear-bound fundamentalists of their time: Galileo Galilei, Joan of Arc, Susan B. Anthony, Martin Luther King Jr., Mahatma Gandhi, Pythagoras, Paracelsus, Hypatia of Alexandria, Jesus of Nazareth, etc.[224] Each of them looked beyond common belief to wonder how the world might be better, if…

Cooperative Tools of the Goddess

To wonder is the receptive (goddess) power of elemental air and so holds the cooperative lessons needed to progress our culture toward a better future. In our yin-yang analogy, this spot of the goddess side of the air polarity is the keyhole to unlocking true mental power and balance. It is through the powers of wonderment that we can reexamine the programs of powerlessness installed by the dominator culture and discover our personal truths so we can each take back our own authority and then work together to solve societal problems as equals.

The Path of Truth

What is truth? What one believes to be true or thinks is true is a matter of perspective. To even construct that last sentence, the words "believe" and "think" were necessary. Both bring us back to functions of the mental body, which are the domains of elemental air.

The *Hermetic Principle of Mentalism* states: "The All is MIND; The Universe is Mental."[225] If the transcendent consciousness of an embodied cosmos is the *Divine Mind* of God/dess, we could poetically describe God/dess as thinking themself into being. They dream of swirling galaxies and solar systems; dreams of ecosystems, bees seeking nectar, the way roots hold the soil, and flowers lean into sunbeams; dreams of electrons spinning within atoms, molecules bonding; dreams of gods and goddesses, of heroes, villains, and

---

224. Albert Van Helden, "Galileo," Encyclopedia Britannica, updated February 19, 2021, https://www .britannica.com/biography/Galileo-Galilei; Hall, *Secret Teachings*, 65, 150; John G. Hargrave, "Paracelsus." Encyclopedia Britannica, updated January 14, 2021. https://www.britannica.com/biography /Paracelsus.

225. Atkinson, *The Kybalion*, 64.

monsters. The Divine Mind holds beautiful utopian fantasies and nightmares of dysto-
pian destruction; all are within the infinite possibility of God/dess. Everything we hold
to be relatively "true" and "real" are thoughts, affected by thought, the effects of thoughts;
"the Universe is Mental." [226]

In this cosmic poem, humans would be a divine thought, too, and we are thinking with
our own spark of Divine Mind. Through our thoughts (mental), feelings (emotional), and
sensations (physical), we have the sentience to integrate all this information (spirit) and
respond with purpose and power (will). This is because we *know* who we are and where
we fit within the grander scheme of things. Witches uniquely realize that we are both the
dreamer and the dream.

The Truth Paradox: Absolute vs. Relative

In *The Kybalion: A Hermetic Philosophy*, a teaching about truth emerges from the *Hermetic Principle of Polarity*, which states "all truths are but half-truths; all paradoxes may
be reconciled."[227] Hermeticists call this the "divine paradox" between the absolute and
relative truths.[228] If everything in the universe is a dream within the Divine Mind and
our material separateness is an illusion, then we arrive at an absolute truth: the only
thing objectively "real" is the God/dess as a whole. Whatever God/dess knows would
be an ineffable, *absolute truth*. However, there must be the polar opposite side of truth
too. Everything humans understand to be "true" here in the Middleworld with our finite
minds and our best attempts at reasoning with mortal senses is a *relative truth*. What we
perceive to be relatively true is based on our point of perspective: what is obvious, touch-
able, provable, measurable?

For magick ever to become objectively "real," the Witch is reminded in *The Kybalion*
to "beware half-truths."[229] An example of this paradox of truth is in the relative illusion
of our material separateness, which is subject to time and impermanence, as opposed to
the absolute reality of our spiritual oneness within God/dess, immortal and infinite. This
may seem impossible to comprehend, but science presents us with a similar example

---

226. Atkinson, *The Kybalion*, 64
227. Atkinson, *The Kybalion*, 67.
228. Atkinson, chapter 6, in *The Kybalion*.
229. Atkinson, *The Kybalion*, 98.

in the structure of the atom. Matter, which humans perceive as being relatively solid and still, is scientifically affirmed to be mostly empty space, information, and forces that are in constant motion. Electrons are both particles and waves of potential.[230] Both are true at the same time in varying degrees. The paradox can be reconciled, but the mental flexibility we call wonderment allows us to consider more than one perspective at the same time. Embrace a subjective reality. Occult studies start with knowing the obvious, observable, scientifically describable *relative truth* of the Middleworld. Then they spiritually seek the hidden, opposite, *absolute truth* on the flip side of the obvious, or what I call *the is-ness*. From this balanced search for the whole truth, Witches derive our own beliefs, as revealed through the course of our practices.

Third Eye Chakra: Rethinking Belief

The Hindu chakra system aligns the heart chakra with elemental air, which makes sense in one context, as cardiopulmonary systems do regulate breathing. However, from the perspective of Hermetic alchemy, the endeavors of expression through speech, insight, and thought processes are aligned with the elemental powers of air. So, for balancing our mental bodies along the path of truth, we'll consider the lessons of the throat and third eye chakras. Through the throat chakra, consciousness emerges as an expression of our personal truth that we share outwardly through our speech, contributions, art, and personal style. But before we can express that truth, we need the insight of the third eye chakra to discern what that personal truth may be.

The third eye chakra, when opened, has clear perception of the truth of things but is blocked by illusion, or in many cases delusion. If you were raised within one of the invasive orthodoxies, you may have been taught that you are inherently flawed, sinful, and in need of salvation. The patriarchal, dominator paradigm installs that *external locus of control* program where everything that happens to us is either a blessing bestowed because we complied or a punishment inflicted because we disobeyed. If you like what you get, you remain indebted to that capricious source. If you don't like what you get, you remain the victim of that capricious source. Both are positions of powerlessness and

---

230. Described by the Double-Slit experiment; Glenn Stark, "Young's Double-Slit Experiment," in "Light," Encyclopedia Britannica, updated October 29, 2020, https://www.britannica.com/science/light/Youngs-double-slit-experiment.

enslavement. Both are delusions that hinder our own divine perception, personal truth, and authority, as well as deny our earthy sovereignty.

Belief is defined as an acceptance of something to be true, that it exists. Beliefs are the framework within which we process all other information and upon which we take action.[231] Therefore, carefully reconsidering one's truth and the beliefs we derive from that truth should be the first task of any magickal practitioner.

One's beliefs are like a computer's operating system, which is installed from birth by our culture. We are programmed by our parents, teachers, bullies, advertising, pop culture, and religious and political leaders. Every message we internalize becomes part of our root programming. Everything else we do in life runs from the platform of that operating system. Even if you eventually reject parts of your culture of origin, that program may still insidiously lurk in the background until you make purposeful changes. This will be challenging. If your base programming denied the possibility of magick, attempting magickal work is as pointless as trying to run a Mac program on a Window's operating system; you will waste a lot of time and energy hacking it, and the outcomes will be glitchy and problematic at best.

Witchcraft is a magickal operating system of wholeness, abundance, sovereignty, and empowerment, coded by the paradox of Divine Truth. The praxis can be a technical manual to help purge the old OS and carefully install a system that supports new spiritual goals. The Witching OS gets all your systems (physical, mental, will, emotional, and spiritual) working harmoniously together so that eventually anything is possible with a simple change of mind.

Exercise 6: Responding to Cognitive Dissonance in Twelve Steps

When new information or insights we receive are in conflict with the beliefs of our old operating program, a form of mental tension creeps in called *cognitive dissonance*. Cognitive dissonance is that anxious feeling we get when confronted with information that is contradictory to our beliefs. Perhaps new scientific evidence disproves a long-held theory, or a relative truth is being expressed by someone else that we've never considered.

231. Joyce Higginbotham and River Higginbotham, *Paganism: An Introduction to Earth-Centered Religions* (Woodbury, MN: Llewellyn Publications, 2007), 45–46.

Our hackles can raise, and offense, frustration, posturing, anger, and violence may result. Ridicule and condemnation are weapons of the fearful to belittle whatever, or whomever, challenges their base programming. Unfortunately, challenging the status quo causes fear for anyone who benefits from the old assumptions. Cognitive dissonance created by freethinkers too often shows up with pitchforks and torches, but we can't let that stop us from discovery and evolving into a better life. It takes significant inner strength to claim and live by our witching truth.

For Witches throughout history, merely living authentically can cause cognitive dissonance in those around us. But we are not immune to that inner conflict as we tread the path of truth. That tension of cognitive dissonance is a good sign that you are making progress. Congratulations! You've just discovered some bit of hidden programming, and this is your golden opportunity to work on it! Rather than reacting, take time to *respond*. This is magick of wonderment in twelve steps.

1. Recognize that there is some kind of problem causing cognitive dissonance.
2. Stop for a moment. As the "Rede of the Wiccae" poem advises, "… speak little, listen much."[232] Best not to fire off defensively or rampage on social media. Put your phone down.
3. Turn to face the challenge. Don't run away! Lean in and look closely. What is actually happening here? Have a face-to-face conversation with whomever else may be involved. Remember the fourth Rule of Personal Sovereignty: *must be present to win*. Listen carefully to the relative truth of the other person's perspective. Ask questions and listen some more. Consider their own right of personal sovereignty.
4. Now, pull way back and look for the bigger pattern in your own life. Has this issue come up before in other ways? Ask lots of questions of yourself. What assumptions are at play here? What bias, what privileges of personal experience impede the perspective of anyone involved? Consider these issues in light of your own right of personal sovereignty.

---

232. Mathiesen and Theitic, *The Rede of the Wiccae*, 52–53.

5. Feel all the feelings without censoring yourself. In your Book of Mirrors, name those feelings. Let them all flow through you and onto the page without judgment or analysis. All these yucky feelings on both sides of this dustup are valid, relatively speaking.

6. Consider the second Rule of Personal Sovereignty: *don't be the problem.* Which party's truths or actions upon those truths is actually the problem in this situation? Is it you? Seek higher guidance through divination, prayer, and meditation to access your own higher consciousness; seek the council of a wise friend, speak to your therapist, priest/ess, or both; make an appointment with a trusted astrologer or diviner for an unbiased reading to make sure it isn't you who've gone off the rails in this situation. Remember the third Rule of Personal Sovereignty: *don't be the weak link.*

7. Hold the space on all that you're discovering without rushing to judgment. Give it the time and attention necessary to undo a lifetime of brainwashing inflicted on everyone within this dominator culture. Cut yourself lots of slack because you are doing very difficult and noble shadow work right now. Remember the first Rule of Personal Sovereignty: *don't burn the Witch.*

8. Cut the other folks some slack because everyone in this dominator culture is traumatized in some way, and everyone who is wounded has lashed out irrationally at some time in some way. Don't burn the other "Witch" at the stake, either.

9. Pretend like you are stepping outside your own brain, watching from a distance as an observer. Which bit of dogma or *fear of a lack of love* is being challenged in this situation? Is that idea even consistent with the rest of your witching paradigm? Or is that a remnant program of an invasive orthodoxy still attempting to control through fear, shame, or guilt?

10. Now, what kind of witching person do you want to be? What kind of life do you want to live? What kind of world do you want to create to bring the most happiness and mutual respect to the most people? Without considering blame or punitive consequences, what next step would actually solve the original problem for all parties?

11. Now, respond appropriately. Can diplomacy find a truce, even if actual peace isn't yet possible? This is not always the same thing as "making nice." Some-

times the solution is disengaging, walking away, and defending your sovereign boundaries at a distance you define. Sometimes that means taking an offensive position and stopping baneful behaviors through intervention, legal action, magickal binding, or the like. What would Divine Love do?

12. To follow up, personally express both the tension and the revised truths you're discovering in some creative way that affirms the growth you've just made: poetry, art, dance, song—make something real and shareable to reflect your realization. *That* discovery is what you can share on your social media feed (or wherever.) This will anchor that idea in a way that reaffirms it for you concretely, using the powers of earth to help balance those of air.

Throat Chakra: Expressing Your Truth

The throat chakra is all about speaking your truth, feeling free to authentically be yourself, and share that openly through all forms of expression: speech, art, dance, how you wear your hair, adorn your body, your personal style, and how you live your life. These are all methods by which we share what is true for each of us. The throat chakra is blocked by lies—even lies of omission. Have you been wounded by the lack of authenticity or acceptance from the world? The throat chakra clamps down and feels like a lump in the throat when we don't feel safe to say or be what we feel.

Redefining your relative truths about the cosmos, yourself, and your capabilities is a process of releasing the fears and limitations of others. Ultimately, it is a natural process of growing up. Fearfully obeying the will of outside authorities is the infantilized mentality that the dominators of the patriarchy practically demand of us. Behaving maturely is a radical act of defiance.

After this reflection, you may find that there isn't much that needs adjusting in your belief system. Your relative truths may already be correct for you and in alignment with your goals. The purpose of this path of truth is to regularly open your mind to the possibility that with more experience and discovery of new information, your relative truth may change over time. We develop mental flexibility by allowing assumptions to be challenged and analyzed. In this way, we just might hone our way closer to glimpsing flashes of absolute, divine truth and attaining enlightenment. This is a multiple-lifetimes-long process. The trick to sovereignty is that you get to decide what best fits for you. Trust your intuition.

✤ Exercise 7: Internalizing Your Locus of Control ✤

I've heard it said that the easiest thing to change is your mind. I beg to differ. It took me a decade to throw off the bindings of the "fear and admonition of the Lord" that dominated my childhood. But internally shifting your frame of mind from *victim* to *victor* can, and must, be done. In this exercise, begin by consciously thinking through and listing what is true and what old ideas need to be transmuted so you can internalize control over your life.

Step 1: Believe in Yourself

To begin, you have sacred permission to understand the world and yourself uniquely from anyone else you know. Choose to perceive the world and your place within it in a healthier and more empowered way than your ancestors ever dared to dream possible. It isn't disloyal to evolve beyond your parents' point of view. This is normal evolution, and it honors your ancestors to strengthen yourself. Believe that you are capable of making these necessary changes. In the culture dominated by the invasive orthodoxies, being saturated in notions of sin and damnation can cause self-defeating thoughts to rattle their chains in our minds like the ghosts of religions past! If deep down you worry that your humanity is somehow shameful, feeble, subordinate, and separate from God/dess, remember that this sorry vibration is anathema to our panentheist teaching of perfect wholeness. You are made of Divine Love; you are whole and complete in infinite, abundant connection to God/dess no matter what.

In your Book of Mirrors, list out what you think is relatively true about the cosmos, divinity, the purpose of life. What is good? What is admirable? How would life and society operate in your idea of the perfect world? Create a personal statement of truth describing your highest ideal. Now, describe your role within the cosmos and your part in achieving that ideal. How can your Witchcraft strive toward making that dream a reality for more people? List all of your admirable strengths that will help achieve that ideal. Reframe every quality in the affirmative, which can include things like, "I learn from my mistakes." Brag. Toot your own horn. Claim all your beauty and skills. Define the awesome Witch you already are and envision your most ideal future Self. Dream big.

Step 2: Internalizing Control

Now, list out ways you can take back the necessary control over your life to accomplish those ideals and become that powerful Witch you've envisioned. What power to change your circumstances do you hold right now? Remembering that you are a dreamer within the dreaming mind of an infinitely powerful God/dess, dream up a best-case scenario. Examples: I can decline this invitation to an argument. I can leave an oppressive relationship behind. Or, I can call this help line for assistance breaking an addiction.

We remain infantilized for as long as we perceive ourselves as being battered about by whims of outside forces. We must internalize the locus of control. There are no scapegoats in Witchcraft that we can blame; no "devil made me do it" as an excuse for the hateful or self-destructive choices you're making *right now*. If so, you're losing "the blame game." The blame game is a primary indicator of a disempowered, external locus of control. In the history of everything, there has never once been a winner of the blame game because both sides get burned at the metaphorical stake.[233]

Step 3: Break the Cycle

Finally, put into new practice your witching beliefs to achieve your ideals in the future. Breaking the cycle of enslavement begins with understanding that other people's wounds and the harm their wounded choices did to you were never actually about you. Abusive behavior tends to ripple out, like stones thrown in a mud puddle. They run in generational cycles, too, because wounded people learn how to wound more people. You have your own choices to make. It sucks, and it does not *excuse* the bad behavior of the dominators in our culture, but it can *explain it*. It's tough, but an explanation can return us to the compassion of Divine Love so we may detach and discover our own peace. Through this detachment, we may shift from the *victim* to *survivor* perspective and actually break the wounding cycle to become the *victor* in our story. To paraphrase an often-repeated nugget of perennial wisdom: "Hatred is like poisoning yourself and waiting for your enemy to die."[234] Transmute the poison into your own antidote; apply liberally.

---

233. Sue Mehrtens, "How to Internalize a Locus of Control, a Locus of Authority and a Locus of Security: A Follow-Up Essay," Jungian Center for the Spiritual Sciences, accessed April 30, 2020, https://jungiancenter.org/how-to-internalize-a-locus-of-control/.

234. Variations of this theme have been attributed to Emmet Fox and repeated by many wise people.

Figure 28: Candle wrap image for air by Heron Michelle

Formulary for Elemental Air

As the Ostaratide wanes toward the Spring Equinox, craft the magickal materials for the airy magick ahead. Craft your incense, oil, and air magick candle, referencing the table below for the elemental correspondences of air, and make substitutions as needed.[235]

---

235. I assembled these element correspondence charts from many sources, but a good reference is *Llewellyn's Complete Book of Correspondences* by Sandra Kynes.

Elemental Correspondences of Air	
Alchemical Symbol	△
Color	Yellow
State of Matter	Gaseous
Direction	East
Time of Day	Dawn
Phase of Life	Birth
Season	Spring
Alchemical Qualities	Warm and moist
Mental Gender	Yang, masculine, gender-fluid
Governs	Mental body: thought, communication, knowledge, wisdom, intellect, inspiration, liminal travel
Projective Power	The power to know
Receptive Power	The power to wonder
Elemental Beings	Sylphs
Elemental Sovereign	Paralda
Magickal Tool	Wand, staff, bell
Consecration	Incense smoke
Planetary	Mercury ☿, Uranus ♅, Jupiter ♃
Days of Week	Wednesday
Astrological Signs	Cardinal: Libra; fixed: Aquarius; mutable: Gemini
Stone	Quartz crystal (clear), citrine, ametrine, aragonite, moldavite, celestite, chrysoberyl, blue tourmaline, tree agate
Metals	Aluminum, mercury, tin
Herbs	Agrimony, bergamot, broom, clover, lavender, lemongrass, peppermint, spearmint, sage, mistletoe, star anise, Spanish moss, meadowsweet

Elemental Correspondences of Air	
Trees/Woods/Barks	Acacia, ash, birch, elm, hawthorn, hazel, linden, sycamore
Resins	Benzoin, copal
Creatures	Gazelle, condor, crow, falcon, raven, hawk, dragonfly, most birds

❧ Exercise 8: Air Formulary Crafting ❧

Auspicious Timing

Look at the time frame you have left until Ostara and pick a time during a waxing lunar cycle, preferably while the moon is in an air sign of Gemini, Libra, or Aquarius, and/or on the day/hour of Mercury (Wednesday).

Needs

See the recipes below for specific materials and equipment for each recipe.

Lay your working altar with enough surface area to spread out, make a mess, and be artistically creative.

Consecration elements, including charcoal in a censer for testing your incense blend. Add anything that aids your connection to air energies: feathers, chimes, etc.

Preparation

Awaken and consecrate your altar with the ritual 1 in chapter 9.

Call upon your spiritual guides to be present and inspire your magickal creations.

For charging any air-drawing materials, chant this charm:

Air Blessing Charm

Powers of air, of Paralda and sylphs!
By Mercury's flight and wing-ed swifts!
Come powers of truth and clarity,
As I will, so mote it be!

❧ Elemental Air Incense—Planetary Mercury Magick ❧

This incense recipe is effective for rebalancing the mental body and any journeys and spells where elemental powers of air or planetary Mercury would aid in manifesting your intention for knowledge, wonderment, communication, inspiration, clarity of thought, etc.

Needs

Mortar and pestle to grind and blend dry ingredients

2 parts base wood—birch bark powder (air)

2 parts resin—benzoin resin

½ part herb—star anise (air, Jupiter)

1 part herb—lavender (air, Mercury)

1 part lemongrass (air, Mercury)

Essential oils—10 drops each of lavender and lemongrass (optional)

2 parts vegetable glycerin to bind

Stones: citrine, yellow aventurine, or clear quartz

Dark-colored jar with lid and opening large enough for your incense spoon; amber brown glass is ideal

Praxis

In your mortar and pestle, grind with a deosil motion all plant ingredients until relatively fine. As you add each ingredient, invite their spirits to aid your airy work and thank them. Add the essential oil (optional) and glycerin, stir to combine and bind. Add stone chips of citrine or another substitute. Draw the alchemical sigil of air in the incense with your index finger or wand. Transfer the blend to the jar, then hold it in your hands.

Chant the air blessing charm three times and charge with the powers of air by picturing a high cliff at the top of the highest mountain peaks. The cold wind whips through; there are only clouds and blue sky above. See the natural energy glowing from that sky in the yellowish light from the east. Direct that light with your mind, like a wind blowing down through your hands, until you envision the blend also glowing yellow.

Label the jar, including the date and the glyph of alchemical air and planetary Mercury ☿ to continue charging. Burn some on your charcoal to test the scent and boost the airy signal while you keep working.

❧ Elemental Air Anointing Oil ❧

This oil may be used to anoint candles, yourself, or other magickal objects to bring them into sympathy with mental goals and any planetary Mercury magick.

Needs

Dark-colored 1-dram bottle with tightly sealing cap. Amber glass is ideal.

9 drops each of lavender and lemongrass essential oil

3 stone chips of citrine, clear quartz, or substitute

Jojoba oil or other carrier oil

Praxis

As you add each ingredient to the bottle, tap on the materials three times and awaken them to their powers of air: knowledge, wonderment, communication, inspiration. Invite their spirits to be part of your magickal team and thank them for all the inspiration they will help you achieve.

When all materials are assembled in the bottle, cap it and swirl the oils together deosil, and charge it with the visualization above. Chant the air blessing charge three times.

Label the bottle with the name, date, and alchemical glyphs of elemental air and planetary Mercury ☿ to continue charging. Anoint your third eye and throat chakra to further align your thoughts with air as you keep working.

❧ Elemental Air Candle ❧

In the same manner you prepared your dedication and earth candle, prepare a seven-day glass-jarred sanctuary candle to channel powers of elemental air.

Needs

Yellow seven-day sanctuary candle in glass jar. They are typically 2.25 x 8 inches tall and take refill insert candles no more than 2 inches wide.

The 7-inch square image from figure 28 can be copied and colored to create a candle wrap, or you may creatively decorate your own piece of lightweight paper.

13-inch length of yellow cord or ribbon

Flat head screwdriver or a power drill with large bit

½ teaspoon prepared air herbal incense

3 drops prepared air anointing oil

3 tiny chips of citrine, clear quartz, or other stone variety (see table for options)

Praxis

On the blank side of the 7-inch square candle wrap paper, write an air gateway opening call. Compose your own or reference the calls provided in ritual 2. If you're not using the image provided in figure 28, decorate the outside of the wrapper with images of elemental air, such as birds, wand or staff, sylphs, feathers, alchemical air glyph, planetary glyph for Mercury ☿, etc.

With the flat head screwdriver or drill, bore out three holes in the wax about an inch deep. Load the candle by poking the air incense into the holes with a chopstick. Top with a stone chip in each hole. Then anoint with three drops of air oil and rub it around the wax deosil with a bare finger.

Wrap the paper wrapper around the jar and tie down with the cord or ribbon. The charging of this candle will take place during the ritual journey to realms of elemental air.

Journey to the Realms of Air

In the same manner as done for the journey to earth, this interactive ritual merges the performance of ritual actions in the outer temple, with a meditative journey which takes place within your astral temple, imagined within the mind's eye. This functional high-alpha brainwave state is called "ritual consciousness."[236] When prompted, intone or speak aloud, light candles, throw incense on the coals, etc. The ritualized journey is

236. Penczak, *Inner Temple of Witchraft*, 87.

best enacted by listening to a recording of the meditation or as someone reads it aloud for you.

✤ Ritual 5: Elemental Air Temple ✤

Our ritual cycle continues by calling the essence of air from the eastern quarter and then taking a guided journey through your astral temple to the airy elemental plane. The goal is to seek partnership with the sylphs and their sovereign, Paralda, receive insights about the magickal tools of air for you, and which plant allies may best aid your path of truth. This temple will be opened solely for air. This experience is most poignant when enacted outside in nature, where you can breathe the fresh air, feel the breeze, and hear the birds in song. High mountaintops are said to be the dwelling places of sylphs. If that isn't possible, indoors will suffice … hopefully you can open a window and set up a fan to blow!

Auspicious Timing
During the second lunar cycle closest to the Spring Equinox, during a waxing lunar phase when the moon is in an air sign: Gemini, Libra, or Aquarius.

Needs
Prepare your altar for air adding any items that evoke airy presence for you: a yellow tablecloth, images of birds, feathers, etc.

Consecration element: offering for the sylphs of burning incense in a censer with sand and a hookah charcoal tab, tongs, small spoon, and a lighter or box of matches

Air herbal incense blend

Air anointing oil

Dedication candle for Spirit

Prepared yellow air candle with yellow cord or ribbon

A feather from a bird large enough to easily hold in your hand[237]

Your Book of Mirrors and a pen

Diagrams of air invoking and banishing pentagrams for easy reference. See figure 24.

---

237. Be advised that it is illegal to possess feathers of birds protected by the Migratory Bird Treaty Act of 1918 (16 U.S.C. 703–712, MBTA), https://www.fws.gov/lab/featheratlas/feathers-and-the-law.php.

An athame if you already have one or just your "natural athame" of the index and middle fingers of your projective hand

Device for playing a recording of the guided journey

Preparation

Begin with a physical cleaning of the ritual space. Bathe and dress in fresh, comfortable clothing, preferably barefoot with hair unbound, or nude as you prefer.

Lay your working altar before you, arranged such that you can meditate comfortably and still reach everything easily.

Anoint yourself with air oil at the throat chakra where your collarbones meet and your third eye chakra on your forehead.

Light your dedication candle to welcome Spirit, who is ever-present.

Light the charcoal and place in the censer in preparation for loose incense burning.

Praxis

Altar Consecration: Light your dedication candle, then awaken and consecrate your altar as taught in ritual 1. Shift consciousness into your branches high in the atmosphere. Breathe deeply and establish the flow of power connecting you to the three realms. Inhale that power as yellow light; exhale it through your projective hand. Hold the jar of incense blend in that hand. Visualize yellow light drawn down from wind to imbue the incense. Say: *I charge this incense as a being of air.* Scoop a teaspoon of incense on the hot charcoal in the censer. As the smoke rises, draw the banishing pentagram of air in the smoke over the altar.

Say: *Powers of air, blow free any impurity from this sacred space.* Envision a yellow energy imbuing the altar.

Hallowing: Walk the perimeter of your circle with the burning incense, wafting and chanting aloud: *I consecrate this circle by the powers of air.* Present the incense to the eastern quarter and say, *As your Witch of air, I greet you with air and ask that you blow free any baneful energies from this circle tonight. So mote it be!*

Temple: Cast your circle with the awen cone of power as taught in ritual 2; close the sphere above and below.

Open the Eastern Gate: As taught in ritual 2, face east. Stand in a posture of air evocation.

Exhale and see yellow light of air beaming from your projective hand. Your receptive hand is prepared to receive that inflowing energy. Stand tall, chin up, shoulders back; speak with authority from the diaphragm.

Say: *Powers of the east! Essence of air! I summon you to this sacred place! Sylphs! Sovereign Paralda of the windy reaches! Be with me now and lend your powers of wisdom, imagination, and communication. Open my mind! Awaken your lessons of knowing and wonderment within me. Come wings of flight and mountain height. Come golden dawning, breezes light and laughter lifting, to focus and inspire this magick. I welcome you with gratitude. Hail and welcome!*

Draw the invoking pentagram of air with the natural athame of your projective hand. See the star glowing with yellow light in the air of the eastern quarter. Encircle the pentagram deosil, turning the lock to open. Draw your fingers toward your lips, pulling in a streamer of elemental air. Kiss your fingers, then with hand over your heart, bow to that direction. A yellow girder now encircles your temple in the east.

Sit down and prepare for meditation. Begin the recording of this guided journey.

❧ Meditation 6: Guided Journey to the Realms of Air ❧

Close your eyes; take a deep breath. Picture your most magickal Self sitting in a comfortable chair in a comfortable room inside your mind. It is quiet and still in your mental sanctuary. Your eyes are now a window on a distant wall of that room. Any distracting noises or stray thoughts are merely birds flying past that distant window … release them without care. (*Pause.*)

There is a skylight above you, and a soft beam of divine light shines down upon your crown chakra. Breathe down the light with three deep breaths. Inhale through the nose and exhale through the mouth … releasing all tension. (*Pause for three breaths.*) You are at perfect ease on all levels. (*Pause.*)

There is a beautiful, ornate door in the floor of your meditation room, a door leading to all possibility. Open that door, finding a spiral staircase descending beyond. With each exhale of your breath, step down, deeper and deeper, descending into your subconscious mind, and deep into your own belly. At the foot of the stairs, you'll arrive at your inner crossroads. Twelve steps down, around and 'round you tread the spiral staircase.

Before you there hangs a looking glass, a portal outward to the astral realms where all things are possible by a mere thought. Picture your Astral Temple upon the glass. (*Pause.*)

Say: *My intention is to journey to my astral temple to seek the elemental plane of air to learn the mysteries of knowing and wonder. I tread the path of truth, seeking a relationship with the beings who govern the essence of air known as sylphs and their sovereign, Paralda. I wish to receive my tool of air and allies of plant or tree to aid my mental balance. I call upon my guides, gods, and ancestors to keep me safe and show me the way. Blessèd be.* (*Pause.*)

On the count of three, step through the portal and arrive on the path to your temple. One, two, three, step through!

You arrive on the astral plane; the great world tree looms large in the distance. This time, take the temple path that lies before you. Down, down, down the path you tread, seeing the glowing light of your temple ahead. Smell the sweet scent of the temple incense burning, enticing you home.

You arrive at the door of your astral temple and enter. This sacred place is perfectly suited to your needs. The pure waters of Divine Love flow cool and refreshing from your place of water. The breeze of divine inspiration blows gently through, sweet and fresh, from your place of air. The sacred flames of your Divine Will glow brightly from your place of fire. Find your way now to the heart of your temple, the earthen altar itself, broad and stable. Stand before your altar in strength.

On the altar several things are spread before you: a yellow candle, a feather, a pot of herbal incense, and a censer with hot coals prepared for your ceremony. Onto that hot coal, sprinkle some incense to call air. As the smoke billows and your sense of smell is stimulated, your airy connections are deepened.

Say aloud: *Welcome, spirit of benzoin and lavender; open the way to the realm of air. Aid me with your powers!* (*Pause.*)

Upon the altar is a feather. Pick up this feather and hold it in your receptive hand.

Shift your attention to the surface of the feather and the way it feels upon the skin of your fingers. Envision the bird soaring through the air with this feather. Reach out with your consciousness just beyond that soft feather to feel the wind.

Air is the invisible realm that magickally supports the visible realm. As you breathe in, you breathe in a connection to the past. This atmosphere has been here since the beginning. Your ancestors breathed this air. As you breathe, let this air be your guide. Place the feather back upon the altar.

Pick up your yellow candle in your projective hand. Remember that connection to the air and channel all this power through your hands into the candle. Tap the glass three times, picturing its consumption of oxygen in flame, until you see it glowing yellow in your mind's eye. Now light the yellow candle.

The light of the temple shifts to golden and opens the mind further, vision lengthening. Your breath stirs as you sense a shift; the powers of air begin to blow nearby. (*Pause.*) In your mind's eye, face the eastern quarter of your temple. Raise your hands to shoulder height, palms outward, fingers splayed like a tree with your branches flowing.

With power in the voice, say aloud: *Powers of air! You who are thought, communication, and intellect! I call upon your elemental beings called sylphs and seek to know your sovereign, Paralda. Open my mind to new possibilities! Grant me entrance into your airy realms! Open the portal and show me the way!*

A gateway in the east appears. See it clearly as you approach the gate; symbols or images adorn the frame. Remember them. (*Pause.*)

You hear sounds of a howling wind and bird call beyond the gate, the flap of wings and branches rustling, the scent of fragrant smoke upon the air. (*Pause.*)

Golden energy pours through the gateway and fills your auric field. Feathered wisps form around the edge; you are protected, like a flight suit. Your density lightens as it resonates with essence of air. Light as the breeze itself, with a thought, you can fly.

Touch the gateway and it shimmers opens. Fly forward through the gate to set gently down on rocky cliffs high in the atmosphere. It is dawning. Take in the details of this environment. Feel the cool wind as it blows. (*Pause.*)

The golden edge of your aura forms a lens. Through this lens you can see so much more. From the wind itself, the sylphs emerge in a flock of fluttering, winged flight. They surround and lift you up. How do they present themselves to you? (*Pause.*)

Take flight with them; as easy as thought, ride the wind with the sylphs wherever imagination takes you. They show you how their powers create the world. Fly with them and open your mind to possibilities. Receive the vision. (*Long pause to journey.*)

The sylphs bring you to a beautiful place within their airy realm, and you land gently where you may have an audience with their sovereign, Paralda. What does this place look like? (*Pause.*)

By singing aloud an intonation of Paralda's name, we set a resonance by which to summon the sovereign to appear. Sing "Paralda" on three long, sustained breaths. Take a deep breath in … Chant aloud: *Pa-ral-da … Pa-ral-da … Pa-ral-da …*

The collective consciousness of airy essence gathers from the surrounding wind and shimmers into form as Sovereign Paralda appears before you. Introduce yourself. (*Pause.*) Remember all the details of how they appear to you. (*Long pause.*)

You ask aloud: *Paralda! I seek your wisdom as I tread the path of truth!* (*Pause.*) Paralda shares their wisdom with you now … (*Long pause.*)

You ask aloud: *Paralda! Please teach me your lessons of knowing. How best do I seek knowledge for my magick? What do I need to know as I seek truth in my life?* Paralda invites you on a journey to reveal their power of knowing. (*Long pause.*)

You ask aloud: *Please teach me the lessons of wonderment. What new questions should be explored? What programming needs to be deleted?* Paralda invites you on a vision journey to learn the power of wonder air lends. (*Long pause.*)

You ask aloud: *Paralda, will you partner with me in my magick?* (*Pause.*)

If yes, you ask Paralda: *Which altar tool of air would best summon the powers of the sylphs and elemental air to my Great Work? Is it a wand or staff? Something else?* Paralda now presents you with that tool. Take in the details very carefully. (*Pause.*) You are shown where and how you might obtain that tool in the Middleworld. Receive the vision. (*Pause.*)

You ask Paralda: *Which tree or plant spirit will best aid my mental balance through elemental air?* Paralda presents you with this gift and a vision to help identify it clearly. You are offered a vision of this healing, which eases your mind. (*Pause.*)

Accept these gifts and visions with gratitude as you bid Paralda farewell. Paralda shimmers and is gone on the wind.

The sylphs flock around you and lift off once more. Follow them on the winds of imagination, back the way you came. Wander through wonderment, allowing the breezes to clarify your thoughts. Allow the powers of air to inspire a fresh vision of your life and truth. (*Long pause.*)

The sylphs land you softly back at your temple gate, and you bid them farewell. As you step back through, the golden flight suit of protection is shed behind you, reabsorbed by the realms of air. Your vibration shifts back into your normal state.

Step back to your altar. Placing your gifts of tool and plant upon the altar, you remember your lessons with perfect clarity. Take a moment to reflect on all that you've learned.

Now it is time to return to the Middleworld. Leave through the temple door, following the path back. Back, back the way you came, seeking out the looking glass, that portal back into your body. See your body through the looking glass. When you pass through this portal you will once more follow the umbilical cord back into your own belly. In three steps, three, two, one, step through!

From those crossroads in your center, ascend the spiral stairway, rising higher and higher, twelve steps to waking consciousness. Emerging back into the meditation room in your mind and closing the ornate door in the floor behind you.

Say aloud: *I am grateful to my guides, gods, and ancestors—all those who kept me safe and showed me the way. Blessèd Be.* Stretch your muscles. Move to the window of your eyes, and then open them to find your outer temple awaiting.

Journal Reflection

In your Book of Mirrors, record the messages from your allies, draw your visions, and explore your thoughts and feelings about the experience. When finished, deconstruct your temple.

Deconstructing the Temple

Close the elemental gateway by standing to face the east in the posture of air, natural athame raised in salute.

Say: *Powers of the east! Essence of air! Sylphs and Sovereign Paralda! I am grateful for your inspiring presence and your aid in these rites. Continue to strengthen my mind and Great Work along the path of truth. For now, I release you to your fair and airy realms. Hail and farewell!*

See the yellow girder and all powers receding back through the gateway of your circle.

Draw the banishing air pentagram with your natural athame, like a key in the lock. As you encircle the star widdershins, see the portal closing and locking.

Once more kiss your athame or fingers, but this time follow through with a thrusting gesture toward the quarter, directing any remaining energy outward to their realm. Bow.

Release the circle by gathering the sphere into your hands, smaller and smaller until it is imagined like a glowing ball over the altar. Charge the ball to further light your way along the Pentacle Path. Shout *Release!* as you toss the sphere upward to the cosmos, clap your hands three times, and say: *The circle is open but never broken. Merry meet, merry part, and merry meet again!*

Magick of Truth

With your alliances in elemental realms of air, plan and enact the following two-part spell to holistically break free from old thoughts and identities that are no longer "true" for you. Then wondrously strengthen your new mental goals and personal truths, balancing both the third eye and throat chakras. Begin at a dark moon while in the Northern Hemisphere the sun passes through the earthy sign of Taurus, or in the Southern Hemisphere the sun passes through watery Scorpio. The second part follows after the moon waxes again, with airy Mercury's aid as you redefine and express your new truth.

❧ Spell 2: Saturn's Reckoning Jar ❧

The purpose of this magickal working is to examine what has been "true" about your life experiences very carefully, to discover what baneful beliefs and delusions still hinder the true perception of your third eye. It roots out which societal programs tried to rob you of internal control, authority, and security. Release attachments to the old ways you knew yourself and former identities that no longer serve your future Self.

This spell is especially effective after major life transitions, such as adopting a new Witchcraft practice, divorce, name change, coming out, gender affirmation, completion of any kind of rehabilitation, etc. Whatever symbolically goes into this jar will be purged from your "operating system." It is being put to karmic order, and laid to rest as surely as a funeral, so be exceedingly careful and ethical about your wording and choices. Remember: Do not burn the Witch; do not be the problem; do as you will, but harm none.

Planetary Influence

Saturn and elemental earth and water to balance airy thoughts with grounded discipline.

Auspicious Timing

The first part of this spell should be enacted during lunar fourth quarter as the moon wanes to dark, preferably on a Saturday or, best yet, when the moon is in Capricorn, ruled by Saturn.

Needs

Prepare your working altar for elemental air magick: consecration elements of air incense in a censer with sand, hookah charcoal tab, tongs, small spoon, a lighter or box of matches, and a bowl of sea salt.

Your dedication, earth, and air sanctuary candles on your working altar

An image printed on paper of the Death card (XIII) from any tarot system you like. This image forms a portal to the energies of radical external transformations you seek, freeing you from old ensnarements and releasing old attachments that hinder your progress.

Glass quart jar with tightly fitting lid

Stack of paper cut down into 2 x 4 inch size. You might need a lot!

Black ink pen

Symbolic representations of any former "truths," identities, or affiliations you intend to leave behind. Examples: symbols of your childhood religion, a key to a former home that represents times best left behind, a name badge, membership card, or pin, an old business card or ID from a former affiliation, marriage, deadname, or identity that you no longer answer to, an old photo of yourself taken when you were not yet in control of your life or not yet in your true form, any unnecessary document or certificate with a name you no longer use, substances of controlling influence over you like a wine cork, pill, cigarette, etc.

3 stems of a rose (pink is ideal) with the sharp thorns intact. Remove the petals to dry on your altar. Save the petals for spell 3: Mercury's truth jar.

3 black tourmaline crystals or any crystal associated with Saturn and root chakra

1 cup of sea salt or more

1 black tea light candle, metal tin removed

A few drops of the elemental earth anointing oil you prepared during the earth lessons

Preparation

Set your working altar and assemble all the materials close at hand with plenty of workspace for writing.

Tape or glue the Death card image to the outside of the jar.

Praxis

Light your dedication candle. Awaken and consecrate your working altar as taught in ritual 1. Hallow yourself and the perimeter of the circle with incense smoke and salt as taught in ritual 2. Anoint your third eye and throat chakras with the air oil.

Cast your circle as taught in ritual 2. Open the gateways to earth and air; light their candles.

Invite to be present your guides, ancestors, and spirit. Call the god Saturn to aid your work if you are comfortable doing so.

Sit, close your eyes, breathe deeply, and go to the meditation room in your mind as taught in meditation 1. Descend through the trapdoor, down the spiral stairs, to arrive at your own center, in a deeply relaxed and mindful state.

On the looking glass, imagine projected there a documentary—like a video retrospective of your life and all that you were taught was "true" in the past. Images flow across the screen: your childhood, your culture, your family, former relationships, living situations, the doctrines you were taught. From this safe distance, allow to emerge a recollection of experiences that impacted your development as a person. (*Long Pause.*)

When have you been made to feel powerless? Or lacking in control over your circumstances? When have you been infantilized or discouraged from trusting your inner truth?

We all have difficult experiences that need to be faced, released, and healed. Whenever a difficult memory emerges on the screen, shift the light until the entire scene is tinted in pink … visualize that pink energy as the warm and comforting unconditional love of the God/dess, easing whatever tensions arise from the memory. Continue until you feel ready to evaluate the problems objectively.

Remember that you are a perfect child of Divine Love.

Consider the nine Divine Love Conditions and the fears that arise from their lack. Now name those difficult circumstances that wounded you in a word or phrase. Poverty? Suffering? Violence? Betrayal? Bigotry? Exploitation? Lies? Oppression of your free will? Abandonment? What "truths" that you'd considered in the past no longer ring true for you? Write each on a slip of paper; include any specific details of your experience from which you seek emotional separation and healing.

When the notions of "blame" or "fault" come up for why these things happened, create a release and cycle-breaking statement on a slip of paper. Something like, "I release the [actions] of [the faulty party] in peace. I break the chains of blame. I am free to make different choices."

Recall any recurring defeating thoughts that tarnish your own self-image. What delusions or worries dim your shine? What toxic programming learned from society needs deleting? Have you ever been criticized? Demeaned? Called a hurtful slur or told you weren't enough? Usually, it is by a bully trying to oppress or manipulate you to ease their own suffering. Follow those hurts back to their source. What toxic societal programs lurk in those shadows? Dogma? Domination? Racism? Sexism? Misogyny? Classism? Ageism? Ableism? Greed? Homophobia? Body-shaming? Slut-shaming? Those are delusions sourced from fear.

On a slip of paper, write out any baneful memory, thought, or idea, any words that do not support the amazing person and Witch you are becoming. Write down any false belief or the harmful effects of those falsehoods that you now banish from your mind and life.

Put all these slips of paper one by one into the jar, naming each with power in the voice, followed by stating aloud: *I banish you!* Shout it, sing it, stomp them into the ground if you like; raise power with all the emotions dredged up through this healing and direct it into the jar.

Add any additional symbols of your former identities or controlling substances that you now release. State aloud: *I release all attachment to that former Self [name, identity]. As I will, so mote it be!*

Snip the thorny stems from the roses (short enough pieces to fit inside the jar); blow gently over them and ask Venus's aid in defending your unconditional Divine Love. Add them to the jar, saying aloud: *By rose's thorn and Venus's scorn, banish bane with justice and love. As below and so above!*

Tap on the three black tourmaline stones, blow gently over them, and ask Saturn's aid in binding and neutralizing all lingering harm. Drop them in the jar, saying aloud: *By tourmaline and Saturn's rings, bind bane with order, defending my borders. As above and so below!*

Pour in the salt, calling the powers of earth to further purify and nullify.

Remove the metal tin from the black tea light candle. Anoint in widdershins motion with the elemental earth oil, and charge to disintegrate the connections that remain between you and all that is now in the jar. Set the black tea light candle carefully on the salt and light it. As it burns down, imagine it drawing all external influences within the jar and nullifying their effect on your future.

Attend the burning candle while meditating for at least 29 minutes. (Representing the years of Saturn's revolution.) Take care to extinguish the flame well before it reaches the salt.

Extinguish the flame by snuffing it out. Piss in the jar like the alpha-dog boss that you are. Don't be shy or squeamish now because it isn't Witchcraft until things get visceral. In this primal way, exert dominance over this territory. Mark the work as your own. To urinate is literally how we detoxify the garbage from the physical body, so it is the perfect symbolic act. Moreover, urine is actually sterile, and the uric acid and ammonia will further break down the contents, slowly continuing the work over time.

Tightly seal the lid on the jar. State with authority: *The work is complete!* Clap your hands three times to release it.

Thank your guides and guardians for their aid. Close the elemental gateways to earth and air; release the circle. Leave the jar on your altar. If you already have a pentacle paten, place the jar on the paten.

Later, on the first day of dark moon cycle, when the moon and sun are conjunct in the same sign, take the jar to a natural wooded place distant from where you live. Find a tree with whom you can establish a working partnership, preferably a species aligned with Saturn. There are many: aspen, beech, cypress, elm, fir, holly, magnolia, pine, and poplar to name a few.[238] Ask Saturn's priest of the plant realm to guard and aid in your gentle transmutation and reordering. Ask assistance in mental discipline as you reprogram. If agreement is made, offer the tree fresh water in thanks, and bury the jar under the tree. Cover the place carefully, arranging as if the earth was never disturbed.

Again, clap three times, stating with authority: *I release you! I release you! I release you! So mote it be!* Turn widdershins on the spot and walk away. Never look back; never visit it again. Hold earth's lesson of silence, and do not speak of it to anyone. Just hold open the space of potential within your thoughts that is now created.

---

238. Sandra Kynes, *Llewellyn's Complete Book of Correspondences: A Comprehensive & Cross-Referenced Resource for Pagans & Wiccans* (Woodbury, MN: Llewellyn Publications, 2013), 382.

❧ Spell 3: Mercury's Truth Jar ❧

The purpose of this magickal working is to seek a new truth. Open your mind to air's receptive power of wonderment. What is your personal truth? What cosmic paradigm really gets your besom flying? The problem is that old belief and new truth don't always match. This magick attends to that realignment. It is here that you build up your new identity as an empowered Witch, ready to have your mind cracked open to the mysteries of a magickal cosmos.

We work to open the throat chakra, which is all about speaking your truth and outwardly expressing your authentic Self. It is blocked by lies, even lies of omission, and in many cases is blocked by the "closet doors" we hide behind out of fear of being rejected or harmed.

The end result of this path of truth is becoming a fully-fledged spiritual adult with authority over your own mind and choices. Whatever symbolically goes into this jar represents your truth. Now is your time to express the wonderous being you're becoming. As "The Charge of the Goddess" suggests, affirm your "highest ideal" so you may "strive ever toward it."[239]

Be careful what you ask for because you will undoubtedly get it, and the universe has a sly sense of humor. Remember: *don't be the weak link*; *must be present to win*; Perfect Love and Perfect Trustworthiness begin with you.

Planetary Influences
Mercury and elemental air and water

Auspicious Timing
The second part of this spell should be enacted a few days after completing spell 2: Saturn's Reckoning Jar, during the next lunar first quarter as the moon tides shift into waxing, preferably on the following Wednesday, or better yet when the moon is in an air sign.

---

239. Valiente, *The Charge of the Goddess*, 12–13.

Needs

Prepare your working altar for elemental air magick: consecration element of air incense in a censer with sand, hookah charcoal tab, tongs, small spoon, and a lighter or box of matches.

Your dedication and air sanctuary candles

Another glass quart jar with lid, small nail, and a hammer. Flip the jar lid over on a cutting board and hammer the nail through the inside, right in the middle. Flip it back over so the sharp point sticks out of the top like a candle spike to hold the votive candle safely.

An image printed on paper of the Magician or Magus card (I) from any tarot deck you like. This image represents the powers of Mercury, our clear communication and flexible mental brilliance, "the Will, Wisdom, and the Word through which the world was created."[240] The trickster Mercury treads the liminal between truth and falsehood, throwing all preconceived ideas and judgments into question.

A stack of paper cut down into 2 x 4 inch size

A blue ink pen

Symbolic representations of your personal truths, powers, and identities. Examples: pentacle or other symbols of your chosen religion, your magickal name if you've taken one already, or a new legal name if applicable. God/dess images. Any affiliation or identity you claim as your own. Be creative.

The dried pink rose petals you've been drying on your altar since performing spell 2: Saturn's Reckoning Jar.

3 citrine crystals, or any stone associated with Mercury and throat chakra

1 cup of various seeds, berries, and dried flowers associated with Mercury and elemental air. Examples: juniper berries, elderberries, various wildflower seeds, dandelion fluff (the seed heads, if seasonal) lavender, honeysuckle, jasmine, chamomile, etc.

A big dollop of honey

A pint of gin, a distilled liquor of juniper berry, spirit of Mercury

1 natural (yellow) 2-inch beeswax votive candle

---

240. Gerd Ziegler, *Tarot: Mirror of the Soul: Handbook for the Aleister Crowley Tarot* (Boston: RedWheel/Weiser, 1988), 16.

Air anointing oil, recipe in the formulary section

A firesafe plate large enough to hold the jar safely and catch any candle wax that drips over the side

Preparation

Lay out your working altar for air with plenty of room to work. Assemble all the materials needed.

Tape or glue the Magician or Magus card image to the outside of the jar. Write your chosen name on that image as well, identifying yourself as the wise and powerful Magus. Rub your fingertip along the inside of your cheek, and then anoint the inside of the jar deosil with your saliva as a taglock to your DNA. This jar now represents and is in sympathy with you. Anything you do to the jar, you do to your future Self.

Consecrate and hallow the altar and yourself as taught in ritual 1. Hallow and cast the circle as taught in ritual 2. Open the gateway to air. Call to be present your guides and protectors, evoking the deities Mercury and Venus if you're comfortable doing so.

Praxis

Sit comfortably, close your eyes, and breathe deeply. Begin in the meditation room in your mind as taught in meditation 1. Descend through the trapdoor in the floor, down the spiral stairs, until you find the looking glass at the center of your being.

Consider these questions: Of what relative truths or identities do you take full possession? Consider the nine Divine Love Conditions that are the birthright of everyone: resources, affection, free will, acceptance, security, trustworthiness, expression, authenticity, and reciprocity. Which of these conditions do you claim more of for your future?

At the looking glass in your mind's eye, imagine projected there a vision of your current circumstances and the future you are building for yourself. See yourself crowned and sovereign at the center of your domain, wisely walking the path of truth. In three steps, pass through the looking glass and arrive on the astral plane: one, two, three, step through! Feel your crown; survey your domain. A web of glowing interconnections flow from you, extending throughout the cosmos, touching everything else.

Recall from the previous exercise any times of lack or wounds from the past when it appeared as though circumstances were out of your control. As the sovereign, extend your connections into the past and fulfill those needs in your imagination.

Through the web you reach out and connect to Divine Love; see all physical resources and structures you need to thrive manifesting on the world tree, like fruits ready for the picking. On a slip of paper, write something like, *I claim control over my body, my health, and the creation of my physical life. I create abundance so I may thrive, and draw to me [list the things you claim].* You may be specific which needs you pluck from the tree, or leave it general. Read the paper aloud and drop it into your jar. See this as an act of internalizing your locus of control.

Through the web reach out and connect to Divine Mind, knowledge, and wonderment. Open to understand your personal truths and identity. Allow time for dreaming big … On a slip of paper, write something like, *I claim authority over my own mind and choices. I seek the truth within myself. I wonder [ask questions for which you seek answers].* You may also claim any personal truths, like, *I am a sacred being, complete within myself and balanced on all levels. I grow into deeper understanding of my place within the cosmic order. I am trustworthy.* What do you know? What do you want to know? Write it on the paper, read it aloud, and drop it into your jar. See this as an act of internalizing your locus of authority.

Through the web reach out and connect to Divine Will, the power of nature, and the spark of divine becoming. Reach out and claim any needed control over your own goals and actions. Claim any discipline needed to conquer baneful habits. Claim energy needed to accomplish your sacred mission and evolve as needed through your actions and choices. Claim self-confidence and the social skills needed to effectively live within society as a contributor. On a slip of paper, write something like, *I claim my free will to pursue happiness and fulfillment in peace. I safely set my own course by my own moral compass for the highest good of all involved, harming none.* Read it aloud and drop it into your jar. See this as an act of internalizing your locus of security.

Add to the jar any additional symbols of your becoming. Name and claim them as you drop each into the jar.

Pick up the dried rose petals, blow gently over them, and ask Venus's aid in your graceful acceptance of her Divine Love. Add them to the jar, saying aloud: *By rose's flower and Venus's bower, I claim my control above and below!*

Pick up and tap on the citrine three times, blow gently over the crystals and ask Mercury's aid in discerning your own truth and communicating effectively. Drop them in the jar, saying aloud:

By citrine's power and Mercury's hour, I claim my voice by will and choice.

Pour in the cup of seeds, berries, and flowers, calling the powers of both Mercury and air to inspire fruitful new thoughts and ideas in beautiful ways. Say aloud:

By airy seed and fruit and tree, I nurture my own authority.

Pour the dollop of honey over all, calling gentle sweetness of loving acceptance and nurturance of your spirit throughout the coming cycle of your growth.

Fill the jar to the top with the gin, a spirit of Mercury, preserving and strengthening the work of your own divine spirit. Screw the lid on tightly.

Anoint the beeswax votive candle in a deosil motion with the elemental air oil and charge it to inspire all transformations represented by the jar. Push the candle carefully onto the nail, holding it securely in place. Set the jar on a firesafe plate that can catch any extra wax, or on your altar paten if you already have one. Light the candle. Spend time meditating and praying with the candle as it burns, softly focused on the flame, allowing the dripping wax to flow down the sides and seal the jar.

Close your eyes and visualize yourself on the astral plane. See yourself upon the looking glass. In three steps return to the Middleworld. One, two, three, step through! You arrive in your own center and take the twelve spiral steps back up, through the trap door in the floor, into the sanctuary of your mind. Move to the window of your eyes and open them to find your outer temple waiting.

When you are ready, thank and release your guides, guardians, and gods, close the elemental gateway to air, and close your circle, charging the sphere of your circle to light your way along the path of truth.

Every day through the remainder of the waxing moon cycle, relight the candle and meditate for a while upon all that you've internalized, all that you are becoming, and the sacred responsibilities required of a sovereign Witch. On the night of the full moon, allow the candle to finish burning completely if it hasn't already. Clap three times saying, *The work is complete. So mote it be!*

Let the jar live on your altar for as long as you see fit, taking gentle care of it. Should you ever feel the need to nurture the working further, anoint and add another yellow candle and attend those meditations again. Should you ever wish to retire this spell jar, bury it in a special place on your property or near to where you live, preferably under a rose or juniper bush. Ask the aid of Venus (rose) or Mercury (juniper) to gently guide your pursuit of truth.

☙ Journal Reflection: The Path of Truth ❧

For your Book of Mirrors review of these lessons, use the Witch's Jewel of Power framework below. Before you switch gears into the fire lessons of the next chapter, record your impressions about the following questions for your future Self to find, like a letter to yourself about where you were at this point along the Pentacle Path. Consider these questions: What truth has been revealed to you through this magick? How are you expressing yourself authentically? By examining your beliefs, in what ways have your perceptions of life changed? In what ways have your long-held beliefs been affirmed as correct for you?

From Air: To Know and to Wonder

- What impactful thing have you learned from this lesson?

- What do you still wonder about that needs further exploration?

From Fire: To Will and to Surrender

- How did you apply your will to these exercises? Did you adapt them to make them your own? What worked or didn't work well for you?

- Was there any expectation, assumption, or fear that needs to be surrendered?

From Water: To Dare and to Accept

- What gut emotional reactions came up for you?

- What surprised you? Which were easy to accept?

- Which do you dare to challenge or overcome?

From Earth: To Be Silent and to Resonate

- Now that the work is done, pay attention to what is going on in your life. How has this work affected your perceptions, actions, dreams? What patterns emerge?

- In what practical ways will you resonate your new awareness into reality?

Chapter 14

Element of Fire and the Path of Power

From the sabbat of high spring at Beltane to high summer at Lammas, we work through the mysteries of elemental fire. This chapter's lessons are divided into two parts: During the 6.5 weeks of the waning Lithatide, we'll explore the projective elemental mystery *to will*. During the 6.5 weeks of the waxing Lammastide, we'll explore the receptive elemental mystery *to surrender*.

The Great Work: Wheel of the Year

Once more, as we tread the path of power, there are three ritual workings to complete, which may be timed to the three lunar tides that crest within this solar period:

1. Crafting formulary materials for fire rituals and spells.

2. Taking a ritual journey to the realms of elemental fire.

3. Performing a spell with planetary Mars for protection and holistic balancing of your will.

Lithatide: Beltane to Litha

As spring wanes, kindle your fires and apply your will by taking action upon your *Great Work* dedication for this year. This is the time to roll up your sleeves and dig into the "doing things" portion of life. Apply your fires to the practical projects that need work: gardening, home repair projects, necessary physical exercise. *Go* and *do* magickal things that further your witching sovereignty (earth) and strive toward your ideals (air). See an issue that needs attention? Take the lead and resolve it. Read the chapter's lessons, complete the exercises, and then prepare your fire magick sanctuary candle and formulary needs for the rituals to follow after Litha.

Lammastide: Litha to Lammas

As summer heats up, shift into the receptive mysteries of fiery surrender by feeding the forge fires of your will. Let go of any old forms that are hindering your progress, like the snake shedding a skin that is too small or the caterpillar undergoing radical transformation in the chrysalis before emerging as a butterfly. However, the trick to fire is in discerning the balance between feeding the beneficial fires and applying them effectively without burning out or blowing up.

Every day of this cycle, clear out one area of dead weight or congestion in your life. Take out the literal or metaphorical trash. Cull possessions for donation or unsubscribe from unwanted email lists—prune back the excesses. Similar to the Catholic season of Lent, give up an undesirable habit or overindulgence for a while just to exert your will to live the healthier lifestyle you choose. Prove to yourself that you're sovereign in your life, not your addictions or obsessions. Perhaps a social media vacation? Or a dietary cleanse (under the guidance of your physician) of some kind to improve your health or better fulfill your ideals? Shortly after Litha, while the waxing moon is in a fire sign, take the ritual journey to the realms of fire, seeking alliances with the salamanders and Sovereign Djin. Seek guidance about the correct tool of fire for you, and an animal spirit guide to aid the balance of your will. Then, find or begin crafting your tool of fire as a continuation of your magick. Apply what you've learned to enact the Shield of Mars spell for protection and balance between personal will and Divine Will.

The Pentacle Path of Power and the Body of the Will	
Chakras	Solar plexus chakra
Regulates	Empowerment
Opened by	Divine Will
Blocked by	Shame
Witchcraft Goal	Sacred mission alignment of wills
Love Conditions	Free will vs. fear of oppression. Acceptance vs. fear of bigotry.
Charm of Affirmation	By the powers of fire and bone, I am who I am and do what must be done.

Mysteries of Elemental Fire

Elemental fire energizes the body of will. Dynamic and aggressive, fire governs our determination, passions, and willpower, spurring our charge into battle like a warrior of Divine Love on a sacred mission. The movement of our muscles is provided by the chemical reactions of our body, releasing our inner metabolic fire. It is also the internal, spiritual fire of divinity within us. Our sense of *sight* is associated with fire since it holds the power of light. In Hermetic alchemy, elemental fire is thought to have a hot and dry nature and anchors the divine masculine end of the spectrum of mental gender.

Fire is the first essence to emerge from Spirit and is the least dense energy of the elemental realms. Fire is a transitional state between matter and energy, between our talents and actions, regulating sex drive and intensity. It is also the curious spark that fuels imagination and drives one to manifest those imaginings. Fire also fuels our work—whether that be one's career or sacred mission, how one creates opportunity, and then makes good use of those opportunities.

Fire Through the Zodiac

The lessons of fire are seen first through the human life cycle and zodiac as cardinal Aries with the emergence of the new infant, expressing the lesson of "I am." Aries is here to teach others that love is about innocence and is here to learn that love requires mutual trustwor-thiness. Later, fire emerges through fixed Leo as the human teenager, expressing, "I will." Leo is here to teach others that love can be ecstatic while learning that love requires humil-ity. Finally, fire emerges as mutable Sagittarius with an exploration of knowledge, express-ing the lesson of "I see." Sagittarius is here to teach others that love requires honesty while learning that love engenders mutual loyalty.[241]

Witch's Jewel of Power: Fire		
	Yang: projective	Yin: receptive
Mystery Teaching	To will	To surrender
Wheel of Year	Beltane through Litha	Litha through Lammas
Planetary Sphere	Sun	Mars

Witch's Jewel of Power: To Will

To will is the projective power of elemental fire. What do Witches mean by *will*? The infamous occultist Aleister Crowley is credited with the Thelemic maxim, "Do what thou wilt shall be the whole of the Law … Love is the law, Love under will. There is no law beyond Do what thou wilt."[242] This maxim is believed to have influenced the Wiccan ethical guideline in the poems "Rede of the Wiccae" and "The Witches' Creed," which advise: "an it harm none, do what ye will."[243]

The projective power *to will* represents how we actualize our personal desire. Through movement, action, strength, and assertion we apply our inner fires to making the things we want actually happen. Without essential fire nothing gets done!

The will is the "engine" of our being—the drive, action, oomph, the verb in the sentence we write with our lives. There is a difference between personal will and Divine Will, what practitioners of Thelema call *True Will*. Personal will may be shortsighted by the whims of the moment. For example, indulgence of eating this entire pizza, desire for the shiny new

---

241. Goodman, *Linda Goodman's Love Signs*, 13.

242. Aleister Crowley, *The Book of the Law* (York Beach, ME: Red Wheel/Weiser, 1976), 9.

243. "Rede of the Wiccae," attributed to Lady Gwen Thompson (Mathiesen and Theitic, *The Rede of the Wiccae*, 52–53), and "The Witch's Creed," a poem by Doreen Valiente (Valiente, *The Charge of the Goddess*, 19–21).

iPhone, lust to shag the sexy beast who just sat down next to me at the bar, compulsion for revenge when I've been harmed. Or maybe it's my determination to keep jogging until I fit into my favorite jeans again or work late to achieve that promotion I deserve at work. In my microcosm, personal will compels me to do whatever it takes to satisfy what my ego wants, and that isn't necessarily a bad thing, but it is just a smaller part of the ultimate thing: a microcosm subset of my will within the macrocosm of Divine Will.

Divine Will compels me toward my destiny, fueling the achievement of my existence's spiritual purpose. Tapping Divine Will starts the flow of power from the creative source, then aligns with personal will, opening the conduit between all three planes: Spiritual, through Mental, down to Physical. The Witch becomes the conductor of that divine power.

Witch's Jewel of Power: To Surrender

The flip side of fire, the passive, receptive, feminine, and less obvious lesson is about **surrender**. In surrender we receive the tools for transforming culture through cooperation. Think about the log on your bonfire. The fuel that is burning must surrender to that catalyst so that its raw material is transformed into something amazing. Nothing set aflame can remain the same. Fire consumes both oxygen (air) and matter (earth), releasing the latent energy as light and warmth. The applied combination of water and fire gives us the powerful steam engine! When we cooperatively surrender to the transformation by Divine Will, all impediments to our sacred mission are burned away. Like tempering a steel blade, our impurities and weaknesses are also transmuted into power. After the forge, the sword that remains is sharper, more resilient, and far more effective. Similarly, essential fire tempers our little egos into more enlightened states of consciousness. With this rarified purpose, Witches are ready for a cooperative interrelationship with society and advancing human evolution.

Surrendering is about getting out of your own way, an attitude of not struggling, not fighting the fire, just letting it burn. With this mystery, I think of our destiny like a river flowing in the direction of our evolution (collectively and individually). In this metaphor, we're captains of our destiny, in command of our "ship." Question is, what is fueling the engines of that ship? When we can appropriately detach from our little ego's expectations of how we are in control, we can fuel our engines with the limitlessness of this divine fire. This allows us to navigate our destiny harmoniously with the flow of nature rather than egotistically rowing against the current.

Cooperative Tools of the Goddess

It is the receptive (goddess) powers of elemental fire that hold the cooperative lessons we need to evolve our culture into a more just and equitable future. Surrender is where the ultimate power of Divine Will can be found. To surrender is letting go of preconceived ideas about how things *should be* done. In surrender, it is possible to release the death grip anyone holds on the helm of the metaphorical ship they captain through their life and work. In surrender, you can relax into the thrill of the ride. This receptive power of fire is how a society can uncoil the tightly closed channel of potential into the ease of nature's greatest source of vitality. Again, our true power is through *opening*.

Surrender is where we rebalance *ease* in the body of the will. Sometimes in order to cure, you have to curse; to heal you must destroy. For example: a rotten tooth must be violently yanked out of your jawbone, because if you don't remove the rot, the infection could kill you. For wellness on all levels there must be a balance of giving and receiving: the toil and sacrifice of the outflowing tide and the enjoyment and satisfaction of the inflowing tide. With true freedom comes great responsibility and sometimes great sacrifice.

The Path of Power

What is power, anyway? In English, this word is used as a noun, verb, and modifier. We might wear a "power suit" when we mean serious business. It could mean the capacity to take action or the potential to create changes, as in "the power of speech." Or, power is viewed as authority, as in "a government in power." It could be an exertion of strength or force, like, "the power of the hurricane." It could also be the mechanical or electrical energy that "powers the lamps." In every instance, elemental fire plays its part.

For Witches, the necessary question about power is not *What is it?* or *How do I use it?* Nay, the important witching question is this: *From whence does power flow?* In both real estate and magick: location, location, location! Once more we go back to psychology's lessons of internalizing the three loci: control, security, and authority. "The Charge of the Goddess" liturgy is a lesson in reclaiming divine empowerment: if power is "that which thou seekest," then the God/dess suggests that we search for it within ourselves.[244]

With earth's lessons we explored control over one's physical survival and circumstances of life. With air's lessons we explored the control over one's relative truth and the

---

244. Valiente, *The Charge of the Goddess*, 12–13.

beliefs those truths speak for their authority. With fire's lessons, we examine the role of free will and how we control our power. We explore how to defend our authority, resulting in self-confidence and an internal sense of security.

The Power Paradox: Domination vs. Cooperation

The paradox of power that Elemental Witchcraft can help to reconcile lies on the range of polarity between the domination and cooperation models of "control" that we've been exploring throughout this work. The power of the God/dess in equal balance is distinguished by how all beings are interconnected within nature (earth), how the Divine Love of the God/dess drives diverse relationships (water), and how we can wondrously imagine new solutions to shared problems within Divine Mind (air). The path of power teaches that the most internally powerful people are aligned within Divine Will (fire). This results in a sacred mission that tends to foster personal empowerment in others. In other words, the most spiritually powerful people have the most cooperative power-sharing partnerships and tend to be the most peaceful, which is the paradox! The mystery lies in the location from whence that person derives their power: internally or externally.

Sue Mehrtens of the Jungian Center writes about how similar this power sharing is to the sharing of love: "Our society regards power as a 'zero-sum thing.' That is, if I have power, then you don't. If you have it, then I don't. But in reality power is like love: the more we share it and empower others, the more power there is in the world."[245] This describes the ultimate goal of the Hermetic Great Work of Magick. First, we empower ourselves from within, then we share that wisdom to jointly solve the big problems, helping others. Internalizing our power is a process of growing up.

❧ Exercise 9: Power Reflection ❧

In Janet Hagberg's book *Real Power: Stages of Personal Power in Organizations* (1984), she brilliantly outlined six stages of the human relationship with power. The first three stages begin the range from the most externalized locations of power.

---

245. Mehrtens, "How to Internalize a Locus of Control."

Step 1: Hagberg's Stages of Power

As you read the summarized stages of power, make notes in your Book of Mirrors about each stage. Then write down examples that exhibit the qualities and behaviors of that stage. Think of people you know or have heard of, like celebrities or historical figures, or government, business, or religious organizations. Even think critically about the Neopagan and Witchcraft leaders you've known or heard about.

1. **Powerlessness:** Feels no personal control over their circumstances or survival. Completely dependent on outside help: children, enslaved or incarcerated people. Often felt by the oppressed, disadvantaged, disabled, and disenfranchised genders and minorities in a society.

2. **Power by Association:** Feels some access to power through their affiliations to others like their parents, spouse, spiritual guru, employer. Or by the promise of a messiah or "magical other" they believe will save them if they earn it.

3. **Power by Achievement:** Feels power from external recognition of achievement; found in symbols of success like titles, credentials, fame, or awards. Or through granting of privileges, like exclusive memberships or security clearances. Or felt by collecting exclusive possessions like designer clothing, sports cars, jets, yachts, or their name on a building. In a shifting social media landscape, perhaps they count power by Twitter and Instagram followers or YouTube subscribers.[246]

Most of capitalist American society, being at levels one and two, tends to think three is the pinnacle of power when really it is the most tenuous. All of these forms of externally affirmed power can be stripped away in an instant of bad weather, stock-market crash, or scandal.

Crises of Awakening

Hagberg describes how moving into the last three levels typically requires some crises or life-altering event: a personal tragedy, near-death experience, profound loss, or spiritual catalyst to kick off self-discovery, which "propels the individual to enter the inner realm of

---

246. Janet O. Hagberg, *Real Power: The Stages of Personal Power in Organizations,* 3rd ed. (Salem, WI: Sheffield Publishing Co., 2003), n.p.

self-knowledge and integrity."[247] Witches call it "the awakening." Mystics sometimes call this a "shamanic initiation crisis."[248] The dreamy illusion of material separateness drops, for even one ecstatic moment, and we're jolted awake into a new light. At that point cosmic unity cannot be ignored, and real power is finally possible. The last three stages of power are increasingly internalized, offering true control, authority, and security.

4. **Power by Reflection:** Feels true power within themselves, expressed as their identity, their core values, and what they stand for. During this process, you don't much care about material things that can easily be destroyed or denied. You can detach your sense of self-worth from relationships and honestly enjoy them without dependence. Folks at stage four know who they are, and their own integrity is ultimately *the authority* that empowers their lives. They can be congruent and fair.

Once you see divinity in your reflection, then increased self-confidence, higher self-esteem, and this broader self-awareness results in an internalized sense of security.

The Steep Path

In order to transition to stage five, we have to hit what Hagberg calls "the Wall."[249] I would wager that to even consider reading this book, you've already hit the Wall in your spiritual life some time back. In witching parlance, we could call the process of moving through the Wall an *initiatory crisis*.[250] Author Vivianne Crowley describes this trip descending the "steep path" into the Underworld to face our fears. This steep path describes the initiatory journey between second- and third-degree Wiccan rites. To successfully navigate the path of power, the God/dess inevitably strips bare all ego attachments so the Witch can internalize control and be empowered by the God/dess within. In Witchcraft we call this magick "shadow work," and it is a lifelong process. However,

247. Hagberg, *Real Power*, 79.

248. Roger Walsh, "The Making of a Shaman: Calling, Training and Culmination," *Journal of Humanistic Psychology* 34, no. 3 (Summer 1994): 12–15, https://doi.org/10.1177/00221678940343003.

249. Hagberg, "Chapter 5: The Wall," in *Real Power*, 121.

250. For example, the Tower tarot card pathworking between Hod (Venus) and Nezach (Mercury) in the Qabala Tree of Life following initiatory rites to the Priest/ess/hood.

significant headway should be made before that Witch can ascend the next wave, ready to responsibly assume the mantel of coven leadership.[251]

The path of power is where personal will is aligned with Divine Will and is forced to confront what the Wall casts in shadow: "our wounds, our hidden addictions ... our childhood pains, our self-absorption."[252] The Witch is asked to let go and flow with their starry destiny, whether they like it or not.

Down the steep path of power, we may feel a lot of inner turmoil, as if we've been abandoned by our God/dess entirely. During my own initiatory crisis, I described it as being dragged through the thorns of Aphrodite's rose garden. But on the other side, we are embraced by their love and grace in a new way.

The techniques of the Pentacle Path of Elemental Witchcraft are designed to help Witches navigate the challenges of their awakening, grow through their shadows, and eventually realize the last two levels of internalized power for themselves. However, Hagberg offers a poignant warning to which we should take heed, especially as Witchcraft trends in popularity around social media influencers. She warns, "You cannot learn Stage Five behavior from Stage Three people."[253] As a Witchcraft retailer, I must unequivocally state that there is nothing you can buy, no expensive class, no exclusive membership, no subscription box or kit of witching parts that will magically bestow a "power by purpose or wisdom" upon you from the outside. Material allies and wise teachers might be helpful, but true empowerment can only be attained through internal realization, direct from Source. Any self-appointed "influencer" who makes grandiose claims or offers expensive guarantees otherwise, is unlikely to have even approached the Wall, nor ever noticed their shadows, so they are most likely still deluded by their personal ego.[254] Again, discernment is key.

5. **Power by Purpose:** Feels power from a clear sacred mission, which more fully attunes them to Divine Will. They've fueled their internal engine from the *cosmic power grid* of divinity. Being "on fire" to achieve one's sacred mission also gives you a reason to get out of bed in the morning. Folks at stage five often

---

251. Crowley, "Chapter 12: The Steep Path," in *Wicca: The Old Religion in the New Millennium*, 207–219.

252. Hagberg, *Real Power*, 121.

253. Hagberg, *Real Power*, 121.

254. Hagberg, *Real Power*, 121.

become some kind of helper, advocate, or activist. They authentically put their powers to work for a better life for everyone and for a better world.

6. **Power by Wisdom:** Effortlessly and humbly feels divine power from within themselves: noted by humility, peacefulness, happiness, compassion, and healing ability. Clearly understands the larger patterns of interconnection as a synergistic, organized whole. Tends to choose modest, simple lifestyles. Their lives become an open conduit of that divine power and creativity to earth as a messenger and teacher.

Power by wisdom approaches the alchemical "opus" of spiritual enlightenment, the perfect alignment of divine selfhood and the potential bliss of reunion with Source after they die, released from further incarnation.

Theoretically, the Witch who attains the sixth stage of wise empowerment could create effortlessly within Divine Will, dream vast possibility within Divine Mind, and love unconditionally within Divine Love with nary a candle necessary to *poof* their dreams into being. That level of natural power might look like a "miracle," "supernatural," or "the paranormal" to those who cannot yet *see* our divine interconnections. Paradoxically, folks at this level of awareness don't even want the external trappings and prestige of "power" anymore. That's how you know they're at level six wisdom. These folks tend to be renowned for their mission of empowering others, for peace, benevolence, and cooperative, mutual respect for all.

Unfortunately for them, folks still operating from the first three power levels tend to deify those wise humans at the sixth stage; they call them gurus, saints, ascended masters, the hidden company, avatars or bodhisattvas. They are given titles like Trismegistus (Thrice Greatest), Christ (Greek: Anointed One), or Buddha (Sanskrit: Awakened One).[255]

Sadly, when the powerless and insecure masses catch a glimpse of true human power shining brightly, they tend to be drawn like moths to a flame but are inevitably burned. Things tend to go badly for all parties from there. Truth is, folks can't hear what these messengers deliver until they are ready to seek it within themselves. The Hermetic and

---

255. "Hermetic Writings," Encyclopedia Britannica, updated September 3, 2013, https://www.britannica.com/topic/Hermetic-writings.; Jaroslav Jan Pelikan and E. P. Sanders, "Jesus," Encyclopedia Britannica, updated March 24, 2021. https://www.britannica.com/biography/Jesus.; Donald S. Lopez, "Buddha," Encyclopedia Britannica, updated February 19, 2020, https://www.britannica.com/biography/Buddha-founder-of-Buddhism.

Wiccan mythos can only offer salvation from the illusions of separateness and powerlessness. However, each Witch must still walk their own Pentacle Path through to completion, figuring out these mysteries for themselves.

Step 2: Reflecting on Your Relationship to Power

To continue exercise 9, consider your own relationship to power throughout your life experiences. Journal in your Book of Mirrors about your own journey along these stages of spiritual awareness. Where are you now? What shadows might be cast by "the Wall" that you must eventually work through? This helps map where you've been along the path of power already. Now, which stage of power is your next goal? What act of will or surrender is being asked of you in order to reconcile the paradox of power for yourself?

The paradox of power reconciles two ends of the spectrum between domination and cooperation, externalized and internalized power. Dominator power gives rise to tyranny, which seizes external control by depriving the *free will* of others—oppressing the god/dess-given right of self-determination of our personal sovereignty. Cooperator power gives rise to humility, which shares control by cultivating the free will of others—defending liberty and the pursuit of happiness through personal sovereignty and self-determination of all members of that society. The more internalized power you wield, the less likely you are to abuse that power, resolving the paradox.

The Solar Plexus Chakra: Sacred Mission

The solar plexus chakra, which is located at the diaphragm—midpoint between navel and heart—is the entry point of essential fires in the body. Imagine your personal fires radiating like the sun at your center. This chakra regulates our empowerment, and when properly opened, feeds the fires of Divine Will into the engines of our personal will. However, the flow of this chakra can be blocked by issues of shame over our actions or bigotry due to any lack of acceptance of our true identities. Any oppression of our free will hinders the flow of energy through the solar plexus and results in a kind of spiritual enslavement.

⚜ Exercise 10: Sacred Mission and Your Saturn Return ⚜

Hagberg's stage five "power by purpose" speaks about our sacred mission. Does what you do with your time and energy even remotely resemble what your Divine Will came here to accomplish? First things first, figure out your sacred mission. Remember that Hermetic philosophy believes that Spirit descended through the celestial mechanism of the stars, called astrology, and was cast into form as you with a very specific set of aptitudes, strengths to offer, and challenges to learn from. When you contribute what you're good at and actively strengthen your weaknesses, that is when you are on task for your sacred mission. Basically, living your best life as your best Self is your job.

One way to figure out what that sacred mission might be is to research your astrological natal chart. Witches typically begin by looking at which zodiac signs the sun and moon were in, and which sign was "rising" over the horizon (also called your ascendant) at the moment of your birth. Which classical planets rule those signs? The elemental energies of those signs, and the characteristics of those planetary rulers, will come naturally for you. However, for our lessons in fire and the path of power, it is helpful to discover how the earthy planet of Saturn is positioned in your natal chart

Saturn is often considered "malefic" in astrology, so it gets a bad rap. Saturn is the strict father-figure of the planetary spheres. He's the disciplinarian and taskmaster: all about responsibility, duty, and work ethic. He's that elder who throws challenges at you as a teaching tool for patience, diligence, and maturity so you'll grow up by overcoming hardships. Planetary Saturn in your chart shows up as what kind of adult you're going to be and how you'll best apply your power in the world. Folks tend to fear things Saturn governs, but there is no avoiding them. Dad'll keep restricting you until you can be self-disciplined on your own.[256] If you face those challenges head on, you are more likely to evolve in character and power, realizing your full potential. To understand Saturn is to understand the true nature of divine life here on Earth.[257] When we align the fires of our will, goals, actions, and how we spend our time with how Saturn's power works for us, life gets easier and more fulfilling.

Step 1: Understanding Saturn

Saturn mediates elemental earth energy into the Middleworld. It forms divine power into societal structures, rules, laws, and systems of cause and effect. When we speak of defending "boundaries" for our security and sovereignty, Witches are tapping Saturn's

---

256. Joanna Martine Woolfolk, *The Only Astrology Book You'll Ever Need* (Lanham, MD: Taylor Trade Publishing, 2006), 264.

257. Dominguez, *Practical Astrology for Witches and Pagans*, 34.

earthy power. Saturn teaches pragmatism, and is felt as the challenge of physical constraints, like the laws of physics, the limitations of the human body, and the march of time toward death. It is by Saturn's hammer and anvil that the metal of our fiery will is wrought into form and put to good use. In an analogy, where our fire is the power of a steam engine, Saturn is like the train and rails that guide where that fire power takes us.

Folks tend to figure out what they really want to do with their lives and finally take the helm of their destiny around the time of their first *Saturn return*, like a cosmic rite of passage into spiritual adulthood. Saturn takes 29.46 years to complete one full lap around the zodiac, which returns it to the same zodiac sign it was in at your birth. It takes 2.5 years to cross each sign, so the effects of one's first Saturn return are felt between ages 27 and 30.[258] The lucky human has three returns through which to mature, with a second return between ages 58–60, and hopefully again in one's late eighties.

Saturn returns are not usually a fun time. They can feel like the boss fight at the end of a videogame level, but then you "level up" and embrace your adult role in life. If you weren't already engaged in your sacred mission, you'll suddenly feel compelled to make big life changes, like change careers, get married or divorced, or have children. At twenty-seven years old, I suddenly wanted to have my first child. By twenty-eight, I'd relocated my family back to my home state and left behind the profession that I spent ten years and countless resources to achieve so I could raise my children myself. That is when I began seeking Witchcraft training in earnest. Without even knowing about Saturn's influence, these choices led me back to the occupation that my natal chart reflected that I'm here to do. It was absolutely the best decision to make the switch; I only wish I'd figured that out sooner. Folks who go ahead and dig into the work that fulfills their sacred mission will be least disrupted by their Saturn returns. It is a straight path to fulfillment, too, because destiny flows with you.

Step 2: Natal Chart

To start this astrological quest of self-discovery, you'll need to acquire your natal chart. To create this chart, you'll need to know the exact location, time, and date of your birth. If you don't know exactly, the approximate time of day can get you close. There are many websites and applications available online that prepare these natal charts for free and provide canned explanations. However, I recommend that you invest in yourself by seeking out a skilled professional astrologer for a full reading.

---

258. Dominguez, *Practical Astrology for Witches and Pagans*, 120.

A complete unpacking of the astrological mechanics involved in a natal chart is beyond the scope of this book. Frankly, it is beyond my own expertise. I recommend Joanna Martine Woolfolk's *The Only Astrology Book You'll Ever Need* as a guidebook to unpacking all the details of your natal chart.

In brief, remember that planets represent their sphere's divine state of being and source of power. In your natal chart, that planet's energy is filtered through which zodiac sign it was in at birth and determines how it influences your life.[259] Ivo Dominguez Jr. calls the breakdown of the zodiac signs the "12 styles of human wisdom and human folly … 12 basic modes of human consciousness."[260] That zodiac "filter" also tunes that planet's energy into its particular element and modality, as we covered in chapter 4. Recap: air lends intellectual qualities, earth lends material qualities, fire lends active qualities, water lends emotional and mystical qualities. Cardinal energy is a self-starter, fixed energy works hard to sustain and serve, mutable energy closes the deal and transmutes into the next cycle.

The next filter to determine how the planet's energy shows up in your life is known as the "house." The houses are the twelve big wedges that divide up the circle of your natal chart. Dominguez describes the houses as the energies of the zodiac signs projected "all the way down to earth" and represent twelve arenas of function in our lives.[261] For example, the fourth house is the arena of family and home life, whereas the eleventh house is the arena of friends and your social life.

Step 3: Researching Saturn's Influence

For this exercise, your task is to determine through which zodiac sign (and corresponding elemental energy and modality) Saturn's influence is being filtered into your life. Find out which planet rules that sign and which deities are associated with that planet for clues to those attributes. Then look into which house's arena that power is made concrete for you. For example: Saturn in Gemini (ruled by Mercury) in the tenth house of career and public standing. This information will indicate your style of adulthood and the general arena in which your sacred mission may be pursued.

Saturn's placement also indicates what kinds of struggles you're tasked to overcome, including the types of health challenges you might develop. This part may seem disheartening, but consider that "forewarned is forearmed," as they say. It's like the weather channel

---

259. Dominguez, *Practical Astrology for Witches and Pagans*, 21.

260. Dominguez, *Practical Astrology for Witches and Pagans*, 21.

261. Dominguez, *Practical Astrology for Witches and Pagans*, 25.

telling you what kind of storm is approaching, when and where it will hit, and what type of damage is likely so that you can prepare and make choices accordingly.

Employing the airy power of knowing, do some more research about what these placements mean for you. In your Book of Mirrors, make notes to fill in a table for yourself like the example given below. Apply what you know about the elemental power and modality of the sign Saturn is in for you to how those energies affected your personality, aptitudes, and motivations. Make note of the house's arena of life and jot down keywords for how those skills and aptitudes, obstacles and health challenges, are typically lived there. You'll no doubt notice that every astrology resource on Saturn's influence includes the potential ways that our fiery sides might twist these qualities to our bane, how we might *burn the Witch*, become *the problem* or *weak link* in society. But it will also give clues to what we're best suited to achieve.

Step 4: Brainstorming Your Sacred Mission

With all these details in mind, employ your airy power of wonder and brainstorm ways to responsibly apply Saturn's structure to your elemental fires to empower your life's sacred mission. What actions would help avoid the potential vices and health challenges? What can be surrendered to the fires of Divine Will so I can move forward? Look over the example chart below and use it to help you fill out your own. See the third column for an example of the thought process of airy wonder.

	Saturn's Placement[262]	What This Means for My Sacred Mission
Zodiac Sign	Gemini: Favorable placement. Versatile intellectual capabilities.	Seek work that requires mental flexibility and endurance, communication, and perception. Writer? Teacher?
Element of Sign	Air: Mental	Powers of knowing: research, academics. Wonderment: innovation, pioneering thought
Modality of Sign	Mutable	Good at methodically integrating data, multitasking, seeing patterns, and transmuting them into new forms—traverses the liminal.

---

262. Woolfolk, *The Only Astrology Book You'll Ever Need*, 267, 297.

	Saturn's Placement [263]	What This Means for My Sacred Mission
Planetary Ruler of Sign, Deities	Ruled by Mercury. Deities: Mercury, Hermes, Thoth.	Intellect, language, magick, mediumship, liminal travel, commerce, handcrafting.
House	Tenth house of career and public standing; community status reputation; all matters outside the home.	Seek a profession outside the home. Let ambitions serve the community, express mental talents outwardly; curate trustworthy public image.
Life obstacles	Early childhood lonliness and sadness; obstacles to early education and realizing identity separate from my parents; obstacles to travel.	Forgive my parents for the challenges of differentiation of my identity and beliefs. Realize obstacles will get easier as I age. Beware obstacles to travel later in life. Take extra care with public communication.
Health obstacles	Chest and lungs	No smoking; attend to cardiopulmonary health through diet and exercise, watch cholesterol, have regular mammograms.
Virtues to employ	Childlike idealism and curiosity; clear-minded, responsible, talents in finance and music; good stamina.	Be persistent and calculating; never stop learning or sharing, keep striving toward my ideals. Trust financial instincts.
Vices to avoid	Cynicism, skepticism, sarcasm, insensitivity, selfishness, overly cautious.	Take chances; try not to be so grim and serious all the time; have faith that success comes with persistence despite early obstacles; be purposefully sensitive to needs of others.

Step 5: Apply Fire

I trust that you're realizing how Saturn's influence has already shown up through your upbringing, life choices of education, jobs, hobbies, and motivations so far. What usage of your time and energy would further bring you the most happiness and fulfillment? In what ways could you share that happy fulfillment to improve the world? What needs to

---

263. Woolfolk, *The Only Astrology Book You'll Ever Need*, 267, 297.

be surrendered so you can move forward? An abusive relationship? The wrong job? An addiction? I promise life will get easier once you surrender those obstacles to the fires of your Divine Will.

Spend time in meditation, divination, and prayer to seek higher guidance on how best to align your personal will with Divine Will. Figure out what adjustments to your course would most effectively use these powers to benefit yourself and everyone your life touches. Then strike out, work hard, and do more of those beneficial things. Elemental fire magick will help.

Figure 29: Candle wrap image for fire by Heron Michelle

Formulary for Elemental Fire

As the Lithatide wanes toward the Summer Solstice, prepare your fiery formulary materials in preparation for the rites ahead. Craft your incense, oil, and fire magick candle. Reference the table below for the elemental correspondences of fire, and make substitutions as needed.[264]

Elemental Correspondences of Fire	
Alchemical Symbol	△
Color	Red
State of Matter	Plasma
Direction	South
Time of Day	Noon
Phase of Life	Youth
Season	Summer
Alchemical Qualities	Warm and dry
Mental Gender	Yang, masculine
Governs	Body of Will: passions, physical energy, action
Projective Power	The power to will
Receptive Power	The power to surrender
Elemental Beings	Salamander
Elemental Sovereign	Djin
Magickal Tool	Athame, sword, thurible
Consecration	Candle
Planetary	♂ Mars, ☉ sun
Day of the Week	Tuesday for Mars, Sunday for sun
Astrological Signs	Cardinal: Aries; fixed: Leo; mutable: Sagittarius

264. I assembled these element correspondence charts from many sources, but a good reference is *Llewellyn's Complete Book of Correspondences* by Sandra Kynes.

Elemental Correspondences of Fire	
Stone	Amber, bloodstone, fire agate, carnelian, golden tiger's-eye, lava rock, ruby, red calcite, fire opal, pyrite, rhodonite, sardonyx, sunstone, golden topaz, red zircon
Metals	Iron, steel, gold
Herbs	Angelica, basil, carnation, clove, dill, ginger, nutmeg, orange, garlic, hyssop, rosemary, marigold, sunflower, rue, St. John's wort
Trees/Woods/Barks	Alder, chestnut, holly, laurel, palm (draconis), walnut, yew, cinnamon
Resins	Dragon's blood, frankincense
Creatures	Bee, lion, red fox, ram, horse, tiger, porcupine

❧ Exercise 11: Fire Formulary Crafting ❧

Auspicious Timing

Look at the time frame you have left until Litha, and pick a day during a waxing lunar cycle, preferably while the moon is in a fire sign of Aries, Leo, or Sagittarius, and/or on the days/hours of Mars (Tuesday) or sun (Sunday.)

Needs

See the recipes below for specific materials and equipment for each recipe.

Lay your working altar with enough surface area to spread out, make a mess, and be artistically creative.

Consecration elements, including charcoal in a censer for testing your incense blend. Add anything that aids your connection to fire energies: iron, extra candles, images of dragons, lava rock, sunstone, hematite stones, etc.

Preparation

Awaken and consecrate your altar as taught in ritual 1.

Call upon your spiritual guides to be present and inspire your magickal creations.

For charging any fire-drawing materials, chant this charm:

Fire Blessing Charm

Powers of fire, salamander, and Djin!
By blade of Mars, controlled within!
Come power, will, and authority!
As I will, so mote it be!

❧ Elemental Fire Incense—Planetary Mars and Sun Magick ❧

This incense recipe is effective for rebalancing the body of the will and any journeys and spells where elemental powers of fire or planetary Mars and sun would aid in manifesting your intention: courage, protection, empowerment, motivation, and success.

Needs

1 part base wood—oak wood powder (earth, sun)

1 part cinnamon bark power (fire, sun)

2 parts resin—dragon's blood resin (fire, Mars)

½ part herb—ginger powder or chips (fire, Mars)

½ part herb—clove powder (fire, sun)

1 part herb—powdered peel of orange or tangerine (fire, sun)

Essential oils—10 drops each of sweet orange and clove (optional)

2 parts vegetable glycerin to bind

Stones: hematite, sunstone, or red aventurine

Dark-colored jar with lid and opening large enough for your incense spoon; red glass is ideal

Praxis

Grind all plant ingredients in your mortar and pestle clockwise until relatively fine. Invite their plant spirits to aid your work; thank them for their aid. Add the essential oil (optional) and glycerin, stir to combine and bind. Add stone chips of hematite or other substitute. Draw the alchemical sigil of fire in the incense with your ring finger, or athame if you already have one.

Charge with the powers of fire by picturing a raging fire, the crackle of wood and air consumed, and the light and heat released through the flickering flames. See the natural energy of that fire glowing with a red-hot light like lava, flowing down through your hands until you envision the blend also glowing red. Chant the fire blessing charm three times to build and direct power into the blend.

Transfer the blend to the jar and label it, include the date and the glyph of alchemical fire and planetary Mars ♂ and sun ☉ to continue charging. Burn some on your charcoal to test the scent and boost the fiery signal while you keep working.

⚶ Elemental Fire Anointing Oil ⚶

This oil may be used to anoint candles, yourself, or other magickal objects to bring them into sympathy with goals regarding your will.

Needs

Dark-colored 1-dram bottle with tightly sealing cap, red glass would be ideal

Mix 20 total drops of essential oil: choose from a mix of orange, clove, or ginger

3 stone chips of hematite, sunstone, or red aventurine

Jojoba oil for longer shelf life or other carrier oil for short-term use

Praxis

As you add each ingredient to the bottle, tap on the materials three times and awaken them to their powers of fire: willpower, surrender, courage, power. Invite them to be part of your magickal team and thank them for all the action they will incite.

When all materials are assembled in the bottle, cap it and swirl the oils together deosil, and charge it with the visualization above. Chant the fire blessing charge three times.

Label it with the name, date, and alchemical sigils of fire and planetary Mars ♂ and the sun ☉ to continue charging.

Annoint your solar plexis chakra with the oil blend to energize your magickal work.

⚶ Elemental Fire Candle ⚶

In the same manner used previously, prepare a seven-day glass-jarred sanctuary candle to channel powers of elemental fire.

Needs

Red seven-day sanctuary candle in glass jar. They are typically 2.25 x 8 inches tall and take refill insert candles no more than 2 inches wide.

The 7-inch square image from figure 29 can be copied and colored to create a candle wrap, or you may creatively decorate your own piece of lightweight paper.

13-inch length of red cord or ribbon

Flat head screwdriver or a power drill with large bit

½ teaspoon prepared fire herbal incense

3 drops prepared fire anointing oil

3 tiny chips of hematite, sunstone, or red aventurine, or substitute

Praxis

On the blank side of the 7-inch square candle wrap paper, write a fire gateway opening call. Compose your own or reference the calls provided in ritual 2. If you're not using the image provided in figure 29, decorate the outside of the wrapper with images of elemental fire, such as dragons or phoenix, athame or sword, salamanders, alchemical fire glyph, planetary glyphs for Mars ♂ and sun ☉, etc.

With the screwdriver or drill, bore out three holes in the wax about an inch deep. Load the candle by poking a bit of fire incense into the holes with a chopstick. Top with a stone chip in each hole. Then anoint with three drops of fire oil and rub it around the wax deosil with a bare ring finger.

Wrap the paper wrapper around the jar and tie down with the cord or ribbon. The charging of this candle will take place during the ritual journey to the realms of elemental fire.

Journey to the Realms of Fire

In the same manner done in previous journeys, this interactive ritual merges ritual actions made in the outer temple with a meditative journey envisioned within your astral temple. This functional high-alpha brainwave state is called "ritual consciousness."[265] When

---

265. Penczak, *Inner Temple of Witchraft*, 87.

prompted, intone or speak aloud, light candles, throw incense on the coals, etc. The ritual-ized journey is best enacted by listening to a recording of the meditation or as someone reads it aloud for you.

❖ Ritual 6: Elemental Fire Temple ❖

We continue the ritual cycle by calling the essence of elemental fire from the southern quarter and then taking a guided journey through your astral temple to the elemental realm of fire. The goal is to seek partnership with the salamanders and Sovereign Djin, receive insights about your magickal tools of fire, and which animal spirit allies may best aid your power and sacred mission.

Unlike complete temple creation, this rite only opens the southern gates of fire. Ele-mental journeys are most impactful when done outside, close to the element. This fire can be safely built in a fireplace, around a bonfire, or in a patio firepit. If outdoors is not possible, add additional red candles to your indoor altar.

Auspicious Timing

Enact this rite during the second waxing lunar cycle, nearest to the Summer Solstice when the moon is in a fire sign of Aries, Leo, or Sagittarius.

Needs

Consecration element: a small red fire candle as offering to the salamanders

Add any items that evoke fire for you: a red tablecloth, images, lava stone

Incense censer with sand and a hookah charcoal tab, tongs, small spoon, and a lighter or box of matches

Dedication sanctuary candle for Spirit

Fire herbal incense blend

Fire anointing oil

Prepared red fire sanctuary candle with red cord or ribbon

An iron nail, railroad spike, or other implement of iron or steel to hold. Hematite stone is another substitution with high iron content.

Your Book of Mirrors and a pen

Diagrams of fire invoking and banishing pentagrams for easy reference. See figure 24.

An athame if you already have one or just your "natural athame" of your projective hand. Ring finger projects the sun's power.

Device for playing a recording of the guided journey

Accessible fire extinguisher, just in case

Drinking water for additional hydration if you get thirsty during the rite

Preparation

Much like an athlete prior to physical exertion, eat a calorie-rich meal with some salt (electrolytes) a few hours before your rite. Hydrate with extra-pure water so that as you channel fire energy, your physical systems will have the extra energy and water to support your fiery work.

Begin with a physical cleaning and organizing of the ritual space and your altar. Bathe and dress in fresh, comfortable clothing, preferably barefoot with hair unbound, or nude as you prefer.

Lay your working altar accessibly before you, arranged such that you can meditate comfortably and still reach everything easily; pay extra attention to safe fire-tending practices. Note that for this initial fire working, there is a separate candle lit in the beginning to consecrate the altar and as offering to the salamanders. This is in addition to the elemental fire sanctuary candle prepared for charging during this rite and can later be used for altar consecrations as well.

Anoint your solar plexus chakra with fire anointing oil at your diaphragm.

Light your dedication sanctuary candle to welcome Spirit, who is ever-present.

Light the charcoal and place in the censer in preparation for loose incense burning.

Praxis

Altar Consecration: Awaken your altar for the element of fire as taught in ritual 1. Shift consciousness into your branches high in the atmosphere, touching the light of the sun. Breathe deeply and establish the flow of power connecting you to the three realms. Inhale that power as red light; exhale it through your projective hand. Hold the red fire consecration candle in that hand. Visualize red light drawn down from the sun itself to imbue the candle. Say: *I charge this candle as a being of fire.* Light the candle. Draw a banishing pentacle with the candle over the altar.

Say: *Powers of fire, burn free any impurity from this sacred space.* Envision a red energy imbuing the altar.

Hallowing: Walk the perimeter of your circle with the candle, chanting, *I consecrate this circle by the powers of fire.* Present the candle to the southern quarter and say, *As your Witch of fire, I greet you with fire and ask that you burn free any baneful energies from this circle tonight. So mote it be!*

Temple: Cast your circle with the awen cone of power as taught in ritual 2; close the sphere above and below.

Open the Southern Gate: As taught in ritual 2, face the south. Stand in a posture of fire evocation, natural athame raised in solute, receptive hand in fist at hip height (see figure 25). Exhale and see the red light of fire beaming from your projective hand. Your receptive hand is prepared to receive the inflowing energy. Stand tall, chin up, shoulders back; speak with authority from the diaphragm.

Say: *Powers of the south! Essence of fire! I summon you to this sacred place! Salamanders! Sovereign Djin of the burning inferno! Be with me now and lend your powers of courage and transformation. Strengthen my power for the work at hand. Awaken your lessons of willing and surrender within me. Come glowing ember and fiery sun; come heat of summer noon and blazing plasma to temper and empower this magick. I welcome you with gratitude. Hail and welcome!*

Draw the invoking pentagram of fire with the natural athame of your projective hand. See the star glowing with red light in the southern quarter. Encircle the pentagram deosil, turning the lock to open. Draw your fingers toward your lips, pulling in a streamer of elemental fire. Kiss your fingers, then with hand over your heart, bow to that direction. A red girder now encircles your temple in the south.

Sit down and prepare for meditation. Begin the recording of this guided journey.

✤ Meditation 7: Guided Journey to the Realms of Fire ✤

Close your eyes; take a deep breath. Picture your most magickal Self sitting in a comfortable chair in a comfortable room inside your mind. It is quiet and still in your sanctuary. Your eyes are now a window on a distant wall of that room. Any distracting noises or stray thoughts are merely birds flying past that distant window … release them without care. (*Pause.*)

There is a skylight above you, and a soft beam of divine light shines down upon your crown chakra. Breathe down the light with three deep breaths. Inhale through the nose and exhale through the mouth … releasing all tension. (*Pause for three breaths.*) You are at perfect ease on all levels. (*Pause.*)

There is a beautiful, ornate door in the floor of your meditation room, a door leading to all possibility. Open that door, finding a spiral staircase descending beyond. With each exhale of your breath, step down, deeper and deeper, descending into your subconscious mind, and deep into your own belly. At the foot of the stairs, you'll arrive at your inner crossroads. Twelve steps down, around and 'round you tread the spiral staircase.

Before you hangs a looking glass, a portal outward to the astral realms where all things are possible by a mere thought. Picture your astral temple upon the glass. (*Pause.*)

Say: *My intention is to journey to my astral temple to seek the elemental realm of fire and to learn the mysteries of will and surrender. I tread the path of power, seeking a relationship with the beings who govern the essence of fire known as salamanders and their sovereign, Djin. I wish to receive my tool of fire and animal allies to aid my empowerment and sacred mission. I call upon my guides, gods, and ancestors to keep me safe and show me the way. Blessèd be.* (*Pause.*)

On the count of three, step through the portal and arrive on the path to your temple. One, two, three, step through!

You arrive on the astral plane; the great world tree looms large in the distance. Take the temple path that lies before you. Down, down, down the path you tread, seeing the glowing light of your temple ahead. Smell the sweet scent of the temple incense burning, enticing you home.

You arrive at your astral temple and enter. This sacred place is perfectly suited to your needs. The pure waters of Divine Love flow cool and refreshing from your place of water. The breeze of Divine Inspiration blows gently through, sweet and fresh, from your place of air. The sacred flames of your Divine Will glow brightly from your place of fire. Find your way now to the heart of your temple, the earthen altar itself, broad and stable. Stand before your altar in strength.

On the altar several things are spread before you: a red candle, a pot of herbal incense, and a censer with hot coals prepared for your ceremony. Onto that hot coal, sprinkle some incense to call fire. As that smoke billows, the aroma awakens your fiery connections.

Say aloud: *Welcome, plant spirits of cinnamon and dragon's blood! Open the way to the realms of earth. Aid me now with your fiery powers!*

Upon the altar is an implement of iron. Pick it up and hold it in your receptive hand. Shift your attention to the surface of the iron against your palm. In your mind's eye, imagine yourself like the blacksmith at a forge, the iron red hot in the burning orange coals. Feel the heat and light. Pull the iron out of the coals and imagine in your other hand a hammer, which beats the soft red iron against the anvil. Feel how the metal, pliable, surrenders to the shape demanded by the hammer. (*Pause.*) Feel also the cold, unyielding iron of the anvil. With power and persistence, the will of the blacksmith shapes and refines the raw material into a formidable blade, sharp and strong. Watch as it takes form. (*Long pause.*) Pull your attention back, back to feel the cool, hard iron in your palms once more. Place it back upon the altar.

Pick up your red sanctuary candle prepared for elemental fire and hold it in your projective hand. Remember that connection to the heat and power of the forge, and channel that fire through your hands into the candle to awaken the potential combustion within it. Tap the glass three times until you see it glowing red in your mind's eye. Light the red candle.

The illumination in the temple also reddens, a flickering play of light and shadow. Your very metabolism quickens, vision lengthening as you sense a shift; the powers of fire are crackling nearby.

In your mind's eye, turn to face the southern quarter of your temple. Hold your fists raised strong to waist height, as though you hold hammer and blade at the forge.

With power in the voice, say aloud: *Powers of fire! You who are catalyst, force, and transmutation, I call upon your elemental beings known as salamanders and seek to know their sovereign, Djin! Ignite and empower my will and sacred mission! Grant me entrance into your fiery realms. Open the portal and show me the way!*

The gateway in the south appears. See it clearly as you approach the gate; symbols and images adorn the frame. Remember them. (*Pause.*)

You hear the crack and roar of burning plasma beyond the gate. Hot, dry, smell of smoke and cinder. Flaring, slink, and molten dance of life and light to pounding rhythm of distant drums.

Red energy glows through the gateway to fill your auric field. Sparking facets form around the edge of your aura. Inside you remain cool and shielded, like wearing a firefighter's suit of protection. Your density shifts lighter with your auric vibration in perfect resonance with the essence of fire. You are completely safe to journey within their realms. (*Pause.*)

Touch the gateway and it shimmers open. Step forward through the portal into a landscape of sand and rock at night. There is a bonfire in the distance … a flame carries you, setting you down by the blazing fire. Watch the flames dancing, consuming and illuminating the darkness. (*Pause.*)

The edge of your aura works like a lens. Now you can see a salamander at the heart of every flame, flickers that leap from the sand. (*Pause.*) How do they present themselves to you? (*Pause.*)

These guardians of essential fire beckon you to join them in their leaping fire dance. You, too, are the heart of fire, and so you follow them. (*Pause.*) There is a pulse; you hear the drumbeat of your heart and the pounding of your blood. In the crackling fugue a chaotic rhythm syncopates. (*Pause.*)

Salamanders dart around this burning landscape in a dance to pounding drumbeats, and you join them … Dancing, dancing … (*Pause.*) Let the fire transmute all fear into courage. All weakness surrenders to be strengthened as you dance, dance, dance … (*Long pause.*)

Salamanders lead you now to a place of power where you will meet Sovereign Djin. There is a pull to face a certain direction, as though a pressure is building. Raise your fisted hands in the posture of fire once more.

By singing aloud an intonation of Djin's name, we set a resonance by which to summon the sovereign. In a mid- to high-range tone, with power in the voice, sing the name Djin on three long, sustained breaths. Inhale and intone: *Djin … Djin … Djin …*

The collective consciousness of fiery essence flickers into view. Djin, the sovereign of fire, appears before you in glorious radiance. Introduce yourself. (*Pause.*) Remember all the details of his appearance for you. (*Pause.*)

You ask: *Djin! I seek your guidance along the path of power in my life. How should I take control and build a secure life?* Djin shares his wisdom with you now. (*Long pause.*)

You ask: *Djin, please teach me the lessons of will. Which sacred mission would best align my personal will with Divine Will for a fulfilled life?* Djin invites you on a journey to receive your sacred mission. (*Long pause.*)

You ask: *Djin, please teach me the lessons of surrender. Which ego attachments must I release to the fires for tempering?* Djin invites you into the tempering white flames, and you see what must be surrendered gently detaching and transmuting into greater strength. (*Pause.*) Release all that does not serve your highest good. Those weaknesses are transmuted into illumination. You are the tempered blade wielded in your own life. (*Long pause.*)

You ask: *Djin, will you partner with me in my magick?* (*Pause.*)

If yes, you ask Djin: *Which altar tool of fire would best summon the powers of the salamanders and elemental fire to my Great Work? Perhaps an athame or sword? Something else?* Djin now presents you with that tool. Remember the details. (*Pause.*) You are shown where and how you might obtain this tool in the Middleworld. Receive the vision. (*Long pause.*)

You ask: *Djin, which animal spirit can best aid my balance of will?* Djin introduces you to an animal spirit who can aid your balance with a vision of what they can teach you. Receive the vision. (*Long pause.*)

Accept these gifts and visions with gratitude as you bid Djin farewell. Djin flickers into smoke and is gone.

The salamanders' flames surge to take you back the way you came, dancing back to the bonfire on the sands at night and the portal back to your astral temple. The salamanders recede into the fires once more. (*Pause.*)

Back to the gate, returning to your temple, you step back through that portal, and the red glowing suit is reabsorbed by the realms of fire.

Step back to the altar. Placing your gift of the tool upon the altar, you remember all the lessons with perfect clarity. Place your hands on the altar and ground all excess energies, allowing the stone to cool and stabilize you once more, returning to a normal, comfortable density. Sit for a moment in the candlelight and reflect on all that you've experienced here. (*Long pause.*) Remember that you can return to your temple and the gates of fire whenever you wish.

Now it is time to return to waking consciousness. Leaving your temple, now follow the path back. Back, back the way you came, seeking out the looking glass, that portal back into yourself. See yourself on that looking glass. Passing through this portal, you will once more follow the umbilical cord. Three steps back into your own belly. Three, two, one, step through!

Take the spiral stairway back up twelve steps, rising higher and higher, returning to waking consciousness. Returning to the little room behind your eyes, closing the trapdoor in the floor behind you.

Say aloud: *I am grateful to my guides, gods, and ancestors—all those who kept me safe and showed me the way. Blessèd Be.* Stretch your muscles. When you are ready to return to your day, refreshed and balanced, walk to the window of your eyes, opening them to return to your outer temple.

Journal Reflection

In your Book of Mirrors, record the messages from your allies, draw your visions, and explore your thoughts and feelings about the experience for as long as you'd like.

Deconstructing the Temple

Close the elemental gateway by standing to face the south in the posture of fire, natural athame raised in salute. See figure 25.

Say: *Powers of the south! Essence of fire! Salamanders and Sovereign Djin! I am grateful for your empowering presence and your aid in these rites. Continue to strengthen my will and Great Work along the path of power. For now, I release you now to your fair and fiery realms! Hail and farewell!*

See the red girder and all powers receding back through the gateway of your circle. Draw the banishing pentagram of fire with your natural athame, like a key in the lock. As you encircle the star widdershins, see the portal closing and locking.

Once more kiss your athame or fingers, but this time follow through like a fencer with a thrusting gesture toward the quarter, brandishing your blade with fierce resolve. Direct any remaining energy outward to their realm. Bow.

Release the circle by gathering the sphere of remaining energy into your hands, smaller and smaller until it is imagined like a glowing ball over the altar. Charge the ball to further light your way along the Pentacle Path. Shout *Release!* as you toss the sphere upward to the cosmos. Clapping your hands as you chant, *The circle is open but never broken, Merry meet, merry part, and merry meet again.*

Magick of the Will

Time to put your new fiery partnerships into action. Spells of fire are most effective when they balance the body of will within your fivefold Self. Again, the holistic nature of existence is interwoven at every level, just as the pentacle depicts. To use this power of Divine Will safely, one must be in healthy balance on all levels.

- **Mental:** Will fuels what vision and ideals you set your mind to accomplishing.

- **Emotional:** Will acts upon the deepest desire of the heart. It is the passion that stubbornly prods you to rise from the mat and keep fighting no matter how many times you are knocked down.

- **Physical:** Will compels you to invest resources, blood, sweat, tears, and bones into your sacred mission.

- **Will:** Divine Will grants the commission as an agent of Divine Love and gives you the authority, firepower, and energy needed to accomplish your goals.

- **Spirit:** When personal will is in alignment with Divine Will, spirit flows freely from microcosm to macrocosm to wield the most powerful tool in creation: magick.

✤ Spell 4: Shield of Mars ✤

With that holistic balance in mind, enact a Shield of Mars spell. Consider this line of the "Rede of the Wiccae" poem: "When misfortune is enow, wear the blue star on thy brow."[266] This instruction hints at the power of the banishing pentagram as a balanced means to establish a shield of protection when there is danger or misfortune. This shield is essential magick for walking the Pentacle Path within the battleground of the dominator culture. This adaptation of a traditional practice uses the combination of earth and fire energy to create energetic armor that deflects all baneful influence.

Planetary Influences
Mars and Saturn, fire and earth

Auspicious Timing
Waxing moon in a fire sign of Aries, Leo, or Sagittarius, day/hours of Mars (Tuesday) or sun (Sunday).

---

266. Mathiesen and Theitic, *The Rede of the Wiccae*, 52–53.

Needs

Add any items to your working altar that evoke a feeling of empowerment and protection

Dedication sancturary candle for Spirit, which is always present

Charged elemental fire and earth sanctuary candles

Fire anointing oil blend

Fire incense blend

Incense censer with sand, and a hookah charcoal tab, tongs and a small spoon, lighter or box of matches

A bowl of sea salt

A bowl of pure water

A steel or iron-bladed athame and pentacle paten if you already have them

Anything iron for protection of Mars—iron nails, a railroad spike, or a hematite stone

An image for reference of the banishing earth pentagram and the fire invoking pentagram. See figure 24.

Drinking water for additional hydration if you get thirsty during the rite

Preparation

Once more, eat a calorie-rich meal with some salt (electrolytes) a few hours before your rite. Hydrate with extra-pure water so that your physical systems can support your fiery work.

Bathe and dress in fresh clothing that is comfortable, feet bare and hair unbound, or nude as you prefer.

Lay your working altar for fire and earth, arranged such that you can meditate comfortably with your materials easily visible and accessible before you.

Praxis

Awaken and consecrate your working altar as taught in ritual 1. Hallow yourself and the perimeter of the circle by the four elements as taught in ritual 2.

Cast your circle with the awen chant, closing the sphere above and below. Open the gateways to earth in the north and fire in the south as taught in ritual 2; light their candles.

Invite to be present your guides, ancestors, and Spirit. Call the gods Saturn and Mars if you are comfortable doing so.

Sit, close your eyes, breathe deeply, and go to the meditation room in your mind from meditation 1. Descend through the trapdoor, down the spiral stairs, to arrive at your own center, in a deeply relaxed and mindful state.

In the looking glass, picture your astral temple. On the count of three, step through the looking glass to arrive at the door to your temple. One, two, three, step through!

You find your astral temple just as you left it. Entering through the door, look around, finding the Sacred Flame you tend still burning brightly. Feel the sweet breeze from your place of air, and smell the incense burning. Feel the cool mist from your place of water and be cleansed. Back to your earthen altar, and you are grounded and centered. (*Pause.*)

Upon the altar, see a paten, a disk-shaped tool with the symbol of the pentacle: the five-pointed star. The points represent the five elements: earth, air, fire, and water in perfect balance with Spirit, encircled. They represent the continuity of Divine Love weaving together the living cosmos. (*Pause.*) The pentacle is also a symbol of humankind in fivefold existence.

Your intention through this exercise is to empower yourself through the fivefold path, build up a shield of protection with the banishing pentagram, and then ignite the fires of Divine Will within you to empower your sacred mission.

Envision yourself at the center of your temple, and physically stand up now in a posture of power and authority: feet shoulder-width apart, chin up, shoulders back. Raise your arms like the branches of a tree. Envision the white light of Spirit opening your crown chakra, flowing freely down through an open channel from crown to root chakra. Exhale down the light of the God. (*Pause.*)

Now, envision a black light of Spirit opening your root chakra, flowing up through the open channel, from root to crown chakra. Inhale up the darkness of the Goddess. (*Pause.*)

Reach up with your right hand into the atmosphere and breathe down elemental air as yellow light. See a sphere of Divine Truth now glowing yellow in your right palm.

Reach up with your left hand into the fiery sun and stars and breathe down elemental fire. See a sphere of Divine Power now glowing red in your left palm. (*Pause.*)

Dig deeply through the roots of your left foot into the foundation of stone and breathe up elemental earth. You stand upon a sphere of Divine Sovereignty now glowing green under your left foot. (*Pause.*)

Dig deeply through the roots of your right foot into the water table and breathe up elemental water. You stand upon a sphere of Divine Love glowing blue under your left foot. (*Pause.*)

See yourself as an embodied pentagram, connected through the center by Divinity in Upperworld, Middleworld, and Underworld. Stand in power, interweaving the liminal places between land, sea, sky, and stars. Cross your arms over your chest, pressing the spheres of truth and power into the solar plexus chakra of your belly. (*Pause.*)

Kneel, touching the spheres of sovereignty and love beneath you. Stand, drawing up the power through your body, once more crossing your arms over your chest, and pressing the spheres of sovereignty and love into the solar plexus chakra in your belly.

Lower your hands and form with your fingers an upward-pointing triangle, the glyph of alchemical fire, and hold this hand position over your solar plexus chakra. Seeing the integrated beams like a rainbow of white light flowing through you. This fivefold power forms a torus of energy extending throughout your auric field.

Say aloud: *I am divine; I am sovereign; I see the truth; I am powerful; I am loving; I am whole and complete within myself. I am a perfect child of the God/dess.*

From your altar, pick up the iron in your projective hand (athame, nail, railroad spike, hematite), extend your index and middle (Saturn) finger along the iron, pointing. Channel the power from above and below through your fingers, like wielding a laser pen in green energy of elemental earth. With the essence of earth, you cast protection from any harms that could interfere with your health, safety, and abundance in the Middleworld, as well as any spiritual interferences to accomplishing your sacred mission. Earth offers grounding and a practical tempering of your fires.

In total, you will draw six banishing pentagrams of earth. This forms a shield on the inside surface of your auric field in all six directions around you: four cardinal directions, below, and above.

With the green light, draw the first banishing pentagram of earth in the air before you: start at the bottom left corner, up to the top point, down to the bottom right, across to the left, across to the right, back down where you began, back to Spirit at the top. Then encircle it widdershins, or counterclockwise, to banish all harm from that boundary.

See the blazing green pentacle before you, protecting your free will and sovereignty from the front. (*Long pause.*)

Now turn 90 degrees to your right (deosil) and repeat, drawing the green pentacle over your right shoulder. (*Long pause.*) Turn 90 degrees deosil again, drawing the green pentacle behind you. (*Long pause.*) Turn 90 degrees deosil again, drawing the green pentacle over your left shoulder. (*Long pause.*) Then draw the green pentacle below your feet (*Long pause.*) and above your head. (*Long pause.*)

Now, take a moment, turning in your mind's eye to see these six pentacles surrounding you, drawn between the worlds, in a place beyond place, in a time beyond time.

Say aloud: *I deflect all that does not serve my highest good. Only love will enter in, and only love will emerge. Within these shields, I am secure, nourished, and balanced on all levels; I am complete within myself, a perfect child of the God/dess.*

Like programming your spiritual security system, you can now set any additional rules and consent for what is welcomed within your auric sphere. Set your intentions for when, how, and who (physical or spiritual beings) may interact with you and under what circumstances. (*Long pause.*)

Your glowing green energetic shield now begins to shift and mold itself to your form, becoming your energetic armor. Imagine your armor in any design and style you like, fitting you perfectly, flexible, like your second skin. (*Pause.*)

Ask your divine guides: *From what threats to my sovereignty, truth, and free will do my shields protect me?* Receive the vision. (*Pause.*)

Ask your divine guides: *Which boundaries should I actively defend with my power?* Receive the vision. (*Pause.*)

Ask your divine guides: *I seek to know my sacred mission. For which divine purpose should my witchery strive?* Receive the vision. (*Pause.*)

Now, shift your attention to your solar plexus chakra and your fires smoldering in the engine of your will. Touch your belly with your fingertips and pull out those fires as a red ray of light. With your iron or natural athame, draw an invoking pentagram of fire over your belly, encircle the star deosil to activate the fiery star, like a sheriff's badge…

Say: *By powers of fire and Divine Will, I claim my badge of sovereign authority!*

Now, with your iron or natural athame, draw an invoking pentagram of fire below your feet; encircle the star deosil to activate, and draw up the molten fire of the earth, tapping into the fiery will of the Goddess… Say: *By fiery powers of the goddess and her Divine Will, I empower my badge of sovereign authority!*

Now, with your iron or natural athame, draw an invoking pentagram of fire above your head; encircle the star deosil to activate, and draw down the plasma fire of the sun, tapping into the fiery will of the God … Say: *By fiery powers of the god and his Divine Will, I empower my badge of sovereign authority!* Envision a column of red light running through you, sourcing divine power above and below. Cast that red star before you, a beacon projected like a knight's shield before you on your receptive side.

Say aloud: *May all that I defend serve Divine Will for the benefit of all involved, harming none.*

Now, from your projective hand, project the beam of red light into a sword, like a Jedi lightsaber. Say aloud: *By the power of Divine Will, I accept their commission as an agent of Divine Love. May all that I create be a benefit in service to the natural order of the Two Who Move as One, harming none. So mote it be!*

You stand in this temple of your own making, armored, shielded, and armed by Divine Will, prepared to safely explore the three worlds. (*Pause.*)

In your mind's eye, shift your attention back to your altar as the center of your astral temple. Upon the altar stone, you find gifts, weapons, tools of some kind to be taken up in power and security within your life. What do you find? (*Pause.*) Offer gratitude for the gifts.

Sit at your physical working altar, and in your Book of Mirrors journal about your discoveries. Draw a sketch of your armor, sword, and gifts.

When it is time to return, leave the temple and in your mind's eye, journey back to the looking glass, returning back the way you came. See yourself upon the looking glass. In three steps you return into your own belly. Three, two, one, step through!

Arrive back at the center of your being at the foot of the spiral stairs. Taking twelve steps back up, return to waking consciousness, and begin to stretch your muscles. At the top of the stairs, close the trapdoor behind you. Cross the room to the window, and when you are ready, open your eyes.

Close your temple by releasing your guides and gods with gratitude. Close the gates to elemental fire and earth with gratitude to Djin and the salamanders and Ghob and the gnomes for their continued aid in empowering your shields and magickal weapons. Extinguish all flames. Release the circle, gathering the remaining sphere of light, charging it and releasing to guide your path with the integrity of the God/dess. Remember that you still wear your armor and remain protected and empowered on all levels wherever you go within the three worlds.

❧ Journal Reflection: The Path of Power ❧

In your Book of Mirrors, use the Witch's Jewel of Power framework below to record your impressions for your future Self to find. Consider these questions: What discoveries have you made about your sacred mission? How are you now applying your fires to that work? Consider your level of motivation, temper, and stage of power. In what ways do you feel more internally empowered now?

From Air: To Know and to Wonder
- What impactful thing have you learned from this lesson?
- What do you still wonder about that needs further exploration?

From Fire: To Will and to Surrender
- How did you apply your will to these exercises? Did you adapt them to make them your own? What worked or didn't work well for you?
- Was there any expectation, assumption, or fear that needs to be surrendered?

From Water: To Dare and to Accept
- What gut emotional reactions came up for you?
- What surprised you? Which were easy to accept?
- Which do you dare to challenge or overcome?

From Earth: To Be Silent and to Resonate
- Now that the work is done, pay attention to what is going on in your life.
- How has this work affected your perceptions, actions, dreams? What patterns emerge?
- In what practical ways will you resonate your new awareness into reality?

Chapter 15
Element of Water and the Path of Love

On the Wheel of the Year, water's mysteries are explored from High Summer through High Autumn, as the elemental journey turns down the path of love. This chapter's lessons are divided into two parts: During the 6.5 weeks of the waning Mabontide, explore the projective elemental mystery *to dare*. During the 6.5 weeks of the waxing Samhaintide, explore the receptive elemental mystery *to accept*.

The Great Work: Wheel of the Year

As we tread the path of love, there are three ritual workings with water, which may be timed to the three lunar tides that crest within this solar period:

1. Crafting formulary materials for water rituals and spells.

2. Taking a ritual journey to the realms of elemental water.

3. Performing a two-part spell with planetary moon for holistic balancing of your emotional health and healing wounds of the heart.

Mabontide: Lammas to Mabon

From Lammas to Mabon, apply the watery mysteries of *daring* and ask which emotional barriers need to be dismantled in order to create the changes you've been working on during this year's Great Work. What impediments need to be overcome in order to regain emotional balance? Consider the wounds of the heart and whatever you are grieving. Consider what societal impediments, taboos, or outmoded restrictions about love and relationships need to be redefined in order to advance your sacred mission in the world. Pursue daring new relationships. Read the chapter's lessons, complete the exercises, and then prepare your water magick sanctuary candle and the formulary materials for the rituals and spells to come.

Samhaintide: Mabon to Samhain

As the autumn cools, shift into the receptive mysteries of *acceptance*. Take stock of all you've harvested so far this year and identify which new mold is coming into form. This mold will shape your new and improved Self and the witching life you've been working for. As you approach the third harvest of Samhain, cease striving and accept the new reality you've created. Allow yourself to settle into this new shape. This time of acceptance also requires that you evaluate which of your personal boundaries might need to be defended in order to maintain your emotional balance. Every day of this cycle, drink plenty of pure water. Doing energy work will require even more hydration or you'll blow out your circuits. Mindfully observe your relationships, remembering the lessons of Perfect Love and accepting the wholeness of the people in your life. Shortly after Mabon, take the ritual journey to the realms of water, seeking alliances with the undines and Sovereign Nicksa, guidance about the correct tool of water for you, and an ancestor ally to aid the balance of your emotional body. Then, seek out or begin crafting your tool of water as a continuation of your magick. Apply what you've learned to enact the two-part lunar spells of emotional healing.

The Pentacle Path of Love and the Emotional Body	
Chakras	Heart Chakra
Regulates	Interdependence
Opened by	Divine Love
Blocked by	Grief of separateness
Witchcraft Goal	Healing from wounds of fear
Love Conditions	Security vs. fear of violation Trustworthiness vs. fear of deception
Charm of Affirmation	By the powers of water and air, I am safe from all harm; I can trust in my care.

Mysteries of Elemental Water

Elemental water forms our emotional bodies and governs shape and form. Water will always form to the shape of its container and is easily molded by intention. Water rules the sense of *taste*, which is one reason why Witches fill their chalices with something tasty to drink as a means of enjoying water's power. In Hermetic alchemy, elemental water is said to have a wet and cold nature and anchors the polarity of fierce feminine power.

Water is the element of the astral plane and the subconscious mind. Ruled by the moon, water is the psychic energy shaped by the other elemental influences yet forms the matrix out of which our reality blooms. Just like physical water, its power flows everywhere, connecting everything.

In water we dive deeply into our intuition, dreams, and visions. These spiritual waters are where our subconscious mind rests. When you're asleep, the watery realm of the astral plane is where your subconscious mind goes to dream. Beyond our body's physical needs for rest, if humans do not sleep, we go certifiably insane after a few days. But it isn't just unconsciousness that we require for our mental health; we have to achieve REM (rapid eye movement) levels of sleep when we dream, where our watery essence is poured back into the astral ocean of Divine Love. That is the true spiritual rest. Maintaining the illusion of separateness is exhausting, and without regular returns to our emotionally and spiritually interconnected realm, we can't recharge.

Water teaches us that existence is cyclical, tidal; there is an ebb and flow of all life. These mysteries are mirrored throughout the cycles of nature, which all begin (cardinal), peak in power (fixed), and decline to be transmuted into something new (mutable.) This is especially true of the 29.5-day cycle of both the moon and menses—full moon corresponding to ovulation and dark moon corresponding to menstruation.

Elemental water is also associated with the sun setting in the west and so is symbolically linked with the liminal transition between realms where endings and beginnings meet. So elemental water is mutable and also dual in nature: born from the water of our mother womb but returning to the astral waters of the Great Goddess, which receive us at death and then prepare us for rebirth. Therefore, water and the west are also associated with themes of death and rebirth.

Water Through the Zodiac

The lessons of elemental water emerge through the human life cycle and zodiac first as cardinal Cancer, as the adolescent who traverses the liminal waters of individuation. Cancer's water expresses as the lessons of "I feel." They are here to teach others that love is about devotion while learning that love requires mutual freedom. Later, water emerges through fixed Scorpio as an exploration of sexual intimacy expressed as the lessons of "I desire." Scorpio is here to teach others that love can be passionate while learning that love requires mutual surrender. Finally, mutable Pisces explores lessons of submission, expressing as the lessons of "I believe." Pisces folks are here to teach others that love is compassionate while learning that "love" comprises everything in the cosmos, without conditions.[267]

Witch's Jewel of Power: Water		
	Yang: projective	Yin: receptive
Mystery Teaching	To dare	To accept
Wheel of Year	Lammas through Mabon	Mabon through Samhain
Planetary Sphere	Neptune	Moon

267. Goodman, *Linda Goodman's Love Signs*, 13.

Witch's Jewel of Power: To Dare

To dare is the projective power of elemental water. Water knows no discrimination; all streams flow together. Water's lessons of daring are about inclusion. There is no drop too precious nor too polluted to be excluded: ocean, rain, holy water, and toilet water alike. Water represents emotions and the heart; it takes daring to open your heart to others. Daring waters teach us how to work together so we can overcome all obstacles. Once gathered together, the tide raises all ships equally. A drop of dew may seem peaceful and powerless. But remember that the persistence of many single drops in a stream can precision drill through solid rock as though it were butter. Many drops of water joined together can become a violent tidal wave of utter destruction: fancy resorts and shanty-towns alike can be indiscriminately rendered into matchsticks.

Water's projective power is one of fearlessness. With the power of elemental water, you can *dare* to overcome all barriers to wholeness before you. Much like a raging river rising up to break the banks and flow over all impediments, the daring power of water is the radical energy to blast through all preconceived limitations and societal injustice. It is this daring that fuels revolutions and movements for change, like the women's suffrage movement of the 1910s and the civil rights movement of the 1960s.

Daring is also the boldness to heal your emotional wounds, strengthen your weaknesses, and seek relationships despite the risk of disappointment. Call on water's power to release those who've wounded you in the past and call up the necessary bravery to stop the cycle of harm from causing further destruction. Through the power of daring water, redefine your boundaries and carve a new path for yourself in life. Like the river tumbles a stone, water can help you smooth over the jagged edges and polish yourself to a spiffy shine.

The projective power of daring breaks the old molds so you can redefine yourself. Daring to overflow the cauldron's edge can only happen after you discover where that edge lies, then you can boldly reach new depths of compassion and intuition. Once the cauldron spills, there is no containing this power.

Witch's Jewel of Power: To Accept

To accept is the receptive power of elemental water. *Acceptance* is an acknowledgment of the present mold that defines you. You have to know who you are right now (the good, the bad, and the ugly) in order to diagnose your wounds, strengthen weaknesses, and put your strengths to work. You have to know where you are so you can chart a course to where you want to be. Acceptance is the first step in any evolutionary path toward emotional maturity.

Consider the Witch's chalice and cauldron, the magickal tools of water; they teach us about defining and honoring boundaries. Acceptance is the "cup" that molds your emotional water. This power is about settling into the circumstances of your body, environment, family, friends, work, etc. It is about acknowledging what is truly happening right now so you can determine what you'd like your life to become. For example, you first have to accept that systemic racism and sexism exist before you can take action to correct the problem.

Cooperative Tools of the Goddess

Once more, it is the receptive (goddess) powers of elemental water that hold the cooperative lessons we need to evolve our culture into a more compassionate future. Acceptance is where ultimate emotional power lies. As an example, consider how Western society regards death. In a dominator culture, threat of death is used as a means of fearful control over others. Death and life are a competition, always striving to thwart death, with phrases often used like "losing the battle" after someone dies from a long illness. Unnaturally thwarting spiritual annihilation after death became an obsession in many ancient cultures. An example being the funerary practices of the Egyptian pharaohs. However, accepting mortality and embracing the mutable phase of the cycle as being natural and necessary releases our power to enjoy life and love. When we can no longer be threatened with death as a means of controlling our choices, we fully embrace water's cooperative power.

Consider the characters of Voldemort in the Harry Potter books and Darth Vader in the Star Wars movies: both characters feared death and became embittered over the loss of love. Both characters turned to baneful magick in an attempt to thwart death, becoming evil villains capable of atrocity. In both tales, evil forces were defeated by rebels whose love, friendship, and unity illustrate how many individual "drops of water" could join together and rise up in a tidal wave to defeat that evil. The heroes of these stories reluctantly became warriors of cooperation and love who bravely risked dying in battle so they could overcome tyranny and restore liberty and sovereignty to loved ones. This truth of loving unity is a human anthem that repeats throughout our culture, illustrating the relationship between acceptance and daring in regard to power.

The Path of Love

Our emotional experience is arguably the most important aspect of being human. In her version of the Wiccan creation myth, Starhawk concludes with "All began in love; all seeks to return to love. Love is the law, the teacher of wisdom, and the great revealer of mysteries."[268] In this metaphor, the physical world is an embodiment of *divine emotion*. It's all love, baby! This is a sweet answer for the questions of existential dread we all ask eventually: What is our human purpose here? My answer: I love, therefore I am.

The panentheist paradigm begins and ends with Divine Love. Ideally, all Witchcraft based in the God/dess is sourced from the heart space. Author Miles Batty wisely described Divine Love as "the principal life force … the language of the Goddess, and Witches speak in her language."[269] If we are made of Divine Love, then the ground of being would be the essence of emotion, like an ocean of feeling. To awaken from the coma of the divisive, self-loathing, dog-eat-dog material world into the enlightenment of the Craft is to realize that we are interconnected with everyone and everything in the cosmos. This message of Divine Love is *way* more inclusive than "love your neighbor as yourself."[270] That may have been the message of the Piscean Age, but Witchcraft for the Age of Aquarius will help us realize that *my neighbors and I are One; we are Divine Love.*

Sadly, divisive messages are on repeat in our modern society, like the death rattle of the patriarchy as the era ends, perpetuated by folks whose awareness hasn't evolved higher than the first three chakras of *what I need*, *what I have*, and *what I want*. Those levels are necessary, but when they are overindulged and out of balance those folks remain emotionally immature. To fully embrace the path of love requires the Witch to wake up and move beyond the selfish, reactionary, entitled stages of childhood.

Too often, wounded and hurting folks wander over to the Witchcraft aisle of the bookstore and seek to *win* the human *race* with magick. If they remain bound by jealousy, hate, or resentment of whomever they still identify as *others*; if they seek power to exploit nature for their exclusive gain; or if they use magick in an attempt to gain superiority over anyone

---

268. Starhawk, *Spiral Dance*, 32.

269. Miles Batty, *Teaching Witchcraft: A Guide for Teachers and Students of the Old Religion* (Longview, TX: Three Moons Media, 2006), 123.

270. Matthew 22:39, Bruce M. Metzger and Roland E. Murphy, eds. *The New Oxford Annotated Bible with the Apocryphal/Deuterocanonical Books, New Revised Standard Edition* (New York: Oxford University Press, 1991, 1994).

else, that impedes them from attaining the truly awesome potential of Modern Witchcraft. That is *dominator culture* thinking, and we don't play that game at Mama's house.

Hermetic Witchcraft requires the Witch to walk the path of love in equal measure to those of truth, power, and sovereignty. Until you at least *want* to mature into a responsible adult, willing to lay little ego aside and get your hands dirty in service to the web of life, then you aren't yet ready for the keys to this magickal arsenal. Moreover, loving and respecting yourself is the most important prerequisite for successful magickal work. Whatever you feel about yourself deep down in your subconscious is exactly what your magick will reinforce. Therefore, the work of elemental water magick and rebalancing the emotional body is to ensure that you feel your sacred place within the greatness of Divine Love. For that we'll have to both identify what wounded our hearts and then heal those wounds.

The Love Paradox: Love vs. Fear

What is Divine Love? Witches seek to reconcile the paradox between unconditional or perfect Divine Love of the God/dess and the necessary conditions of human relationships as we navigate the illusion of our separateness.

Going back to the God/dess's Thealogy of Perfection in chapter 3, the paradox resolved by the path of love is *Perfect Love* vs. *fear of a lack of love*. It all comes down to how we experience the nine Divine Love Conditions and the fear that arises from not having them. When those fears come true, our hearts are wounded, which is why we call emotional pain being "heartbroken." To be denied these basic human needs for too long is traumatizing. That trauma causes anxiety and anger. That anger twists and festers inside us until it emerges as paranoia and hatred.

Fear of a lack of love too often leads to abusive relationships where bigotry, hostility, and aggression dam up the waters of Divine Love. Like wounded animals, sometimes folks lash out and impose the same transgressions that they've suffered onto other people. This is their pitiable way of either getting what they need the hard way or exacting revenge as a means to lessen their pain. The deprivation of Divine Love is how bullies are made. Wounded people tend to wound other people.

These harmful behaviors announce one's wounds, much like a giant billboard advertising what wounded them in the first place. Like Shakespeare said in *Hamlet*, "The lady doth protest too much, methinks!"[271] This is called *projection* by psychologists, where a person projects their own fears onto the world around them, incorrectly assuming the worst in people. Projections announce our shadow-selves like fanfare, calling out those things we hate most about ourselves.

When wounds are still in charge of someone's behavior, they might become the jerk who demands everyone else change to assuage their fear rather than facing whatever terror of rejection still binds them. For example, the conservative, "family values" preachers or lawmakers who loudly condemn homosexuality and work overtime to impede LGBTQ+ equality under the law only to later be scandalously exposed as being a closeted, self-loathing homosexual themselves. Their hate proceeds from fear of being cast out from their god's love simply for loving whom they love. That spiritual violence is a tragedy our God/dess is here to heal.

Mahatma Gandhi is credited as saying, "The enemy is fear. We think it is hate; but, it is fear."[272] Folks hate what they fear, and that fear, on some level, comes from the wounds inflicted by a lack of the nine Divine Love Conditions. The divine paradox holds in the balance two simultaneous truths: we are unified within one God/dess of unconditional Divine Love, and we are separate individuals upon the material plane, *and* healthy relationships must hold safe boundaries that do not transgress our diversity and individuality. A way to show unconditional love for anyone who violates your healthy boundaries is at a peaceful distance that you are allowed to define. In witching terms, through the promise of Perfect Love and Perfect Trustworthiness.

To realize this universal truth allows us to remain centered in compassion, thus reconciling the paradox. Elemental water grants us permission to fully accept ourselves and all others for exactly as we are, without judgment. Elemental water also grants us permission to redefine the societal landscape to be radically inclusive, ensuring that unconditional Divine Love, as experienced through the nine Divine Love Conditions, is accessible by all beings. And we can include everyone without kill-or-be-killed ranking through a competition for resources. In this way, the paradox between unity within God/dess and diversity upon Earth is also embraced.

---

271. William Shakespeare, *Hamlet*, Act 3, Scene 2 (Washington, DC: Folger Shakespeare Library, n.d.), accessed August 27, 2021. http://shakespeare.folger.edu/shakespeares-works/hamlet/act-3-scene-2/.

272. Attributed to Mahatma Gandhi.

Heart Chakra: Healing Wounds of Fear

The fourth chakra of the heart is the central chakra out of the seven major energy centers of the body. In the swirling green light of the heart space, the lower three chakras of personal awareness overlap the upper three chakras of societal and cosmic awareness. Although in the Hindu system the heart chakra is associated with elemental air, in Hermetic Witchcraft remapping, the emotional center aligns with elemental water.

To balance the emotional body and fully activate our heart chakras, Witches are tasked to first heal the emotional wounds inflicted by fear. The fearful lack of any Divine Love Condition impedes the flow of chi through the heart chakra. This leaves us feeling powerless and without internal control. Through a shift into the compassion of the heart chakra, you can regain your power.

✤ Exercise 12: Mending the Broken Chalice ✤

The Witchcraft of the path of love asks you to identify what fears wound you emotionally so you can mend the vessel of your broken heart. Before you can properly interact with others in sovereignty, truth, and power, you'll need a whole, healed, and openly flowing heart. You can't properly pour from an empty chalice, either. Through the Witchcraft of the exercises and rituals of water, Witches strive to become the strong vessel through which the Perfect Love of the God/dess can flow into the Middleworld.

To accomplish this feat, recognize how those wounds drive fearful behavior, then conquer your fears. Renew your connection to the Divine Love of the God/dess, which is boundless. Break the wounding cycle through acts of compassion and grace. Regain your power to enjoy your own life, then fight the good fight of restoring balance within your sphere of influence so others may enjoy the same freedoms. A tall order, to be sure, but we are Witches. If Witches won't accept this mission, who else do we expect to do it?

Witches tend to the path of love and water last because through the strengthening of the other elemental bodies first, you've been strengthening your emotional vessel all along. Imagine your heart like a chalice with sturdy edges formed from your other four bodies: physical, mental, will, and Spirit. You began molding your emotional waters through the earthy magick of your physical body in establishing sovereign control over your life and aligning your moral compass through development of a strong character and the passions you most enjoy. Hopefully, your physical health is improved too. Then, you continued molding your emotional waters through the airy magick of thoughts, honing your beliefs about your sacred worthiness and expression of your truth, resolving cognitive dissonance with grace. Through the fiery magick of will, you internalized your true power and accepted your sacred mission. Those flames fired the furnace of your spirit to temper the vessel of your heart stronger than ever. Your capacity for powerful emotion, directed through the Great Work of Magick, expands with each lap of the Pentacle Path until at last you are prepared to channel the greatness of the Two Who Move as One and their Divine Love through your heart chakra.

The *Hermetic Principle of Vibration* states: "Nothing rests; everything moves; everything vibrates."[273] Our state of mental and emotional health sets the frequency at which our consciousness is vibrating. *Like attracts like*, as they say. If you look at the world through fear-colored glasses, you will only see those things that scare you. Fear becomes a self-fulfilling prophecy.

Step One: Understand How Fear Cracks Your Chalice

Fear cracks the chalice of the heart through a dynamic of *love* vs. the *fear of a lack of Divine Love*. This is typically called "having your heart broken," but our hearts are broken by all kinds of things beyond just romantic love. Being denied any of the nine Divine Love Conditions hurts our feelings. Fear sets in that we'll be hurt again. Our feelings then vibrate with "wounded consciousness," and we take up constant vigilance in vain hope to never be hurt again. If this goes on long enough, we begin to project our fear onto the other people around us. Paranoia now assumes the worst in everyone. Taken to the extreme, we may lash out with bullying behaviors to ease that tension. We may be trying to protect ourselves but end up wounding other people in turn: boundary violations, gossiping, doxxing, cursing, hexing. Worst case scenario, other forms of spiritual, emotional, and physical violence may result. In which case, the target of this violence retaliates defensively right back at us! So, we suffer more of the same aggressions in kind, reinforcing our worst fears. When this scenario plays out, an identity in victimhood is affirmed, becoming a self-fulfilling prophecy. This sad cycle of woundings repeats all the way to "the dark side."

The cosmos is a mirror that reflects above and below, but we also see the outer world as a mirror of our inner selves. If we are spiritually betrayed by a world that does not fulfill its promise of Divine Love to us, the spiritual suffering is chaotic and excruciating. That kind of pain blocks our link of interconnection with others, making it difficult to

---

273. Atkinson, *The Kybalion*, 131.

empathize. That emotional pain may be cast outward as a way to fulfill the reciprocity of the mirror. Only this time, mirroring the fear rather than the love.

Do you recognize any of your own behaviors or the behaviors in our communities recently that are reflected in the cycle above? When folks lash out from their wounds, they are gushing their emotions all over the place through the "cracks" in the chalice of their hearts. These cracks are made evident by their inappropriate boundary violations. Because we are all interconnected, everyone is affected on some subconscious level when any part of us suffers. Who wants to suffer like those guys over there? Enter: *survival of the fittest* and a race of mean girls and bullies evolves to take over the government. If we want to rise above that dog-eat-dog race and the domination through warfare to regain our cooperative power, change starts with our individual choices. We must respond by loving in a radically different way. Witches are good at being radically different. So, back to good ol' Witchcraft!

Step Two: Identifying Wounded Consciousness

To balance the emotional body carefully, consider each of the nine Divine Love Conditions listed below. Look around the world today—at politics and social movements, at your own relationships and feelings—and notice how you're being affected.

Nine Divine Love Conditions and Wounded Consciousness

1. **Resources:** If I am wounded by a lack of physical resources, I vibrate with poverty consciousness. I might project harm through greed, theft, hoarding, gluttony, etc.

2. **Affection:** If I am wounded by a lack of the affection I prefer, I vibrate with deprivation consciousness. I might project harm through nonconsensual sexual deviancy like sexual assault, rape, self-harm, pedophilia, stalking, violence toward those perceived as rejecting me, etc.

3. **Sovereignty:** If I am wounded by a lack of free will, I vibrate with slavery consciousness. I might project harm through unjustified internment, false imprisonment, conservatism, restriction of immigrants, cruelty of animals, disregard for civil rights, etc.

4. **Acceptance:** If I am wounded by fear of a lack of acceptance, I vibrate with bigotry consciousness. I might project harm through self-denigration, racism, homophobia, transphobia, nationalism, xenophobia, etc.

5. **Security:** If I am wounded by a lack of security, safety, or privacy, I vibrate with victim consciousness. I might project harm through physical violence, invasion of privacy, bullying, terrorism, threats, etc.

6. **Expression:** If I am wounded by a lack of expression, convinced that my contributions aren't worthy of consideration, I might vibrate with imposter consciousness. I might project that harm through demeaning the contributions of others, anti-intellectualism, silencing through censorship, book burning, conspiracy theories, gerrymandering, election tampering, etc.

7. **Trustworthiness:** If I am wounded by a lack of trustworthiness, I vibrate with paranoid consciousness. I might project that harm through betrayal, distrust, gossip, backstabbing, espionage, more conspiracy theories, and assuming everything is out to get me, etc.

8. **Authenticity:** If I am wounded by a lack of authenticity, I vibrate with exploited consciousness. I might project harm through lying, cheating, subterfuge, conning others for my own gain, etc.

9. **Reciprocity:** If I am wounded by a lack of reciprocity, I vibrate with betrayal consciousness. I might project harm by working overtime to beat everyone else to the punch. Maybe it's just rude and inconsiderate entitlement, like littering. Maybe it festers into malevolent crimes? The worst "evils" result from thwarting the natural order of Divine Love, such as a disregard for human life. Why bother doing the right thing if deep down you can't imagine anyone else honoring their end of the social bargain?

Step Three: Radical Love Affirmations to Mend Your Chalice

Reality manifests to match the song your heart is singing. If your heart is still singing one of the tales of woe listed above, no matter what your magickal petition paper says, more of the woeful consciousness will be delivered. In your Book of Mirrors, reflect how you may be impacted by these conditions right now. Then, write a list of affirmations that can heal those wounds and reprogram your state of consciousness. You'll need these affirmations for spell 5: healing the wounded heart at dark moon later this chapter.

Affirmations are a magickal way to reprogram old mental and emotional garbage and forge new neurological pathways between your head and heart. Affirmations are a tool of air for communicating throughout all levels of yourself, sending a memo all the way to

Divine Mind. It takes repeating them many times, with power, until you not only believe them on all levels, but you feel them on all levels. Then your heart can vibrate at Divine Love consciousness.

Remember that you have no control over how other people choose to treat you, but you can choose how you respond to them and have all the control over how you treat other people. That is the witching task of Perfect Trustworthiness; affirm *your* beneficial intentions and become a strong link in the chainmail of society.

Figure 30: Candle wrap image for water by Heron Michelle

Formulary for Elemental Water

As the summer wanes toward the autumnal equinox, prepare the magickal materials for the watery magick ahead. As you've done in previous chapters, craft an incense, oil, and water magick candle, referencing the table below for the elemental correspondences of water, and make substitutions as needed.[274] For this element of water, also prepare charged mother waters from the directions below.

Elemental Correspondences of Water	
Alchemical Symbol	▽
Color	Blue
State of Matter	Liquid
Direction	West
Time of Day	Dusk
Phase of Life	Adulthood
Season	Autumn
Alchemical Qualities	Cold and moist
Mental Gender	Yin, female
Governs	Emotional body: dreams, visions, emotions
Projective Power	The power to dare
Receptive Power	The power to accept
Elemental Beings	Undine
Elemental Sovereign	Nicksa (Necksa)
Magickal Tools	Chalice, cauldron, scourge
Consecration	Salted water
Planetary	Moon
Day of Week	Monday

---

274. I assembled these element correspondence charts from many sources, but a good reference is *Llewellyn's Complete Book of Correspondences* by Sandra Kynes.

Elemental Correspondences of Water	
Astrological Signs	Cardinal: Cancer; fixed: Scorpio; mutable: Pisces
Stones	Amethyst, aquamarine, angelite, azurite, chalcedony, chrysocolla, blue calcite, blue lace agate, iolite, dioptase, lapis lazuli, larimar, blue kyanite, moonstone, opal, pearl, rose quartz, sapphire, selenite, sodalite
Metals	Copper, silver
Herbs	Apple, aloe, blackberry, chamomile, cardamom, gardenia, geranium, grape, heather, lemon balm, passionflower, rose, eucalyptus, jasmine, lotus, orris root, mugwort, reeds, strawberry, star anise, thyme, valerian
Resins	Myrrh
Trees/Woods/Barks	Apple, aspen, beech, birch, mimosa, mesquite, myrtle, olive, white willow, sandalwood
Creatures	Bat, trout, salmon, dolphin, crab, whale, most aquatic creatures, beaver, hare, otter, raccoon

❧ Exercise 13: Water Crafting Formulary ❧

Auspicious Timing

Look at the time frame you have left until Mabon and pick a day during a waxing lunar cycle, preferably while the moon is in a water sign of Cancer, Scorpio, or Pisces, and/or on the days/hours of the moon (Monday.)

Needs

See the recipes below for specific materials and equipment for each recipe.

Lay your working altar with enough surface area to spread out, make a mess, and be artistically creative.

Consecration elements, including charcoal in a censer for testing your incense blend. Add anything that aids your connection to water energies: shells, images of the ocean or merfolk, etc.

Preparation

Awaken and consecrate your altar as taught in ritual 1.

Call upon your spiritual guides to be present and inspire your magickal creations.

For charging any water-drawing materials, chant this charm:

Water Blessing Charm

> *Powers of water, of Nicksa and undines!*
> *By lunar tides and astral dreams!*
> *Come daring love and unity!*
> *As I will, so mote it be!*

❧ Elemental Water Incense—Planetary Moon Magick ❧

This incense recipe is effective for rebalancing the emotional body and any journeys and spells where elemental powers of water or planetary moon would aid in manifesting your intention for daring, acceptance, love, compassion, healing, and psychic work.

Needs

Mortar and pestle to grind and blend dry ingredients

2 parts base wood—white willow bark powder (water, moon)

2 parts resin—myrrh resin powder (water, moon)

½ part herb—jasmine or gardenia flower (water, moon)

½ part herb—thyme or eucalyptus (water, moon)

1 part herb—powdered peel of lemon (water, moon)

Essential oils—9 drops each of lemon and eucalyptus

2 parts vegetable glycerin to bind

Stone chips: moonstone, amethyst, or aquamarine

Dark-colored jar with lid and opening large enough for your incense spoon; cobalt blue glass is ideal

Praxis

In your mortar and pestle, grind with a deosil motion all plant ingredients until relatively fine. As you add each ingredient, invite their spirits to aid your watery work and thank them. Add the essential oil and glycerin, stir to combine and bind. Add stone chips of moonstone or a substitution. Draw the alchemical sigil of water in the incense with index finger or wand if you have one already.

Chant the water blessing charm three times, and charge with the powers of water by picturing the churning rapids in a river or the crashing waves along the ocean shore. See the natural water energy glowing a cool, misty blue. Direct that light with your mind, like a current of water flowing down through your hands, until you envision the blend also glowing blue.

Transfer the blend to the jar and label it, including the date and the glyph of alchemical water and planetary moon ☽ to continue charging. Burn some on your charcoal to test the scent and boost the watery signal while you keep working.

⚜ Elemental Water Anointing Oil ⚜

This oil may be used to anoint candles, yourself, or other magickal objects to bring them into sympathy with emotional or psychic goals.

Needs

Dark-colored 1-dram bottle with tightly sealing cap, cobalt blue glass is ideal

Mix 9 total drops of essential oil: choose from a mix of eucalyptus, lemon

3 stone chips of moonstone, amethyst, aquamarine or substitute

Jojoba oil for longer shelf life, or olive oil for short-term use

Praxis

As you add each ingredient to the bottle, tap on the materials three times and awaken them to their powers of water: daring, acceptance, emotions, intuitions, dreams, and healing. Invite their spirits to be part of your magickal team and thank them for all the intuition they bring.

When all are assembled in the bottle, cap it and swirl the oils together deosil. Chant the water blessing charm three times to build and direct power into the blend and charge it with the visualization above. Label it with the name, date, and alchemical sigils of water and planetary moon ☽ to continue charging. Anoint your heart chakra to further align your emotions with water energy as you keep working.

⚜ Elemental Water Candle ⚜

In the same manner used previously, prepare a seven-day glass-jarred sanctuary candle to channel powers of elemental water.

Needs

Blue seven-day sanctuary candle in glass jar. They are typically 2.25 x 8 inches tall and take refill insert candles no more than 2 inches wide.

The 7-inch square image from figure 30 can be copied and colored to create a candle wrap, or you may creatively decorate your own piece of lightweight paper.

13-inch length of blue cord or ribbon

Flat head screwdriver or a power drill with large bit

½ teaspoon prepared water herbal incense

Chopstick or toothpick

3 drops prepared water anointing oil

3 tiny chips of moonstone, amethyst, aquamarine, or substitution

Praxis

On the blank side of the 7-inch square candle wrap paper, write a water gateway opening call. Compose your own or reference the calls provided in ritual 2. If you're not using the image provided in figure 30, decorate the outside of the wrapper with images of natural water, such as sea creatures, undines (merfolk), shells, alchemical water glyph, planetary glyph for moon ☽, etc.

With the screwdriver or drill, bore out three holes in the wax about an inch deep. Load the candle by poking a bit of water incense into the holes with a chopstick. Top with a stone chip in each hole. Then anoint with three drops of water oil and rub it around the wax deosil with a bare finger.

Wrap the paper wrapper around the jar and tie down with the cord or ribbon. The charging of this candle will take place during the journey to realms of elemental water later on.

Charged Mother Waters

Mother waters are magickal preparations made from waters collected from natural sources, which are then charged and preserved for later use: in altar bowls, spiritual baths, and spells. Just add nine drops of any mother water to a larger quantity of fresh water, and according to the Law of Contagion, the magickal properties are then transferred throughout and remain sympathetically linked to the original source of water in nature.[275]

For all magickal waters, preserve with a 50 percent dilution of brandy prior to bottling them. Brandy is an alcohol made from a variety of distilled fruits, which also have magickal associations. These can be chosen for their elemental or planetary properties. Grape brandy is clear, associated with the moon, and elemental water.

Auspicious Timing

For all kinds of mother waters, collect the water from nature whenever possible, paying special attention to the zodiac sign of the sun at the moment rain or snow falls to be collected, as that filter of energy will also impress upon the water. Leave prepared waters to charge under a full moon, preferably during a water sign.

Daring Mother Water

Use daring waters in magick meant to destroy emotional boundaries, overcome discrimination, and carve a new path through material hindrances. For example, dissolve a petition paper describing that which must be overcome in a jar of daring water and white vinegar. Daring waters would be collected during the high winds of hurricanes, at ocean edges where it is chiseling the rocks, or wild river rapids collected where whitewater churns. This can be tricky business; take great care.

---

275. Penczak, *Inner Temple of Witchcraft*, 162.

Needs

8 ounces naturally collected "daring" waters

8 ounces of grape brandy, or an equal quantity to the water for 50 percent dilution

Clear or blue pint jar with lid

A small quartz crystal, or sunstone for fire

Praxis

Boil the water prior to preserving and bottling so that elemental fire adds to the power. For an extra boost, add sunstone or a substitution of stones with elemental fire to charge the waters. Water plus fire becomes a powerful steam engine!

Pour water and brandy into a clear or blue glass jar, add the stone, and leave in direct moonlight overnight. Charge with elemental visualizations and charms as described previously. Label with the date, and glyphs of water, moon, and the sun sign under which it fell or was collected.

Acceptance Mother Water

Acceptance mother waters are best collected from snow as it softly settles and collects in a vessel left outside, preferably a cauldron. A gentle rain caught in a glass bowl will also fulfill most magickal acceptance purposes. Use this water in work intended to help define or defend boundaries and come to terms with emotional circumstances beyond your control. For example, add 9 drops of acceptance mother water to a bowl of tap water and an intention paper stating an emotional attachment that needs releasing. Freeze the water, then allow the frozen bowl of water to melt slowly on your altar during a dark moon for gentle easing.

Needs

8 ounces naturally collected "acceptance" waters

8 ounces of grape brandy, or an equal quantity to the water for 50 percent dilution

Clear or blue pint jar with lid

A small quartz crystal, or green calcite for earth

Praxis

Pour water and brandy into a clear or blue glass jar, add the stone, and leave in direct moonlight overnight. Charge with elemental visualizations and charms as described previously. Label with the date, and glyphs of water, moon, and the sun sign under which it fell or was collected.

Journey to the Realms of Water

Continue the ritual cycle in a similar manner to previous interactive elemental journeys, where parts are done within the mind's eye in a typical meditation. But when prompted, you will be asked to perform ceremonial actions. This functional high-alpha brainwave state is called "ritual consciousness."[276] The ritualized journey is best enacted by listening to a recording of the meditation or as someone reads it aloud for you.

❧ Ritual 7: Elemental Water Temple ❧

This ritual creates an elemental temple of water, opening from the western quarter, and then taking a guided journey through your astral temple to the elemental water plane. The goal is to seek partnership with undines and Sovereign Nicksa, asking to receive insights about your tool of water, and which ancestral spirit ally may best aid the balancing of your emotional body. Elemental journeys are most impactful when done outdoors, close to the element in nature. If possible, locate your rite near naturally flowing water, like a river, stream, lake, or at the beach.

Auspicious Timing

During the second lunar cycle closest to the autumnal equinox, during a waxing moon in a water sign: Cancer, Scorpio, or Pisces.

Needs

Consecration element: water bowl as an offering to the undines, add a small seashell

Three pinches of sea salt

---

276. Penczak, *Inner Temple of Witchraft*, 87.

Add any items that evoke water for you: a blue tablecloth, sea images, additional seashells, etc.

A conch or other larger shell through which you may "listen" to the ocean

An incense censer with sand and a hookah charcoal tab, tongs, small spoon, and a lighter or box of matches

Water herbal incense blend

Water anointing oil

Dedication sanctuary candle for Spirit

Prepared blue water candle with blue cord or ribbon

Your Book of Mirrors and a pen

Diagrams of water invoking and banishing pentagrams for easy reference. See figure 24.

An athame if you already have one or just the "natural athame" of your projective hand

Device for playing a recording of the guided journey

Preparation

Begin with a physical cleaning and organizing of the ritual space and your altar. Bathe and dress in fresh, comfortable clothing, preferably barefoot with hair unbound, or nude as you prefer.

Lay your working altar before you, arranged such that you can meditate comfortably and still reach everything easily.

Anoint your own heart chakra with water anointing oil at your heart.

Light your dedication candle to welcome Spirit, who is ever-present.

Light the charcoal and place in the censer in preparation for loose incense burning.

Praxis

Altar consecration: Awaken your altar for the element of water. Shift consciousness into your roots deep within the earth below, finding the water table. Breathe deeply and establish the flow of power connecting you to the three realms. Inhale that watery power as blue light; exhale it through your projective hand. Hold the bowl of water. Add three pinches of sea salt, or scoops with tip of your athame if you already have one. Stir by drawing the earth banishing pentagram with your athame or finger into the water itself, which banishes all earthly impurity from the water. Say: *I purify this water as an offering of water and banish all impurity.* With fingers or athame tip, sprinkle three splashes of water over the altar.

Say: *Powers of water, wash free any impurity from this sacred space.* Envision a blue energy imbuing the altar.

Hallowing: Walk the perimeter of your circle with the bowl of salted water, sprinkling and chanting: *I consecrate this circle by the powers of water.* Present the water to the western quarter and say: *As your Witch of water, I greet you with water and ask that you wash free any baneful energies from this circle tonight. So mote it be!*

Temple: Cast your circle with the awen cone of power as taught in ritual 2. Close the sphere above and below.

Open the Western Gate: As taught in chapter 10, face the west. Stand in a posture of water evocation, natural athame raised in salute, with receptive hand forming cup at shoulder height (see figure 25). Exhale and see blue light of water beaming from your projective hand. Your receptive hand is prepared to receive this inflowing energy. Stand tall, chin up, shoulders back; speak with authority from the diaphragm. Visualize the ocean waves crashing against the shore. See the blue light beaming from your athame or fingers.

Say aloud: *Powers of the west! Essence of water! I summon you to this sacred place! Undines! Sovereign Nicksa of the ocean depths! Be with me now and lend your powers of intuition and emotion. Strengthen my heart for the work at hand. Awaken your power of daring and acceptance within me. Come crashing wave and foggy dusk, come glistening dew and river rapids to buoy and carve the way for this magick. I welcome you with gratitude. Hail and welcome!*

Draw the invoking pentagram of water with the natural athame of your projective hand. See the star glowing with blue light in the air of the western quarter. Encircle the pentagram deosil (clockwise), unlocking. Draw your fingers toward your lips, pulling in a streamer of elemental water. Kiss your fingers, then with hand over heart, bow to that direction. A blue girder now encircles your temple in the west.

Sit down and prepare for meditation. Begin the recording of this guided journey.

⚜ Meditation 8: Guided Journey to the Realms of Water ⚜

Close your eyes; take a deep breath. Picture your most magickal Self sitting in a comfortable chair in a comfortable room inside your mind. It is quiet and still in your sanctuary. Your eyes are now a window on a distant wall of that room. Any distracting noises or stray thoughts are merely birds flying past that distant window … release them without care. (*Pause.*)

There is a skylight above you, and a soft beam of divine light shines down upon your crown chakra. Breathe down the light with three deep breaths. Inhale through the nose and exhale through the mouth … releasing all tension. (*Pause for three breaths.*) You are at perfect ease on all levels. (*Pause.*)

There is a beautiful, ornate door in the floor of your mental sanctuary, a door leading to all possibility. Open that door, finding a spiral staircase descending beyond. With each exhale of your breath, step down, deeper and deeper, descending into your subconscious mind, and deep into your own belly. At the foot of the stairs, you'll arrive at your inner crossroads. Twelve steps down, around and 'round you tread the spiral staircase. (*Pause.*)

Before you hangs a looking glass, a portal outward to the astral realms where all things are possible by a mere thought. Picture your Astral Temple upon the glass. (*Pause.*)

Say aloud: *My intention is to journey to my astral temple to seek the elemental realms of water to learn the mysteries of daring and acceptance, to swim the path of love, seeking a relationship with the beings who govern the essence of water known as undines and their sovereign, Nicksa. I wish to receive my tool of water and ancestral allies to aid my emotional balance. I call my guides, gods, and ancestors to keep me safe and show me the way. Blessèd be. (Pause.)*

On the count of three, step through the portal and arrive on the path to your temple. One, two, three, step through!

You arrive on the astral plane; the great world tree looms large in the distance. Take the temple path that lies before you. Down, down, down the path you tread, seeing the glowing light of your temple ahead. Smell the sweet scent of the temple incense burning, enticing you home.

You arrive at the door of your astral temple and enter. This sacred place is perfectly suited to your needs. The pure waters of Divine Love flow cool and refreshing from your place of water. The breeze of Divine Inspiration blows gently through, sweet and fresh, from your place of air. The sacred flames of your Divine Will glow brightly from your place of fire. Find your way now to the heart of your temple, the earthen altar itself, broad and stable. Stand before your altar in strength.

On the altar several things are spread before you: a blue sanctuary candle, a pot of herbal incense, and a censer with hot coals prepared for your ceremony. Onto that hot coal, sprinkle some incense to call water. As that smoke billows, the aroma awakens your watery connections; your blood stirs.

Say aloud: *Welcome, plant allies of willow and myrrh, chamomile and jasmine. Aid me now with your watery powers!*

Upon the altar is also a bowl of salted water, with a seashell. Place your fingers into this water, touching the shell. Allow your focus to sink deeply into the water itself. Consciousness can travel anywhere, so like looking through a microscope, you zoom in, your consciousness small enough to take a swim in the bowl. (*Pause.*)

There is no such thing as matter, only energy so dense as to be perceived. (*Pause.*) You are also made of energy; there is no difference between you and the water. Feel the coolness and fluidity against your skin. Note how the water displaces to receive you, flowing gently around to accept your finger. Allow your consciousness to fill the bowl, remaining level and smooth. (*Pause.*)

Water is flexible, rising to the occasion. Water is accepting, it does not discriminate. It fills every space and molds itself to the situation. Safe as your mother's womb. Listen now as the water teaches you its lessons of fluidity. (*Long pause.*)

On your altar, you find a conch or large shell. Pick it up and place it to your ear to listen. Like the beating of your own heart and the pumping of your own blood waters, hear the echoing tide of the ocean. Dive deeply into this water, feel powerful waves, feel the pull of the moon to swell and recede, churn and crash … fearless … dynamic. Listen as the water tells you of her cycles. (*Pause.*)

Like refocusing the microscope, pull back now, larger, to hold the shell in your hand and see your altar laid before you. Pick up your blue candle and hold it in your projective hand. Remember the power of the ocean and channel that water through your hands into the candle to awaken the potential to melt within it. Tap the glass three times until you see it glowing blue in your mind's eye. Light the blue candle.

A blue light also glows through the temple, darkening. Feel the cool, wet waters rippling nearby—dripping, echoing, hear the burble and splash. Waving light reflects on the walls. Your blood pounds in response, vision lengthening as you sense a shift; the powers of water are crashing nearby.

In your mind's eye, turn to face the western quarter of your temple. Raise the open cups of your hands to shoulder height, receptive like the crescent moon.

With power in the voice, say aloud: *Powers of Water! You who are mystery and emotion. I call upon your elemental beings called undines and their sovereign, Nicksa! Guide me along the path of love. Grant me entrance into your watery realms. Open the portal and show me the way! Hail and welcome!*

A gateway now appears in the west. It calls you like the crash of waves. See it clearly as you approach the gate. Symbols and images adorn the frame. Remember them. (*Pause.*)

The veil between you and the realm of water is like moonlight shimmering across a dark ocean cove. Blue light pours through the portal to fill your auric field with the energetic essence of water. Your vibration shifts into fluid waves, forming the safety of a dive suit around you. Like a fish you may now swim through fluid space with the speed of feeling.

Feel the power of that water inviting you through the gateway. Touch the gateway and it shimmers open. Like a diver, plunge straight through that mirrored surface into the depths of the blue ocean. Look around through the blue water, powerful and deep. (*Pause.*)

Like a diver's mask, your energetic shield acts like a magickal lens. Through this lens you see the undines approaching, like a school of curious fishlike beings. You see them clearly all around you now, fluidity incarnate, grace and fierce beauty. How do the undines present themselves to you? (*Pause.*)

Gathering you into their school, communicating through telepathy, you swim easily together. Safely, the undines guard you from all harm. Ask to know the mysteries of their shadowy realms… Ask the undines to guide you as you face all your fears of the heart. (*Pause.*) They encourage you on, and so you dive together. Dive. Dive into your deepest emotional depths. (*Long pause.*)

The undines lead you now to a special place of power to meet Sovereign Nicksa. Like whale song, you sing to call the sovereign ruler of elemental water. On each of three long breaths, in two syllables, intone *Nick-sa*. Deep breath in. Chanting aloud: *Nick-sa… Nick-sa… Nick-sa…*

The collective consciousness of elemental water coalesces into view. Nicksa, the sovereign of the sea, appears before you in fierce beauty. Introduce yourself. Remember all the details of their appearance before you. (*Pause.*)

You ask aloud: *Nicksa! I seek your guidance along the path of love in my life. What fears of a lack of love have wounded me in the past, cracking the chalice of my heart? (Pause.) I seek healing, mending, and balance within Divine Love.* Nicksa approaches, and the glowing essence of water's emotional healing flows through your emotional body like an embrace, healing your heart.

You ask aloud: *Nicksa! What emotional impediments in my life can the power of water help me dare to overcome?* Nicksa shares their wisdom with you now. (*Long pause.*)

You ask aloud: *Nicksa! What boundaries of my life should I accept to mold me into new form?* Nicksa invites you to join them on a vision journey, showing how their power flows through your emotional life. (*Long pause.*)

You ask aloud: *Nicksa! Will you partner with me in my magick?* (*Pause.*)

If yes, you ask Nicksa: *Which altar tool of water best summons the powers of undines and elemental water into my Great Work? Perhaps a chalice or cauldron? Something else?* Nicksa presents you with this tool. From which vessel will you drink in their power? You see it clearly now. (*Pause.*) You are shown where and how you might acquire this vessel in the Middleworld. Receive the vision. (*Long pause.*)

You ask Nicksa: *Which Underworld or ancestral guide can best aid my emotional balance?* Nicksa introduces you to an ancestral guide who can aid your emotional balance with a vision of what they can teach you. Receive the vision. (*Long pause.*)

Accept these gifts and visions with gratitude as you bid Nicksa farewell. Nicksa ripples into shadow and is gone.

The undines swim around you again, inviting you to explore with them the boundless waters of earth, traveling the interconnected waterways, wherever you wish to explore. (*Long pause.*)

As you swim with the undines through the ocean, your emotional burdens wash away until you are buoyant, lighter, and less substantial. Together you rise like water vapor into the clouds, clean and unfettered. (*Pause.*) Together you condense and rain down to nourish the plants … each drop of rain gathered in, no exceptions; all drops of rain find your way into the creeks, into rivers. (*Pause.*) You burble up as freshwater springs … flowing through your interconnected relationships with others. Ebb and flow, following the tributaries back to the ocean. (*Pause.*)

The undines guide you back to the gateway of your astral temple. Bid them farewell with your gratitude, and they depart. Swim through the dark mirror of the gateway. The blue shielding of your dive suit remains behind, and you shift easily back to your normal, comfortable density.

Step back to the altar. Placing the gift of your tool upon the altar, you remember the lessons of water with perfect clarity. Sit for a moment in the candlelight and reflect on your experiences in the realms of water. (*Long pause.*) Remember that you can return to your temple and the gates of water whenever you wish.

Now it is time to return to waking consciousness. Leaving your temple, follow the path back to the looking glass. Back, back the way you came, seeking the portal back into yourself. See yourself on that looking glass. Passing through this portal you will once more follow the umbilical cord. Three steps back into your own belly. Three, two, one, step through!

Take the twelve steps of the spiral stairway back up, rising higher and higher, returning to waking consciousness. Returning to the little room behind your eyes, closing the trapdoor in the floor behind you.

Say aloud: *I am grateful to my guides, gods, and ancestors—all those who kept me safe and showed me the way. Blessèd be.* Stretch your muscles. When you are ready to return to the outer temple, refreshed and balanced, move to the window of your eyes and then open them.

Journal Reflection
In your Book of Mirrors, record the messages from your allies, draw your visions, and explore your feelings about the experience for as long as you'd like.

Deconstructing the Temple
Close the elemental gateway by standing to face the west in the posture of water, natural athame raised in salute.

Say: *Powers of the west! Essence of water! Undines and Sovereign Nicksa! I am grateful for your healing presence and your aid in these rites. Continue to heal my heart and empower my Great Work along the path of love. For now, I release you to your fair and fluid realms. Hail and farewell!*

See the blue girder and all powers receding back through the gateway of your circle. Draw the banishing pentagram with your athame or fingers, like a key in the lock. As you encircle the star widdershins, see the portal closing and locking.

Kiss your athame or fingers, but this time follow through like a fencer with a thrusting gesture toward the quarter, brandishing your blade with fierce resolve, directing any remaining energy outward to their realm. Bow.

Release the circle by gathering the sphere of remaining energy into your hands, smaller and smaller, until it is imagined like a glowing ball over the altar. Charge the ball to further light your way along the Pentacle Path. Shout *Release!* as you toss the sphere upward to the cosmos, clapping your hands, and say: *The circle is open but never broken. Merry meet, merry part, and merry meet again.*

Magick of Love

With the lessons of the undines and Nicksa fresh upon your heart, plan a holistic spell to balance your emotional body within your fivefold Self. The name of this game is self-care and pampering! The spells of emotional healing to follow include two major workings that span between the third dark moon of the autumn season, continuing through the two weeks of the waxing lunar cycle, to be concluded at the following full moon. In preparation for those spells, you'll need the water herbal incense, anointing oil, and charged acceptance mother water from exercise 12 in the water formulary section of this chapter. You'll also need to prepare a few additional formulary materials in advance: an "Emotional Purification Bath Sachet" with the planetary powers of the moon and Venus, and a "Triumph of the Heart Body Butter" with Venus and the sun.

❧ Emotional Purification Bath Sachet ❧

A bath sachet makes a big "tea bag" for your bathwater, lending plant spirits aligned with the moon and Venus energies to create a magickal potion to bathe in.

Planetary Influence
Moon and Venus magick

Auspicious Timing
Assemble your materials any Monday (moon) or Friday (Venus), preferably while the moon is in a water sign of Cancer, Scorpio, or Pisces.

Need

½ cup of sea salt

½ cup of Epsom salt

Large muslin bag filled with:

Rose petals or lavender: love, protection, sleep, peace, and tranquility

Hyssop: spiritual opening, cleansing and purification; lightens vibrations

Angelica root: Exorcism, protection, healing

Lemon peel: water, cleansing, purification, removal of blockages, spiritual opening

Praxis

Add all ingredients to the muslin bag, cinch it closed, then hold between the hands. Awaken and charge for emotional healing with the visualizations and charms provided in the formulary of water section of this chapter.

❧ Triumph of the Heart Body Butter ❧

A body butter is a lot like a lotion to soften and seal the skin, minus the water content. Body butters infuse herbs into a combination of oils, which are half liquid and half solid at room temperature. Once they cool, a soft butter-like consistency allows them to be easily applied to the skin. Magickally charge this potion by the powers of Venus and the sun, and when absorbed into your skin, it boosts your emotional vibration with loving, successful happiness.

Planetary Influence

Venus and sun magick

Needs

8-ounce jar with lid

A chopstick for stirring

½ cup jojoba oil

One vanilla bean, split open—Venus, love

Dried peel of a small orange or tangerine—sun, happiness, empowerment

Handful of dried red or pink rose petals, organically grown for consumption—Venus, love

10 drops rose absolute (optional)

2 teaspoons of vitamin E oil

Small, tumbled rose quartz stone

½ cup unrefined African shea butter or coconut oil

Praxis

Pour the jojoba oil into the jar. Add the vanilla bean, peel, and dried rose petals to the oil, seal the jar, and allow the oil to infuse in a warm, dark place for at least a week. (The top of the water heater is a good choice.) The oil should completely cover the plant material.

After it infuses, strain out the plant material and add the vitamin E oil, rose quartz, and the rose absolute.

Gently melt the raw African shea butter or coconut oil by placing the original container it came in into a larger bowl filled with hot water. This will warm the oil indirectly. When liquified, add a half cup of melted shea or coconut oil to the jar of infused jojoba. Seal the jar with the lid and swirl it together deosil while calling upon Venus and the sun to awaken their powers of self-love, contentment, and happiness within the blend. Refrigerate for five minutes. Take it out and stir it with a chopstick. Refrigerate for another five minutes and repeat stirring until cool, solid, and whipped together. The end result will have a semi-soft consistency like butter. A body butter remains solid at room temperature but melts easily with body temperature to be absorbed by the skin. Charge the blend with the elemental power of water using the visualizations and charms provided in the water formulary section of this chapter. Date and label your creation to keep charging, including the sigils for Venus ♀, sun ☉, and alchemical water. Use within the month, or for longer shelf life, store it in the refrigerator.

❦ Spell 5: Healing the Wounded Heart at Dark Moon ❦

The first part of this two-week-long working kicks off at dark moon with a purification bath, releasing attachment to old emotional wounds. Create a small working altar to water in your bathroom as adjacent to your bathtub as possible. The back of the toilet is actually ideal if you consider that it is a source of flowing water.

Planetary Influence
Moon and Venus magick

Auspicious Timing
On the eve of the dark moon while she is still waning, preferably within the thirteen hours preceding exact conjunction of sun and moon in the same sign. If you're following the wheel in the Northern Hemisphere, dark moon in Scorpio is ideal. In the Southern Hemisphere, dark moon in Taurus, ruled by Venus.

Needs
Self-lighting charcoal rounds, incense censer with sand, tongs, small spoon, lighter or matches

Elemental water incense blend

Bowl of salted water as offering for the undines

1 black 4-inch chime candle (banishment) in a safe candle holder

Awl, nail, or pin to inscribe candle

Dedication sanctuary candle for Spirit

Your charged blue elemental water sanctuary candle

A small plate

Emotional Purification bath sachet in muslin bag

Triumph of the Heart body butter

½ cup dried rose petals

9 drops acceptance mother water

Your Book of Mirrors turned to the list of affirmations written for exercise 11: Mending the Broken Chalice

Preparation

Lay your water altar. Light your dedication candle. Ignite the charcoal and add some water incense to the censer. Hallow yourself and the room with smoke. Cast a small circle, open the gateway to elemental water, and light the blue sanctuary candle. Call upon the God/dess and your guides to be present for your spell.

Praxis

Facing west, with the awl or pin, inscribe the black candle with words and symbols that describe the wounds for which you seek emotional healing. Anoint the candle from the base to the tip with the elemental water oil, pointing away from your heart area. Lay the oily candle on the small plate, and sprinkle some of the incense over the candle. Rub the herbs into the inscriptions. Focus all your pain into this candle until it becomes the wounds from which you seek release.

Breathe in power from above and below and declare your intentions aloud. Say: *I call upon the love of the Great God/dess and the powers of elemental water! Nicksa, undines! Aid me now! I accept the lessons taught by the emotional wounds of the past.* (Name them specifically if you'd like.) *Now I dare to release all baneful attachment to those wounds so that my heart may be restored to wholeness by the grace of Divine Love!*

> Chant: *By candle black and darkening moon,*
> *fears of lack dissolve, old heart strings hewn*
> *by water's resolve, to sing love's tune.*

Light the candle. Repeat the chant at least three times, building power while you draw a hot bath. Add the bath sachet and swirl the bag through the water widdershins, creating a whirlpool. Add nine drops of acceptance mother water.

State your intention that this bath serves to purify your emotional body of all baneful attachments to the wounds caused by the fears of the lack of Divine Love in the past.

> Chant: *By water I am purified*
> *to ebb the bane by lunar tide.*
> *Undines! Ease my emotional pain,*
> *accepting fears for daring love regained.*

Soak in the bath and meditate on your emotional wounds inflicted from those fears. Visualize your emotional body like blue light, now flowing freely with the blue energetic light of the bath water. Allow yourself to think the angry thoughts. Feel the hurt feelings. Call to mind any lingering attachments to people and circumstances that inflicted those wounds. Like emotional toxins, they must be released into a widdershins swirl of blue light. This purifying potion you're sitting in draws all the poison out, leaving you healthier and better balanced. See the toxins drawn out of your emotional body into the water. Cry it out. Soak for as long as it takes to let it all go. Pray; listen.

When ready, open the drain and sit there as you watch all the toxic feelings drain away completely.

> Chant: *By water's daring flow, above and below,*
> *I banish all doubt, within and without.*
> *So mote it be!*

Now stand up and take a regular cleansing shower. Shampoo, shave, scrub away all that old, dead skin from the past. Really scour yourself into a shine! I also recommend a haircut at some point soon and possibly even a fresh start on a beard. Our dead hair and skin hold our experiences and memories within them. If you want to disconnect from who you were and things that happened in the past, releasing the hair that was made during that time can help speed that process.

Towel off and apply the Triumph of the Heart body butter into your damp skin—face to toes. See it forming an emollient barrier for your entire physical body but also a spiritual protective boundary. Massage it into your muscles using deosil (clockwise) motions as you repeat your affirmations from exercise 11. Make statements of gratitude for the aid you are receiving. Dress in fresh clothes that are light and cheerful colors for you.

Close the gateway to elemental water. Release your guides and temple with gratitude. Allow the black candle to burn away completely.

✤ Spell 6: Heart of Wholeness at Full Moon ✤

The second part of the spell begins the next day as the moon shifts to waxing again. Rise each morning of the waxing tide and prepare yourself for each day in your special way. Use your Triumph of the Heart butter to moisturize as needed. Dress in your favorite clothes, aftershave, makeup, jewelry, or whatever empowers you. Every day at your altar, repeat your daily affirmations and anoint your heart chakra with water oil.

Planetary Influence
Venus and sun

Auspicious Timing
Conclude the spell during the next full moon, preferably within thirteen hours of full, while still waxing.

Needs
To construct a poppet, cut 2 layers of blue fabric into a roughly human shape, think of a traditional gingerbread man cookie-shape 9 inches tall. Recycled denim or old shirt material is fine. Leave a wide enough opening in the neck for a small stone to pass through into the head space.

Pink embroidery thread and needle

3 dried rose petals

A personal concern, or a taglock. This can be a strand of your hair, a nail clipping, or your personal sigil, etc.

1 small rectangle of blue intention paper that can be easily rolled into a scroll to fit inside the poppet

Small rose quartz stone (heart chakra, Venus, self-love)

Small blue calcite stone (for emotional healing)

½ cup dried rose petals

3 myrrh tears

A small shallow box, like a cigar box, or a dish

Preparation
Lay your working altar with all ingredients for your poppet easily accessible with work space to be creative.

With the pink thread, sew the 2 layers of blue fabric poppet around the outside from inner ankle around to the inner ankle of the other leg. Leave the inseam of the legs open, creating a charm bag for loading.

Anoint your own heart chakra with water anointing oil at your heart.

Light your dedication candle to welcome Spirit, who is ever-present.

Light the charcoal and place in the censer in preparation for loose incense burning.

Praxis

Awaken and consecrate your altar as taught in ritual 1. Consecrate the bowl of salted water as an offering to the undines. Hallow yourself and the space with the water incense smoke. Hallow the perimeter of the circle with the salted water. Cast your circle as taught in ritual 2.

Open the gates to elemental water and call upon the aid of the undines and Nicksa. Light your blue elemental water sanctuary candle. Invite to be present your guides, ancestors, and God/dess.

On the rectangle of blue paper, write your intention for emotional balance and fulfillment in the future. Here is my example: *My heart is restored to wholeness through the Divine Love of the God/dess. I walk their path of love with grace. By waxing moon, as daring waters flow, I am restored to balanced ease. I can love again with compassion, Perfect Love, and Perfect Trustworthiness. For the highest good of all involved, harming none. So mote it be.*

Holding the lit blue water candle, read your intention paper aloud.

To charge and stuff your poppet, hold each stone and ingredient, tap and meditate on what each one can bring to you, then add it to the poppet. First, add your personal concern or your tag-lock: a token, your sigil, or a strand of your hair, etc. Say to your poppet, *I name you [your name]. We are one in sympathy.*

Anoint the blue calcite stone in water oil, tap it three times, and blow over the stone.

Say: *Awake, awake, awaken to your powers of balance.*

Picture yourself tapped into that full moon above and her light flowing through you to the stone. Hold it in your palm; imagine yourself restored to wholeness. Then stuff it into the head of the blue poppet.

Anoint the rose quartz stone in water oil, tap it three times, and blow over the stone.

Say: *Awake, awake, awaken to your powers of peace.*

Imagine yourself glowing with pink light. Drop it into the heart of the blue poppet.

Hold the three myrrh tears in your palm. Tap them three times; blow over them.

Say: *Awake, awake, awaken to your powers of emotional healing.*

Add them to the body of the poppet.

Hold the three rose petals in your palm. Tap them; blow over them.

Say: *Awake, awake, awaken to your powers of love.*

Add them to the body of the poppet.

Repeat your intention statement above. Roll up the paper tightly and add it to a leg of the poppet. Finish sewing closed the poppet's legs and tie off the thread with nine knots.

Anoint the poppet's heart area with the elemental water oil. Hold it over the burning incense smoke to be purified and charged one step further. Blow gently into the poppet's mouth, as though resuscitating into life. Whisper this charm into the poppet's ear:

> *Poppet and me in sympathy,*
> *What love to you, is love to me.*
> *By triple moon, grow three by three*
> *As I do will, so mote it be!*

Sprinkle the remaining rose petals in the shallow box or dish. Lay the poppet on that bed of roses and leave to charge on your altar, making sure no one else has access to see or touch it. If privacy is an issue, store the closed box under your bed. You may add to the box or dish any symbols or items of loving nurturance that are meaningful to you.

Close your temple, releasing all guides, and closing the elemental gateway to water with gratitude. Extinguish all candles.

Care nightly for the poppet, continuing through to the next full moon, repeating your intention regularly. Open your spirit to the moon's light and meditate while holding your poppet. Occasionally add another drop of oil into the poppet's heart to "feed it." Visualize that the moon's watery energy is growing within you, restoring your emotional well-being.

Remember that you are a perfect child of the God/dess, and your spiritual guides are all around you, cheering you along the Pentacle Path of love. You are never forsaken. Lean into this path with your whole heart. Take excellent care of yourself, eat nutritious food and drink plenty of fresh water, and get adequate rest and exercise. Attend to your hygiene and beauty routines and indulge in life's simple pleasures with treats and pampering. Express love and appreciation abundantly to everyone in your life, and feel it returning to you. The lesson of the heart I've learned from Aphrodite is this: The heart that is opened from the sharing of love is opened and prepared to receive love.

Whenever you feel the working is sufficiently complete, give thanks for the fulfillment of the spell, and then tuck the poppet somewhere private near where you sleep, like under the mattress.

✤ Journal Reflection: The Path of Love ✤

The deep waters of emotion can be especially challenging and may take many turnings of the wheel to fully explore their depths and applications in your life. Both challenges and victories are equally important to record for your future Self to reflect upon. For your Book of Mirrors review, use the Witch's Jewel of Power framework below. Record your impressions about the following questions for your future Self to find. How do you love yourself? What are you grieving? What emotional wounds still need attention? What practical expressions of Perfect Love and Trustworthiness will you continue to offer the world at large?

From Air: To Know and to Wonder

- What impactful thing have you learned from this lesson?

- What do you still wonder about that needs further exploration?

From Fire: To Will and to Surrender

- How did you apply your will to these exercises? Did you adapt them to make them your own? What worked or didn't work well for you?

- Was there any expectation, assumption, or fear that needs to be surrendered?

From Water: To Dare and to Accept

- What gut emotional reactions came up for you?

- What surprised you? Which were easy to accept?

- Which do you dare to challenge or overcome?

From Earth: To Be Silent and to Resonate

- Now that the work is done, pay attention to what is going on in your life.

- How has this work affected your perceptions, actions, dreams? What patterns emerge?

- In what practical ways will you resonate your new awareness into reality?

Chapter 16
Quintessence of Spirit and the Path of Completion

The journey down the Pentacle Path seeks completion through the mysteries of quintessence, the fifth essence of Spirit. The timing for this path is a little different than in previous chapters. After the conclusion of water's elemental mysteries at Samhain, the Great Work for this Wheel of the Year is technically complete for this turning and is beginning anew. Assuming, that is, that your integrated ritual practice also celebrated the Great Goddess with each lunar esbat and the God with each solar sabbat. However, along the Pentacle Path of Elemental Witchcraft, the final stroke is one of completion as we return to the fifth point. This top point represents the wholeness of divinity both within matter and transcendent as Spirit, or God/dess.

In this chapter we'll map these mysteries to the top and bottom points of the Witch's Jewel of Power to explore the projective mysteries as the Great God through the Wiccan Rede and the receptive mysteries as the Great Goddess as the two keys to the Witch's temple: Perfect Love and Trust.

The Great Work: Completion Within the Wheel of the Year

As we explore the path of completion, there are three ritual workings that may be timed to the three lunar cycles between Samhain and Imbolc or at your own pace.

1. Once you have assembled your elemental altar tools, the first magick of this chapter is to consecrate those tools to their divine purpose.

2. Craft the formulary materials for the ritual journey to balance the Great Goddess and God within.

3. The culminating esbat rite integrates all the temple-creating techniques you've learned so far, using your consecrated chalice and athame (and optionally the pentacle paten and wand) for the Simple Feast, a ceremony also known as the Symbolic Great Rite.

The Pentacle Path of Completion and the Spiritual Body	
Chakras	Crown Chakra
Regulates	Wholeness
Opened by	Completion within God/dess
Blocked by	Ego-attachment
Witchcraft Goal	Integration of anima and animus, light and shadow
Love Conditions	Reciprocity vs. fear of betrayal
Charm of Affirmation	By the Two Who Move as One, I am complete through interconnection. Open channel, flowing free, blessed on all levels, So mote it be!

Mysteries of Quintessence

This fifth element is known by many names: ether, spirit, akasha, prima materia, or *quintessence*. It is symbolized on the pentacle as both the top point of the star but also as the surrounding circle. Quintessence is not an elemental essence like those we've previously studied; it is beyond the four material elements, the "background unity" from which they come into form.[277] Quintessence is the synergistic culmination of earth, air, fire, and water, which is greater than the sum of its parts. It is the transcendence of them all as the Spirit of the natural world.

Alchemist Robert Allen Bartlett describes quintessence as "a vast ocean of energy and everything seen and unseen is part of it. The alchemists called this energy the 'Celestial Fire,' Prima Materia, the First Matter, Chaos, and many others. Everything around us, though it seems separate and different from ourselves is One only One. All is from One is the First Law of Hermetics."[278] As a Witch, I consider quintessence to be the collective consciousness and love of *the Two Who Move as One*: the God/dess.

Witch's Jewel of Power: Spirit as Goddess and God		
	Yang: projective	Yin: receptive
Mystery Teaching	Wiccan Rede: "Do as ye will, so as it harms none."	Perfect Love and Perfect Trust
Wheel of Year	Solar cycles	Lunar cycles
Planetary Sphere	Sun	Moon

Witch's Jewel of Power: Spirit as Yang and Yin

Recall that our Jewel of Power symbol discussed in chapter 6 is the Platonic solid known as an octahedron or a *bipyramid*. Two individual pyramids, their square bases flat together as a mirror to each other: the upward-pointing *yang pyramid* symbolizes the projective mysteries of the Great God, and the downward-pointing *yin pyramid* symbolizes the receptive mysteries of the Great Goddess. Remembering that each face of the pyramid is a triangle, these echo the alchemical symbols for the elements by primary mental gender. Each pyramid's vertex holds a key to the mystery of a Witch's divine power.

Yang: Projective Vertex of the Great God

Within the persistent illusion of our separateness here in the Middleworld, the yang half of the jewel speaks to us as individuals on our personal journey. Remembering the

---

277. Greer, *The New Encyclopedia of the Occult*, 151.

278. Bartlett, *Real Alchemy*, 20.

origins of this teaching from Eliphas Levi, the traditional cornerstones to achieving the *Powers of the Sphinx* were to discover these elemental powers within oneself.[279] Remember that you are the incarnation of divinity on Earth, and then empower yourself as a sovereign within your kingdom. The magus is charged to assume the authority of their own mind (air) and take up the weapons of their will (fire), overcome fears of existence, power, and responsibility (water), and then actively carve out their place in the world, defending those boundaries (earth.)

Like the Emperor (IV, Aries) card in the tarot: yang mysteries ask us to become the wise and benevolent leaders of our own lives through innovation and taking charge. However, there must be balance. The Emperor is considered wise because he leads through generous service and serves by leading, making contributions for the greater good. The first two Rules of Witchcraft for Personal Sovereignty come into play: don't burn the Witch and don't be the problem.

God Spirit Mystery: Harm None

The directive from the God that is symbolized by the top vertex is found in the "Rede of the Wiccae" poem attributed to Lady Gwen Thompson. "Eight words the Wiccan Rede fulfill—an it harm none do what ye will."[280] This isn't a man-made law. There is only divine guidance and the free will to take it or leave it at your own risk. The word *rede* comes from the Old English word "raed," which meant *advice* or *counsel*.[281] Consider this message to be advice for a successful life, passed down by magi who likely learned it the stupid way and are trying to help others avoid the baneful effects of what they cause.

This guideline speaks to our personal process of evolution and our self-determination. The projective mysteries of the God are symbolized by the wand and blade of the magus, the thrust of creation: to cast our lot in enchantment and carve out our place in the world, which we then defend by banishing all that would deter our progress. It is alright to insist upon our place of safety, dignity, and respect, to claim our right to comfort and enjoyment here in this Middleworld. Self-care isn't selfish; it is the necessity of putting on your own oxygen mask first before assisting others in need.

---

279. Levi, *Transcendental Magic*, 30.

280. Mathiesen and Theitic, *The Rede of the Wiccae*, 52–53.

281. "Rede," Online Etymology Dictionary, Douglas Harper, accessed December 22, 2020, https://www .etymonline.com/word/rede.

This liturgy calls for the free pursuit of happiness, but that free will is tempered by sovereign responsibility. "Harm none," includes yourself and anything else in the interconnected universe. The big question to interpret becomes, what is harm? When I asked this question of divinity, their counsel in reply was this: If your actions attempt to deny the natural flow of Divine Will, that is harmful. Harm is the intentional impediment of the nine Divine Love Conditions. Harmful actions are sourced by *fear of a lack of love.*

Witches include air, water, plants, animals, the very minerals of the earth, and the ecosystem that supports us all as living parts of this web we all depend on to survive and thrive. In the second line of the "Rede of the Wiccae" poem, Witches are also advised to "Live an let live—fairly take an fairly give" within the web.[282] Poison any part of that web, and we are all poisoned. Starve any part of the web, and we all wither. In other words, don't crap the bed we're all sleeping in!

In short, pursue your happiness and fulfillment in alignment with your Divine Will. Live your destiny your way. Achieve your sacred mission according to your own discretion. Just remain beneficial within your sphere of influence, and don't impede other folks' free pursuit of their happiness, either. It's basically the golden rule—to extend the same considerations to others that you expect for yourself.

Yin: Receptive Vertex of the Great Goddess

The lessons of the Great Goddess are represented by the vertex of the downward pointing pyramid. Within the Goddess, we return to the ultimate receptive mystery of the paten, chalice, and cauldron as the womb of creation. With the Goddess's mysteries, we turn our attention outward to our interconnections within the web. Here we return to the cooperator tools. We are tasked to release our preconceptions and let in the fresh air of new ideas. We do so by listening to outside input (air), surrender ego-attachment as we engage with catalyzing powers (fire), accept all forms of Divine Love as they are offered through interrelationships (water), and then share that power to create a stronger, more compassionate world (earth).

Like the Empress card (III, Venus) in the tarot: Witches become the compassionate sovereign of our larger earthly family. We do so through nurturance of Self, which will passively radiate harmony and wholeness from all levels of our being. In balance, we are tasked to actively create and share beauty, to offer grace and mercy without discrimination or judgment.

---

282. Mathiesen and Theitic, *The Rede of the Wiccae*, 52–53.

The goddess vertex aligns our loftiest and high-minded spiritual values to the most down-to-earth and practical forms. The Witch as magus acts as the creative channel to birth Divine Love into material reality where people can feel that love, benefit from love, utilize love in a real way so they may thrive. Those real ways begin with the nine Divine Love Conditions. This is where the last two Rules for Personal Sovereignty come back into play: don't be the weak link and must be present to win.

Like a chalice of water poured back into a vast ocean, as we explore the Great Goddess's mysteries all self-imposed barriers between ourself, divinity, and our fellow cosmic travelers melt away. Animal, vegetable, or mineral in the matrix of the eternal goddess, all are *one* vast being. We flow with destiny as we evolve into a more enlightened state, both blessed in our divine natures and vastly interconnected to every possible resource because the Goddess is an inexhaustible fount of possibility.

Goddess Spirit Mystery: Perfect Love and Perfect Trust

In Wiccan rites, in order to enter the temple of our sacred circle, the sword-bearer stops each Witch at the gate and challenges them at sword point. Saying:

> You who stand on the threshold between the pleasant world of mankind
> and the Terrible Domains of the Outer Spaces, do you have the courage
> to enter? For it would be better to rush upon my blade and perish than
> to make the attempt with fear in your heart. How do you enter? [283]

There are two keys to open the door of this Witch's temple, and they are encoded within the first lines of "The Rede of the Wiccae" as "In Perfect Love and Perfect Trust." [284]

The divine counsel in these lines warns a Witch not to come to the crossroads of the God/dess unless you've properly prepared yourself through the balance of the Pentacle Path. Meaning you come of your sovereign free will with an open mind and a fearless heart; you're trustworthy to channel Divine Love unconditionally to all who join you at their crossroads. For those who answer correctly, the sword and besom are laid across the threshold, over which the Witch jumps the liminal boundary into the temple and is greeted with a third key: the kiss or a warm embrace and a "Merry meet."

---

283. The Sojo Circle's adaptation from the traditional Wiccan liturgy provided by Vivianne Crowley in *Wicca: The Old Religion in the New Millennium*, 111.

284. Mathiesen and Theitic, *The Rede of the Wiccae*, 52–53.

Perfect Love: Acknowledges yourself and others as sovereign, with dignity and worth, whole within both light and shadow. A promise of Perfect Love embodies the Divine Love Conditions of acceptance, free will, resources, affection, and expression: we care, you are important, you are worthy to co-create with the gods, we will not abandon you just because you might be having an off day. However, Perfect Love is a powder keg unless it is tempered by the most important part of that statement about Perfect Trust.

Unconditional love does not mean unconditional relationships. Nor does it mean that you have to like every aspect or behavior of every person in your community. Sadly, there are many Witches in the early laps of their own Pentacle Path who are still sourced from fear. You still need a solid sense of discretion and healthy boundaries. You can respect a newcomer's inner divinity, warts and all, while still being smart about your safety. Again, discretion and clear communication are key.

Perfect Trust: Sets the strong boundaries in place that make a safe environment for all that unconditional love you'll be offering. To pledge that you enter with Perfect Trust is a statement that *you* are trustworthy. Your own trustworthy intentions should be easy enough to promise to anyone at any time, but most of all to the Witches that join you on sacred ground.

Perfect Trust embodies the Divine Love Conditions of security, authenticity, trustworthiness and reciprocity. This is the social contract between members that promises that the care you are extending to them will be returned to you in equal measure *to the best of their ability.* This is the trust that they are honest and authentic in their dealings with you and that they will not transgress against your boundaries while expecting the same from you in return, *to the best of your ability.* This is reciprocity; the social contract is a two-way street and promises that you are all trying to live up to your shared ideals. If one of you misses the mark, then you will respectfully help them get back into your good graces … without burning them at the stake, slandering them on social media, nor cursing them into a toad.

"Sure, Heron!" you say. "What if some jerk refuses to uphold their end of this social contract?" When it becomes clear they do not share your ideals—habitually doing trust-breaking things, burning the Witch, being the weak link, and refusing to show up and work it out? Fools! Then Witches of good conscience have a boundary to defend. This is water's lesson of acceptance brought into practice. Accept this situation, define that boundary, and peacefully sever ties. Remove their access to harm you further. You have no control over other people, but you should have control over your own affiliations.

"The Rede of the Wiccae" addresses this issue in the twenty-first couplet: "With the fool no season spend or be counted as his friend."[285] Or, as I often say: *Namaste away!* Which translates to: "The spirit in me releases your spirit in peace to pursue happiness at a distance that I will now define until you can do better."

The Path of Completion

The path of completion is a remembering of our fivefold nature within quintessence. To be in balance within our spiritual body is to awaken from the illusion of separateness. To be complete is to fully realize our interconnections throughout divinity, throughout time and space, and within our previous incarnations. To attain spiritual balance is to seek the God/dess within and eventually embrace our *wholeness*. Like a living yin-yang symbol, we balance our dark and light, day and night, the bane and balm, horror and beauty, projective and receptive qualities we possess. All these things are a part of being an incarnate God/dess. Wholeness is perfection; we are perfectly human.

The Completion Paradox: Unity vs. Diversity

The paradox reconciled through Spirit's completion resolves the polarity of unity and diversity. Once more, this mystery teaching goes back to the "divine paradox" between the *absolute truth* and the *relative truth* of God/dess; between the monolith oneness (Hermeticists call the *One only One*) and the simultaneous radical diversity of individuals incarnated into this apparent separateness. To reconcile this paradox, we must hold as equally evident that 1) every possible thing, seen and unseen, sentient and otherwise, is absolutely one being: Divine Love. Therefore, no kind of person is greater-than or lesser-than anyone else manifested in the cosmos. There could be no superior race, no dominant sex, no "chosen people," and 2) the ultimate purpose is to parse God/dess into diverse individual forms to discover the relative truths in every nitty-gritty nook and cranny of possible make, model, identity, lifestyle, and demographic. Nature is compelled to seek further diversification!

The illusion of our separateness serves the very useful purpose of relationship. We create ripples of interference patterns as we interact with each other, whether that be love or tension, and God/dess learns from those interactions. As we awaken into the absolute truth of our unity, we naturally evolve into inclusivity of relative truths too. All bigotry and

---

285. Mathiesen and Theitic, *The Rede of the Wiccae*, 52–53.

phobias about each other fall away. In this way, the paradox between unity within God/dess and diversity upon Earth can be equally embraced. In Oneness we are a beautiful kaleidoscope of diversity.

Crown, Earth Star, and Soul Star Chakras: Divine Alignment in Three Worlds

The Crown Chakra at the top of the head regulates our connection to divine consciousness, connecting our human mind with Divine Mind. Beyond the best-known seven chakras, there are a total of twelve chakras within our auric field, with transpersonal chakras connecting us further to divinity, above and below. I correspond the crown chakra to the *anima mundi*, Latin for "soul of the world."[286] The crown chakra regulates our individual divine consciousness within this current incarnation. See figure 13.

The Earth Star Chakra is below the feet, connecting to the planetary energy of our Mother Earth Goddess in her most material form. It is through the earth star gate that planetary power first ascends, feeding through our root chakra to snake through the seven main chakras along our spines to the crown of our heads. I correspond this chakra to the *corpus mundi*, Latin for "body of the world."[287] The earth star chakra regulates our interconnection of divine consciousness manifesting as our physical bodies.

The Soul Star Chakra is above the crown chakra and is called the "seat of the soul," which connects to cosmic-level consciousness and Divine Love. Through the soul star gate, we may access the information of the astral (lunar) realm, known as the akashic records, which are an energetic archive of all human experience. This includes the accumulated soul experiences of our own past lives.

The Stellar Gateway at the top of our auras feeds all our subtle bodies. I imagine the sunlight of Father Sky God beaming down through the stellar gateway. I correspond this chakra to the *spiritus mundi*, Latin for "vital force of the world."[288] The steller gateway regulates our interconnection to the vital, spiritual force of God/dess, which empowers all.

---

286. Greer, *The New Encyclopedia of the Occult*, 24

287. Greer, *The New Encyclopedia of the Occult*, 113.

288. Greer, *The New Encyclopedia of the Occult*, 450.

These chakras easily align with our Witch's Jewel of Power mysteries as the top- and bottom-most vertices (see figure 15) and the Hermetic three-world paradigm of Upperworld, Middleworld, and Underworld (see figure 13).

⚜ Exercise 14: Balancing God/dess Within ⚜

The end goal in balancing our spiritual body is to consciously connect that channel of power running through us individually to the ultimate cosmic power source: God/dess above and below. At each lap of the Pentacle Path, we've opened one of the "channel locks" along the many layers of fivefold Self. On the path of completion, complete that channel opening. Through the spiritual body we tap into divine power from earth star ascending all the way to soul star and the stellar gateway beyond. Which descends again around the torus field to rise again through our open channel in a continuous spiral of rejuvenation and creation. The more freely flowing and conscience this connection becomes, the more effective managers of human life we become because we also gain a broader, more transcendent view of life's patterns.

The ultimate mystery teaching of the Witch's Jewel of Power is the sacred marriage between the God and Goddess within ourselves. From there, the journey is personal, complex, and no two humans will have the same experience. The mystery of the Jewel is attainment of balance within yourself, within your environment here in *the below* and in your relationship with divinity and spiritual realms of *the above*. Through this God/dess alignment, the harmony of nature can flow most powerfully through every aspect of your life.

Spiritual imbalance happens when we forget our inherently divine nature but also when we neglect either our god or goddess powers. Remember that polarity and mental gender are spectrums of possibility like a slider bar, not an either-or toggle switch. Balancing our spirits has little to do with our biological sex, so don't get hung up on that. The God/dess is every possibility of the rainbow, and so are we. So, rather than talking about what is masculine or feminine, Witches are better served to consider their wholeness within the *projective and receptive* phases of a cycle. Thus, the trick to balancing our spiritual bodies is to embrace our full range from the projective side of thought (air) and action (fire) and to the receptive side of feeling (water) and creating (earth), and then to strengthen the weaker qualities over time until we can be a powerhouse in all four arenas.

✢ The Simple Feast—Symbolic Great Rite ✢

Wicca's ceremonial chalice blessing for the Simple Feast, which is descriptively called "cakes and wine" or "cakes and ale," magickally balances the Goddess and God within us. This rite enacts the symbolic mysteries of the *heiros gamos*, the Great Rite of sexual union.

The sacred marriage *in token* is symbolically enacted with the traditional altar tools, primarily the chalice and the athame. Ultimately, this iconic Wiccan ritual attempts to reconcile the ancient Neolithic-era tensions created between the gylanic earth goddess cultures and the patriarchal warrior god cultures who invaded and subsumed them, as described by Riane Eisler's *The Chalice and the Blade*.[289] This magick reconciles our inner God/dess and can potentially reconcile the equal power of goddess and god within the culture too.

The chalice, a tool of water, represents the womb of the Goddess as the receptive principle, filled with a "spirit" made from a fruit or grain. The athame, a tool of fire, represents the phallus of the God and the projective principle. Upon the pentacle paten, the tool of earth, a delicious cake, cookie, or bread is blessed for each celebrant and charged to both nurture their bodies and to be enjoyed. This is a fulfillment of the God/dess's promise of Divine Love. Though the cakes are traditionally blessed with the athame touching them with a drop of blessed wine, another option is to use the wand, a tool of air, whose purpose is to cast enchantment. Adding the fourth altar tool brings all four elemental energies to complete this fivefold rite of union.[290]

The Simple Feast blessing is called the Great Rite *in token*, because the symbolic actions are in sympathy with the *actual* great rite of sexual coupling that produces new babies. However, this magick extends far beyond the obvious hetero-sexiness. This magickal act is in sympathy with the sacred union of the land and her people: of anima mundi, spiritus mundi, and corpus mundi, or the soul, spirit, and body of the divine world.[291] It is a magickal act of internalizing the creative union of goddess and god, whose metaphorical coupling literally sustains us. God/dess is the culmination of sunlight, soil, water, and atmosphere, planning and toil, nurturing and harvesting. Their Divine Love produces the fruits, grains, nuts, and meats that are passed all the way up the food chain from sunlight to chocolate chip cookie. Each link in that chain is a fulfillment of their promise of Divine

---

289. Eisler, chapter 4, in *The Chalice and the Blade*.

290. Vivianne *Crowley, Wicca,* 188.

291. Greer, *The New Encyclopedia of the Occult,* 24.

Love through sacrifice and gratitude, *fairly taking, and fairly giving*, as the "Rede of the Wiccae" advises.[292] The Simple Feast ceremony serves to remind Witches of their charge.

The "cakes" can be any small cookie or pastry, often in a crescent moon shape, or a piece of fruit, chocolate bonbon—anything you like. The chalice is typically filled with a fermented "spirit," like a fruit wine, beer or ale, or other blended "potion." If alcohol is not ideal for you, purified water, herbal tea, or juice can be chosen for their magickal associations. Consuming these blessed foods then helps a Witch to internalize that magick of divinity.

During the ritualized journey to balance spirit later this cycle, the ceremony of the Simple Feast will be enacted. If you don't already have the altar tools of chalice, athame, pentacle paten, and wand, now would be a meaningful time to collect yours and conse-crate them to their sacred purpose prior to the rite.

Consecration of Altar Tools

At this point in this Elemental Witchcraft system, you will have already created the nec-essary charged elemental candles, incense, and oil blends that were part of each element working. This rite is a culmination of the ritual techniques and temple-building you will have explored up until now.

⚜ Ritual 8: Elemental Tool Consecration ⚜

Auspicious Timing

The waxing or full moon immediately following the conclusion of four classical elemental lessons or part of your Yule sabbat celebration. It can be especially meaningful to rededicate your tools to their sacred purpose each Winter Solstice as the first steps toward rededica-tion to the Great Work through the next Wheel of the Year.

Needs

The elemental tools you intend to consecrate

Consecration elements of bowl of salt, bowl of water, fire candle, censer with char-coal tab for incense, small spoon, and tongs

Dedication sanctuary candle for Spirit, which is always present

---

292. Mathiesen and Theitic, *The Rede of the Wiccae,* 52–53.

Representations of Spirit as God/dess that are meaningful to you, perhaps an image or statuary

The four corresponding charged elemental candles

The four corresponding element incense blends and anointing oils

Preparation

Physically clean and organize the ritual space. Bathe and dress in fresh, comfortable clothing, preferably barefoot with hair unbound, or nude as you prefer.

Lay your altar with intention.

Light your dedication candle to welcome Spirit, who is ever-present.

Light the charcoal and place in the censer in preparation for loose incense burning.

Praxis

Awaken and consecrate your altar as taught in ritual 1. As taught in ritual 2, hallow yourself and the circle perimeter with the four elements, cast your circle, and open the four elemental gateways to the quarters, lighting their candles. Call upon God/dess and your guides to be present.

Purification

Taking a tool in your dominant hand, pass it through the smoke of the corresponding elemental incense; see the energies of air infusing and clarifying the object of all ideas and thoughts.

Say: *I purify this [tool] with the powers of air.*

Pass through or near the flame of the fire candle, seeing the energies of fire infusing and burning away all previous will or intentions from the object.

Say: *I purify this [tool] with the powers of fire.*

Touch the object to the water or anoint with a drop of water with your fingers, seeing the energies of water washing free any previous emotions or psychic impressions from the tool.

Say: *I purify this [tool] with the powers of water.*

Touch the tool to the salt, seeing the energies of earth ground free any previous ownership or purpose from the object.

Say: *I purify this [tool] with the powers of earth.*

Pass the tool through the flame or light of the Spirit candle and touch to the representation of Spirit on the altar, seeing the white light of God/dess neutralizing all previous history of the object, leaving it clean and prepared to receive new purpose in alignment with Divine Will.

Say: *I purify this [tool] with the powers of Spirit.*

Dedication

Say: *This [type of object] will serve as my [name of tool] and be my tool of [element it will channel].* Example: *This dish will serve as my paten pentacle and be my tool of earth.*

Charge the specific tool with the specific quality from "The Charge of the Goddess." The following table has a suggestion for that language.

	Tool	Witch's Jewel of Power Mystery	Charge of the God/dess
Earth	Pentacle Paten	I infuse this paten with earth's projective powers of silence.	I charge this paten to manifest my magick, empowered by nature's balance.
	Besom	I infuse this besom with earth's receptive powers of resonance.	I charge this besom with reverence, defending my sovereignty in Perfect Divine Trust.
Air	Wand	I infuse this wand with air's projective powers of knowledge.	I charge this wand to inspirit my magick, casting enchantment with mirth.
	Staff	I infuse this staff with air's receptive powers of wonderment.	I charge this staff to create within the Divine Mind, defending my sovereignty with strength.
Fire	Athame	I infuse this athame with fire's projective powers of the will.	I charge this athame to empower my magick, banishing fear with humility.
	Sword	I infuse this sword with fire's receptive powers of surrender.	I charge this sword to empower through Divine Will, defending my sovereignty with honor.

	Tool	Witch's Jewel of Power Mystery	Charge of the God/dess
Water	Chalice	I infuse this chalice with water's projective power of daring.	I charge this chalice as a fountain of beauty, which will flow through my magick.
	Cauldron	I infuse this cauldron with water's receptive power of acceptance.	I charge this cauldron as a fountain of Perfect Divine Love, defending my sovereignty with compassion.

Touch the tool now to the corresponding consecration material (salt for earth, incense smoke for air, flame for fire, water for water). Spiritually tap your consciousness into the appropriate elemental energy by mentally returning to that place in your astral temple and remembering your connections to that plane. Both feel and visualize that color of energy (green/earth, yellow/air, red/fire, blue/water) infusing the matter of the tool and becoming a gateway to channel that power in the future.

Anoint the tool with the appropriate elemental oil blend.

Now, touch the tool to the deity image or Spirit candle on the altar, feeling the blessings and power of divinity flow into the object.

Say: *Only the purest divine energy may enter and work through this [tool]. Together, may all that we do be for the highest good of all involved, harming none. So mote it be!*

Repeat this ceremony for all of your altar tools. Raise a cone of power, chanting and dancing deosil with your tools in hand, first a few laps with the wand and athame, chanting:

> *By magick wand and fiery blade,*
> *Truth be known and will be bade!*
> *Sylph and dragon, wind and flame,*
> *As I do dream, my will proclaimed!*

Then chant a few laps with the chalice and pentacle paten.

> *By chalice deep and paten round,*
> *Daring love and silence found!*
> *Gnome and undine, land and sea,*
> *As I do will, so mote it be!*

Deconstruct the Temple

Conclude the rite and close the temple as taught in ritual 2. Release Spirit and guides with gratitude. Close the elemental gateways widdershins beginning in the north.

Gather the circle into a small sphere, charge to light your path in the future, and release to the cosmos.

Say: *The circle is open but never broken! Merry meet, merry part, and merry meet again!*

Figure 31: Candle wrap image for God by Heron Michelle

Figure 32: Candle wrap image for Goddess by Heron Michelle

Formulary for Spirit as God/dess

During the next waxing lunar cycle, craft your magickal materials for the rituals and magick of Spirit to come. Reference the table below for additional correspondences and make substitutions as needed to suit what materials are regionally available and affordable for you.[293]

---

293. I assembled these element correspondence charts from many sources, but a good reference is *Llewellyn's Complete Book of Correspondences* by Sandra Kynes.

Correspondences of ether (aether) as goddess/yin and god/yang		
	Goddess/yin	God/yang
Color	Black/Silver	White/Gold
Celestial Body	Moon	Sun
Mental Gender	Yin, feminine	Yang, masculine
Governs	Spiritual body	Spiritual body
Witch's Jewel of Power Mystery	Two keys to the temple	The Wiccan Rede
Elements	Water, earth	Air, fire
Primary Magickal Tools	Chalice, cauldron, moon crown	Athame, sword, horned crown
Ritual Cycles	Thirteen esbats of the lunar cycle	Eight sabbats of the solar cycle
Chakra	Root, earth star chakra	Crown, soul star chakra, stellar gateway
Primary Stones	Jet, rainbow moonstone, selenite, smoky quartz	Amber, golden topaz, sunstone, clear quartz
Primary Metals	Silver	Gold
Herbs	Apple, blackberry, cardamom, gardenia, geranium, grape, heather, iris, lily, rose, jasmine, lotus, mugwort, reeds, star anise, pomegranate	Angelica, broomcorn, calendula, carnation, chamomile, cinnamon, clove, corn, mistletoe, marigold, rosemary, sunflower
Resins	Myrrh	Frankincense
Trees/Woods/Barks	Apple, mimosa, mesquite, myrtle, olive, rowan, white willow	Ash, birch, cedar, hazel, juniper, bay laurel, oak, walnut
Creatures	Raven, horse, bear, cat, cattle, hare, crow, owl, peacock, heron, snake, moth, spider	Deer, dung beetle, goat, bull, lion, ram, rooster, eagle, hawk, crane, lizard

❧ Exercise 15: Spirit Formulary Crafting ❧

Auspicious Timing

Waxing lunar cycle, within thirteen hours of an exact full moon, when sun and moon are in opposition.

Needs

See the recipes below for specific materials and equipment for each recipe.

Make sure you have enough surface area at your working altar to spread out and be artistically creative.

Consecration elements, including a hookah charcoal in an incense censer with sand, tongs, small spoon, and lighter or matches.

Add anything that aids your connection to divinity of nature: statuary, images of deities, the sun and moon, etc.

Preparation

Awaken and consecrate your altar with the ritual 1 in chapter 9.

Call upon your spiritual guides, goddess, and god to be present and inspire your magickal creations.

For charging any spirit-drawing materials, chant this charm of making:

Spirit Blessing Charm

> *Quintessence of Spirit! The Two Who Move as One!*
> *Silver shining moon, balance golden rays of sun!*
> *Come powers of completion and perfect unity,*
> *From heart to Heart, and will to Will, so mote it be!*

❧ Spirit Incense ❧

Long has the fragrant resin of myrrh been associated with the moon, feminine divinity, and night forces. Just as frankincense resin has been associated with the sun, masculine divinity, and day forces. An equal blend of the two makes the perfect spirit incense for evoking the *Two Who Move as One.*

Needs

Small jar

1 tablespoon myrrh resin tears or powder (Goddess)

1 tablespoon frankincense resin tears or powder (God)

Praxis

Awaken each resin to its divine power and add each to the jar. Tap into nature's power, envisioning the Great God/dess as the *Two Who Move as One* in loving embrace of earth and water meeting sky and sunlight, or the earth balanced between the moon and sun. Chant the charm of making to empower the blend to balance divinity and invoke Spirit within the temple. Label the jar with the name and date, and glyphs of sun, moon, pentacle, or yin-yang.

❖ Spirit Anointing Oil ❖

Blend this oil to restore the balance of the Great God/dess to any being or object upon which it is anointed.

Needs

Dark-colored 1-dram bottle with tightly sealing cap

9 drops myrrh essential oil, for the nine phases of the lunar cycle

8 drops frankincense essential oil, for the eight sabbats of the sun

Jojoba oil, for longer shelf life, or another carrier oil, for short term use

Optional: a stone chip of both smoky and clear quartz

Praxis

Tap the bottle of each essential oil and awaken to their divine power and add to the bottle. Connect to nature's power, as done above. Fill the vial the rest of the way to the top with the jojoba oil. Add stone chips to charge. Envision, chant the charm of making, and empower blend as described above, to balance divinity and evoke Spirit. Label the bottle with the name and date, and glyphs of sun ☉, moon ☽, pentacle, or yin-yang.

❖ Goddess and God Sanctuary Candles ❖

In the same manner used previously, prepare two seven-day glass-jarred sanctuary candles to channel the powers of Spirit as Goddess and God.

Needs

White seven-day sanctuary candle in glass jar. They are typically 2.25 x 8 inches tall and take refill insert candles no more than 2 inches wide.

Black seven-day sanctuary candle in glass jar. They are typically 2.25 x 8 inches tall and take refill insert candles no more than 2 inches wide.

A 7-inch square image from figure 31a to envision the God in his many aspects. Can be copied and colored to create a candle wrap, or you may creatively decorate your own piece of lightweight paper.

A 7-inch square image from figure 31b to envision the Goddess in her many aspects. Can be copied and colored to create a candle wrap, or you may creatively decorate your own piece of lightweight paper.

13-inch length of white or gold cord or ribbon

13-inch length of black or silver cord or ribbon

Flat head screwdriver or a power drill with large bit

½ teaspoon prepared spirit incense

3 drops frankincense essential oil

3 drops myrrh essential oil

3 tiny chips each of clear quartz and smoky quartz, or substitution

Praxis

Goddess Candle: On the blank side of the 7-inch square candle wrap paper, write an evocation prayer to the Great Goddess. Compose your own or reference the calls provided in ritual 2. If you're not using the image provided in figure 31b, decorate the outside of the wrapper with images of goddesses of the earth, ocean, and the moon, include the planetary glyph for moon ☽, yin and yang, etc.

With the screwdriver or drill, bore out three holes in the wax about an inch deep. Load the candle by poking a teaspoon of spirit incense into the holes with a chopstick.

Top with a smoky quartz stone chip in each hole. Then anoint with three drops of myrrh oil and rub it around the wax deosil with a bare finger.

Wrap the paper wrapper around the jar and tie down with the black or silver cord or ribbon. The charging of this candle will take place during the journey to realms of Spirit later on.

God Candle: On the blank side of the god 7-inch square candle wrap paper, write an evocation prayer. Compose your own or reference the calls provided in ritual 2. If you're not using the image provided in figure 31a, decorate the outside of the wrapper with images of gods of the sky, sun, grains, and horned animals, include the planetary glyph for sun ☉, yin and yang, etc.

With the screwdriver or drill bore out three holes in the wax about an inch deep. Load the candle by poking a teaspoon of spirit incense into the holes with a chopstick. Top with a clear quartz stone chip in each hole. Then anoint with three drops of frankincense oil and rub it around the wax deosil with a bare finger.

Wrap the paper wrapper around the jar and tie down with the white or gold cord or ribbon. The charging of this candle will take place during the journey to realms of Spirit later on.

Journey to the Realms of Spirit

In a religious ceremony devoted to a God/dess of nature, it is ideal to create this temple outdoors, weather permitting. For this culminating rite, I encourage you to write your own gate-openings and evocations to the Goddess and God, or to speak directly from the heart in the ecstasy of the moment. I offer the language included here as inspiration; do as ye will. This rite concludes with the Symbolic Great Rite ceremony, otherwise known as the Simple Feast. Also included in this ritual is the ceremonial usage of the four traditional elemental altar tools on the assumption that you have them consecrated and available. Adapt as needed to what you have.

As before, this interactive ritualized journey is best enacted by listening to a recording of the meditation or as someone reads it aloud for you.

⚜ Ritual 9: Spirit Temple of Goddess and God ⚜

Auspicious timing

Any full moon in a water or earth sign while the sun is in an air or fire sign. However, I recommend revisiting this balancing rite each year just prior to Summer Solstice. In the Northern hemisphere, the sun is in Gemini, almost to his "full" peak, and the waxing moon is in the water sign of Scorpio, almost to her full peak. In the Southern hemisphere, the sun and moon will be in the opposite signs.

Needs

Add to your Spirit altar anything that invokes a balanced divinity for you: a combo of black and white tablecloths, statuary of goddess and god, images of sun and moon, etc.

Dedication sanctuary candle for Spirit, which is ever-present

Prepared black and white sanctuary candles for the Goddess and God

Four elemental sanctuary candles from previous exercises

Altar consecration tools: red candle, bowl of salt, bowl of water, incense censer with sand, and a hookah charcoal tab, tongs and a small spoon, lighter or box of matches

Spirit herbal incense blend

Spirit anointing oil blend

Consecrated tools: athame and chalice filled with wine, beer, juice, or purified water; pentacle paten (or a plate) holding enough "cakes" for the celebrations and to make libations in offering; wand

Bookmarked page to recite "The Charge of the Goddess" by Doreen Valiente, included in chapter 3

Preparation

Prepare the vessel of your body by getting plenty of rest, eating healthy food, and getting adequate hydration of pure water throughout the day leading up to this ritual.

Bathe and dress in fresh, loose-fitting clothes, your hair unbound, barefoot as you are able (weather and location permitting).

Lay your altar as an artistic expression of beauty and reverence.

Make space to place the elemental sanctuary candles around you in the four cardinal directions. Consider outlining the edge of your circle with flour (god) and flowers (goddess).

Anoint the base of your spine and the crown of your head with the spirit anointing oil.

Light your dedication sanctuary candle to welcome Spirit, who is ever-present.

Light the charcoal and place in the censer in preparation for loose incense burning.

Praxis

Awaken and consecrate the altar as taught in ritual 1. As taught in ritual 2, hallow yourself and the circle perimeter by the four elements; cast your circle with the awen cone of power chant while walking the perimeter with your wand or athame; close and charge the sphere of your temple, above and below.

Open the four elemental gateways as taught in ritual 2, lighting their corresponding elemental sanctuary candles and setting them in the four cardinal directions around your circle.

Evoke the ancestors of land, blood, and spirit, as taught in ritual 2.

Evocation of Spirit: At the altar, standing in pentacle pose with open palms turned upward, say aloud: *Great Spirit: You who dwell within all things, I welcome you. You who are boundless potential and infinite diversity, the dreamer and the dream, guide this magick. Hail and welcome!*

Light the black goddess candle. Stand in Goddess branches pose, and raise your opened hands as if to cup the moon above.

Say aloud: *Great Goddess, in the dust of whose feet are the hosts of heaven, whose body encircles the universe, welcome! You who are the beauty of the green earth, the white moon among the stars, and the mystery of the waters. Awaken as my heart's desire! Great Goddess, I seek you within and without, in perfect balance. Flow through these rites. Hail and welcome!* Draw down your hands to cross them over your chest. See figure 21.

Light the white god candle. Now raising your dominant hand in salute to the heavens as if drawing down the sun and your receptive hand pointing toward the earth in open channel pose. See figure 21.

Say aloud: *Great God, in the fires of your Will burns a thousand suns, whose seed brings forth our sustenance, welcome! You who are the power of the wild hunt and the shorn grain of sacrifice, graciously given. You who are the mysteries of death and the miracle of rebirth. Awaken as my soul's fire! Great God, I seek you within and without, in perfect balance! Empower these rites! Hail and welcome!* Cross your hands over your chest.

Sit down comfortably before your altar and begin the recording of the guided journey.

✤ Meditation 9: Guided Journey to Meet Goddess and God ✤

Close your eyes; take a deep breath. Picture your most magickal Self sitting in a comfortable chair in comfortable room inside your mind. It is quiet and still in your sanctuary. Your eyes are now a window on a distant wall of that room. Any distracting noises or stray thoughts are merely birds flying past that distant window … release them without care. (*Pause.*)

There is a skylight above you, and a soft beam of divine light shines down upon your crown chakra. Breathe down the light with three deep breaths. Inhale through the nose and exhale through the mouth, releasing all tension. (*Pause for three breaths.*) You are at perfect ease on all levels. (*Pause.*)

There is a beautiful, ornate door in the floor of your mental sanctuary, a door leading to all possibility. Open that door, finding a spiral staircase descending beyond. With each exhale of your breath, step down, deeper and deeper, descending into your subconscious mind, and deep into your own belly. At the foot of the stairs, you'll arrive at your inner crossroads. Twelve steps down, around and 'round you tread the spiral staircase. (*Pause.*)

Before you hangs a looking glass, a portal outward to the astral realms where all things are possible by a mere thought. Picture your Astral Temple upon the glass. (*Pause.*)

Say: *It is my intention to journey to my astral temple to seek the path of completion within Spirit. I call my guides, gods, and ancestors to keep me safe and show me the way. Blessèd be.* (*Pause.*)

On the count of three, step through the portal and arrive on the astral plane on the path to your astral temple. One, two, three, step through!

You arrive upon the astral plane and take the familiar temple path that lies before you. Down, down, down the path you tread, seeing the glowing light of your temple fires ahead. Smell the sweet scent of the incense calling you home.

At last, you arrive. Enter the temple door, finding it just as you left it. At your place of water, feel the cool mist of the waters flowing. Feel the air blowing freely throughout. Find your place of fire and the sacred flames you tend glowing brightly. Find your place of earth, the altar itself, and stand before it. Softly open your eyes and gaze upon your Middleworld altar, and in your mind's eye, see it in your astral temple too.

In a prayerful way, say: *Great Spirit of Nature, I seek balanced union within the Two Who Move as One. The vessel of my body is properly prepared. My mind opened to Divine Mind. My will aligned to Divine Will. My heart opened to Divine Love. Guide my spirit as I walk the path of completion!*

A portal appears, and through it you see the axis mundi, the great world tree. Approach and step through. (*Pause.*)

You stand before the world tree, whose wide branches hold the cosmos and all the heavens and whose deep roots hold the planet and all the Underworld. Step up onto its knobby roots and lay your hands on the broad trunk of the tree. You hold the Middleworld in your palms. Feel the pulse of creation, the heartbeat of the cosmos. Your heartbeat. (*Pause.*)

You, too, are the axis mundi between the worlds. Your body is the Middleworld of matter, like the trunk. Your subtle bodies of mind, heart, will, and spirit touch the cosmos, above and below, within and without. You and the tree are in harmony. (*Pause.*) Step into the tree. Find your roots from the base of your spine, from the soles of your feet; follow your roots as they dig deeply into the cool, quiet darkness of the Underworld.

As you exhale, breathe down your roots. Push them deep into the earth, into the topsoil, beyond the stones to find bedrock. In the bedrock your roots tap into the green energy of mineral nourishment. Breathe up this green light, up through your roots. (*Pause.*) The green light fills your physical body completely, offering stability, structure, healing, strength. Breathe in the green light and remember the elemental realm of earth. Remember your allies of gnomes and Sovereign Ghob. Remember their silence and resonance upon the path of sovereignty. Your physical body is an open channel of divinity, whole and at ease. (*Long pause.*)

Exhale and push your roots further down, deeper into the earth, deeper and deeper until your roots find the water table. In this underground pool of cool water, there is a blue energy of liquid refreshment. Breathe up this blue light through your roots. The blue light fills your emotional body completely, offering acceptance, unconditional love, healing, and compassion. Breathe in the blue light and remember the realm of elemental water. Remember your allies of the undines and Sovereign Nicksa. Remember their daring and acceptance along the path of love. Your emotional body is an open channel of divinity, whole and at ease. (*Long pause.*)

Exhale and push your roots deeper and deeper still, seeking out the core of the planet earth. Passing through the gateway of the earth star chakra, roots tap into planetary consciousness, finding a complex pigment of all colors. Find the Great Goddess, the nurturing creatrix of all. She wraps you in her arms like a hug. Reflecting in this darkness, you find the moon, shining full in the balanced dance with the sun.

Ask the Great Goddess to reveal herself to you in a form that is correct, gentle, and understandable for you at this time. Receive the vision. (*Long pause.*)

Ask the Great Goddess to show you which of her qualities are strong within you. Receive the vision. (*Long pause.*)

Ask the Great Goddess to show you which of her qualities need rebalancing within you. Receive the vision. (*Long pause.*)

Ask the Great Goddess how you can best fulfill her charge for perfect, unconditional love? How can you fulfill her charge for Perfect Trustworthiness? Receive the vision. (*Long pause.*)

From the core of the earth, breathe up her dark sustenance through your roots, nourishing your spirit on all levels…like a comforting favorite meal only Mama can make. Breathe up her dark power and feel your inner goddess awakening. (*Pause.*) Draw up her fierce beauty throughout your body as her luminescence flows up the trunk of your tree, filling you completely, all the way to your crown. Your chakras spin open as she ascends, seeking her lover. Luminesce with the restful darkness of the Goddess. You are whole and complete within her Divine Love. (*Long pause.*)

Find your branches rising into the air. Feel the sway of the wind as ideas move freely, like birds in flight. Push outward into the atmosphere until you tap the yellow, airy energy of thought. Breathe down the yellow light of air to fill your mental body completely, offering wonderment, inspiration, truth, and wisdom. Breathe in the yellow light and remember the elemental realms of air. Remember your allies of the sylphs and Paralda. Remember knowing and wonderment along the path of truth. Your mental body is an open channel of divinity, whole and at ease. (*Long pause.*)

Exhale and push your branches higher and further, your leaves leaning into the sunlight, feeling the heat of the sun and stars beyond. Push your branches further outward, following the light until you tap a red, fiery energy. Breathe down this red light, absorbed through your leaves, flowing down into your belly, stoking the furnace of your Will. These fires fuel your passions and ambitions and invigorate your sacred mission. Breathe down glowing red light and remember the realms of elemental fire. Remember your allies of the salamanders and Djin. Remember their lessons of will and surrender along the path of power. Your body of will is an open channel of divinity, whole and at ease. (*Long pause.*)

Exhale and push out even further to pass through the Soul Star Gateway, tapping cosmic consciousness and your memories throughout all your lifetimes. (*Pause.*) Push upward and outward again, through the Steller Gateway, traveling with the speed of a dream within the Divine Mind, deep into the cosmos. (*Pause.*) Touch the sun; the divine light of the Great God shines through you as a bolt of inspiration, offering order, wisdom, protection, and encouragement. He provides all you need to survive and thrive … a good father anticipating your needs …

Ask the Great God to reveal himself to you in a form that is correct, gentle, and understandable for you at this time. Receive the vision. (*Long pause.*)

Ask the Great God to show you which of his qualities are strong within you. Receive the vision. (*Long pause.*)

Ask the Great God to show you which of his qualities need to be rebalanced within you. Receive the vision. (*Long pause.*)

Ask the Great God in which ways should you apply your Divine Will? How can you do better to fulfill his counsel to harm none? Receive the vision. (*Long pause.*)

Draw down the power of the God, his power as white light flows down throughout your body. Like lightning strike seeking the ground he seeks his lover. Your chakras spin open as his power descends, and your inner god awakens. Radiate with the bright potential of the God. You are whole and complete within his Divine Love. (*Long pause.*)

On a circulating breath, goddess and god energies merge within your heart. Inhale, and the dark goddess ascends from the Underworld to swirl around your heart. Exhale, and the bright god descends from the heavens to swirl around your heart. (*Pause.*)

Inhale, and the Goddess nourishes you through her holy darkness. (*Pause.*) Exhale, and the God inspires you through his holy light. (*Pause.*)

Their power of creation conjoins within your heart, darkness and light, yin and yang, the *Two Who Move as One* in perfect balance. You are whole and complete, a perfect child of the God/dess. (*Long pause.*)

It is time to return and step free of the world tree. (*Pause.*) Step back through the portal, back into your astral temple.

Reflect for a moment on all that you've seen. It is time to leave the astral temple and return to the outer temple. Following the path back, back the way you came, seeking out the looking glass, that portal back into yourself. See yourself on that looking glass. Passing through this portal you will once more follow the umbilical cord. Three steps back into your own belly. Three, two, one, step through!

Take the spiral stairway back up, rising higher and higher, returning to waking consciousness. Returning to the little room behind your eyes, closing the trapdoor in the floor behind you. Stretch your muscles, move to the window of your eyes, and then open them, finding the blazing altar of your outer temple laid before you. Stand and prepare for the Simple Feast.

❧ Simple Feast: Ceremony of the Symbolic Great Rite ❧

Pick up the athame in your projective hand and point it aloft to the heavens.

Say aloud: *On the outer planes, to create new human life the outward flowing energy of man must be received by the fertile womb of woman.*

Pick up the chalice in your receptive hand, holding it low, presenting to the Underworld.

Say aloud: *But on the Inner Planes, the Goddess is complete within herself. She is that which precedes; she is with us from the beginning and is that which is attained at the end of desire.*[294]

Set the tools back on the altar and pick back up in the opposite hands. (Slowly lower the athame into the cup.) Say aloud: *As the athame is to the God. So the chalice is to the Goddess, and when conjoined they bring forth blessedness. They are the womb and tomb, the spark and tinder, the dreamer and the dream fulfilled. Goddess and God, held in perfect balance within me as the Two Who Move As One. Blessèd be!* Draw the invoking pentacle of earth in the wine, circling deosil thrice as a blessing.

Into the water dish, pour out a libation, saying: *For the Goddess, God, and ancestors, I offer this libation with my gratitude.*

Pick up the paten of cakes in your receptive hand and the wand in your projective hand. Dip the wand into the wine and touch a drop of blessed wine to each cake. Say: *God/dess, bless these cakes as spiritual nourishment, bestowing health of body, strength of will, joy of heart, and peace of mind. Through this feast the God/dess fulfills their promise of Perfect Love.*

A libation cake is given into the water bowl. Say aloud: *For the Goddess, God, and ancestors. I offer this libation with my gratitude.*

As if toasting, hold the chalice aloft and say aloud: *I am a goddess! May I never thirst. Blessèd be!* Take a drink and savor it!

Hold the cake and say aloud: *I am a god. May I never hunger. Blessèd be!* Enjoy eating that cake, fully present in the sumptuous delight of your senses!

---

294. Valiente, *The Charge of the Goddess*, 12–13.

Take some time for prayer and reflection in the candlelit company of the God/dess. Read aloud "The Charge of the Goddess" poem.

Journal Reflection

In your Book of Mirrors, record the messages from Spirit, draw your visions, and explore your thoughts and feelings about the experience.

Release the temple; saying: *Great Spirit, Goddess, and God, the Two who Move as One, through whom I am complete. Ancestors of land, blood and spirit who guard and guide me, I am grateful for this journey and for your lessons of balance. I know that you walk ever with me as I tread the path of completion. Hail and farewell!* Extinguish the black and white candles.

Close the elemental gateways starting in the north and continuing widdershins, extinguishing their candles as the gateways are sealed.

Release the circle by gathering the sphere into your hands, smaller and smaller. Charge it to further light your way along the Pentacle Path. Shout *Release!* as you toss the sphere upward to the cosmos, clapping your hands, and saying: *The circle is open, but never broken. Merry meet, merry part, and merry meet again.*

The Magick of Completion

Rather than providing ready-made spells for balancing your completion within God/dess, the challenge I lay before you, dear reader, is to design your own. Consider this the practicum exam at the end of the course, meant to apply your mastery of the subject. However, the only person you have to impress here is yourself. Your good opinion of your magickal capabilities is the only thing that matters. You've trod the path of sovereignty and taken the helm of your ship and can navigate by your own stars. You've trod the path of truth and know best what you need to do for your growth. You've trod the path of power and internalized control, realizing you have the necessary authority to best fulfill your sacred mission. Hopefully this self-confidence brings you a greater sense of security too. You've trod the path of love, healing emotional wounds so that you may channel the Divine Love of the God/dess through all that you do. There is no one in the three worlds who knows better than you do what next magick should come. So, put to use all the lessons and techniques you've learned thus far, keep the parts that work well for you, adapt what needs adapting to suit your style. If we've accomplished nothing else in our time together, please accept your sacred authority to practice beneficial Witch-craft, done your way, in personal relationship with nature.

The first part of this magick, regardless of your sex or gender identity, is to strengthen your completion within goddess. Invite the receptivity of feminine divinity to emerge from within yourself by nurturing your emotional and creative side.

❦ Exercise 16: Strengthening the Goddess—Anima ❦

As you begin magickal planning to strengthen your inner goddess, here are some timing and activities to consider.

Auspicious Timing

Plan goddess magick by lunar cycles. Work during the waxing period through full moon for strengthening. Work through the waning to dark moon phase for releasing and resting in her strength. Friday (Venus) and the waxing crescent phase are excellent for aspects of the Maiden Goddess archetype. Monday (moon) and the full moon phase empower aspects of the Mother Goddess archetype. Saturday (Saturn) and the waning crescent through dark moon phase empowers aspects of the Crone Goddess archetype.

Full moons when the sun-moon opposition are both in an earth and water sign would be ideal, so look to when the sun is in Capricorn, Pisces, Taurus, Cancer, Virgo, or Scorpio, and then look for a day when the moon is also in one of those signs.

Elemental Magick

Put your magickal materials of earth and water magick to good use again, and they will naturally have ingredients that also bring goddess power to the party.

The Change

Author Vivianne Crowley suggests in her book *Wicca: The Old Religion in the New Millennium* that the mystery for a predominantly "masculine" Witch who seeks to know the Goddess is to stop hunting for her and invite her to emerge willingly from within. "By the well-spring of your being I await you always. Behold I have been with you from the beginning."[295] The Goddess invites you to lay down your weapons, shed your armor,

---

295. Vivianne Crowley, *Wicca*, 201–202.

cease striving, and rest. Be present in silence and quiet observation, fully embodied in the moment. Cultivate your artistry and creativity, intimacy and sensuality; indulge in nurturance and pampering your body and heart; engage the senses of touch (earth), taste (water), and intuition (spirit.)

Practical Magick for Receptive Balance

- Practice active listening with a friend or partner. Active listening is when you not only listen intently to what someone is expressing to you, but then you repeat that back in your own words as a means to make sure you genuinely understand their feelings.

- Say "I love you" and "thank you" out loud as often as possible—to your friends, lovers, folks you just met; tell the tree that shades your car, your houseplants cleaning the air, your neighbor's friendly dog, the worms in your compost bin. By doing so, you affirm the God/dess within them all, and affirm their important interconnection with your life.

- Create visual art and write poetry and music without any expectation of that art being "sold" or requiring that it be "good." Just express yourself creatively as an offering to the Goddess.

- Prepare nourishing food and share that with your friends, loved ones, or neighbors. Bless the food in gratitude to God/dess as provided but also as a magickal charge for your own nurturance.

- Talk about your feelings with a trusted friend or loved one, allowing yourself to be vulnerable, and then open your mind receptively to their feedback. If you've never experienced talk therapy with a professional counselor, this is a good time to seek guidance.

- What kinds of movies or music really touch your heart? Enjoy those purposefully and cry all you want to cry. Let all your water flow.

- Dig your hands into practical, material work of nurturing living beings.

  - Plant a flower or vegetable garden; seek out the spark of consciousness and ancient wisdom within plants, minerals, and animals.

  - Care for animals and any children in your life. Do so from a place of soul recognition. Engage with children on their level, remembering their timeless souls returned most recently from Spirit, and they remember that unity without the filters that hinder other adults. Ask them sincere questions, then pay close attention to their wisdom; let them be your teacher.

- Explore issues of mutual consent and physical touch separate from sexuality. Begin by offering therapeutic touch to friends and loved ones without any strings attached. Ask for a hug when you need one, allow heartfelt exchanges without expectation. Men in Western society are especially touch starved and need to relearn platonic touch beyond just the business handshake. Consent is key, and for that, learning to clearly communicate needs and respect wishes among friends is much-needed magick.

- Pamper your physical body through grooming and preening because feeling outwardly nurtured is very important to self-love.

- Build psychic skills through subjective practices of divination, like scrying in smoke, fire, the black mirror, or a black cauldron filled with water.

- As a Great Work dedication, celebrate the lunar cycles of esbats on full and dark moons, working specifically with the feminine pagan deities and their mythos throughout the Wheel of the Year.

❧ Exercise 17: Strengthening the God—Animus ❧

For magickal planning to strengthen your inner god, consider the following timing activities and elemental associations to spark your imagination.

Auspicious Timing

Plan god magick by solar cycles. In Wiccan mythology, the Oak King rules the waxing light half of the year from Winter Solstice (Yule) while the days grow longer until their peak at Summer Solstice (Litha). The Lord of Light and Horned God are associated with waxing tides of nature through winter and spring. Sunday (sun), Tuesday (Mars), and Thursday (Jupiter) correspond to strengthening and building his projective nature.

The Holly King rules the waning dark half of the year from Summer Solstice (Litha) while the days grow shorter until their ebb at Winter Solstice (Yule). Lord of Darkness, Sacrificial King, and Trickster/Magus/Psychopomp gods of the Underworld are associated with waning tides of nature through summer and autumn. Saturday (Saturn) and Wednesday (Mercury) correspond to diminishing and resting in his receptive power.

Aim for lunar tides when the sun and moon are both in air and fire signs. So, plan spells when the sun is in Aquarius, Aries, Gemini, Leo, Libra, or Sagittarius, and then look for a day when the moon is also in one of those signs.

Elemental Magick

Your magickal materials for air and fire also naturally have ingredients that empower the God's power in your magick.

The Change

Wiccan author Vivianne Crowley also suggests that the mystery for the primarily "feminine" Witch who seeks to balance their inner god is to cease waiting for a "knight on a white charger who will rescue her."[296] Go forth on the perilous quest to seek out the wild god within yourself, because he is "that which is attained at the end of desire."[297] Regardless of your physical sex or gender identity, for the purpose of strengthening your own god aspects, you are invited to take up your weapons, don your armor, and go fight the good fight. Strengthen your intellectual, leader, and warrior side; speak up, strike out, and defend your boundaries; study, explore big cerebral ideas; strive outwardly through activism and take needed action in the world to create the changes you know are just.

Practical Magick for Projective Balance:
- Engage your muscles through some form of martial art training or dancing. Drum your hands off around a bonfire; turn up your favorite ecstatic music and thrash, mosh, boogaloo, get your sweet bootie up and *get down to it.*
- Explore skills of the diplomat. Run for an office or volunteer for a leadership position in your community, school, or coven. Throw your name in the ring for that promotion you want at work. Step up to whatever metaphorical plate you've been training for and swing for the fences. Project yourself into the business at hand.
- Explore your passion, whether that be a hobby, area of academic interest, or a skill. Dive in and stoke those fires!

---

296. Vivianne Crowley, *Wicca*, 202.

297. Valiente, *The Charge of the Goddess*, 12–13.

- Organize a class and teach about your passion to others.
- Express yourself. Say what you need to say. Start a blog or a YouTube channel. Write that book. Find your voice and a microphone and communicate what's in your head and heart with others.
- Try your hand at the more formalized structures of ceremonial magick and ritual practice, like Qabala or laboratory alchemy! Learn one of the objective systems of divination, like tarot card reading, astrology, or Norse runes.
- Explore your sexual desires with a willing partner (or partners). Go Bacchanal wild, *as ye will*, all as worship to your inner god.
- As a Great Work dedication, celebrate the solar cycles of the eight sabbats, working specifically with masculine pagan deities and their mythos throughout an entire Wheel of the Year.

We have been so long oppressed by this patriarchal culture of the West, which would deny women their intellect, deny men their feelings, and deny anyone on the rainbow of nonbinary gender expression any validation at all![298] The beautiful work of Modern Witchcraft is to fulfill our own unique blend of spiritual wholeness and govern our diverse selves through "beauty and strength, power and compassion, honour and humility, mirth and reverence," as the incarnate God/desses we came here to be.[299]

Divination for Divine Guidance

As a means of active listening to the divine guidance of the God/dess, I recommend any Witch become proficient in some means of divination that uses an objective symbol set: tarot, runes, the ogham, throwing bones, etc. There just comes a time in every Witch's life when trusting your subconscious to give you the blunt, honest truth about practical things needs a more concrete form of communication.

I'm a huge fan of the tarot cards, specifically the Thoth Tarot by Aleister Crowley and Lady Frieda Harris. By design, these images already integrate perfectly to Hermetic systems of astrology, Qabala and elemental magick.

---

298. Vivianne Crowley, *Wicca*, 212.

299. Valiente, *The Charge of the Goddess*, 12–13.

The following tarot spread was developed through my personal elemental practice to help guide the way of the Great Work of Magick system presented in this book. It handily mirrors the elemental lessons learned through the Witch's Jewel of Power, answering these queries: Where am I upon the Pentacle Path? What do I do next to fulfill my sacred mission in this life?

This Jewel of Power spread is like asking your divine GPS system to drop that "current location" pin and then give you recommendations about the surroundings and advice about where to head next. It advises which detours to take, which traffic jams to avoid, what kind of snacks to pack for the trip! Remember that "human life" *is* your Great Work, so it could help clarify just about any situation to come up for you all year long. Whatever you ask the God/dess to help you achieve at dedication is what they are providing as a fulfillment of your request. It isn't always clear how *this* fits into that *cosmic plan*. This tarot reading will help. Repeat it every dark moon if you like. Even if you aren't already proficient with tarot, find yourself a deck you like and a good book to go with it. Then do your best to figure it out. We all start somewhere, and this is your moment.

❧ Exercise 18: Witch's Jewel of Power Tarot Reading ❧

Shuffle your deck in a random turning of card direction. Pull a center section out, rotate it the opposite direction, lay those cards back on top, then shuffle the deck back together. Repeat this process many times while calling upon your guides and gods to provide direction for your Great Work.

Draw the first five cards from the top and lay them in the order shown in figure 32. Be sure to pick them all up and lay them all down with the same movements; do not *consciously try* to correct their direction. However, if you subconsciously, accidentally rotate one of them oddly, just leave it; the God/dess intervened.

This spread *does not* read "reversals" of the card's intended meaning. Just interpret the primary meaning of the card, no matter which direction it is laying. However, if the card landed upside down, the meaning of the *position* changed. Upright cards are read for the yang/projective/god mystery of the Witch's Jewel of Power. Inverted cards are read as the yin/receptive/goddess mystery of the Jewel.

Read this entire spread like a love note from God/dess.

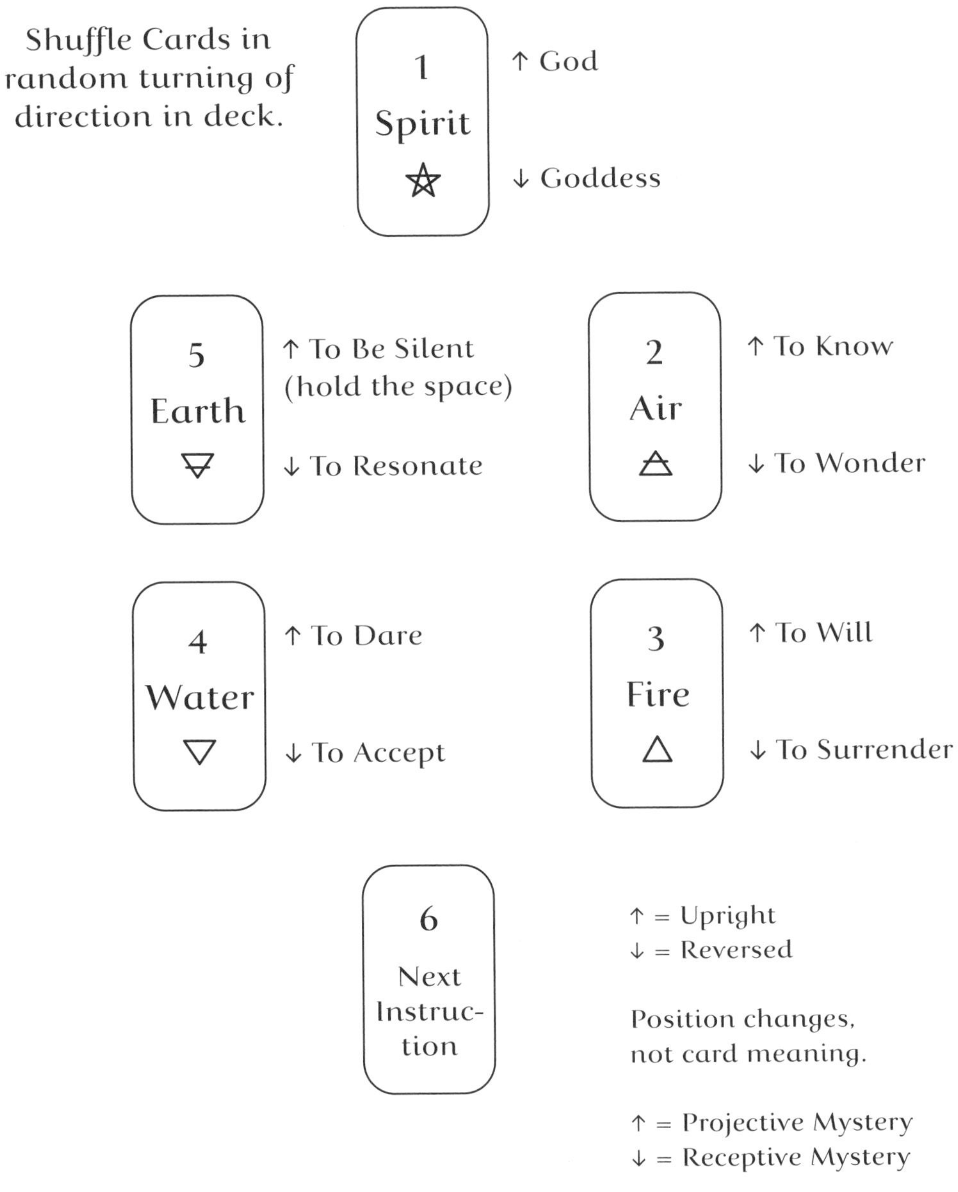

Shuffle Cards in
random turning of
direction in deck.

1 **Spirit** ☆	↑ God ↓ Goddess

5 **Earth** ▽	↑ To Be Silent (hold the space) ↓ To Resonate

2 **Air** △	↑ To Know ↓ To Wonder

4 **Water** ▽	↑ To Dare ↓ To Accept

3 **Fire** △	↑ To Will ↓ To Surrender

6 Next Instruc- tion	↑ = Upright ↓ = Reversed Position changes, not card meaning. ↑ = Projective Mystery ↓ = Receptive Mystery

Figure 33: A Witch's Jewel of Power tarot spread

#1 Card: Personal or Societal Focus of Message

If the Spirit position (#1) is upright, they are addressing your *personal work* of *internal transformation*. Apply this entire reading to how you should be focusing your magickal work on yourself and your internal processes. How should you behave? The God says: "An it harm none, do what ye will." [300]

If the Spirit Position (#1) is reversed, they are addressing your *external work of interconnection and societal transformation*. Apply this entire reading to how you should engage in external processes and interdependent relationships. How do you play nicely with others? The Goddess says: *In Perfect Love and Perfect Trust.* Save the meaning of the Spirit card until the end.

#2 Card: Mental Balance: The Message from Elemental Air

If the Air Card (#2) is upright, you already understand what you need to *know* about [subject matter of card].

If the Air Card (#2) is reversed, release what you think you know about [subject matter of card] and open your mind and *wonder* what new information or perspective you need in this area of your life.

#3 Card: Balance of the Will: The Message from Elemental Fire

If the Fire Card (#3) is upright, apply your personal *will* for change; work to achieve [subject of card].

If the Fire Card (#3) is reversed, cease striving to win the battle you've been fighting and *surrender* to the transformational fires of [subject of card] being applied to you.

#4 Card: Emotional Balance: The Message from Elemental Water

If the Water Card (#4) is upright, *dare* to overcome the emotional boundaries you're encountering and carve a new emotional landscape like the [subject of card].

If the Water Card (#4) is reversed, *accept* the emotional boundaries of [subject of card] and allow them to mold you into this new form.

---

300. Mathiesen and Theitic, *The Rede of the Wiccae*, 52–53.

#5 Card: Physical Balance: The Message from Elemental Earth

If the Earth Card (#5) is upright, your previous work is being born: be patient in *silence* and hold open the space to receive [subject of card].

If the Earth Card (#5) is reversed, time to tune in to a new frequency; set a new intention in *resonance* with [subject of card].

#1 Card: Spiritual Balance: *Now* Interpret the Message from God/dess

God/dess is creating Divine Love through your Great Work process and can be felt or perceived right now as [subject of card].

Remember that Divine Love of God/dess is perfect; it is the *complete circle*, which means sometimes it's a spanking, sometimes a hug, sometimes a new car, and sometimes you're grounded. However, all of it is because you are loved, and somehow, ultimately, this is what is necessary for your development right now. (Let's hope it isn't The Tower card too often!)

#6 Card: Next Instruction

After reading the first five cards, spread the remaining deck out in a line and ask for the next instruction. *Okay, God/dess, I'm picking up what you're layin' down, but what am I supposed to do about it?* Then cast your eyes softly over the line of cards and pull out the one that screams out to you. Read the face meaning of the card regardless of direction and consider this a warning or hot tip about the next move you should make

❧ Journal Reflection: The Path of Completion ❧

The process of integrating the God/dess within yourself never ends. In fact, the longer we work at it, and the older and wiser we progress, the easier this magick of completion feels. So keep at it! The path of completion is a lifelong endeavor of embracing both shadow and light within us. However, there is always some incremental progress as we actively engage our spirituality. What strides have you made in your relationship with God/dess this turning of the wheel? In what ways have your ideas and identity surrounding gender and sexuality been influenced? In what ways have your intellect and feelings been challenged or encouraged? Record those thoughts and feelings for your future Self to find.

From Air: To Know and to Wonder

- What impactful thing have you learned from this lesson?

- What do you still wonder about that needs further exploration?

From Fire: To Will and to Surrender

- How did you apply your will to these exercises? Did you adapt them to make them your own? What worked or didn't work well for you?

- Was there any expectation, assumption, or fear that needs to be surrendered?

From Water: To Dare and to Accept

- What gut emotional reactions came up for you?

- What surprised you? Which were easy to accept?

- Which do you dare to challenge or overcome?

From Earth: To Be Silent and to Resonate

- Now that the work is done, pay attention to what is going on in your life.

- How has this work affected your perceptions, actions, dreams? What patterns emerge?

- In what practical ways will you resonate your new awareness into reality?

Chapter 17
The Path of Return

The *path of return* refers to the natural return of consciousness back to its Source, to eventually remerge with the God/dess. Like a homing beacon, after our spirits incarnate here in the Middleworld, we instinctually seek reunion with the wholeness that our dreaming minds remember from before the womb. The work of the initiate of these mysteries is to awaken from spiritual slumber, to surrender attachment to our limited human egos, so that we may rediscover our divine nature and somehow ease the ache of separation we feel on Earth.

By happenstance, some shock of life trips us back into brief, ecstatic reunion. For me, it was the vision of the Goddess attending me during a difficult childbirth—when I perceived the array of my ancestors and progeny surrounding me throughout time. In the blink between worlds, I contributed to the ecstacy of creation and faced down the fear of death to emerge victorious. What did it for you? What divine blast tripped all your breakers, ignited your witchflame, and jolted you onto the quest?

It is said that due to the transient nature of the elements, the four major existential fears that humans face are these: a fear of death, a fear of responsibility for themselves and their own freedom, a fear of aloneness, and a fear of meaning.[301] The difference between the esoteric (inner) paths and exoteric (outer) paths is whether you're seeking salvation from these fears from an outside source or from within yourself. Characteristics of progress along this esoteric path of return would look like the internalized loci of control, authority, and security. That internal power would be harmonious with nature, cooperative and humble, gentle but fierce. I think these qualities describe a witch who is "soft of eye an light of touch," someone who speaks little and listens much.[302] Someone who is fully present to win, doesn't burn the Witch, is the solution to any problem, and is a strong link in the chainmail of our society.

Enlightened folks who've made progress along the path of return—the Witches that really *get it*—are already restoring the cooperative culture of the God/dess where they live. Every time we cast a balanced circle, call upon both Goddess and God, and bless the Simple Feast, our magick reconciles the tensions between chalice and blade humanity has suffered since the Neolithic era. I'm guessing that Spirit emerged through the Wiccan movement last century with the intention to dismantle the harms of this dominator culture. Perhaps in the coming Age of Aquarius the Great Work of Magick we're all working will level up humanity so we can realize the post-apocalyptic *Star Trek* dream of Gene Roddenberry rather than this *Mad Max Beyond Thunderdome* trajectory we seem to be on now.

But that is the endgame; with every turning of the wheel, and after each lap of the Great Work, we emerge a whole and (hopefully) improved Witch. A bit wiser, more loving, more powerful, more sovereign and complete within Divine Love than we were when we started. In Witchcraft for the Middleworld, the path of return is foremost about your personal growth toward mastery of this thing called life. As we grow in connection with our world, we get better at living effectively and can better enjoy the simple wonders of

---

301. Urvun D. Yalom, *Existential Psychotherapy*, cited by Mark Stavish, M.A. "Problems on the Path of Return: Pathology in Kabbalistic and Alchemical Practices." Accessed February, 12, 2020. https://hermetic.com/stavish/essays/problems-return.

302. Mathiesen and Theitic, *Rede of the Wiccae*, 52–53.

everyday existance. Anything is possible once we understand the elemental powers that weave our human experience together and how to tap into their flow for our benefit. Elemental Witchcraft is a practice that keeps on giving, year after year, in higher and lower octaves, with infinite creative applications.

By ritually reconnecting to the four elements and Spirit in your astral temple when you celebrate esbats, sabbats, and your daily meditation practice, you continue to strengthen all the connections and partnerships you've established this year. Maintain your open channel of alignments to spirit, earth, air, fire, and water through everything you do. If so, planting a garden in spring will become just as powerful magick as is the Grand Sabbat. Witchcraft is a process. The minute you think you've mastered it, the cosmos will throw you a curveball and knock you right off any man-made pedestals. Just keep showing up at the crossroads ready to work on yourself, and you can't help but succeed.

Conclusion

As you weave your way back in conclusion of this lap of the Great Work, consider how far you've come. Go back and re-read your intention statement from the candle scroll you prepared for dedication in your Book of Mirrors this year. Read the letter you wrote to this current you, and then spend time reading through all of your entries for the year. How far have you progressed? Where would you like to journey next?

Be proud of your accomplishments! For every question you asked and answered, for every problem you solved, and every random act of beauty and compassion you shared, I applaud you! Even be proud of those times you got lost in the thickets because every experience hones your understanding. Even if the thing you learned was that these techniques weren't your cup o' tea, at least *now you know* and can check that off of the list of things to try.

On a personal note, know that I'm proud of you, dear reader. Thank you for treading the Pentacle Path of Elemental Witchcraft with me this year. Thank you for the heroic journey to wholeness you've invested in yourself! In the coming years of your Great Work of Magick, I encourage you to revisit these elemental lessons with each turn of the wheel. Integrate them as you celebrate the overlapping solar and lunar cycles, and discover the profound depths each lap of our spiritual travel reveals. From wherever the path leads you, send me a postcard! I'd love to know what new wonders you've discovered. Thank you for doing the good witching work. It is a better place because you are here.

May the luminous shine from within the Witch's Jewel of Power kindle our collective witchflame brighter, so that Witches yearn for more beauty, more challenge, and more enjoyment of this adventure we call life. May we hunger to learn more, go further, and love more deeply than before. Ever onward, may we all continue our destiny's quest, seeking the path of return…

In Perfect Love and Trust,
~Heron Michelle
Greenville, NC, June 11, 2021
heronmichelle.com

Acknowledgments

With this book, my lifelong dream and sacred mission is at last realized. There are many devoted Witches, priests and priestesses, authors, mentors, and friends who helped bring this Great Work of Magick into form. To these folks I owe deep gratitude: To Gerald Gardner, father of Modern Witchcraft, who taught me how to create my own eclectic spiritual practice, but also to be honest about where it all comes from. To Doreen Valiente, mother of Modern Witchcraft, who taught me to boundary-check Witches on an ego-trip, and to progress the Craft with integrity.

To Christopher Penczak, whose brilliant books, workshops, and mentorship during a pilgrimage to the temple ruins of Xunantunich taught me what responsible divine service and community-building should look like. To Timothy Roderick for writing his thoughtful foreword and for his innovative "widdershins spirals" of elemental powers. They sowed the seeds that bloomed into the Pentacle Path of Elemental Witchcraft presented here.

To Tylluan, Justin Bullard, Diana Rice, Panya, Kari Starwise Powell, Kayla Cole, Preston Craddock, Donna Clifton, Alisa Brewer, Anna Meadows Helvie, Doug Helvie, Spanish Moss, and Thalia, whose friendship, witching hour "vortex" conversations, the loan of books, classes, pilgrimage companionship, invitations to public rituals, and encouragement lit the beacons so I could find my own witching path.

To every seeker to pass through the classroom of The Sojo Circle Coven; your questions, contributions, and "bananas" moments forged this tradition. To Jana Webweaver Madden and Epona Petra for reviewing early drafts and being supportive priestesses whenever I hit the Wall. To Courtney Varnadoe for her sustainable herbalism lessons, Jupiter Melchizedek and Melanie Godley for astrology and folk magick lessons, Jennifer Lantigua for technical expertise, and to the whole Sojo staff for brilliantly running the shop so I could go write it all down.

To Jan Bailey, my creative writing teacher at the Fine Arts Center High School who taught me to think critically and find the poetry in everything. To Jason Mankey, for his endorsement and offering me that shot at a Patheos Pagan blog. To Heather Greene, my Llewellyn acquisitions editor and gentle book midwife, and to Hanna Grimson for excellence in copyediting.

To Amy Blackthorn, Dr. Vivianne Crowley, Ivo Dominguez Jr., Canu Nodiad, Raina Starr, Miles Batty, and Mat Auryn for graciously reviewing and endorsing the book in advance. To Julia Belham-Payne at the Doreen Valiente Foundation for permission to reprint "The Charge of the Goddess" and Theitic for permission to reprint the "Rede of the Wiccae."

Most of all, I thank Lipbone Redding, my best friend and belovèd, who one day blew the lid off my mental cauldron when he said, "You know what? We'll never smash the patriarchy if we keep using their patriarchal weapons," and then gave me his copy of Eisler's *The Chalice and The Blade*.

Thank you all.

Glossary

Agency: In the social sciences, agency refers to an expression of personal power through one's own thoughts and actions. People with agency think for themselves, and take action to shape their own life experiences, and manage their own life trajectory.

Akashic Records: A term from Spiritualism describing the collective memory of all "events, actions, thoughts, and feelings that have occurred since the beginning of time … imprinted on akasha, the astral light … a reservoir of occult power, an ocean of unconsciousness to which all are linked, making prophecy and clairvoyance possible."[303]

Alchemy: From Greek and Arabic root words *Al-khemia*, roughly translated as "The Black Arts of Egypt" and describes the practical application of Hermetic philosophy to both spiritual and physical evolution; to transmute and rarify baser substances into those of greater value.[304]

Androcracy: A more precise term for patriarchy as a dominator culture proposed by Riane Eisler. A social system that is ruled by men through threat of force. Derived from the Greek roots *andros*, or "man" and *kratos*, or "ruled."[305]

Apogee: Astronomy term meaning the point in the orbit of a satellite, like the moon, which is furthest away from the earth.

Athame: Pronounced many ways: ah-THAW-may, or ATH-a-may, or a-THAY-me. Witchcraft term for a double-edged, black-handled magickal blade of a metal that contains iron associated with planetary Mars; traditional altar tool used to direct magickal power, "cut" between dimensions, and banish enchantments; conducts essence of elemental fire or sometimes air, depending on the tradition.

Baphomet: A panentheistic symbol of the Hermetic principles designed by nineteenth-century French occultist Eliphas Levi; a hermaphroditic figure, with female torso, goat head and legs, animal features merging the four elements with a torch of flames, wings of air, scales of water, and fur and hooves of land; details represent the operations of alchemy.[306] Caduceus of Hermes as a phallus; seated in posture of esoterism with one hand pointing up to the white moon of Chesed and one hand pointing down to black moon of Geburah, illustrating the accord between mercy and justice and the axiom "As above, so below"; pentagram on forehead with spirit point ascending, flaming torch of Divine Mind from crown. Levi's Baphomet is often conflated with the Sabbatic Goat, or Goat of Mendes of the Knights Templar,

303. "Akashic record," Encyclopedia Britannica, updated January 29, 2015, https://www.britannica.com/topic/Akashic-record.

304. Bartlett, *Real Alchemy*, 12–13.

305. Eisler, *The Chalice and the Blade*, 105.

306. Levi, *Transcendental Magic*, xxii, 174, 290.

and more recently adopted by the Satanic Temple of Detroit, Michigan, as a symbol of their "non-theistic movement aligned with Liberty, Equality and Rationalism."[307]

Book of Mirrors: A Witch's personal journal where they reflect on their spiritual experiences.

Book of Shadows: A Witch's manual of practical information describing ritual and magickal practices: instructions, lore, techniques, charms, formulary recipes, rituals, mythology, principles, laws, etc. Similar to the *grimoires of ceremonial magicians.* This term was originally applied by Wiccan founder, Gerald Gardner, to a Witch-craft coven's operating text, which is passed to new initiates of the tradition. Doreen Valiente reported that Gardner most likely derived this term from an article in *The Occult Observer* magazine, vol 1, no. 3, about an unrelated form of divination described in an ancient Sanskrit manuscript.[308]

Conjunction: Term from astronomy describing the coincidence of more than one planet, star, moon, or other celestial body along the same longitude. Example, at dark moon, both sun and moon are in conjunction.

Cultural Transformation Theory: Term coined by anthropologist Riane Eisler in *The Chalice and the Blade.* Describes human culture as holding two basic models for societal organization: dominator model and partnership model. Dominator model focuses on ranking of one gender over another, venerates violence and fear of death. Partnership models focus on linking relationships in egalitarian cooperation of all genders, venerates peacefulness and life-giving.

Deity: A gender-neutral word for a specific god or a particular aspect of divinity. This can be a catchall word for all god-forms.

Divinity: A collective, gender-neutral term for the quality of godliness, spiritual, holy, sacred; can refer collectively to higher vibrational beings, such as angels, gods, god-desses, and the Mighty Dead.

Eclectic: Keeping what one considers to be the best elements from a variety of estab-lished systems; forging a new system from their many parts.

---

307. "Church of Satan vs. Satanic Temple," The Satanic Temple, accessed June 13, 2021, https://thesatanic temple.com/pages/church-of-satan-vs-satanic-temple.

308. Valiente, *The Rebirth of Witchcraft*, 51.

Egregore: A shared thought form around a symbol, thought, idea, or vision held among a group of people who agree upon its function and which creates an energetic construct that takes on a spiritual agency of its own over time.

Esbat: Witchcraft ritual celebrating the lunar cycles and divine feminine mysteries.

Formulary: A collection of formulas or recipes for blending materials used in religious ceremonies and magickal spells, or a detailed list of medicines for specific uses.

Gnosis: Spiritual knowledge through personal experience of divine truth. From the Greek adjective *gnostikos* "leading to knowledge" or "pertaining to knowledge."[309]

Great Work of Magick, The: A term from Hermetic alchemy referring to processes of intentional self-improvement through ritualized magick with the purpose to awaken awareness of our manifest divinity and fulfill our spiritual destiny in each life toward eventual reunification with our spiritual source. Our ultimate human destiny being spiritual enlightenment, which collectively aids in the evolution of nature as a whole.

Grimoire: A magickal operation manual used in ceremonial magick. See also Book of Shadows.

Gylany: A more precise term for a partnership (cooperative) culture, proposed by Riane Eisler. Derived from the Greek *gyne*, or "woman," *andros* for "man," connected by the letter *l* from the Greek verb *lyein* or *lyo,* meaning "resolve, or dissolve," and "linking" the sexes in equal cooperation.[310]

Hermes Mercurius Trismegistus: Pronounced her-MEEZ mer-CURE-ee-us TRIS-ma-GIS-tus. Translates to "Thrice-Greatest" Hermes. Associated in Hermetic mythology with the Egyptian god Thoth and later syncretized with the Roman god Hermes and Greek god Mercury.

Hierarchy: system of human rankings equated by superiority or inferiority and imposed through threat of force or control of resources.

Liminal: A boundary or threshold that transitions between two sides of an area, process, or cycle. Examples: A hedge between properties, a shore or riverbank, dawn or dusk, death and birth.

---

309. Michael Williams, "Gnosticism," Encyclopedia Britannica, updated March 19, 2019, https://www .britannica.com/topic/gnosticism.

310. Eisler, *The Chalice and the Blade*, 105.

Lunation: A unit of time, lunar month, the 29.5-day orbit of the moon around the earth.

Macrocosm: The total, complex universe as a whole, as opposed to a microcosm.

Magick: Engaging consciously and purposefully within the flow of nature's power and channeling that power for desired changes through symbolic actions, visualizations, partnering with spiritual allies, speaking of intentions, and other meditation and ritual techniques that aid the shifting of one's consciousness.

Magus: From the ancient Persian term for a singular sorcerer or priest; plural noun is *magi*. Used in this text referring to any practitioner of magick.

Matriarchy: A form of social organization based in supremacy of females in leadership, in which the mother is head of the family, with descent and inheritance through the female line (matrilineal) and family residence remaining with mother's family or tribe (matrilocal).

Microcosm: Any miniature of the world or universe, a smaller model of the macrocosm.

Mythology: collection of stories created by a culture to explain life and the world. These tell the stories of the gods, spirits, important people, and history of that culture's religion.

Neopagan: see Pagan.

Occult: From the Latin *occultusanum*, means "secret," hidden wisdom and interconnections found beneath the obvious, surface reality.[311]

Opposition: Term from astronomy describing two heavenly bodies that are on opposite sides from each other along the same celestial longitude. Example: at full moon, sun and moon are on exactly opposite sides of the earth.

Ordo Templi Orientis, O. T. O: Order of the Temple of the East, an occult religious organization that began in Europe with roots in Freemasonry and Western esoteric philosophy. Leadership was assumed by renowned magician Aleister Crowley in 1912 and since incorporated the philosophies of his religion of Thelema.

Orthodoxy: Right belief. Ideology that defines what an adherent must believe as a prerequisite to play for their team. Typical of the monotheistic, patriarchal religions such as Judaism, Christianity, and Islam.

---

311. Roderick, *Wicca, A Year and a Day*, 5.

Orthopraxy: Right Action: Ideology that suggests doing particular practices. Typical of Witchcraft, that offers time-tested techniques through which you will be challenged to think for yourself. Then, through experience and divine revelation, a Witch can discover what they believe on their own.

Pagan: A modern religious movement that excavates the religious beliefs and ritual practices of indigenous cultures, typically earth-centered with a reverence for diverse aspects of divinity within nature.

Panentheism: From the ancient Greek meaning *all-in-god*, a term coined by German philosopher Karl Christian Friedrich Krause (1781–1832) in 1828.[312] Describes an ancient Neoplatonic paradigm that believed in both the immanence of divinity within nature and the cosmos, but also having a transcendent consciousness of divinity as a whole. Other examples include Hindu, Buddhist, and Taoist philosophies.

Pantheon: A family or grouping of individual deities linked through a common culture or mythology.

Paranormal: Meaning outside of normal perceptions or events that cannot be explained in scientific terms, typically referring to spiritual phenomena.

Patriarchy: A social organization marked by the supremacy of males in leadership in which the father is head of the family with descent and inheritance through the male line (patrilineal), and family residence remains with father's family or tribe (patrilocal).

Perigee: Astronomy term for nearest point to earth along the orbit of a satellite, like the moon.

Power: Subtle spiritual energy that flows through nature, creating everything and interconnecting everything within the cosmos. To be powerful in a witching sense is to unite with and openly channel that flow in harmony with nature's inherent power. Also called chi, ki, prana, mana, the Force, etc.

Sabbat: From the same root words as sabbath or holy day. A Witch's ritual celebration of an auspicious moment along the solar cycle, demarking eight divisions of the earth's orbit around the sun, the seasonal changes, and the high point of each season.

---

312. "Karl Christian Friedrich Krause," Encyclopedia Britannica.

Scientific Pantheism: A paradigm that deeply reveres the universe and nature, joyfully embraces life, the body, and the earth as sacred, but with a naturalistic approach without any belief in a transcendent divinity or "supernatural" power. Promotes an ethic of respect for human and animal rights and for sustainable lifestyles that protect the environment.

Secular Humanism: Any philosophy based in human values without reference to spirituality or religion.

Supernatural: Meaning "above nature," typically referring to spiritual phenomena.

Syncretic or Syncretism: Results from the attempt to blend and reconcile varying and sometimes opposing principles and practices within philosophy and religion.

Syzygy: Astronomy term referring to the position of two or more heavenly bodies in a straight line. For example, at eclipses, the earth, sun, and moon are in perfect syzygy alignment.

Thealogy: From the Greek root word *theas*, meaning goddess; the study of religion from a feminist viewpoint, which is inclusive of feminine divinity in equal balance to male divinity.

Thelema: Religious esoteric tradition founded by English occultist Aleister Crowley.

Theurgy: Greek root word *theourgos*, meaning "miracle worker"; a non-platonic system of magick and ritual practice performed to evoke deities with the goal of divine union or to seek their divine aid.

Wheel of the Year: A modern Neopagan ritual cycle that begins and ends at Winter Solstice when the sun enters Capricorn. Typically, this cycle includes the eight solar holidays celebrating the division of the earth's orbit through the twelve signs of the zodiac, four seasons, and twelve to thirteen full moons, which occur within the same time frame.

Wicca: A modern Neopagan religion based in Western European esoterism and folklore, affirming a divinity within nature as both female and male deities, performing magick, and emphasizing a ritual cycle based on the seasons and the life cycle. Originated with an Englishman named Gerald Gardner in the mid-1900s.

Witchcraft: An orthopraxy of rituals and magickal techniques based in the divinity of nature with whom spiritual partnerships may be made to achieve desired goals.

Zodiac: An astrological term for the imaginary map of our stellar neighborhood, dividing into twelve equal sections the band of outer space surrounding the earth as perceived throughout our yearly orbit around the sun.

Further Reading

I encourage you to dig deeply into the roots of modern witchery by reading the original written works of the founders and their memoires and biographies: Gerald Gardner, Doreen Valiente, Robert Cochrane, Maxine and Alexander Sanders, etc. Then look into the foundation texts that inspired them by Eliphas Levi, Cornelius Agrippa, Aleister Crowley, Manly P. Hall, Dion Fortune, Charles Godfrey Leland, Sir James George Frazer, and Robert Graves. There's a long list of titles, but to see what they say for yourself will help put this modern movement into perspective. Start with *The Rebirth of Witchcraft* (Robert Hale, 1989) where Doreen Valiente documents her personal account of how the Witchcraft movement emerged in England, including her experiences in both Gerald Gardner's and Robert Cochrane's covens.

For a study of the archeological origins of early goddess worshipping cultures and the shift into patriarchy throughout the West, check out Marija Gimbutas's *The Goddesses and Gods of Old Europe, 6500–3500 BC: Myths and Cult Images*, Riane Eisler's *The Chalice and the Blade*, and Merlin Stone's *When God Was a Woman*.

To fully explore the beauty and meaning of Neopaganism as it compares and contrasts to the invasive orthodoxies, I recommend *Paganism: An Introduction to Earth-Centered Religions* by Joyce and River Higginbotham.

To better understand the seven Hermetic principles, their influences, history, and impact, I found Philip Deslippe's introduction to the 100th anniversary edition of *The Kybalion* by William Walker Atkinson to be inspiring (Jeremy P. Tarcher/Penguin, 2008). Best yet, read a modern translation of *The Corpus Hermeticum* for yourself.

For a beautiful integration of Jungian psychology to the three-degree initiatory process of British Wicca, I learned just about everything I know from Dr. Vivianne Crowley's *Wicca: The Old Religion in the New Millennium* (Thorsons, 1996).

For more of the sacred poetry of Wicca, Doreen Valiente's *The Charge of the Goddess, Expanded Edition* (2014) is a delight. *The Rede of the Wiccae: Adriana Porter, Gwen Thompson and the Birth of a Tradition of Witchcraft* (Olympian Press, 2005) by Robert Mathiesen and Theitic offers a thorough history and analysis of the Wiccan Rede.

To further your ritual practice according to astrological timing, I recommend Ivo Dominguez Jr.'s book *Practical Astrology for Witches and Pagans: Using the Planets and the Stars for Effective Spellwork, Rituals, and Magickal Work* (Weniser Books, 2016). To better understand your natal chart, every witching library needs Joanna Martine Woolfolk's *The Only Astrology Book You'll Ever Need* (Taylor Trade Publishing, 2006).

For further exploration of the receptive powers of the elements, see Timothy Roderick's original presentation of those concepts in *Dark Moon Mysteries* (Llewellyn Publications, 1996) and furthered in *Apprentice to Power* (The Crossing Press, 2000).

For Wiccan rituals at the solar sabbats, see Jason Mankey's *Witch's Wheel of the Year* (Llewellyn Publications, 2019). For beautiful storytelling of the Wiccan God/dess mythos throughout the Wheel of the Year, find Miles Batty's *The Green Prince's Father* (Three Moons Media, 2008).

For every possible magickal correspondence, I recommend Sandra Kynes's book *Llewellyn's Complete Book of Correspondences: A Comprehensive & Cross-Referenced Resource for Pagans & Wiccans* (Llewellyn Publications, 2013).

For the meanings of the Thoth tarot deck by Aleister Crowley and Lady Frieda Harris, I recommend *Tarot: Mirror of the Soul: Handbook for the Aleister Crowley Tarot* by Gerd Ziegler (Weiser Books, 1988).

To thoroughly unpack the six stages of power, especially in an organizational setting like a coven, I found Janet Hagberg's *Real Power: The Stages of Personal Power in Organizations*, 3rd ed. (Sheffield Publishing Co., 2003) to be very enlightening.

Bibliography

Agrippa of Nettesheim, Henry Cornelius. *Three Books of Occult Philosophy: The Foundation Book of Western Occultism*. Edited by Donald Tyson. Translated by James Freake. St. Paul, MN: Llewellyn Publications, 1993.

"Akashic record." Encyclopedia Britannica. Updated January 29, 2015. https://www.britannica.com/topic/Akashic-record.

Albertus, Frater. *The Alchemist's Handbook: Manual for Practical Alchemy*. Boston: Weiser Books, 1974.

Atkinson, William Walker (Three Initiates). *The Kybalion: The Definitive Edition*. Edited by Philip Deslippe. New York: Jeremy P. Tarcher/Penguin, 2008.

Bartlett, Robert Allen. *Real Alchemy: A Primer of Practical Alchemy.* 3rd rev. ed. Lake Worth, FL: Ibis Press, 2009.

Batty, Miles. *The Green Prince's Father.* Longview, TX: Three Moons Media, 2008.

———. *Teaching Witchcraft: A Guide for Teachers and Students of the Old Religion.* Longview, TX: Three Moons Media, 2006.

Beyer, Catherine. "Alchemical Sulfur, Mercury and Salt in Western Occultism." Learn Religions. Updated July 3, 2019. https://www.learnreligions.com/alchemical-sulfur-mercury-and-salt-96036.

Blackthorn, Amy. *Blackthorn's Botanical Magic: The Green Witch's Guide to Essential Oils for Spellcraft, Ritual, and Healing.* Newburyport, MA: Weiser, 2018.

Bohm, David. *Wholeness and the Implicate Order.* London: Routledge Classics, 1980.

Buckland, Raymond. *The Witch Book: The Encyclopedia of Witchcraft, Wicca, and Neo-paganism.* Detroit: Visible Ink Press, 2002.

Cabot, Laurie. *Power of the Witch: The Earth, The Moon, and the Magical Path to Enlightenment.* With Tom Cowan. New York: Delta Book, 1989.

"Chapter 3: Understanding the Impact of Trauma." In *Trauma-Informed Care in Behavioral Health Services*, Treatment Improvement Protocol (TIP) Series 57, HHS Publication No. (SMA) 13-4801, Rockville, MD: Substance Abuse and Mental Health Services Administration, 2014. https://www.ncbi.nlm.nih.gov/books/NBK207191/.

"Church of Satan vs. Satanic Temple." The Satanic Temple. Accessed June 13, 2021. https://thesatanictemple.com/pages/church-of-satan-vs-satanic-temple.

Clifton, Chas. *Her Hidden Children: The Rise of Wicca and Paganism in America.* Oxford: AltaMira Press, 2006.

Cole, Nicki Lisa. "How Sociologists Define Human Agency." ThoughtCo. January 22, 2019. https://www.thoughtco.com/agency-definition-3026036.

Crowley, Aleister. *Liber Aleph vel CXI: The Book of Wisdom or Folly […].* York Beach, ME: S. Weister, 1991.

———. *Magick in Theory and Practice.* New York: Castle Books, 1929.

———. *The Book of the Law.* York Beach, ME: Red Wheel/Weiser, 1976.

Crowley, Vivianne. *Wicca: The Old Religion in the New Millennium.* London: Thorsons, 1996.

Culp, John, "Panentheism," *The Stanford Encyclopedia of Philosophy*, ed. Edward N. Zalta, fall 2020 ed., updated June 17, 2020, https://plato.stanford.edu/entries /panentheism/.

Cunningham, Scott. *Wicca: A Guide for the Solitary Practitioner*. St. Paul, MN: Llewellyn Publications, 1989.

D'Este, Sorita, and David Rankine. *Practical Elemental Magick: Working the Magick of the Four Elements in the Western Mystery Tradition.* London: Avalonia, 2008.

———. *Wicca Magickal Beginning: A Study of the Possible Origins of the Rituals and Practices Found in this Modern Tradition of Pagan Witchcraft and Magick.* London: Avalonia, 2008.

Dominguez, Ivo Jr. *Practical Astrology for Witches and Pagans: Using the Planets and the Stars for Effective Spellwork, Rituals, and Magickal Work.* San Francisco, CA: Weiser Books, 2016.

Ebeling, Florian. *The Secret History of Hermes Trismegistus: Hermeticism from Ancient to Modern Times.* Translated by David Lorton. Ithaca, NY: Cornell University Press, 2007.

Eisler, Riane. *The Chalice and the Blade: Our History, Our Future.* San Francisco: Harper Collins Publishers, 1995.

El-Abbadi, Mostafa. "Library of Alexandria." Encyclopedia Britannica. Updated July 17, 2020, https://www.britannica.com/topic/Library-of-Alexandria.

"Empedocles." Encyclopedia Britannica. Updated March 7, 2021. https://www .britannica.com/biography/Empedocles.

Gandhi, Mahatma. *The Collected Works of Mahatma Gandhi*. Gandhi Sevagram Ashram, New Delhi, Publications Division Government of India, 1999, vol. 13, chapter 153, page 241. Accessed Dec. 17, 2020. http://www.gandhiashramsevagram.org /gandhi-literature/mahatma-gandhi-collected-works-volume-13.pdf.

"Gardner, Gerald Brousseau." World Religions Reference Library. Encyclopedia.com. April 15, 2021. https://www.encyclopedia.com/religion/encyclopedias-almanacs -transcripts-and-maps/gardner-gerald-brousseau.

"Genius." Encyclopedia Britannica. Updated January 16, 2012. https://www.britannica .com/topic/genius-Roman-religion.

Gilchrist, Cherry. *Alchemy: The Great Work*. San Francisco: Weiser Books, 2015.

Gimbutas, Marija. *The Goddesses and Gods of Old Europe, 6500–3500 BC: Myths and Cult Images.* New and updated edition. Los Angeles: University of California Press, 1982.

Goodman, Linda. *Linda Goodman's Love Signs: A New Approach to the Human Heart.* New York: Harper Collins Publishers, HarperPerennial edition, 1992.

Graves, Robert. *The White Goddess: A Historical grammar of Poetic Myth.* Edited by Grevel Lindop. New York: Farrar, Straus and Giroux, 2013.

Greer, John Michael. *The New Encyclopedia of the Occult.* St. Paul, MN: Llewellyn Publications, 2003.

"Gregorian Calendar." Encyclopedia Britannica n.d. https://www.britannica.com/topic/Gregorian-calendar.

Grimassi, Raven. *The Wiccan Mysteries: Ancient Origins & Teachings.* St. Paul, MN: Llewellyn Publications, 1997.

Hagberg, Janet O. *Real Power: The Stages of Personal Power in Organizations.* 3rd ed. Salem, WI: Sheffield Publishing Co., 2003.

Hall, Manly P. *The Secret Teachings of All Ages: An Encyclopedic Outline of Masonic, Hermetic, Qabbalistic and Rosicrucian Symbolical Philosophy*, 50th anniv. ed. Los Angeles: The Philosophical Research Society, Inc, 1977.

Hamaker-Zondag, Karen. *Psychological Astrology: A Synthesis of Jungian Psychology and Astrology.* York Beach, ME: Sam Weiser, Inc., 1990.

Hargrave, John G. "Paracelsus." Encyclopedia Britannica. Updated January 14, 2021. https://www.britannica.com/biography/Paracelsus.

Hauck, Dennis William. "Working with the Elements." Accessed June 6, 2021. https://azothalchemy.org/elements.htm

"Hermetic Writings." Encyclopedia Britannica. Updated September 3, 2013. https://www.britannica.com/topic/Hermetic-writings.

Heselton, Philip. *Doreen Valiente Witch.* United Kingdom: Doreen Valiente Foundation and The Centre for Pagan Studies, Woodbury, MN: Llewellyn Publications, 2016.

Higginbotham, Joyce, and River Higginbotham. *Paganism: An Introduction to Earth-Centered Religions.* Woodbury, MN: Llewellyn Publications, 2007.

Junius, Manfred M. *Spagyrics: The Alchemical Preparation of Medicinal Essences, Tinctures, and Elixirs.* Rochester, VT: Healing Arts Press, 2007.

"Karl Christian Friedrich Krause." Encyclopedia Britannica. Updated May 2, 2021. https://www.britannica.com/biography/Karl-Christian-Friedrich-Krause.

Keyes, Ralph. *The Quote Verifier: Who Said What, Where, and When*. New York: St. Martin's Griffin, 2006.

Kynes, Sandra. *Llewellyn's Complete Book of Correspondences: A Comprehensive & Cross-Referenced Resource for Pagans & Wiccans*. Woodbury, MN: Llewellyn Publications, 2013.

Labouré, Denis. "The Seven Bodies of Man in Hermetic Astrology." Translated by Michael Edwards. *The Traditional Astrologer* 4 (1994): https://www.skyscript .co.uk/7bodies.html.

"La Ceiba: The Sacred Tree of Life." Na'atik Instituto De Lenguas Culturas. Accessed June 6, 2021. https://www.naatikmexico.org/ceiba-tree/.

Lachman, Gary. *The Quest for Hermes Trismegistus: From Ancient Egypt to the Modern World*. Edinburgh: Floris Books, 2011

Leendert van der Waerden, Bartel, and Christian Marinus Taisbak. "Euclid." Encyclopedia Britannica. Updated on January 5, 2021. https://www.britannica.com/biography /Euclid-Greek-mathematician.

Levi, Eliphas. *The History of Magic: Including a Clear and Precise Exposition of its Procedure, Its Rites, and Its Mysteries*. Translated by A. E. Waite. York Beach, ME: Samuel Weiser, 1999.

———. *Transcendental Magic: Its Doctrine and Ritual*. Translated by A. E. Waite. London: George Redway, 1896.

Lopez, Donald S. "Buddha." Encyclopedia Britannica. Updated February 19, 2020. https://www.britannica.com/biography/Buddha-founder-of-Buddhism.

Mangen, Anne, and Jean-Luc Velay. "Digitizing Literacy: Reflections on the Haptics of Writing." *Advances in Haptics*, edited by Mehrdad Hosseini Zadeh. *IntechOpen* (April 1, 2020): https://doi.org/10.5772/8710.

Mankey, Jason. *Witch's Wheel of the Year: Rituals for Circles, Solitaries & Covens*. St. Paul, MN: Llewellyn Publications, 2020.

Mathiesen, Robert, and Theitic. *The Rede of the Wiccae: Adriana Porter, Gwen Thompson and the Birth of a Tradition of Witchcraft*. Providence, RI: Olympian Press, 2005.

Mehrtens, Sue. "How to Internalize a Locus of Control, a Locus of Authority and a Locus of Security: A Follow-Up Essay." Jungian Center for the Spiritual Sciences. Accessed April 30, 2020. https://jungiancenter.org/hot-to-internalize-a-locus-of -control/.

Melton, J. Gordon. "Wicca." Encyclopedia Britannica. Updated February 2, 2021. https://www.britannica.com/topic/Wicca.

Metzger, Bruce M. and Roland E. Murphy, eds. *The New Oxford Annotated Bible with the Apocryphal/Deuterocanonical Books, New Revised Standard Edition* New York: Oxford University Press, 1994.

"Pan." Encyclopedia Britannica. Updated April 23, 2020. https://www.britannica.com /topic/Pan-Greek-god.

Patterson, Thomas C., Michael Douglas Coe, Geoffrey H. S. Bushnell, Gordon R. Willey, Jacques Soustelle, William T. Sanders, John V. Murra, Victor Wolfgang von Hagen. "Pre-Columbian civilizations" Encyclopedia Britannica. Updated November 18, 2020. https://www.britannica.com/topic/pre-Columbian-civilizations.

Pelikan, Jaroslav Jan, and E. P. Sanders. "Jesus." Encyclopedia Britannica. Updated June 16, 2021. https://www.britannica.com/biography/Jesus.

Penczak, Christopher. *Ascension Magick: Ritual, Myth & Healing for the New Aeon.* Woodbury, MN: Llewellyn Publishers, 2007.

———. *Magick of Reiki: Focused Energy for Healing, Ritual & Spiritual Development.* Woodbury, MN: Llewellyn Publications, 2009.

———. *The Inner Temple of Witchcraft: Magick, Meditation, and Psychic Development.* St. Paul, MN: Llewellyn Publications, 2004.

———. *The Outer Temple of Witchcraft: Circles, Spells, and Rituals.* St. Paul, MN: Llewellyn Publications, 2004.

———. *The Temple of Shamanic Witchcraft: Shadows, Spirits and the Healing Journey.* St. Paul, MN: Llewellyn Publications, 2005.

———. *The Three Rays of Witchcraft: Power, Love and Wisdom in the Garden of the Gods.* Salem, NH: Copper Cauldron Publishing, 2010.

"Qi: Chinese Philosophy." Encyclopedia Britannica. Updated May 7, 2020. https://www .britannica.com/topic/qi-Chinese-philosophy.

"Rede." Online Etymology Dictionary. Douglas Harper. Accessed December 22, 2020. https://www.etymonline.com/word/rede.

Rice, Addison. "Gemstone Toxicity Table." International Gem Society, n. d. https://www.gemsociety.org/article/gemstone-toxicity-table/.

Roderick, Timothy. *Apprentice to Power: A Wiccan Odyssey to Spiritual Awakening.* Freedom, CA: The Crossing Press, 2000.

———. *Dark Moon Mysteries: Wisdom, Power, and Magic of the Shadow World.* St. Paul, MN: Llewellyn Publications, 1996.

———. *Wicca, A Year and a Day: 366 Days of Spiritual Practice in the Craft of the Wise.* St. Paul, MN: Llewellyn Publications, 2005.

Salaman, Clement, Dorian van Oyen, William D. Wharton, Jean-Pierre Mahe. *The Way of Hermes: New Translations of* The Corpus Hermeticum *and* The Definitions of Hermes Trismegistus to Asclepius. Rochester, VT: Inner Traditions, 2000.

Sanders, Maxine. *Fire Child: The Life and Magick of Maxine Sanders, 'Witch Queen.'* Oxford: Mandrake, 2007.

Scott, Sir Walter, ed. and trans. *Hermetica: The Ancient Greek and Latin Writings Which Contain Religious or Philosophic Teachings Ascribed to Hermes Trismegistus.* Boston: Shambhala Publications, 1993.

Shakespeare, William. *Hamlet.* Washington, DC: Folger Shakespeare Library, n.d. Accessed August 27, 2021. http://shakespeare.folger.edu/shakespeares-works/hamlet/act-3-scene-2/

Sheldrake, Rupert. "Morphic Resonance and Morphic Fields—An Introduction," Rupert Sheldrake. Accessed June 4, 2021. https://www.sheldrake.org/research/morphic-resonance/introduction.

Simms, Maria Kay. "Planetary Hours: The Method and the Magick for Quick Timing Decisions." Llewellyn. October 30, 2003. https://www.llewellyn.com/journal/article/534.

Snuffin, Michael Osiris. Hermetic Library. "On the Powers of the Sphinx: Part 2: Aleister Crowley." 2002. Accessed June 6, 2021. https://hermetic.com/osiris/onthepowersofthesphinx2.

Starhawk. *The Spiral Dance: A Rebirth of the Ancient Religion of the Great Goddess.* 10th anniv. ed. San Francisco: HarperSanFrancisco, 1989.

Stark, Glenn. "Young's Double-Slit Experiment" in "Light." Encyclopedia Britannica. Updated October 29, 2020. https://www.britannica.com/science/light/Youngs-double-slit-experiment.

Stavish, Mark. "Problems on the Path of Return: Pathology in Kabbalistic and Alchemical Practices." Hermetic Library. February, 12, 2020. https://hermetic.com/stavish/essays/problems-return.

Stone, Merlin. *When God Was a Woman.* London: Harcourt Brace Jovanovich Publishers, 1976.

Talbot, Michael. *The Holographic Universe.* New York: HarperCollins, 1991.

"The White Goddess." Encyclopedia Britannica. Updated February 02, 2020. https://www.britannica.com/topic/The-White-Goddess.

"Thoth." Encyclopedia Britannica. Updated February 13, 2020. https://www.britannica.com/topic/Thoth.

"Three Philosophical Principles." Organic Unity. Accessed May 31, 2021. http://www.organic-unity.com/top-menu/the-three-philosophical-principles/.

Tolkien, J. R. R. *The Hobbit: Alan Lee Illustrated Edition.* Boston, MA: HMH Books, 1997.

Tyler, Nichola, Roxanne Heffernan, and Clare-Ann Fortune. "Reorienting Locus of Control in Individuals Who Have Offended Through Strengths-Based Interventions: Personal Agency and the Good Lives Model," *Frontiers in Psychology* (September 15, 2020), https://doi.org/10.3389/fpsyg.2020.553240.

Valiente, Doreen. *An ABC of Witchcraft Past and Present.* Custer, WA: Phoenix Publishing Inc., 1973.

———. *The Charge of the Goddess: Expanded Edition with New and Previously Unpublished Poems.* The Doreen Valiente Foundation, 2014.

———. *The Rebirth of Witchcraft.* London: Robert Hale, 1989.

———. *Witchcraft for Tomorrow.* Custer, WA: Phoenix Publishing Inc., 1987.

Van der Waerden, Bartel Leendert, and Christian Marinus Taisbak. "Euclid." Encyclopedia Britannica. Updated January 5, 2021. https://www.britannica.com/biography/Euclid-greek-mathematician.

Van Helden, Albert. "Galileo." Encyclopedia Britannica. Updated February 19, 2021. https://www.britannica.com/biography/Galileo-Galilei.

Von Hellfeld, Matthias. "Christianity Becomes the Religion of the Roman Empire—February 27, 380." DW. November 16, 2009. https://p.dw.com/p/JJNY.

Walsh, Roger. "The Making of a Shaman: Calling, Training and Culmination." *Journal of Humanistic Psychology* 34, no. 3 (Summer 1994): 7–30. https://doi.org/10.1177/00221678940343003.

"Week." Encyclopedia Britannica. Updated April 20, 2020. https://www.britannica.com/science/week.

Williams, Michael. "Gnosticism." Encyclopedia Britannica. Updated March 19, 2019. https://www.britannica.com/topic/gnosticism.

Woolfolk, Joanna Martine. *The Only Astrology Book You'll Ever Need.* Lanham, MD: Taylor Trade Publishing, 2006.

Yalom, Urvun D. *Existential Psychotherapy*, cited by Mark Stavish, M.A. "Problems on the Path of Return: Pathology in Kabbalistic and Alchemical Practices." Accessed February, 12, 2020. https://hermetic.com/stavish/essays/problems-return.

"Yggdrasill." Encyclopedia Britannica. Updated February 7, 2018. https://www.britannica.com/topic/Yggdrasill.

Zeigler, Gerd. *Tarot: Mirror of the Soul: Handbook for the Aleister Crowley Tarot.* Boston: Red Wheel/Weiser, 1988.

Zöllner, Frank. "Agrippa, Leonardo and the Codex Huygens." *Journal of the Warburg and Courtauld Institutes* 48 (1985): 229–234. Accessed June 6, 2021. https://doi.org/10.2307/751218.

To Write to the Author

If you wish to contact the author or would like more information about this book, please write to the author in care of Llewellyn Worldwide Ltd. and we will forward your request. Both the author and publisher appreciate hearing from you and learning of your enjoyment of this book and how it has helped you. Llewellyn Worldwide Ltd. cannot guarantee that every letter written to the author can be answered, but all will be forwarded. Please write to:

Heron Michelle
℅ Llewellyn Worldwide
2143 Wooddale Drive
Woodbury, MN 55125-2989

Please enclose a self-addressed stamped envelope for reply,
or $1.00 to cover costs. If outside the U.S.A., enclose
an international postal reply coupon.

Many of Llewellyn's authors have websites with additional information and resources. For more information, please visit our website at http://www.llewellyn.com.